Object-Oriented Software in Ada 95

To my wife Corinna Lord and mother Margaret Smith

Weiss

JOIN US ON THE INTERNET VIA WWW, GOPHER, FTP OR EMAIL:

WWW: http://www.thomson.com
GOPHER: gopher.thomson.com
FTP: ftp.thomson.com
EMAIL: findit@kiosk.thomson.com

WebExtra^{sm}
The source code for all the example programs
used in this book, additional material on Ada 95,
plus up-to-date information on the Web, is available
by pointing your web browser to
http://www.thomson.com/itcp.html

A service of I(T)P

Object-Oriented Software in Ada 95

Michael A Smith
Department of Computing
University of Brighton

INTERNATIONAL THOMSON COMPUTER PRESS
I⊤P An International Thomson Publishing Company

London • Bonn • Boston • Johannesburg • Madrid • Melbourne • Mexico City • New York • Paris
Singapore • Tokyo • Toronto • Albany, NY • Belmont, CA • Cincinnati, OH • Detroit, MI

Object-Oriented Software in Ada 95

Copyright © 1996 M A Smith

I ⓣ P   A division of International Thomson Publishing Inc.
The ITP logo is a trademark under licence

British Library Cataloguing-in-Publication Data
A catalogue record for this book is available from the British Library

Library of Congress Cataloging-in-Publication Data
A catalog record for this book is available from the Library of Congress

First printed 1996

Commissioning Editor Samantha Whittaker

Cover Designed by Button Eventures
Typeset in 10/12 Times by the author using Word 5.1 on a Macintosh
Printed in the UK by Alden Press, Oxford

ISBN 1-85032-185-X

International Thomson Computer Press
Berkshire House
High Holborn
London WClV 7AA
UK

International Thomson Computer Press
20 Park Plaza
14th Floor
Boston MA 02116
USA

http://www.thomson.com/itcp.html

Imprints of International Thomson Publishing

Contents

Preface

This book is aimed at students and programmers who wish to learn the object-oriented language Ada 95. The book illustrates the language by showing how programs can be written using an object-oriented approach. The book treats Ada 95 as a language in its own right and not just as an extension to Ada 83.

The first chapter provides an introduction to problem solving using an object-oriented design methodology. The methodology illustrated in this introductory chapter is based on Fusion.

The next three chapters concentrate on the basic constructs in the Ada 95 language. In particular the use of types and subtypes is encouraged. By using types and subtypes in a program the compiler can help spot many errors and inconsistencies at compile-time rather than run-time.

The book then moves on to discuss the object-oriented features of the language, using numerous examples to illustrate the ideas of encapsulation, inheritance and polymorphism. A detailed case study of the design and implementation of a program using an object-oriented design methodology is included.

An introduction to the tasking features of Ada is included. Finally a text user interface API is developed to illustrate in a practical way the use of object-oriented components in a program. Several programs that use this interface are shown to illustrate the processes involved.

Exercises and self assessment questions are suggested for the reader at the end of each chapter to allow the reader to practise the use of the Ada components illustrated and to help reinforce, the reader's understanding of the material in the chapter. Answers to many of the practical exercises are given at the end of the book.

I would in particular like to thank: Prof. Dan Simpson for encouragement and the loan of some of the computing equipment used in the preparation of this book, Corinna Lord, Franco Civello, Jonathan Durrant, John English, Garth Glynn, Phil Siviter and Richard Mitchell for many helpful suggestions and comments. In particular to Corinna for putting up with my many long hours in the 'computer room' and her many useful suggestions on the presentation and style used for the material in this book.

The source code for all the the example programs used in this book are available using anonymous FTP at the URL `ftp://ftp.bton.ac.uk/pub/mas/ada95`. Alternatively, contact the author by email at the address given below with a request for the source code. World Wide Web pages which include the source code for all the programs in the book plus additional material on Ada 95 is at the web URL `http://www.bton.ac.uk/ada95/home.html` or alternatively see the WebExtra at `http://www.thomson.com/itcp.html`.

Michael A. Smith
Brighton, October 1995

M.A.Smith@brighton.ac.uk

The example programs shown in this book use the following conventions:

Item in program	Example	Convention used
Attribute of an object or type	`Integer'Last`	Starts with an upper-case letter.

Class	`package Class_cell is`
	`   type Cell is private;`
	
	`private`
	
	`end Class_cell;`
		Is declared as a package prefixed with the name 'Class_'. The class name is given to the private type that is then used to elaborate instances of the class.

Instance method: function or procedure	`display(the:in Cell)`	The function or procedure is in lowercase and the first parameter passed to it is an instance of the class which is named `the`.
Instance attribute: a data item contained in an object.	`balance: float;`	Is in lowercase and is declared in the private part of the package.
Class attribute: a global data item that is shared between all instances of the class	`the_ref_count: Integer;`	Is in lowercase starting with `the_` and is declared in the private part of the package.
Constant or enumeration	`MAX`	Is in uppercase.
Function or procedure	`deposit`	Is in lowercase.
Package	`Pack_account`	Starts with 'Pack_'.
Formal parameter	`amount`	Is in lower case.

Protected type	`protected type PT_ex is`
	`   entry put(i:in T);`
	`   entry get(i:out T);`
	`end PT_ex;`
		Starts with 'PT_'

Reserved word	`procedure`	Is in bold lower-case.

Task type	`task type Task_ex is`
	`   entry start;`
	`end Task_ex;`
		Starts with 'Task_'.

Type or subtype	`Colour`	Starts with an upper-case letter.
Variable name	`mine` `p_ch`	Is in lowercase. An access value for an item will start with 'p_'.

Glossary of terms used

Access type
A type used to elaborate an access value

Access value
The address of an object.

Actual parameter
The physical object passed to a function, procedure, entry or generic unit. For example, in the following statement the actual parameter is number.

```
print( number );
```

Ada 83
The version of the language that conforms to ANSI/MIL-STD 1815A ISO/IEC 8652:1983, 1983. Ada 83 is superseded by Ada 95. The language is named after Ada Augusta the Countess of Lovelace, daughter of the poet Lord Byron and Babbage's 'programmer'.

Ada 95
The version of the language that conforms to ANSI/ISO/IEC 8652:1995, January 1995. The ISO standard was published on 15th February 1995. Ada 95 is now often referred to as Ada

Ada class
In Ada the terminology class is used to describe a set of types. To avoid confusion this will be termed an Ada class.

Allocator
An allocator is used to claim storage dynamically from a storage pool. For example, storage for an Integer is allocated dynamically with:

```
p_int := new Integer;
```

Base class
A class from which other classes are derived.

Class

The specification of a type and the operations that are performed on an instance of the type. A class is used to create objects that share a common structure and behaviour.

The specification of a class Account is as follows:

```
package Class_account is
  type Account is tagged private;
  procedure statement( the:in Account );
  -- Other methods on an instance of an Account
private
  type Account is tagged record
    balance_of: Money := 0.00; -- Instance attribute
  end record;
end Class_account;
```

Class attribute

A data component that is shared between all objects in the class. In effect it is a global variable which can only be accessed by methods in the class. A class attribute is declared in the private part of the package representing the class. For example, the class attribute the_interest_rate in the class Interest_account is declared in the private part of the package as follows:

```
private
  type Interest_account is new Account with record
    accumulated_interest : Money := 0.00;
  end record;
  the_interest_rate: Float := DAILY_INTEREST_RATE;
end Class_interest_account
```

Class method

A procedure or function in a class that only accesses class attributes. For example, the method set_rate in the class Interest_account which sets the class attribute the_interest_rate is as follows:

```
procedure set_rate( rate:in Float ) is
begin
  the_interest_rate := rate;
end set_rate;
```

Note: As set_rate *is a class method an instance of the class is not passed to the procedure.*

Controlled object	An object which has initialization, finalization and adjust actions defined. A limited controlled object only has initialization and finalization defined as assignment is prohibited.
Discriminant	The declaration of an object may be parameterized with a value. The value is a discriminant to the type. For example, the declaration of corinna is parameterized with the length of her name.

```
type Person( chs: Str_range ) is record
  name  : String( 1 .. chs );
  -- Other data members
end record;

corinna : Person(7);
```

Dynamic-binding	The binding between an object and the message that is sent to it is <u>not</u> known at compile-time.
Elaboration	At run-time the elaboration of a declaration creates the storage for an object. For example:

```
mike : Account;
```

creates storage at run-time for the object mike.

Encapsulation	The provision of a public interface to a hidden (private) collection of data procedures and functions that provide a coherent function
Formal parameter	In a procedure, function, entry or generic unit the name of the item that has been passed. For example, in the procedure print shown below the formal parameter is value.

```
print( value:in Integer ) is
begin
  -- body
end print;
```

Generic

A procedure, function or package which is parameterized with a type or types that are used in the body of the unit. The generic unit must first be instantiated as a specific instance before it can be used. For example, the package `Integer_io` in the package `Ada.Text_io` is parameterized with the integer type on which I/O is to be performed. This generic unit must be instantiated with a specific integer type before it can be used in a program

Inheritance

The derivation of a class (derived class) from an existing class (base class). The derived class will have the methods and instance/class attributes in the class plus the methods and instance/class attributes defined in the base class. In Ada this is called programming by extension. The class `Interest_account` that is derived from the class `Account` is specified as follows:

```
with Class_account use Class_account;
package Class_interest_account is
  type Interest_account is tagged private;
  procedure set_rate( rate:in Float );
  procedure add_interest(the:in out Interest_account);
  -- Other methods
private
  type Interest_account is new Account with record
    accumulated_interest : Money := 0.00;
  end record;
  the_interest_rate := 0.00026116; -- Class attribute
end Class_account;
```

Instance attribute

A data component contained in an object. In Ada the data components are contained in a record structure in the private part of the package.

```
type Account is tagged record
  balance_of: Money; -- Instance attribute
end record;
```

Instance method

A procedure of function in a class that accesses the instance attributes (data items) contained in an object. For example, the method `balance` accesses the instance attribute `balance_of`.

```
function balance( the:in Account ) return Money is
begin
  return the.balance_of;
end balance;
```

Instantiation
The act of creating a specific instance of a generic unit. For example, the generic package `Integer_io` in the package `Ada.Text_io` can be instantiated to deliver the package `Pack_int_io` which performs I/O on an `Integer` as follows:

```
package Pack_int_io is
  new Ada.Text_io.Integer_io( Integer );
```

Then a programmer can write

```
Pack_int_io.put( people );
```

to write the contents of the `Integer` object `people`.

Message
The sending of data values to a method that operates on an object. For example, the message 'deposit £30 in account `mike`' is written in Ada as:

```
deposit( mike,  30 );
```

Note: The object to which the message is sent is the first parameter.

Meta-class
An instance of a meta-class is a class. Meta-classes are not supported in Ada.

Method
Implements behaviour in an object. A method is implemented as a procedure or function in a class. A method may be either a class method or an instance method.

Multiple inheritance
A class derived from more than one base class. Multiple inheritance is not directly supported in Ada.

Object
An instance of a class. An object has a state that is interrogated / changed by methods in the class. The object mike that is an instance of `Account` is declared as follows:

```
Account mike;
```

Overloading   When an identifier can have several different meanings. For example, the
                   procedure `put` in the package `Ada.Text_io` has several different
                   meanings. Output a `Character` object, output a `String` object etc.

Polymorphism   The ability to send a message to an object whose type is not known at
                   compile-time. The method selected depends on the type of the receiving
                   object. For example the message `'display'` is sent to different types of
                   picture elements that are held in an array.

```
display( picture_element(i) );
```

Rendezvous   The interaction that occurs when two tasks meet to synchronize and
                   possibly exchange information.

Representation   Directs the compiler to map a program item onto specific hardware
clause   features of a machine. For example, `location` is defined to be at
                   address `16#046C#`.

```
mc_address : constant Address :=
                  to_address( 16#046C# );

location : Integer;
 for location'Address use mc_address;
```

Static binding   The binding between an object and the message that it is sent to it is
                   known at compile-time.

Type   A type defines a set of values and the operations that may be performed
                   on those values. For example, the type `Exam_mark` defines the values
                   that may be given for in exam in English.

```
type Exam_mark is range 0 .. 100;

english : Exam_mark
```

1 Problem solving

This chapter looks at problem solving using an object-oriented approach. In programming, it is all too easy to believe that because you can write a small computer program without resorting to any analysis and design techniques, then solving a large problem will also be possible without any analysis and design techniques.

1.1 A problem, the model and the solution

To implement any solution to a problem, we must first fully understand the problem. Then when we understand the problem, a solution can be formulated. There are many different ways of achieving an understanding of a problem and its solution. Usually this will involve modelling the problem and its solution using either a standard notation or a notation invented by the implementor. The advantage of using a standard notation is that other people may inspect and modify the description of the problem and its proposed solution. For example, in building a house, an architect will draw up a plan of the various components that are to be built. The client can view the plans and give their approval or qualified approval subject to minor modifications. The builders can then use the plan when they erect the house (Figure 1.1)

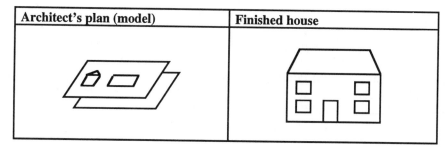

Architect's plan (model)	Finished house

Figure 1.1 An architect's plan and the finished house.

Writing a computer program involves the same overall process. First we need to understand the task that the computer program will perform. Then we implement a solution using the model that we have created.

However, an easy pitfall at this point is to believe that the model used for the solution of a small problem can be scaled up to solve a large problem. For example, to cross a small stream we can put a log over the stream or if we are fit we can even jump over the stream. This approach to crossing a stream however, will not scale up to crossing a large river. Likewise to build a 100 storey tower block, an architect would not simply take the plans for a house and instruct the builders to build some extra floors.

In software the same problems of scale exist; the techniques that we use to implement a small program cannot usually be successfully used on a large programming project. The computer literature is full of examples of software disasters that have occurred when a computer system has been started without a full understanding of the problem that is to be solved.

1.1.1 Responsibilities

Since our earliest days we have all been told that we have responsibilities. Initially these responsibilities are very simple, but as we get older, so the responsibilities increase. Responsibility is a charge, trust or duty to look after something. At an early age this can be as simple as keeping our room neat and tidy. In later life, the range and complexity of items that we have responsibility for increase dramatically.

A student for example, has the responsibility to follow a course of study. The lecturer has the responsibility of delivering the course to the students in a clear and intelligible manner. The responsibilities of the student and lecturer are summarized in tabular form below:

Responsibilities of a student	Responsibilities of a lecturer
Follow the course of study.	Deliver the course.
Perform to the best of their ability in the exam / assessment for the course.	Set and mark the assessment for the course.
	Attend the exam board for the delivered course.

Software too has responsibilities. For example, a word processing program has the responsibility of entering the user's typed text correctly into a document. However, if the text that is entered into the word processor is incorrect or meaningless, then the resultant document will also be incorrect. It is not the role of the word processor to make overall decisions about the validity of the entered text. In early computing literature a common saying was "Garbage in garbage out": even though the software package implements its responsibilities correctly, the results produced may be meaningless. Some of the responsibilities of a simple word processor are shown below:

Responsibility of a word processor
Format text typed into the document according to the prevailing set style.
Spell and grammar check the document when required.
Manage the printing of a copy of the document.

1.1.2   An object

An item that has responsibilities can be thought of as an object. The world that we live in contains many different objects. For example, in an office which deals with telephone sales the following objects can be found.

Computer	Order processing software
Fax machine	Sales people (Andy, Bob, Charles, Dave)
Inventory of stock	Telephones (One per person)
Manager (Elaine)	Terminals (One per person)

Note: There may be objects that share the same responsibilities. For example, in the sales office there are four sales people. Each sales person has the same responsibilities. Likewise each telephone has the same responsibility.

In the sales office customers phone in an order. The sales person who is contacted then uses the computer system to check if the product is available. If available, the customer is asked for a credit card number and their address. The sales person uses the computer system to check the validity of the customer's credit card for the transaction. If the credit card is valid then the computer system will instruct a warehouse to send the product to the customer's chosen address.

Each of the objects in the sales office has responsibilities, some of which are listed below:

Object	Responsibility
Computer	Run programs. Provide access to the internet.
Fax machine	Send a copy of an image to another fax machine. Act as a simple photocopier.
Inventory	Record current stock levels.
Manager (Elaine)	Ensure the smooth running of the office. Sort out problems that cannot be solved by either Andy, Bob, Charles, or Dave. Be able to take over the responsibilities of a sales person should the need arise.
Order processing software (Order soft)	Checks if goods are held in stock. Checks on the validity of a customer's credit card. Records orders and sales of stock. Issues instructions to the warehouse to dispatch goods to customers.
Sales people (Andy, Bob, Charles, Dave)	Handle enquires from customers. Check if customer's credit card is valid. Enter orders onto computer system.

Object	Responsibility
Telephone	Provide a voice connection to another telephone. Remember commonly-used numbers for future easy dialling.
Terminal (One for each person)	Send and receive data from a computer system. Display the received information onto screen.

Notice that in addition to their own responsibilities, a manager also has the responsibilities of a sales person. Thus, a manager can behave like a sales person if the need arises.

In producing a job description for a manager, the responsibilities linked to their occasional need to act as a sales person can be obtained from the job description of a sales person. The effort to produce the job description is therefore greatly reduced by including the contents of an existing job description document.

The objects in the description of a sales office do not have to be physical; for example, the document processed by a word processor is an object. Likewise the inventory of stock that is to be sold is an object. The representation of the internal state of the object will vary depending on how the object is implemented. The users of the object do not need to know how the hidden internal state of the object has been implemented.

1.1.3   A class

In understanding the world we often categorize similar items into a class. For example, in zoology there is the class of birds and the class of reptiles. We use a collective class name when describing several instances of the class. For example, we might talk about the birds in the aviary. However, when we talk about an individual instance of a bird, we tend to use the object's name. For example, George is the bird at the top of the aviary.

Objects that belong to the same class have the same responsibilities. For example, in the sales office described above, Andy, Bob, Charles, and Dave all belong to the same class, that of sales person. Elaine however, belongs to a different class as she has different overall responsibilities. This is illustrated in Figure 1.2.

Objects in the class sales person	Objects in the class manager
Andy, Bob, Charles, Dave	Elaine

Figure 1.2 Objects in the classes sales person and manager.

1.1.4 Inheritance

A class may be inherited from another class. The class manager has the relationship 'is a' to the class sales person. An object in the class manager can be used as if it were an object in the class sales people. This is illustrated in Figure 1.3.

Class hierarchy	Responsibilities
Sales person ← Manager	Handle enquiries from customers. Check if customer's credit card is valid. Enter orders onto computer system. Ensure the smooth running of the office. Sort out problems that cannot be solved by a sales person. Handle enquiries from customers. Check if customer's credit card is valid. Enter orders onto computer system.

Figure 1.3 Class hierarchy for the two classes sales person and manager.

The class manager is said to be 'derived' from the class sales person. The class sales person is termed the base class. A class that is derived from another class does not have to have all the responsibilities of the base class. It may for example, modify one or more of the responsibilities that are inherited from the base class.

1.2 Modelling the process

In defining the working of an office, one approach would be to split the office into individual objects and give each object a set of responsibilities. In some cases objects will have the same responsibilities. For example, the sales people Andy, Bob, Charles, and Dave will each have the same responsibilities. A collection of objects that all have the same responsibilities is called a class. An instance of a class is an object. Andy, Bob, Charles and Dave are instances of the class sales people.

Individual objects may interact with other objects in performing their function. For example, an individual sales person will interact with most of the other objects in the office. The computer will interact with the phone system when internet access is required. By giving each object specific responsibilities, the efficient and correct operation of the whole system can be ensured.

1.3 Fusion

A methodology for analysing and designing a solution to a problem using object-oriented techniques is fusion. Fusion is a second generation object-oriented methodology which builds on many of the first generation object-oriented methodologies. An object-oriented methodology models a system using objects as the basic building components of the system. Fusion was designed by Coelman *et al.* and is fully described in their book *Object-oriented development: The fusion method.*

In fusion, there are various steps or stages to go through before a detailed description of the overall process emerges. These steps, greatly simplified, are illustrated in the following pages.

1.3.1 Analysis

The output of the analysis stage is an object model representing the whole system. The object model shows the interaction between the various objects that make up the system. For example, the sales office is represented by the object model illustrated in Figure 1.4. The part of this model that is to be implemented on a computer system is termed the system object model.

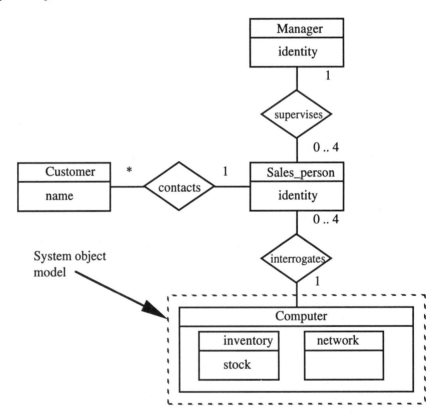

Figure 1.4 Object model for a sales-office.

Note: Some of the minor objects - telephone, fax machine, etc. - have been excluded from the model. The inventory and network are part of the computer-system.
The actual system to be implemented, the system object model, is shown enclosed in a dotted line.
The objects Customer, Manager *and* Sales_person *are outside the system object model, hence they will not form part of the implemented system.*

In the above diagram, the symbols illustrated in Figure 1.5 below are used:

Symbol	Explanation
Customer name	An object. In this case a Customer, the internal state of which is their name.
* contacts 1	Relationship. A customer contacts a sales person. The * on the left hand side indicates that there may be any number of customers contacting a sales person. The 1 on the right hand side indicates that the contact will be to a single sales person

Figure 1.5 Symbols used in the object diagram.

1.3.2 Data dictionary

The data dictionary lists the major items used to describe the system.

Name	Kind	Description
Computer	Class	Processes the transactions generated by a sales person.
Customer	Class	A customer who makes an order
Interrogates	Relationship	The interrogation of the computer system by a sales person
Inventory	Class	The list of products held in stock
Manager	Class	Ensures the smooth running of the people and equipment in the office.
Contacts	Relationship	The ordering of a product from a sales person.
Sales person	Class	Processes an order for a stock item.
Supervises	Relationship	Oversees the effective working of the sales people.
Network	Class	The means by which contacting is made with the credit card computer and the warehouse.

Note: The class name is used in the data dictionary rather than the individual object names. In some cases, for example the computer system, there is only one instance of the class.

1.3.3 Interface model

The behaviour of the above system is represented by the interface model. This shows the interactions that can take place in the system. The interface model shows the interface of the system to external agents: in this case the sales person processing the order with the computer system and the other computers that deal with credit card validation and the requesting of the goods to be sent to the customer. The interface model for the computer system is illustrated in Figure 1.6.

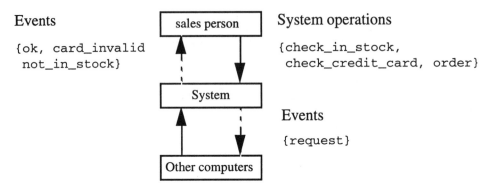

Events   sales person   System operations

{ok, card_invalid   {check_in_stock,
 not_in_stock}   check_credit_card, order}

                              System

                                                    Events

                                                    {request}

                              Other computers

Note: An input event is shown as a solid line and an output event is shown as a dotted line.

Figure 1.6 Interface model for a sales office.

An event diagram shows graphically the passing of messages between the different objects in the system. Time flows downwards in the diagram. The scenario for the system described above is shown below in Figure 1.7.

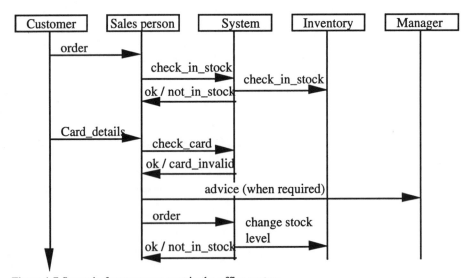

Figure 1.7 Scenario for messages sent in the office system.

1.3.4 Life cycle model

To show the communications in the system, a life cycle model is used. The life cycle model shows the states that the system goes through.

Each day 0 or more contacts with customers are processed by a sales person. The contact with the customer will involve checking with the computer system that the product the customer wishes to order is in stock, then using the computer system to process the order.

```
life_cycle:  Contact*
Contact  = check_in_stock . ( #ok.Process | #not_in_stock )
Process  = check_credit_card . ( Do_Order | #card_invalid )
Do_Order = order.(#ok|#not_in_stock)
```

Note: Output events are shown prefixed with a #.

The life cycle model uses the following notation:

Notation	Explanation
*	Zero or more occurrences of the item. For example a sales person will process 0 or more contacts with a customer in a day.
+	One or more occurrences of the item.
.	Followed by After checking the stock level the order is processed.
|	Alternative An order is processed or the customer is told that there are no items in stock.

1.3.5 Operation model

The operation model specifies the behaviour of the system. This is done in terms of state changes to the system. The operation model lists the following:

Item	Description
Operation	The name of the operation modelled. This comes from the life cycle model.
Description	A description of the operation in English
Reads	The input that the operation uses
Changes	The items that are changed by the operation
Sends	The event returned from the performance of the operation
Assumes	Any assumptions about the state of items before the operation is performed
Result	A description in English of the new state of the item after the operation has been performed

The operation model forms a contract of what to implement. The assumed description is a precondition that must be satisfied before the operation is performed. The results description is a postcondition that must be satisfied after the operation has been performed.

For example, the operation model for the system actions in the above system are:

Operation	check_in_stock
Description	Check if an item is in stock
Reads	Supplied product description
Changes	
Sends	Sales staff {`in_stock`, `not_in_stock`}
Assumes	That the inventory for the products held in stock is valid
Result	The state of the stock for a particular item

Operation	check_credit_card
Description	Check if the customer's credit card is valid and this purchase can be made using the card
Reads	Supplied credit card details
Changes	
Sends	Sales staff {`ok`, `not_ok`}
Assumes	That the credit card check is valid
Result	The validity of the credit card

Operation	order
Description	Order an item held in stock
Reads	Supplied product description, customer's address, credit card details
Changes	Inventory
Sends	Sales staff {`ok`, `not_ok`}
Assumes	That the inventory for the products held in stock is valid
Result	If the order can be satisfied and the credit card is valid then the stock level is adjusted and an order is initiated

Note: The state changes to the system are all managed by the computer system.

1.4   Computer programming and Ada

Early computers were programmed directly in the machine code instructions of the computer system. The next step was for a programmer to use mnemonics for each machine code instruction. This language was termed an assembly language. The mnemonics that make up the assembly language are then translated by the computer into the appropriate binary patterns. A program in an assembly language to calculate the cost of 15 cinema tickets would have the form:

```
LD          TICKET          ; Load into accumulator cost of a single ticket
MULT        #15             ; Multiply by 15
ST          COST            ; Store accumulator into cost
```

In an assembly language there is a one-to-one correspondence between each code line and a machine code instruction.

Later, when computers had both more memory and a greater processing speed, problem-oriented or high-level languages were developed. These high-level languages allowed a programmer to express a program in problem-oriented statements. These high-level language statements were then translated by a compiler into the machine code instructions of the machine. It is usual for each line of a high-level language to be translated into many machine code instructions.

It was fashionable in the early days of high-level languages for many organizations to have their own language or at least a variant of an existing language. Each manufacturer would have their own slightly modified version of the popular languages implemented on their machine. The consequences of this to any organization are:

- Programs are not easily ported to a new machine.
- Staff have to be expert at several languages.

In 1968 at a NATO conference the term software engineering was introduced to describe the discipline of producing programs that would be engineered rather than crafted. This was a reaction to software that was delivered late, over budget or not able to meet its specification.

Nicholas Worth in 1969 developed the language Pascal to enable students to develop good programming practice. A major theme of this language was that errors should be caught by the compiler before the program was executed. If errors did occur in the running program they should be trapped when possible by the run-time system.

In 1974 the DOD (United States Department Of Defense) initiated a program to produce a minimum number of high-level languages for the department's embedded computer systems. It soon became apparent that no existing language was totally suitable. In 1977 the DOD requested proposals for a new high-level language and 14 were received. Later in the year the DOD awarded four contracts for further design work to be carried out. Interestingly each of these languages was based on the language Pascal. To avoid biases in the selection process each language was colour coded. The green language was selected at a meeting on the 2 May 1979 as the winner.

After some debate Ada was chosen for the name of the new language in honour of the first programmer Ada (Byron) Lovelace. Ada (1815-52), the daughter of Lord Byron, assisted the British mathematician Charles Babbage with his work on the analytical engine. The Ada language was adopted as ANSI/MIL-STD 1815A in 1983.

Ada 83 was revised in 1995 to include features that were deemed necessary for developing software in the late 20th, early 21st century. In particular the following features were enhanced: object-oriented components, real-time extensions, interoporability with other languages and distributed components.

Ada is used mainly, though not exclusively, in the following broad areas:

- Defence and related areas
- Megaprogramming
- Safety / mission critical applications
- Teaching of programming

Figure 1.8 Charts the development of computing and programming languages.

When	Computer History	Programming Languages	European History
1830	Analytical Engine 1834		
			Victorian era, 1837-1901
...			
1955			
		FORTRAN 1957	EEC Founded 1957
		COBOL 1959	
1960		Algol 60	
1965			
		Simular 67	
	ARPANET		
1970		Pascal 1970 C 1972	
	Unix 1st Edition 1971	Smalltalk 1972	Great Britain, Ireland, and Denmark join EEC 1973
	Ethernet 1969		
1975			
		Ada 1979	
1980	The IBM PC 1981		Greece joins EEC 1982
	BSD 4.2 1983	Ada 83 standard	
1985		C++	Spain and Portugal join EEC 1986
	Internet worm 1988		
1990	Windows 3.0 1990		Re-unification of Germany 1990 Maastricht Treaty 1991
1995	Windows 95 1995	Ada 95 standard	Sweden, Austria, and Finland join EU 1995

Figure 1.8 Time chart of computer history

1.4.1 Ada 95, the structure

The Ada 95 programming language is split into two distinct sections: a core language that must be implemented and a series of annexes that may or may not be implemented. The annexes extend the language into problem specific areas. The annexes to the language are:

Annex	Contents of annex:
System programming	The provision of features that will allow the interfacing of an Ada program to external environments. For example, the interfacing of Ada code to a peripheral device or to components of the operating system interface.
Real time systems	The provision of features that will allow the control of real-time processes.
Distributed systems	The provision of features that will allow a system to extend beyond a single address space in a single machine.
Information systems	The provision of features that will allow an Ada program to communicate with programs or systems written in C or COBOL.
Numerics	The provision of features that will allow the construction of numerically intense applications
Safety and security	Restrictions to the language to minimize insecurities and areas in which compromises to validation and verification would be made.

Note: The annexes rarely extend the syntax of the language; rather they provide extra packages to enable the particular area to be performed.

1.5 Self-assessment

- Explain why the solution to a small problem may not always scale up to solve a much larger and complex problem.

- Describe the responsibilities of:
  (a)   A TV set.
  (b)   A football coach.
  (c)   The EU or US President.
  (d)   An actor playing the role of Hamlet in a play.

- What is the difference between a class and an object?

- Identify several objects and classes around you at the moment. Can you find any common responsibilities that any of the objects or classes has?

- What classes do the following objects belong to? Identify which classes are derived from other classes?

cat	cow	crayon	dog	elephant
house	hut	ink pen	museum	office block
pencil	sheep	wolf		

1.6 Exercises

Produce an object model, data dictionary, interface model, life cycle model and operation model for the following scenarios.

- *Cinema ticket sales*
  The operation of the issuing of tickets at a cinema. At the local cinema, a customer buys a ticket from the sales person. The sales person enters details about the number of tickets required and for which performance into a computer terminal. The computer terminal tells the sales person if seats are available and if so, the cost of the seats. The customer pays the sales person and the terminal issues the appropriate number of tickets. The computer will inform the sales person when no tickets for a particular performance are available.

- *Video recorder*
  The operation of a video recorder. A video recorder consists of a control panel, clock and memory unit and record playback transport system. A user sets the video recorder by interacting with the control panel. The clock has a memory that allows up to four start and stop times to be set. The record, playback transport system performs the following actions, play, record, fast forward, rewind and ejection of the video tape.

2 Ada introduction: Part 1

This chapter looks at some simple Ada programs, and presents the basic control structures of the language. The data types `Integer` and `Character` are used to introduce these structures.

2.1 A first Ada program

The first program presented is a simple one that writes the message 'hello world' onto the user's terminal.

```
with Ada.Text_io;
use  Ada.Text_io;
procedure helloworld is
begin
  put("Hello World"); new_line;
end helloworld;
```

Note: The example programs in this book are shown with reserved words in bold to aid readability. As the name suggests, reserved words can only be used for their intended purpose. Strange error messages can occur when a reserved word is inadvertently used by the programmer as the name of an object in a program. Reserved words are entered as normal text when writing a program. Section B.1, Appendix B lists all the reserved words in the Ada programming language.

When compiled and run, this program will display on a user's terminal the message:

```
Hello World
```

In the above program, the reserved words **begin** and **end** are used to bracket the body of the procedure `helloworld`. In Ada, a procedure can be a self-contained program unit that may be independently compiled. In the above example, the single procedure `helloworld` forms a complete program that may be compiled and run by an appropriate Ada compiling system.

The statement `put("Hello World");` is responsible for outputting the greeting to the terminal. Used in conjunction with `new_line`, which outputs a new line character to the terminal, these procedures are defined and implemented by the library package `Ada.Text_io`.

Note: *The* **end** *keyword is followed by the name of the procedure, in this example* helloworld *The compiler checks for this to ensure that the procedure's extent agrees with the programmer's view.*

One of the important concepts in Ada is the idea of encapsulating items together to form a package which may be re-used in other programs. The library package Ada.Text_io is provided on Ada systems to allow the input and output of textual information to and from the user's program. This library package is introduced to a procedure by means of the statements **with** Ada.Text_io; **use** Ada.Text_io; the details of which will be explained later.

Figure 2.1 illustrates the components of an Ada program.

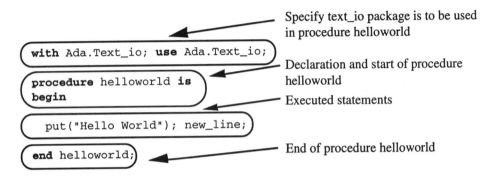

Specify text_io package is to be used in procedure helloworld

Declaration and start of procedure helloworld

Executed statements

End of procedure helloworld

Figure 2.1 Components of an Ada program.

2.2   The case of letters in a program

In Ada, the case of characters used in reserved words and identifiers is unimportant; the compiler will take begin Begin or even BeGiN to mean exactly the same thing. The only place where the case of a letter matters is in string and character constants. The above program for example, could have been written as:

```
WITH Ada.Text_IO; USE Ada.Text_io;

PROCEDURE HelloWorld IS
BEGIN
  Put("Hello World"); New_Line;
END helloworld;
```

2.3 Format of an Ada program

In Ada, like in many other languages, white space is used mainly as a way of neatly laying out a program so that everyone, including the author, may clearly see the structure and purpose of the statements. There are many conventions for the layout of an Ada program and there are even programs which will reformat an Ada program for you.

The program illustrated above could have been written as:

```
with Ada.Text_io; use Ada.Text_io; procedure helloworld is begin
put("Hello World"); new_line; end helloworld;
```

although it is now more difficult to see exactly what the code is supposed to achieve. The only place where white space character(s) or a new line are needed, is between words that contain alphabetic characters. Naturally, any strings that contain white space characters will be output containing these white space characters. However a newline character is not allowed in a string.

A line of an Ada program can be up to 200 characters long and implementors may, if they wish, allow longer lines. A consequence of this is that names of items in an Ada program are considered unique if the first 200 characters are different.

2.3.1 Variable names

A variable name must start with a letter and can then be followed by any number of letters and digits and the underscore character. However, two underscore characters cannot occur next to each other and an underscore character must not start or finish a variable name.

2.3.2 Comments

In Ada, comments may be introduced into a program by preceding the remainder of the line containing the comment, with two - characters. For example, a possible comment to the above program might be:

```
-- This program writes the message
--      "Hello World" to a users terminal
```

2.4   A larger Ada program

A program to produce a countdown is shown below. In this program, various constructs which affect the flow of control are introduced.

```
with Ada.Text_io; use Ada.Text_io; -- Use Ada.Text_io
procedure main is
  count : Integer;                  -- Declaration of count
begin
  count := 10;                      -- Set to 10
  while count > 0 loop              -- loop while greater than 0
    if count = 3 then               -- If 3 print Ignition
      put("Ignition"); new_line;
    end if;
    put( Integer'Image( count ) ); -- Print current count
    new_line;
    count := count - 1;             -- Decrement by 1 count
    delay 1.0;                      -- Wait 1 second
  end loop;
  put("Blast off"); new_line;       -- Print Blast off
end main;
```

In this program an integer variable `count` is declared which contains the current value of the countdown. This is achieved with the declaration `count : Integer;`. The Ada statement `delay 1.0;` causes a pause of one second in the program.

Note: Declarations of items are allowed in any order in Ada 95.
        `Integer'Image( count )` delivers `count` as a character string. This is necessary as the package `Ada.Text_io` only implements input and output on a character or a string.

When run, this program will produce the following output:

```
10
 9
 8
 7
 6
 5
 4
Ignition
 3
 2
 1
Blast off
```

This is similar to the commentary used during the take-off procedures of early space missions.

2.5 Repetition: `while`

```
while count > 0 loop

  -- Repeated statements

end loop;
```

The above construct repeatedly executes the statements between **loop** and **end loop** while the condition `count > 0` is true.

*Note: The mandatory **end loop** terminates the **while loop**. In Ada, most constructs are terminated by a mandatory termination keyword(s). This prevents the kind of errors that can occur in other languages when an extra statement is added in the belief that it forms part of the construct. It also allows the compiler to check that the user has constructed a program correctly by matching the start and end of each construct.*

2.6 Selection: `if`

```
if count = 3 then
  put("Ignition"); new_line;
end if;
```

The **if** statement allows a statement or statements to be executed only if the condition is true. In the above example, the statements `put("Ignition"); new_line;` will only be executed when count is equal to 3.

*Note: The mandatory **end if** terminates the **if** statement.*

An **else** part may also be included, in which case statement or statements which follow it are obeyed if the condition is false. For example:

```
if count = 3 then
  put("Count is 3"); new_line;
else
  put("Count is not 3"); new_line;
end if;
```

*Note: The else part of an **if** statement is optional. However, if it is included it must be followed be at least one statement.*

The rather inelegant nested **if** structure below:

```
if count = 3 then
  put("Count is 3"); new_line;
else
  if count = 4 then
    put("Count is 4"); new_line;
  else
    put("Count is not 3 or 4"); new_line;
  end if;
end if;
```

can be rewritten using the following **elsif** construct:

```
if count = 3 then
  put("Count is 3"); new_line;
elsif count = 4 then
  put("Count is 4"); new_line;
else
  put("Count is not 3 or 4"); new_line;
end if;
```

*Note: For the statements in the **else** part to be obeyed, all the conditions in the **if** and **elsif** parts must be false.*
There may be many elsif components in an if statement, but only one else.

2.7   Other repetition constructs

2.7.1   for

In Ada, a loop may be constructed in which a variable is varied by one unit between two values. For example, the code to print out the numbers from 1 to 10 can be written using a **for** statement as follows:

```
for count in 1 .. 10 loop
  put( Integer'Image( count ) );
end loop;
new_line;
```

When run, this would produce:

```
1 2 3 4 5 6 7 8 9 10
```

*Note: The variable count is declared by the **for** statement and is visible only for the extent of the **for** loop. It is a read only item and therefore cannot be written to.*

The values may be stepped through in reverse order by inserting the keyword **reverse** after the keyword **in**. For example:

```
for count in reverse 1 .. 10 loop
   put( Integer'Image( count ) );
end loop;
new_line;
```

When run, this would produce:

```
10 9 8 7 6 5 4 3 2 1
```

Note: *The range must evaluate to a possible list of values for the body of the* **for**
     loop *to be executed. For example:*

```
for count in reverse 10 .. 1 loop
   --
end loop;
```

would not execute the body of the **for** *loop.*

In the program below the two loops produce identical results:

```
with Ada.Text_io; use Ada.Text_io;
procedure main is
   count    : Integer;              -- count as Integer object
   COUNT_TO : constant Integer := 10; -- integer constant
begin
   count := 1;
   while count <= COUNT_TO loop      -- While loop
     put( Integer'Image( count ) );
     count := count + 1;
   end loop;
   new_line;

   for count in 1 .. COUNT_TO loop   -- count declared here
     put( Integer'Image( count ) );
   end loop;
   new_line;

end main;
```

When run, this would produce:

```
1 2 3 4 5 6 7 8 9 10
1 2 3 4 5 6 7 8 9 10
```

Note: For the **for** *loop a new count is declared which is visible only for the extent of the loop.*

2.7.2 loop

Another way of writing the above loop is by using the infinite looping construct **loop end loop**. As this construct repeats for ever, an exit mechanism is provided to short-circuit the loop. This escape mechanism is the **exit** statement, which causes an immediate exit from the loop. Older programmers will recognise this as a restricted version of the goto statement. The loops seen earlier in sections 2.5 and 2.7.1 could have been expressed using a **loop** construct as follows:

```
with Ada.Text_io; use Ada.Text_io;
procedure main is
   count     : Integer;                -- count as Integer object
   COUNT_TO : constant Integer := 10; -- integer constant
begin
   count := 1;
   loop
     put( Integer'Image( count ) );
     exit when count = COUNT_TO;       -- Exit loop when ...
     count := count + 1;
   end loop;
   new_line;

end main;
```

When run, this would produce:

```
1 2 3 4 5 6 7 8 9 10
```

The exit from the **loop** is accomplished by adding a condition to the **exit** statement, in this case **when** count = 0 .

Note: The **loop** *construct can be used when it is necessary to execute the code at least one-time.*
An **exit** *statement may be used to exit from a while loop and a for loop.*

2.8 Other selection constructs

2.8.1 case

The previous series of **if then else** statements in section 2.6 can be replaced by the following **case** statement:

```
case count is
   when 3       => put("Count is 3"); new_line;
   when 4       => put("Count is 4"); new_line;
   when others => put("Count is not 3 or 4"); new_line;
end case;
```

In Ada, a **case** statement must take account of all values that the control variable may take: hence the **when others** component in the above statement. Had it not been present, then a compile-time error would have been generated.

A character variable may be declared which can hold a character from the Ada character set. The following **case** statement would print out a classification of the character held in the object ch.

```
ch := 'a';
case ch is
   when '0' | '1' | '2' | '3' | '4' |
        '5' | '6' | '7' | '8' | '9'   =>
     put("Character is a digit");
   when 'A' .. 'Z' =>
     put("Character is upper case English letter");
   when 'a' .. 'z' =>
     put("Character is lower case English letter");
   when others     =>
     put("Not an English letter or digit");
end case;
new_line;
```

In this **case** statement two ways of combining case labels are introduced.

Case component	Description	Explanation
|	Or	For example, '0' | '1' will match the character '0' or the character '1'
..	Range	For example, 'A' .. 'Z' will match any character in the range Capital A to Capital Z.

The fragment of program code combined with appropriate declarations and compiled would produce when run:

```
Character is lower case English letter
```

2.9 Input and output

In Ada, input and output are performed by a variety of standard packages. The full implications of the package construct are discussed fully in Chapters 5 and 17 which describe in detail the I/O packages. For the moment, the discussion about input and output will concentrate solely on character data.

Text is output to the terminal using the put procedure. This procedure may take a parameter which is either a character or a character string. For example, to output hello the user could write either:

```
put("hello");
```

or

```
put('h'); put('e'); put('l'); put('l'); put('o');
```

Note: A string is use to represent a sequence of characters. A string is enclosed in " " whilst a character is enclosed in ' '. In this way the compiler can distinguish between a character 'A'and a string of a single character "A".

To input a character into the variable ch of type Character, the user could write:

```
get(ch);
```

A simple program to copy its input, character-by-character to the output source, could be as follows:

```
with Ada.Text_io; use Ada.Text_io;-- Using Ada.Text_io
procedure cat is
  ch : Character;                    -- Current character
begin
  while not end_of_file loop        -- For each Line
    while not end_of_line loop       -- For each character
      get(ch); put(ch);              -- Read / Write character
    end loop;
    skip_line; new_line;             -- Next line / new line
  end loop;
end cat;
```

The above program uses the following input and output functions or procedures.

Function/Procedure	Effect
end_of_file	Delivers true when the end of the file is reached, otherwise it delivers false.
end_of_line	Delivers true when all the characters have been read from the current input line, otherwise it delivers false. NB. This does not include the new line character.
skip_line	Positions the input pointer at the start of the next line. Any information on the current line is skipped.
new_line	Write the new line character to the output stream NB. On some systems new line is represented by two characters when output.

If compiled to the executable file `simple_cat`, the same program could be run on a Unix or MSDOS system to implement a simple software tool to print the contents of the file `about_ada`. To list the contents of the file `about_ada` to the terminal using an MSDOS system, a user could type:

```
simple_cat < about_ada
```

Note: On a DOS or Unix system the command `simple_cat  <  about_ada` *runs the program* `simple_cat` *taking its input from the file* `about_ada`.

2.10 Access to command line arguments

When a program is executed it is possible to access any arguments given on the same line as the program name. For example, the following program `echo` has two command line arguments:

```
echo Hello there!
```

If the program `echo` is compiled with the package `Ada.Command_line` then the programmer has available the following function calls:

call of function	Returns
argument_count	The number of command line arguments. In this case, two.
argument(1)	A string representing the first command line argument. In this case "Hello".
argument(2)	A string representing the second command line argument. In this case "there!".

Note: It would be an error detected at run-time to access `argument(3)`.

The code for the program echo is as follows:

```
with Ada.Text_io, Ada.Command_line;
use  Ada.Text_io, Ada.Command_line;
procedure echo is
begin
  for i in 1 .. argument_count loop
    put( argument(i) );
    if i /= argument_count then
      put(" ");
    end if;
  end loop;
  new_line;
end echo;
```

Note: See how the package Ada.Command_line has been used here.

2.10.1   Putting it all together

If compiled to the executable file echo, the program could be run on a Unix or MSDOS system to implement the command echo as follows:

```
% echo Hello there!
```

Which when run would write:

```
Hello there!
```

2.11 A better cat program

By using, the package Ada.Command_line a better version of the cat program can be written. In this new version the files to be listed to the terminal are specified after the executable program name.

The following procedures and functions are used to control the reading of data from a file.

Function/Procedure	Effect
open	Opens an existing file. A file descriptor to this file is returned as the result. A file descriptor is of type: File_type in the package Ada.Text_io.
close	Close the open file.

Function/Procedure	Effect
end_of_file end_of_line skip_line get	As previously described but this time the effect is not on the normal input stream, but on the input of data from a file. The extra first parameter denotes the file descriptor attached to the file.

This new program is as follows:

```
with Ada.Text_io, Ada.Command_line;
use  Ada.Text_io, Ada.Command_line;
procedure main is
   fd  : Ada.Text_io.File_type;      -- File descriptor
   ch  : Character;                  -- Current character
begin
   if argument_count >= 1 then
      for i in 1 .. argument_count loop
         open( File=>fd, Mode=>IN_FILE, Name=>argument(i) );
         while not end_of_file(fd) loop  -- For each Line
            while not end_of_line(fd) loop-- For each character
               get(fd,ch); put(ch);       -- Read / Write character
            end loop;
            skip_line(fd); new_line;    -- Next line / new line
         end loop;
         close(fd);
      end loop;
   else
      put("Usage: cat file1 ... "); new_line;
   end if;
end main;
```

2.11.1   Putting it all together

Which when compiled to the executable file cat can be run as follows on an MSDOS or Unix system:

```
% cat file1.txt file2.txt
```

Note: *If a file does not exist then the program will fail with an uncaught exception condition. Chapter 12 describes how such exceptional conditions may be caught and processed in a program.*

2.12 Characters in Ada

In Ada there are two distinct types used for holding characters. These are:

Type	An instance of this type
`Character`	Can hold 256 distinct characters. Characters with internal code 0-127 are from the ASCII character set. The ASCII standard is equivalent to ISO 8859.
`Wide_character`	Can hold 65336 different characters. The characters are defined in ISO 10646 BMP

Note: Many computer systems use the ASCII character set to represent data held internally or transmitted.
In Ada 83 variables of type `Character` *are restricted to holding only 128 different character values compared to Ada 95's 256.*

These types are defined as enumeration types in the package standard. A consequence of this is that characters like 'A' are enumerations of both `Character` and `Wide_character`. The effect is that a programmer cannot write:

```
if 'A' = 'A' then    ...   end if
```

as the character 'A' could belong to the type `Character` or `Wide_character` which the compiler cannot resolve from the statement.

2.13 Self-assessment

- What is the purpose of the package `Ada.Text_io`?

- What are the disadvantages of the **exit** statement?

- Why did the designers of Ada make the control variable in a **for** loop read only?

- Why might the omission of **when others** in a **case** statement cause a compile-time error?

- Can every **loop end loop** statement be expressed as a **while end loop** statement which does not have an **exit** statement? For example, the following program illustrates a **loop end loop**:

```
procedure main is
  count     : Integer := 1;
  COUNT_TO : constant Integer := 10;
begin
  loop
    put ( Integer'Image ( count ) );
    exit when count = COUNT_TO;
    count := count + 1;
  end loop;
  new_line;
end main;
```

Is the converse true? Explain your answer.

- What are the major differences discussed so far between Ada and other programming languages known to you?

- Why might an Ada 95 program using a Character variable not compile using an Ada 83 compiler?

- How may command line arguments be accessed from a program?

2.14 Exercises

Construct the following programs:

- Numbers
  A program to print the first 20 positive numbers (1, 2, 3, etc.).

- Times table
  A program to print out the 8 times table so that the output is in the following form:

```
8 * 1   =      8
8 * 2   =      16
8 * 3   =      24
.   .   .
8 * 12  =      96
```

- Series
  A program to print out numbers in the series 1 1 2 3 5 8 13 ... until the last term is greater then 10000.

- Character table
  A program to print the characters represented by the numbers 32 to 126.

  Hint:
  If a variable `number` is of type `Integer` then
  `Character'Val(number)` will deliver the character which is represented internally by the value contained in number.

- Table
  A program to print out the square, cube and 4th power of the first 15 positive numbers.

3 Ada introduction: Part 2

This chapter looks at declarations and use of scalar data items in Ada. One of Ada's key contributions to programming is the ability to declare data items that can only take a specific range of values. Ada's strong typing ensures that many errors in a program will be detected at compile rather than run-time.

3.1 Introduction

So far, only objects of type Integer or Character have been introduced. An Integer object stores a number as a precise amount with no decimal places. The exact range of values that can be stored is implementation defined. A user can find out this range by employing the attributes 'First and 'Last on the type Integer. In addition the attribute 'Bits returns the size in bits of an Integer object. The following program prints these attributes for an Integer type.

```
with Ada.Text_io; use Ada.Text_io;
procedure main is
begin
  put("Smallest integer ");
  put( Integer'Image( Integer'First ) ); new_line;
  put("Largest integer  ");
  put( Integer'Image( Integer'Last ) ); new_line;
  put("Size in bits of an Integer is ");
  put( Integer'Image( Integer'Size ) ); new_line;
end main;
```

Note: The attribute 'First is pronounced 'tick first'.

When compiled and run on two different machines, this would produce:

Machine using a 16 bit word size	Machine using a 32 bit word size

```Smallest integer -32768```
```Largest integer   32767```
```Integer (bits)   16```
	```Smallest integer -2147483648```
	```Largest integer 2147483647```
	```Integer (bits) 32```

3.2 The type `Float`

An instance of the type `Integer` holds numbers to an exact value. In the solution of some problems the numbers manipulated will not be an exact value. For example, a person's weight is 80.23 kilograms. The data type `Float` elaborates an object which can hold a number which has decimal places. Thus in a program a person's weight can be held in the object `weight` which is declared as follows:

```
weight : Float := 80.23;
```

A `Float` is implemented as a floating point number. A floating point number holds a value to a specific number of decimal digits. This will in many cases be an approximation to the exact value which the programmer wishes to store. For example, a 1/3 will be held as 0.333 ... 33. The following table shows how various numbers are effectively stored in floating point form to 6 decimal places:

Number	Scientific notation	Floating point form
80.23	$0.8023 * 10^2$	+802300 +02
0.008023	$0.8023 * 10^{-2}$	+802300 -02
0.333333	$0.333333 * 10^0$	+333333 +00

Note: In reality the floating point number will be held in binary.

The main consequence of using a floating point number is that numbers are held to an approximation of their true value. Calculations using floating point numbers will usually only give an approximation to the true answer. However, in many cases this approximation will not cause any problems. An area where this approximation will cause problems is when the value represents a monetary amount.

The attributes `'First`, `'Last` and `'Size` may also be applied to objects of type `Float`. In addition the attribute `'Digits` returns the precision in decimal digits of a number stored in a `Float` object. For example, the following program:

```
with Ada.Text_io; use Ada.Text_io;
procedure main is
begin
  put("Smallest Float ");
  put( Float'Image( Float'First ) ); new_line;
  put("Largest  Float ");
  put( Float'Image( Float'Last ) ); new_line;
  put("Float (bits)    ");
  put( Integer'Image( Float'Size ) ); new_line;
  put("Float (digits) ");
  put( Integer'Image( Float'Digits ) ); new_line;
end main;
```

Note: `Float'Image` delivers a string representing a floating point number in scientific notation.

when compiled and run on two different machines would produce:

Machine using a 32 bit word size	Machine using a 64 bit word size
| ```
Smallest Float  -3.40282E+038
Largest  Float   3.40282E+038
Float (bits)     32
Float (digits)   6
``` | ```
Smallest Float  -1.79769313486232E+308
Largest  Float   1.79769313486232E+308
Float (bits)     64
Float (digits)   15
``` |

3.2.1   Other Integer and Float data types

Some implementations of Ada may provide data types that offer a greater precision than the in-built types of `Integer` and `Float`. If these are provided they will be called `Long_Integer`, `Long_Float`, `Long_Long_Integer` etc.

3.3   New data types

Using an object of type `Integer` to hold numeric values may be a useful approach, but it does not lead to a program that is machine independent. For example, during its execution a program could create values which were not containable in a particular machine's `Integer` object. If this happened, then the program would fail with a run-time error of 'Constraint_Error'.

Ada provides an elegant solution to this problem. It allows a user to define a new data type, which has a specific range of values. For example, the following declaration defines a new data type `Distance` which will hold the distance between two places:

```
type Distance is range 0 .. 250_000;
```

Note: If the compiler cannot provide an object which can hold such a range, a compile-time error message will be generated.

`Distance` is a new type, instances of which may not be mixed with instances of other types. The following table shows some examples of type declarations in Ada.

Type declaration	An instance of T will Declare
type T is range 0 .. 250_000;	An object which can hold whole numbers in the range 0 .. 250_000.
type T is digits 8;	An object which can hold a floating point number which has a precision of 8 digits.
type T is digits 8 **range** 0.0 .. 10.0;	An object which can hold a floating point number which has a precision of 8 digits and can store numbers in the range 0.0 .. 10.0.

3.3.1   Type conversions

To convert between compatible scalar types the type name of the required type is used to convert an object to the required type. For example, the following program converts an object of type `Apples` into an object of type `French_apples`.

```
procedure main is
   type Apples          is range 0 .. 100;
   type French_apples is range 0 .. 100;
   number : Apples;
   number_from_france : French_apples;
begin
   number := 10;
   number_from_france := French_apples( number );
end main;
```

It is, however, up to the programmer to determine whether the conversion is meaningful. Conversion however can only take place between types that are compatible.

3.3.2   Universal integer

To avoid tedious type conversion when dealing with constants, Ada has the concept of a universal integer. The compiler will automatically convert a universal integer to an appropriate type when used in an arithmetic expression. In Ada all integer numeric constants are regarded as being of type universal integer. Likewise all floating point constants are regarded as a universal float.

3.3.3   Constant declarations

To make a program more readable, all values other than 0 or 1 should normally be given a symbolic name. This helps to improve the readability of a program and allows the programmer to change the value by means of a single textual change. For example, the capacity of a car park could be described as:

```
MAX_PARKING_SPACES : constant := 100;
```

This describes `MAX_PARKING_SPACES` as a universal integer. However, if the declaration had been:

```
MAX_PARKING_SPACES : constant Parking_spaces := 100;
```

then `MAX_PARKING_SPACES` would be a constant of type `Parking_spaces`.

Note: The latter declaration will restrict the places where MAX_PARKING_SPACES can be used to only those places where a value of type Parking_spaces can occur.

3.4 Modified count-down program

The countdown program shown in section 2.4 can be rewritten, restricting count to the values 1 to 10 as follows:

```
with Ada.Text_io; use Ada.Text_io;      -- Use Ada.Text_io
procedure main is
  type Count_range is range 1 .. 10;
begin
  for count in reverse Count_range loop
    if count = 3 then                    -- If 3 print Ignition
      put("Ignition"); new_line;
    end if;
    put( Count_range'Image( count ) ); -- Print current count
    new_line;
    delay 1.0;                           -- Wait 1 second
  end loop;
  put("Blast off"); new_line;           -- Print Blast off
end main;
```

Note: *Even though* count *is of type* Count_range, *it can be compared with the integer constant 3.*

The use of the type Count_range *in the* **loop** *statement. This confines the loop to the range of values that an instance of* count_range *can take.*

The use of

    Count_range'Image(count)

to deliver a character representation of the contents of count. Remember count *is of type* Count_range.

3.5 Input and output in Ada

One of the stumbling blocks in writing programs in Ada is the complexity involved in outputting integer and floating point numbers. Ada 95 provides two packages:

-     Ada.Integer_Text_IO
-     Ada.Float_Text_IO

explicitly for this purpose.

The programs in this book use the single package Simple_io which in effect is a combination of the above two packages plus the package Ada.Text_io. The definition of the package Simple_io is given in section C.3 in Appendix C. If you do not wish to use the package Simple_io then simply replace the package with the above three packages. For example:

A program which begins:

```
with Simple_io;
use  Simple_io;
procedure main is
```

would need to be changed too:

```
with Ada.Text_io, Ada.Float_Text_IO, Ada.Integer_Text_IO;
use  Ada.Text_io, Ada.Float_Text_IO, Ada.Integer_Text_IO;
procedure main is
```

Chapter 17 describes how specific packages are instantiated to output instances of other types.

3.5.1 Output of floating point numbers

A floating point number is output using the overloaded procedure `put`, though by default this displays the number in scientific notation. Extra parameters to `put` are used to control the output form of the floating point number. These parameters are used together or individually. The main parameters to control the format are named `fore`, `aft` and `exp`. For example, to output the contents of the `Float` object `num` that contains 123.456 the following versions of `put` may be used:

put statement	Output	Notes
put(num);	1.23456E+02	1
put(num, fore=>4, aft=>2, exp=>0);	1.23	2
put(num, fore=>4, aft=>2, exp=>3);	1.23E+02	3

Note: Section C.5, Appendix C contains a description of the package Ada.Text_io *and shows other forms of the* put *statement.*

Notes:

1			*Scientific notation by default.*
2	*aft*	*=>2*	*Number of places after the decimal point.*
	fore	*=>4*	*Number of places before the decimal point.*
			This includes any sign character such as –.
	exp	*=>0*	*No exponent hence non scientific notation.*
3	*exp*	*=>3*	*Scientific notation with three places for the exponent.*
			This includes any sign character such as –.

3.5.2 Output of integer numbers

In the output of an integer number the parameters `base` and `width` can be used together or individually to control the format of the output. For example, to output the contents of the Integer object num which contains 42 the following versions of put may be used:

put statement	Output	Notes
put(num);	42	1
put(num, base=> 8, width=>5);	8#52#	2

Notes:

1	*Output in the default field width.*	
2	base =>8	*Output base: in this case octal.*
	width =>5	*Field width for the number.*

3.6 Conversion between **Float** and **Integer** types

Because Float and Integer are two separate types, instances of these types may not be mixed. This initially can cause problems as often we informally mix whole numbers and 'floating point numbers' together. For example, the following program prints a conversion table for whole pounds to kilograms:

```
with Simple_io; use Simple_io;
procedure main is
begin
  for i in 1 .. 5 loop
    put( i ); put(" Pounds = " );
    put( Float(i) / 2.2046, exp=>0, aft=>2 );
    put( " Kilograms" ); new_line;
  end loop;
end main;
```

Note: The explicit conversion Float(i) *converts the* Integer *object i to an instance of a* Float.

When run, this will give the following output:

```
1 Pounds =   0.45 Kilograms
2 Pounds =   0.91 Kilograms
3 Pounds =   1.36 Kilograms
4 Pounds =   1.81 Kilograms
5 Pounds =   2.27 Kilograms
```

The conversion process may be used in reverse to convert a floating point number to an integer form. The effect of this conversion is to round away from zero, so that:

Float object f contains	Integer(f) delivers
1.5	2
1.3	1
−1.5	−2
−1.3	−1

3.7 Type safety in a program

By using the type mechanism, errors in a program can be detected at compile-time. For example, a program which processes distances in miles and kilometres can be made safer by defining separate types for miles and kilometres as follows:

```
type Miles      is digits 8 range 0.0 .. 25_000.0;
type Kilometres is digits 8 range 0.0 .. 50_000.0;
```

Note: The range of values is adequate to accommodate any distance between two points on the earth.

A program which processes distances between cities could be defined as follows:

```
with Simple_io; use Simple_io;
procedure main is
   type Miles      is digits 8 range 0.0 .. 25_000.0;
   type Kilometres is digits 8 range 0.0 .. 50_000.0;
   london_paris       : Miles;
   paris_geneva       : Kilometres;
   london_paris_geneva: Kilometres;
begin
   london_paris := 210.0;   -- Miles
   paris_geneva := 420.0;   -- Kilometres
   london_paris_geneva :=
         kilometres( london_paris * 1.609_344 ) + paris_geneva;
   put("Distance London - Paris - Geneva is " );
   put( Float( london_paris_geneva ), aft=>2, exp=>0 );
   put( "Km" );
   new_line;
end main;
```

*Note: There is an explicit conversion of a distance in miles to kilometres using the type conversion kilometres(london_paris * 1.609_344).*

The contents of london_paris_geneva has been converted to a Float so that it can be printed using the package Simple_io. Chapter 17 describes how user defined types may be output.

The parameters to put when outputting a floating point number control the number of decimal places output and the format of the number. Section C.3, Appendix C lists the parameters used in outputting numbers .

If by accident a programmer wrote:

```
london_paris_geneva := london_paris + paris_geneva;
```

then the Ada compiler would detect a type mismatch at compile-time. London to Paris is in miles and Paris to Geneva is in kilometres.

3.8 Subtypes

The type mechanism can on occasion, be restricting as a programmer wants the range checking provided by the type mechanism but does not want to have to keep explicitly performing type conversions. A subtype of a type provides the range checking associated with a type, but instances of a type and its subtypes may be freely mixed in expressions.

For example, the speed of various forms of transport can be defined using the type and subtype mechanism as follows:

```
type     Speed_mph     is range 0 .. 25_000;
subtype Train_speed   is Speed_mph range 0 .. 130;
subtype Bus_speed     is Speed_mph range 0 .. 75;
subtype Cycling_speed is Speed_mph range 0 .. 30;
subtype Person_speed  is Speed_mph range 0 .. 15;
```

A subtype is derived from an existing type and constrains the values that can be assigned to an instance of the subtype. The compiler will enforce this constraint either by performing a compile-time check or by generating code to check the constraint at run-time. Of course, the subtype inherits all the operations that can be performed on an instance of the type.

Instances of a type and its subtypes may be freely mixed in arithmetic, comparison and assignment operations. For example, using the above type and subtypes declarations for the speed of various forms of transport, the following code can be written:

```
with Ada.Text_io; use Ada.Text_io;
procedure main is
   --        Type and subtype declarations for speeds
   t0715  : Train_speed;   -- 07:15 Brighton - London
   b0720  : Bus_speed;     -- 07:20 Brighton - London
begin
   t0715 := 55;   -- Average speed Brighton - London (Train)
   b0720 := 35;   -- Average speed Brighton - London (Bus)
   if t0715 > b0720 then
     put("The train is faster then the bus");
   else
     put("The bus is faster then the train");
   end if;
   new_line;
end main;
```

Note: It is of course an error to mix instances of subtypes which are derived from different types.

3.8.1 Types vs. subtypes

Criteria	Types	Subtype
Instances may be mixed with	only instances of the same type	only instances of a type and subtypes derived from the type
May have a constraint	Yes	Yes

3.9 More on types and subtypes

In Ada only subtypes have names. The consequence of this is that the declaration:

```
type    Speed_mph    is range 0 .. 25_000;
```

is effectively treated as:

```
type    Anonymous    is -- implementation defined
subtype Speed_mph    is Anonymous range 0 .. 25_000;
```

The anonymous type from which `Speed_mph` is derived can be obtained by using the attribute `'Base`. The attribute `'Base` refers to the anonymous base type from which a type or subtype has been originally derived. For example, the range of the anonymous type from which `Speed_mph` is derived is printed with the following code:

```
put("Base range of the type Speed_mph is ");
put( Speed_mph'Base'First ); put( " .. " );
put( Speed_mph'Base'Last ); new_line;
```

Note: An instance of the base type can be declared by using the type declaration `Speed_mph'Base`.

3.9.1 Root_integer and Root_real

The model of Ada's arithmetic is based on the anonymous types `Root_integer` and `Root_real`. These types are in effect used as the base types from which all integer and real types are derived. The following table summarizes the properties of `root_integer` and `root_real`.

Root type	Range / precision	Minimum range
`root_integer`	`System.min_int ..` `System.max_int`	$1 .. 2^{15}-1$
`root_real`	`System.max_base_digits`	2. digits

All the arithmetic operators are defined to operate on, and deliver instances of, their base type.

3.9.2 Type declarations: root type of type

In declaring a type for an integer, there are two distinct approaches that can be taken. These are illustrated by the two type declarations for an `Exam_mark`.

```
type Exam_mark is new Integer range 0 .. 100;
type Exam_mark is range 0 .. 100;
```

The first declaration defines `Exam_mark` to be a type derived from `Integer` with a permissible range of values 0 .. 100. Its base type will consequently be that of `root_integer` as `Exam_mark` is derived from `Integer`.

The second declaration defines `Exam_mark` to be a type, the values of which are in the range 0 .. 100. It is derived from `root_integer` but the base range of the type does not have to be that of `root_integer`. Some implementations may implement an instance of this type and its base type in a single byte. The following table illustrates the base type of the types described above:

type Exam_mark is	Base type	Minimum range of root type
`new` Integer `range` 0 .. 100;	`root_integer`	$1 .. 2^{15}-1$
`range` 0 .. 100;	Implementation defined	Implementation defined but must hold 0 .. 100

When performing arithmetic with an instance of a type's base type, no range checks take place. This allows an implementor to implement the base type in the most efficient or effective way for a specific machine. However, the exception `Constraint_Error` will be generated if the resultant arithmetic evaluation leads to a wrong result. For example, the exception `Constraint_Error` is generated if an overflow is detected when performing calculations with the base type.

3.9.3 Arithmetic with types and subtypes

In a program dealing with a student's exam marks, the following program is written to average the marks for a student taking English, Maths and Computing:

```
with Ada.Text_io; use Ada.Text_io;
procedure main is
  type Exam_mark is new Integer range 0 .. 100;
  english  : Exam_mark;
  maths    : Exam_mark;
  computing: Exam_mark;
  average  : Exam_mark;
begin
  english   := 72;
  maths     := 68;
  computing := 76;
  put("Average exam mark is ");
  average := (english+maths+computing) / 3
  put( Integer'Image(average )  );
  new_line;
end main;
```

In executing the statement:

```
average := (english+maths+computing) / 3;
```

the expression:

```
(english+maths+computing) / 3
```

will generate a result which is in the range 0 .. 100. However, the component of the statement english+maths+computing will generate a temporary result which is outside the range of Exam_mark.

In Ada the arithmetic operations are defined to process instances of the root types. In evaluating english+maths+computing, english+maths will deliver a temporary object of type root_integer (Exam_mark'Base) which is then added to computing. The result of the addition is divided by 3 at which point a range check is performed on the temporary result before it is assigned to the object average.

Of course, for this to work the root_integer type must be sufficiently large to hold the sum of english+maths+computing. Remember, this will be of type root_integer which has a range of $-2^{15} .. 2^{15}-1$.

3.9.4 Warning

If the declaration for Exam_mark where replaced by:

```
type Exam_mark is range 0 .. 100;
```

then the above program would fail with a Constraint_Error if the base type of Exam_mark were to be implemented in a single byte.

3.9.5 Constrained and unconstrained types

In Ada there are no named typed only subtypes. The Integer and Float types are derived from root_integer and root_float respectively. Range checks only apply to constrained subtypes, but overflow checks always apply. For example, using the declaration of Exam_mark:

```
type Exam_mark is new Integer range 0 .. 100;
```

the following properties hold.

Declaration	Instance is	Commentary
Exam_mark	Constrained	Constrained to the range 0 .. 100.
Exam_mark'Base	Unconstrained	No range checks applied to assignment of this variable. An implementor may allow this to have a range greater than the base range of the root type
Integer	Constrained	Constrained to the base range of Integer, which is implementation dependent.
Integer'Base	Unconstrained	No range checks apply; may have a range greater than Integer.

Note: *Regardless of whether an item is constrained or unconstrained, overflow checks will always apply. Thus, the result obtained will always be mathematically correct.*
Take note of the the difference between Integer and Integer'Base. Instances of the type Integer are constrained to the base range of the type, whilst instances of Integer'Base are not.

3.9.6 Implementation optimizations

An Ada compiler is allowed to represent an instance of a base type to a greater precision than is necessary. For example, with the following declarations:

```
type Exam_mark is new Integer range 0 .. 100;
type Temporary is Exam_mark'Base;
english : Exam_mark;
total   : Temporary
```

the variable `total` may be implemented to hold numbers of a greater range than is allowed by an `Integer` declaration. This is to allow compiler writers the opportunity to perform optimizations such as holding a variable or intermediate result in a CPU register which may have a greater precision than the range of normal `Integer` values. Of course, overflow checks will be performed at all times, so the mathematical result is always correct.

The danger is that a program which compiles and runs successfully using a particular compiler on a machine may fail to run successfully when compiled with a different compiler on the same machine, even though both compilers have the same range for an `Integer`.

3.10   Compile-time and run-time checks

The following program declares data types to represent: (a) the number of windows in a room, (b) the capacity of a lecture room in seats, and (c) the capacity of a tutorial room, again in seats. In this program, various assignments are made, some of which will fail to compile, some of which will fail in execution.

```
procedure dec is
  MAX_WINDOWS      : constant Integer := 6;
  type Windows_in_room  is range 0 .. MAX_WINDOWS;

  LECTURE_SIZE     : constant Integer := 80;
  type Lecture_room     is range 0 .. LECTURE_SIZE;

  TUTORIAL_SIZE  : constant Lecture_room := 20;
  subtype Tutorial_room is Lecture_room range 0 .. TUTORIAL_SIZE;

  windows_in_504 : Windows_in_room;    -- Windows
  people_in_504  : Lecture_room;       -- Size of lecture room
  people_in_422  : Tutorial_room;      -- Size of tutorial room
begin
  windows_in_504 := 3;
  windows_in_504 := 80;                -- Error / Warning

  people_in_504  := 15;
  people_in_422  := people_in_504;

  people_in_504  := windows_in_504;    -- Error (Type Mismatch)

  people_in_504  := Lecture_room( windows_in_504 );  -- Force

  people_in_504  := 50;
  people_in_422  := people_in_504;     -- Constraint error (R-T)
end dec;
```

The compilation or execution of the following lines will fail for the following reasons:

Line	Reason for failure
windows_in_504 := 80;	The range of values allowed for the object `Windows_in_504` does not include 80. This will usually be detected at compile-time.
people_in_504 := windows_in_504;	The objects on the LHS and RHS of the assignment statement are of different types and will thus produce a compile-time error.
people_in_422 := people_in_504	Will cause a constraint error when executed. In this example, the error could in theory be detected at compile-time.

Note: Depending on the quality of the compiler, some errors which in theory could be detected at compile-time, will only be detected at run-time.

This shows the strength of Ada's strong type checking: problems in a program can be identified at an early stage of development. However, careful planning needs to be made when writing a program. Decisions about which distinct data types to use and which data types should be a subtype of others are particularly important.

3.10.1   Subtypes Natural and Positive

The Ada language pre-defines the following subtypes:

```
subtype Natural  is Integer range 0 .. Integer'Last;
subtype Positive is Integer range 1 .. Integer'Last;
```

3.10.2   Declare

The following program manipulates details about the memory of various components in a PC. As each of the memory components is a **subtype** of Memory, instances of these subtypes can be mixed together in arithmetic expression and the result assigned to `total_memory`. The program introduces the **declare** construct. This construct allows a variable or variables to be declared in the middle of executable Ada statements. The scope of any items declared using **declare** is simply the statements between the **begin** and **end** components of the construct.

```
with Ada.Text_io; use Ada.Text_io;
procedure dec is
  Kb : constant := 1024;               -- Universal Integer
  Mb : constant := Kb * Kb;            -- Universal Integer

  type Memory  is range 0 .. 64 * Mb;

  subtype Cache_memory      is Memory range 0 .. 512 * Kb;
  subtype Video_memory      is Memory range 0 .. 4 * Mb;
  subtype Disk_cache_memory is Memory range 0 .. 16 * Mb;

  pc_main_memory : Memory;             -- Main memory
  pc_memory_cache: Cache_memory;       -- Memory cache
  pc_video_memory: Video_memory;       -- Video memory
  pc_disk_cache  : Disk_cache_memory;  -- On Disk controller
begin
  pc_main_memory := 32 * Mb;           -- 32Mb of memory
  pc_memory_cache:= 256 * Kb;          -- 256kb cache memory
  pc_video_memory:= 4 * Mb;            -- 4Mb of video memory
  pc_disk_cache  := 8 * Mb;            -- 8Mb of disk cache

  declare
    total_memory: Memory;
  begin
    total_memory := pc_main_memory + pc_memory_cache +
                    pc_video_memory + pc_disk_cache;
    put("pc_main_memory :");
    put( Memory'Image(pc_main_memory)  ); new_line;
    put("pc_memory_cache:");
    put( Cache_memory'Image(pc_memory_cache) ); new_line;
    put("pc_video_memory:");
    put( Video_memory'Image(pc_video_memory) ); new_line;
    put("pc_disk_cache  :");
    put( Disk_cache_memory'Image(pc_disk_cache) ); new_line;
    put("total_memory   :");
    put( Memory'Image(total_memory) ); new_line;
  end;

end dec;
```

Note: The use of the image attribute such as `Memory'Image(pc_main_memory)`
       converts in this case the object `pc_main_memory` into a string which can be
       printed by `Ada.Text_io`.

When run, this would produce:

```
pc_main_memory : 33554432
pc_memory_cache: 262144
pc_video_memory: 4194304
pc_disk_cache  : 8388608
total_memory   : 46399488
```

3.11 Enumerations

In writing a program dealing with different classifications of an item it is good programming practice to give meaningful names to each of the different classifications that an item may have. For example, in a program that deals with colours, an incorrect approach would be to let each colour take a numeric value, as follows:

```
with Ada.Text_io; use Ada.Text_io;
procedure main is
  car_colour : Integer;
begin
  car_colour := 1;

  case car_colour is
    when 1       => put("A red car"); new_line;
    when 2       => put("A blue car"); new_line;
    when 3       => put("A green car"); new_line;
    when others  => put("Should not occur"); new_line;
  end case;
end main;
```

*Note: Remember the **when others** is required as a case statement and must cover all possible values.*

This however, is not very elegant and can lead to confusion about which colour 1 represents. There is also the danger that a non valid colour will be assigned to the object car_colour. By using an enumeration, specific names can be given to the colours that a car may have. The declaration for the enumeration Colour is as follows:

```
type Colour is (RED,BLUE,GREEN);
```

The type Colour is then used to elaborate objects which can only take the values of RED, BLUE or GREEN. The enumeration type Colour is used as follows in the re-writing of the previous code fragment:

```
with Ada.Text_io; use Ada.Text_io;
procedure main is
  type Colour is (RED,BLUE,GREEN);
  car_colour : Colour;
begin
  car_colour := RED;

  case car_colour is
    when RED    => put("A red car"); new_line;
    when BLUE   => put("A blue car"); new_line;
    when GREEN  => put("A green car"); new_line;
  end case;
end main;
```

*Note: As the only possible values that can now be assigned to car_colour are either RED, BLUE or GREEN, the **case** statement can be simplified.*

3.11.1   Enumeration values

As well as symbolic names enumerations may also be character constants. For example, the type `Character` is an enumeration made up of the characters in the standard ISO character set.

Thus the type `Character` is conceptually defined as:

```
type Character is ( nul, soh,              -- etc
                    ' ', '!', '"',          -- etc
                    '@', 'A', 'B', 'C',    -- etc
                  );
```

Note: The package standard contains conceptual definitions of all the pre-defined types. Section C.4, Appendix C contains a listing of the package standard.

A programmer can define his/her own enumerations containing characters. For example, the following is an enumeration type declaration for a binary digit.

```
type Binary_digit is ( '0','1' );
b_digit : Binary_digit := '0';
```

3.11.2   The attributes `'Val` and `'Pos`

The position of a specific enumeration in a type is delivered with the attribute `'Pos` whilst the representation of an enumeration n'th value is delivered by `'Val`. These attributes are usefully used on the pre-defined enumeration `Character` to deliver respectively the character code for a specific character and the character representing a value. For example, the following program prints the character code for 'A' and the character representing character code 99.

```
with Ada.Text_io; use Ada.Text_io;
procedure main is
begin
  put("Character 'A' has internal code ");
  put( Character'Pos('A') ); new_line;
  put("Code 99 represents character    ");
  put( Character'Val(99) ); new_line;
end main;
```

Which when run will print:

```
Character 'A' has internal code     65
Code 99 represents character    c
```

3.12   The scalar type hierarchy

The types that are used in arithmetic operations are derived from the scalar types, with the only exception of the enumerated types. Even though they are considered part of the hierarchy, they may not be used in arithmetic operations. The type hierarchy is illustrated in Figure 3.1

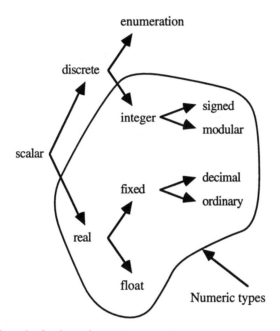

Figure 3.1 Type hierarchy for the scalar types.

Component	Example declaration	Note
Scalar		
discrete		
Enumeration	**type** colour **is** (RED, GREEN, BLUE);	1
Integer	**type** Miles **is range** 0 .. 10_000;	
Signed		
Modular	**type** Byte **is mod** 256;	2
Real		
Fixed		
Ordinary	**type** Miles **is delta** 0.1 **range** 0.0 .. 10.0;	3
Decimal	**type** Miles **is delta** 0.1 **digits** 8;	
Float	**type** Miles **is digits** 8 **range** 0.0 .. 10.0;	4

Note 1   *The enumeration types include the inbuilt types* `Character, Wide_character` *and* `Boolean`.

Note 1   *The enumeration types include the inbuilt types*
         Character, Wide_character *and* Boolean.

Note 2   *A modular type implements modular arithmetic. Thus, the following*
         fragment of code:

```
type Byte is mod 256;
count : Byte := 255;
begin
  count := count + 1;
```

would result in count *containing 0.*

Note 3   *A fixed point number is effectively composed of two components: the*
         whole part and the fractional part stored in an integer value. This can
         lead to more efficient arithmetic on a machine which does not have
         floating point hardware or where the implementation of floating point
         arithmetic is slow. It also provides a precise way of dealing with numbers
         that have a decimal point.
         An alternative notation for a decimal fixed point type is:
                 type *Miles* **is delta** *0.1* **digits** *8* **range** *0.0 .. 10.0;*
         However, even though all compilers must parse this type declaration they
         only need to support it if the compiler implements the Information systems
         Annex.

Note 4   *A floating point number.*
         An alternative type declaration is: **type** *Miles* **is digits** *8; which defines the*
         precision 8 digits but not the range of values that may be stored.

3.12.1   The inbuilt types

Ada provides the following inbuilt types.

Type	Classification	An instance of the type
Boolean	Enumeration	Holds either True or False.
Character	Enumeration	Holds a character based on the ISO 8859-1 character set. In which there are 256 distinct characters.
Float	Float	Holds numbers which contain a decimal place.
Integer	Integer	Holds whole numbers.
Wide_character	Enumeration	Holds a character based on the ISO 10646 BMP character set. In which there are 65536 distinct characters.

The implementation minimum values for these types are given in section B.6, Appendix B.

3.13 Arithmetic operators

The arithmetic operators in Ada 95 are:

+	Addition
-	Subtraction
*	Multiplication
/	Division

The following arithmetic operators are defined on integer values only:

mod	Modulus
rem	Remainder

The operators **mod** and **rem** are similar, and will give identical results when both operands have the same sign. The operator **rem** gives a remainder corresponding to the integer division operation /. The consequence of this is that as integer division truncates towards 0, the absolute value of the result will always be the same regardless of the sign of the operands. **mod** meanwhile gives the remainder corresponding to a division with truncation towards minus infinity.

The following tables illustrate the result of using mod and rem. With both operators an RHS (Right Hand Side) of 0 will cause the exception Constraint_error to be raised. The resultant exception Constraint_error is indicated by the message Err in the tables.

```
mod   | -5  -3   0   3   5          rem   | -5  -3   0   3   5
-----------------------------        -----------------------------
 -5   |  0  -2  Err  1   0           -5   |  0  -2  Err -2   0
 -3   | -3   0  Err  0   2           -3   | -3   0  Err  0  -3
  0   |  0   0  Err  0   0            0   |  0   0  Err  0   0
  3   | -2   0  Err  0   3            3   |  3   0  Err  0   3
  5   |  0  -1  Err  2   0            5   |  0   2  Err  2   0
```

3.13.1 Exponentiation

The operator ** is used to raise a real or integer value to a whole power, which must be greater or equal to zero.

**	Exponentiation

The effect of using ** for different powers of integer values is shown in the table below. The exception Constraint_error is raised for a negative RHS.

```
**   | -3  -1   0   1   3
--------------------------
-3   | Err Err  1  -3 -27
-1   | Err Err  1  -1  -1
 0   | Err Err  1   0   0
 1   | Err Err  1   1   1
 3   | Err Err  1   3  27
```

The implementation of a ** b can be performed by multiplication in any order.
Hence a**4 could be implemented as a*a*a*a or (a*a)**2.

3.13.2 Monadic arithmetic operators

-	Negation
+	Positive form

These deliver the expected results.

3.14 Membership operators

The membership operators are:

in	is a member of
not in	is not a member of

These operators check if a value is a member of a subtype or range. For example, to check if a letter belongs to the upper case alphabetic characters the following code may be used:

```
if ch in 'A' .. 'Z' then
   put("Character is Upper case Alphabetic"); new_line;
end if;
```

Alternatively, to check if an item is not a member of the upper case alphabetic characters, the code would be:

```
if ch not in 'A' .. 'Z' then
   put("Character is not Upper case Alphabetic"); new_line;
end if;
```

The membership test can also be used to check if a value is in the range of a subtype. For example:

```
with Ada.Text_io; use Ada.Text_io;
procedure main is
  subtype Exam_mark is Integer Range 0 .. 100;
  mark : Integer;
begin
  get( mark );
  if mark in Exam_mark then
    put("Valid mark for exam"); new_line;
  end if;
end main;
```

*Note: However, if Exam_mark had been declared as a type then a compile-time error would be generated, as the type of operands of **in** are not compatible.*

3.15 Use of types and subtypes with membership operator

A program to convert a person's height in inches to metres is shown below:

```
with Simple_io; use Simple_io;
procedure main is
  METRES_IN_INCH : constant Float := 0.0254;     -- Conversion
  MAX_HEIGHT     : constant Float := 120.0;      --
  subtype Metres is Float range 0.0 .. MAX_HEIGHT*METRES_IN_INCH;
  subtype Inches is Float range 0.0 .. MAX_HEIGHT;
  height_inches : Float;                          -- Data
  height_metres : Metres;                         -- Converted
begin
  put("Enter person's height in Inches ");
  get( height_inches );                           -- Get data
  if height_inches in Inches then                 -- Sensible
    height_metres := height_inches * METRES_IN_INCH;  -- Convert
    put("Height in Metres is        ");
    put( height_metres, exp=>0, aft=>2 ); new_line;
  else
    put("Height not valid"); new_line;            -- Error
  end if;
end main;
```

In the program, subtypes have been used to help check the consistency of the input data and so that internal consistency checks can be performed on calculations. The person's height is read into the variable height_inches which is of type Float. Validation against the range of the subtype Inches is then performed. The height in inches is then converted to metres and assigned to height_metres. As height_metres is of subtype Metres, a range check is performed on the assigned value. No conversion is required when height_metres is output as its type Metres is a subtype of Float.

An example of a user's interaction with the program is shown below:

```
Enter person's height in Inches 73.0
Height in Metres is             1.85
```

3.16 Relational operators

The logical comparison operators are:

=	equal
/=	not equal
<	less than
>	greater than
<=	less than or equal
>=	greater than or equal

The relational operators are used to establish the truth of a relationship between two values. The result is of type `Boolean`. For example:

```
with Ada.Text_io; use Ada.Text_io;
procedure main is
  temperature : Integer;   -- Temperature in Centigrade
  hot         : Boolean;   -- Is it hot
begin
  get( temperature );
  if temperature > 24 then
    put("It's warm"); new_line;
  end if;
  hot := temperature > 30;
  if hot then put("It's hot"); new_line; end if;
end main;
```

3.16.1 `Boolean` operators

Boolean values may be combined with the following operators:

and	logical and Note: Both LHS and RHS evaluated
or	logical or Note: Both LHS and RHS evaluated
and then	logical and Note: RHS only evaluated if LHS TRUE
or else	logical or Note: RHS only evaluated if LHS FALSE

For example, the following program prints a message on Christmas day.

```
with Ada.Text_io; use Ada.Text_io;
procedure main is
  day,month : Natural;
  christmas : Boolean;
begin
  get( day ); get( month );
  if day = 25 and month = 12 then
    put("Happy Christmas"); new_line;
  end if;
  christmas := day = 25 and month = 12;
end main;
```

By using **and then** or **or else** only the minimal evaluations will be performed to determine the truth of the Boolean expression. For example, the following two fragments of code are equal in effect:

if month = 2 **and then** day = 29 **then**
   — The 29th of February
end if;
	if month = 2 **then**
	  if day = 29 **then**
	    — The 29th of February
	  end if;
	end if;

Note: *The RHS of the condition will only be evaluated if month = 2 is true.*
*In some cases the correct evaluation of the RHS of an **and** or **or** Boolean operator will depend on the evaluation of the LHS of the operator.*

Section B.3.1, Appendix B contains a list of the priority of all the operators.

3.16.2 Monadic **Boolean** operators

The inverse of a Boolean value is obtained by using the operator:

not	not

This delivers the inverse of the Boolean expression or Boolean value. For example:

```
if not month = 2 then
  put("Month is not February"); new_line;
end if;
```

3.17 Bitwise operators

These are used for operating on modular quantities. Most programs will only occasionally require the use of these operators.

and	bitwise and
or	bitwise or

For example, using the declarations:

```
K : constant := 1024;
type Word16 is mod 64 * K;
pattern : Word16;
```

the following code:

• sets the top nibble of the two byte word `pattern` to zero.

```
pattern := pattern and 16#FFF#;
```

• sets bit 9 in the two byte word `pattern` to 1.

```
pattern := pattern or 2#0000001000000000#;
```

Note: The constant to base 16 is 16#FFF# and to base 2 is 2#0000001000000000#. Section B.4, Appendix B describes how to declare constants to different bases.

3.18 Self-assessment

• Why is it not always appropriate to hold a value using an instance of a `Float`?

• How in a program can you find out the smallest value that can be stored in an instance of `Long_Integer`?

• What are the benefits of user defined types and subtypes in a program?

- Why does the following program fail?

```
program main is
  type Miles       is new Integer range 0 .. 100;
  type Kilometres is new Integer range 0 .. 100;
  london_brighton    : Miles := 50;
  TO_BRIGHTON        : constant Kilometres := 2;
  distance_to_london : Miles;
begin
  distance_to_london := london_brighton + TO_BRIGHTON;
end main;
```

- What is the difference between a type and a subtype?

- Why are the concepts of universal integer and universal float important?

- How can you convert a value of one type to that of another?

- Using the type declarations:

```
type Miles       is new Integer range 0 .. 10_000;
type Kilometres is range 0 .. 100;
```

what are the ranges of the following variables:

```
london_brighton : Kilometres'Base;
london_newyork  : Miles'Base;
```

- How can the use of enumerations help improve a program's clarity?

3.19 Exercises

Construct the following programs using types and subtypes where appropriate:

- Is prime
  A program to say if a number is prime. A prime number is a positive number which is divisible by only 1 and itself.

- *Series*
  A program to print out numbers in the series 1 1 2 3 5 8 13 ... until the last term is greater than 10000.

- Times table general case
  Write a program to print a times table for any positive number.

  You may wish to use the following approach.
  The input procedure get may take its input from a string. The following
  statement: get (argument (1), number, last); will convert the
  number held as characters in the string 'argument (1)' into an integer
  number in the variable number. The argument last denotes the position in
  the string of the last character processed. Chapter 28 gives a full description of
  the input and output procedures available in Simple_io.

- *Temperature*
  A program to convert a Fahrenheit temperature to Centigrade. The formula for
  converting between Fahrenheit and Centigrade is:

  Centigrade temperature = (Fahrenheit temperature - 32)/1.8

- *Weight*
  A program to convert a person's weight input in pounds to kilograms.
  Assume that there are 2.2046 pounds in a kilogram.

- *Grades*
  A program to read in a student's name of 20 characters followed by his/her
  exam mark. The output to be the student's name followed by grade. For
  example, marks in the range 100-70 get an A grade, 60-69 a B grade, 50-59 a
  C grade, 40 - 49 a D grade and 0 - 39 an F grade. Thus if the input was:

  ```
  Andy                  74
  Bob                   46
  Charles               56
  Dave                  67
  ```

  the output would be:

  ```
  Andy                  A
  Bob                   D
  Charles               C
  Dave                  B
  ```

4 Procedures and functions

This chapter introduces procedures and functions. They allow a programmer the ability to abstract code into subprogram units that then may be re-used in different parts of a program or even other programs. This re-use of code, however, is at a very basic level. Other mechanisms, in particular the **package**, allow a much greater flexibility in promoting code re-use in programs.

4.1 Introduction

A function or procedure is a grouping together of one or more Ada statements into a subprogram unit, which can be called and executed from any appropriate part of a program. Functions and procedures allow a programmer a degree of abstraction in solving a problem. However, related procedures and functions are more powerfully used when combined with related data items to form a class. The concepts and uses of a class are discussed fully in Chapter 5.

4.2 Functions

A function is a subprogram unit that transforms its input value or values into a single output value. For example, a function to convert a lower case character to its upper case equivalent is:

```
function  to_upper_fun( c:in Character ) return Character is
  answer   : Character;
  diff_A_a: constant Natural :=
                     Character'Pos('a') - Character'Pos('A');
begin
  if c in 'a' .. 'z' then
    answer := Character'Val( Character'Pos(c) - diff_A_a );
  else
    answer := c;
  end if;
  return answer;
end to_upper_fun;
```

Note: *The function's parameters may only import data into the function: they may not be used to export information back to the caller's environment. Thus, a function is a unit of code that transforms its input into a new value that is returned to the caller.*

As the parameter c can only be used to import data into the function, it may not be written to.

The character codes for the English upper- and lower-case characters are:

```
'a' => 97      'A' => 65
'b' => 98      'B' => 66
'c' => 99      'C' => 67
etc.
```

As there is a constant distance between an English lower-case letter and its upper-case equivalent it is easy to convert any English lower-case letter to its upper-case form.

The major components of the above function are illustrated in Figure 4.1

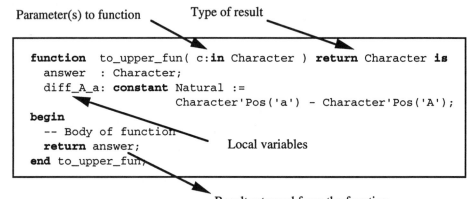

```
function  to_upper_fun( c:in Character ) return Character is
   answer   : Character;
   diff_A_a: constant Natural :=
                    Character'Pos('a') - Character'Pos('A');
begin
   -- Body of function
   return answer;
end to_upper_fun;
```

Parameter(s) to function   Type of result   Local variables

Result returned from the function

Figure 4.1 Major components of a function.

The function to_upper_fun may be used with a procedure as follows:

```
with Ada.Text_io, to_upper_fun;
use  Ada.Text_io;
procedure upper is
   ch : Character;                    -- Read / Write object
begin
   while not end_of_file loop         -- For each line
     while not end_of_line loop       -- For each character
        get(ch);                      -- Read character
        put( to_upper_fun(ch) );      -- Write as upper case
     end loop;
     skip_line; new_line;             -- move to next line, new line
   end loop;
end upper;
```

*Note: The statement **with** Ada.Text_io, to_upper_fun; allows access to the code of the function to_upper_fun.*
The package Ada.Characters.Handling contains the function to_upper which performs a similar process to the above function.

When compiled, the above program acts as a very simple software tool to convert a file into all upper-case characters. For example, on a Unix or DOS system, if the file file.dat contained the text:

```
Ada 95 contains object-oriented programming constructs.
```

then running the program taking input from the file file.txt:

```
% upper < file.dat
```

would produce the following output:

```
ADA 95 CONTAINS OBJECT-ORIENTED PROGRAMMING CONSTRUCTS.
```

Note: With MSDOS or Unix, the syntax upper < file.dat instructs the program upper to run taking its input from the file file.dat.

4.2.1 Separate compilation of functions

It is usual for such a small program as illustrated in section 4.2 to be compiled as a unit. However, the function to_upper_fun and the procedure upper may be compiled separately as self-contained units. The two separately compiled units may then be linked together to form an executable program. This is made possible because the two subprogram units are treated by the Ada compiling system as independent units, allowing them to be re-used in other programs developed at a later stage.

4.2.2 Local variables

When a variable is declared inside a function, its lifetime is that of the function. When the function is entered, space for any local variables is created automatically on a run-time stack. On exit from the function, the space created for the local variables is returned to the system.

4.3 Procedures

A procedure is a program unit that, unlike a function, does not return a result. If information has to be returned to the calling environment this is done instead by writing to a formal parameter that has been declared as mode **out**. Writing to the formal parameter of a procedure updates the value of the actual parameter passed to the function. The full implication of modes of a parameter are discussed in section 4.5.

```
procedure to_upper_proc( c:in out Character ) is
   diff_A_a: constant Natural :=
                     Character'Pos('a') - Character'Pos('A');
begin
   if c in 'a' .. 'z' then
      c := Character'Val( Character'Pos(c) - diff_A_a );
   end if;
end to_upper_proc;
```

Note: A procedure can only export values back to the caller's environment by writing to a parameter that has mode **out** *or* **in out***.*

The major components of a procedure are illustrated in Figure 4.2.

Parameter(s) to procedure

```
procedure to_upper_proc( c:in out Character ) is
   diff_A_a: constant Natural :=
                     Character'Pos('a') - Character'Pos('A')
begin
   -- Body of procedure
end to_upper_proc;              Local variables
```

Figure 4.2 Components of an Ada procedure.

This procedure may then be used in a program as follows:

```
with Ada.Text_io, to_upper_proc;
use  Ada.Text_io;
procedure upper is
   ch : Character;                    -- Read / Write object
begin
   while not end_of_file loop         -- For each line
      while not end_of_line loop      -- For each character
         get(ch);                     -- Read character
         to_upper_proc(ch);           -- Convert to upper
         put( ch );                   -- Write character
      end loop;
      skip_line; new_line;            -- move to next line, new line
   end loop;
end upper;
```

when run, this program would produce the same output as the previous program.

Note: There is a standard library function (`to_upper`) to convert a character into upper case.

4.4 Formal and actual parameters

In describing the parameter passing mechanism the following terminology is used:

Terminology	Commentary
Formal parameter	The parameter used in the declaration of a function or procedure. For example, in the function `to_upper_fun` the formal parameter is `c`.
Actual parameter	The object passed to the function or procedure when the function or procedure is called. For example, in the procedure `upper` the actual parameter is `ch`. If this is an expression then the object passed will be the result of evaluating the expression.

In discussing functions and procedures it is important to distinguish between the actual parameter passed to a function and the formal parameter used in the body of the code of the function or procedure. This relationship is shown in Figure 4.3.

Formal parameter (c)

```
function to_upper_fun(c:in Character) return Character is
   -- Declarations
begin
   -- Body of function
end to_upper_fun;
```

```
with Ada.Text_io, to_upper_fun;
use  Ada.Text_io;                    Actual parameter ( ch )
procedure upper is
   ch : Character;
begin
   ch := 'a';
   ch := to_upper_fun( ch );
   put( ch );
end upper;
```

Figure 4.3 Formal and actual parameters of a function.

4.5   Modes of a parameter to a function or procedure

In Ada, as in many languages, objects can be passed to a procedure in several different ways depending on how the object is to be accessed. The simplest and by far the safest mode to use, is **in**. This allows an object to be imported into the procedure, but the user is prevented by the compiler from writing to the object.

A procedure can export information to the actual parameter when the formal parameter is described by mode **out**. Naturally for this to happen, the actual parameter's mode must allow the object to be written to. It must therefore not be an expression or object which has a mode of **in** only.

A function in Ada however, is only allowed to have parameters of mode **in**. The different ways that a parameter may be passed to a function or procedure is summarized in the table below:

Mode	Allowed as a parameter to	Effect
in	a function or procedure	The formal parameter is initialized to the contents of the actual parameter and may only be read from.
in out	a procedure only	The formal parameter is initialized to the contents of the actual parameter and may be read from or written to. When the procedure is exited, the new value of the formal parameter replaces the old contents of the actual parameter.
out	a procedure only	The formal parameter is **not** initialized to the contents of the actual parameter and may be read from or written to. When the procedure is exited, the new value of the formal parameter replaces the old contents of the actual parameter. In Ada 83 an **out** formal parameter may not be read from.

Note: *The implementation of the above for simple objects is usually performed by copying the contents of the object, whilst for large objects the compiler may implement this by using references to the actual object.*

4.5.1   Example of mode **in out**

A procedure swap which interchanges the contents of the actual parameters passed to it is as follows:

```
procedure swap(first:in out Integer; second:in out Integer) is
  temp : Integer;
begin
  temp := first;
  first := second; second := temp;
end swap;
```

4.5.2 Putting it all together

The function swap may then be used in a program as follows:

```
with Simple_io, swap;
use  Simple_io;
procedure main is
  books_room_1 : Integer;
  books_room_2 : Integer;
begin
  books_room_1 := 10; books_room_2 := 20;
  put( books_room_1 ); put (" "); put( books_room_2 ); new_line;
  swap( books_room_1, books_room_2 );
  put( books_room_1 ); put (" "); put( books_room_2 ); new_line;
end main;
```

which when run produces:

```
10 20
20 10
```

4.5.3 Summary of access to formal parameters

Formal parameter specified by: (using as an example an Integer formal parameter)	Write to formal parameter allowed	Read from formal parameter	Can be used as a parameter to
item: Integer	✗	✓	procedure or function
item: **in** Integer	✗	✓	procedure or function
item: **in out** Integer	✓	✓	procedure only
item: **out** Integer	✓	✓	procedure only

4.6 Recursion

Recursion is the ability of a procedure or function to make a call on itself from within its own code body. Whilst this initially may seem a strange idea, it can lead to very elegant code sequences that otherwise would require many more lines of code. In certain exceptional cases recursion is the only way to implement a problem.

An example of a recursive procedure to write a natural number using only character based output is sketched in outline below:

Write a natural number: (`write_natural`)
- Split the natural number into two components
  - (a)   The first digit (remainder when number divided by 10)
  - (b)   The other digits (number divided by 10).

For example:
123 would be split into:
3   (first digit)
12   (other digits).

- If the other digits are greater than or equal to 10 then write the other digits by recursively calling the code to write a decimal number.

- Output the first digit as a character.

The sequence of calls made is

Call	Implemented as
`write_natural( 123 )`	`write_natural(12);` output first digit 3
`write_natural( 12 )`	`write_natural(1);` output first digit 2
`write_natural( 12 )`	output first digit 1

This process is diagramatically expressed in Figure 4.4.

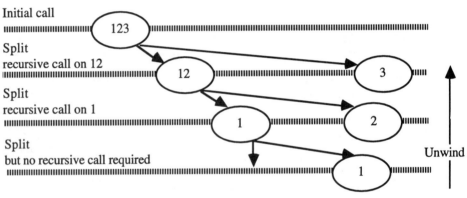

Figure 4.4 Illustration of recursive calls to print the natural number 123.

The process works by solving a small part of the problem, in this case how to output a single digit, then re-executing the code to solve the remainder of the problem, that is, to output the other digits. In this particular example, the recursive call is made before the solution of the remainder of the problem. This still works as the problem to be solved 'the number to be output' is reduced in size in each recursive call.

However, for recursion to work, the code must reduce the problem to be solved before recalling itself recursively. If this does not take place then endless recursive calls will ensue, which will cause eventual program failure when the system cannot allocate any more memory to support the recursion. Stack space is used on each recursive call to store any parameters or local variables plus the function / procedure support information.

4.6.1   The procedure `write_natural`

The procedure `write_natural`'s implementation is shown below:

```
with Ada.Text_io; use Ada.Text_io;
procedure write_natural( num : Natural) is
   first_digit   : Natural;              -- Unit digit
   other_digits  : Natural;              -- All except first digit
begin
   first_digit  := num rem 10;           -- Split 1234  =>    4
   other_digits := num / 10;             --                =>  123
   if num >= 10 then                     -- Print other digits
      write_natural( other_digits );     -- Recursive call
   end if;
   put( Character'Val( first_digit + Character'Pos('0') ) );
end write_natural;
```

4.6.2   Putting it all together

The function `write_natural` could be used in a program as follows:

```
with Ada.Text_io, write_natural;
use  Ada.Text_io;
procedure main is
begin
   write_natural( 123 );    new_line;
   write_natural( 12345 ); new_line;
end main;
```

which when run would produce:

```
123
12345
```

4.7   Overloading of functions

Overloading is a process that allows several items providing different facilities to have the same name. The compiler chooses the appropriate definition to use from the context of its use.

This is best illustrated by an example where the overloaded item is a procedure. Firstly, three different procedures are defined which each have a different action. The action is to identify and print the contents of their single parameter.

```
with Simple_io; use Simple_io;
procedure is_a_int( an_int:in Integer ) is
begin
  put("The parameter is an Integer:  value = ");
  put( an_int ); new_line;
end is_a_int;

with Simple_io; use Simple_io;
procedure is_a_float( a_float:in Float ) is
begin
  put("The parameter is a Float:     value = ");
  put( a_float ); new_line;
end is_a_float;

with Simple_io; use Simple_io;
procedure is_a_char( a_char:in Character ) is
begin
  put("The parameter is a Character: value = ");
  put( a_char ); new_line;
end is_a_char;
```

Note: The package Simple_io *provides several different definitions for* put *depending on the object to be output.*

The individual procedures have unique names so that they can be identified and re-used in a program. This is a consequence of each procedure being a separate compilation unit. However, Ada allows the renaming of a procedure or function. By choosing the same name a user can overload a particular name with several different definitions. For example, a program unit can be written which renames the three different procedure names (is_a_int, is_a_float, is_a_char) with the same overloaded name is_a.

```
with Simple_io, is_a_int, is_a_float, is_a_char;
use  Simple_io;
procedure main is
  procedure is_a( p:in Integer )    renames is_a_int;
  procedure is_a( p:in Float )      renames is_a_float;
  procedure is_a( p:in Character )  renames is_a_char;
begin
  is_a( 'A' );
  is_a( 123 );
  is_a( 123.45 );
end main;
```

Note: It is possible to write several functions or procedures with the same name directly by using the package construct.

When run this would print the type and value of the argument passed to is_a.

```
The parameter is a Character: value = A
The parameter is an Integer:  value = 123
The parameter is a Float:     value = 123.450
```

Of course, for this to happen, the actual function called must be different in each case. The name is_a is overloaded by three different functions. The binding between the called function and its body is worked out by the compiler at compile-time using the type of parameters passed to resolve any conflicts.

4.8 Different number of parameters

As the compiler can distinguish between overloaded names, several functions that deliver the maximum or larger of their parameters can be written. With re-use in mind the first function max2 can be written which delivers the maximum of the two Integer parameters passed to it.

```
function max2( a,b:in Integer ) return Integer is
begin
  if a > b then
    return a;        -- a is larger
  else
    return b;        -- b is larger
  end if;
end max2;
```

This function max2 can be re-used in a function max3 that will deliver the larger of three parameters passed to it.

```
with max2;
function max3( a,b,c:in Integer ) return Integer is
begin
  return max2( max2( a,b ), c );
end max3;
```

Then the following code can be written:

```
with Simple_io, max2, max3;
use  Simple_io;
procedure main is
   function max(a,b:in Integer)    return Integer renames max2;
   function max(a,b,c:in Integer) return Integer renames max3;
begin
  put("Larger of 2 and 3 is "); put( max(2,3) ); new_line;
  put("Larger of 2 3 4   is "); put( max(2,3,4) ); new_line;
end main;
```

which when run produces:

```
Larger of 2 and 3 is 3
Larger of 2 3 4   is 4
```

Note: *The overloading of names in an Ada program can provide a simpler interface for a programmer. However, the overuse of overloading can lead to programs that are difficult to maintain and debug.*

4.9   Default values and named parameters

If a default value is given to a parameter, it may be omitted by a programmer when they write the call to the function or procedure.

For example, the function sum whose four parameters have a default value of zero returns the sum of these parameters. The procedure answer_is prints the first parameter with an additional message when the second parameter has the default value TRUE.

```
function  sum( p1:in Integer := 0;
               p2:in Integer := 0;
               p3:in Integer := 0;
               p4:in Integer := 0  ) return Integer is
begin
  return p1 + p2 + p3 + p4;
end sum;

with Simple_io; use Simple_io;
procedure answer_is( n:in Integer;
                     message:in Boolean := TRUE ) is
begin
  if message then put("The answer = "); end if;
  put( n );
  if message then new_line; end if;
end answer_is;
```

Note: *Parameters to the function* sum *are given a default value of 0, if a value has not been supplied by a caller of the function.*

Any parameter to a function or procedure may be specified either by position or by name. For example, the second parameter to the function answer_is can be specified in the following ways:

```
answer_is( sum, TRUE );            -- By position
answer_is( sum, message => TRUE ); -- By name
```

Note: If a parameter is specified by name, then all subsequent parameters must be specified by name.

4.9.1   Putting it all together

The procedures `sum` and `answer_is` can be used in a program as follows:

```
with Simple_io, sum, answer_is;
use  Simple_io;
procedure main is
begin
  answer_is( sum );
  answer_is( sum( 1, 2 ) );
  answer_is( sum( 1, 2, 3 ) );
  answer_is( sum( 1, 2, 3, 4 ), message => FALSE );
  new_line;
end main;
```

The code that is actually compiled for the procedure `main` above is:

```
procedure main is
begin
  answer_is( sum( 0, 0, 0, 0 ), TRUE );
  answer_is( sum( 1, 2, 0, 0 ), TRUE );
  answer_is( sum( 1, 2, 3, 0 ), TRUE );
  answer_is( sum( 1, 2, 3, 4 ), FALSE );
  new_line;
end main;
```

which is more complex for the writer to construct and for a maintainer to follow.

Note: The syntax `message => FALSE` *is used for specifying a parameter by name. The syntax for the call of the function* `sum` *when no parameters are specified has no brackets. This can lead to confusion as a reader of the code would not know from the context if* `sum` *was a simple variable or a function call.*

When run the above program produces:

```
The answer = 0
The answer = 3
The answer = 6
10
```

Note: Procedures and functions may be nested. The advantage of this approach is that a single program unit may be decomposed into several smaller units and yet hide the internal decomposition.

4.10 Self-assessment

- From a programming safety point of view, what are the advantages of passing parameters by mode **in**?

- Why is parameter passing using mode **in out** required, if values can already be passed back as the result of the function?

- When might overloading of function names be used?

- What are the disadvantages of overloading names in a program?

- What is the difference between a function and a procedure? Can a procedure which exports several values through the parameter mechanism be easily made into a function? Explain your answer.

4.11 Exercises

Construct the following subprograms and programs:

- The function what_is_char which accepts as a parameter a character and returns its 'type' as defined by the enumeration :
type Char **is** (DIGIT, PUNCTUATION, LETTER, OTHER_CH);

- Using the function what_is_char write a program to count the number of digits, letters and punctuation characters in a text file.

  Hint:
  Nest the function what_is_char inside a procedure which processes input received by the program.

- Write a procedure order3 which takes three parameters of type Float and re-orders the parameters into ascending order.

- Write a program which finds the average of three rainfall readings taken during the last 24 hours. The program should print the average of the samples plus the readings in ascending order. For example, if the input data was:
4.0 6.0 5.0
then the program should produce output of the form:
Rainfall average   is : 5.00
Data values (sorted) are : 4.00 5.00 6.00

5   Packages as classes

This chapter introduces the package construct. A package is an elegant way of encapsulating code and data that interact together into a single unit. A package may be used in a variety of ways. This chapter, however, will promote its use to define classes.

5.1 Introduction

The world in which we live is populated by many devices and machines that make everyday living easier and more enjoyable. The TV, for instance, is viewed by almost every person in the country, yet few understand exactly what happens inside 'the box'. Likewise, there are many millions of motorists who drive regularly and do not need a detailed knowledge of the workings of a car to make effective use of it.

To many people, their knowledge of a car is as shown in Figure 5.1.

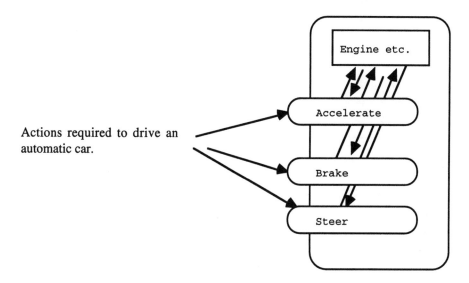

Figure 5.1 Basic understanding of working of an automatic car.

The details of what happens inside the car are not important for most day-to-day driving.

In essence the world is populated with many objects which have an interface that allows the humblest of persons to make effective use of the item. We sometimes criticize the interfaces as being ineffective and difficult to use, yet in most cases we would prefer to use the objects as they stand, rather than having to perform the task by other means.

Likewise in the software world, there are objects that a user or programmer can make effective use of without having to know how the object has been implemented. On a very simple level an Ada program may declare objects to hold floating point numbers, which can then be used with arithmetic operations to sum, multiply, etc. these values. Most programmers however, do not know the exact details of how these operations are performed; they accept the interface provided by the programming language.

At one point it was fashionable for programming languages to provide a rich set of data types. The designers of these languages hoped the data types provided would be adequate for all occasions. The problem was, and still is, that no one language could ever hope to provide all the different types of item that a programmer may need or wish to use.

Ada gives a programmer the ability to declare new data types, together with a range of operations that may be performed on an instance of the type. Naturally, a programmer may also use types and operations on these types that have been defined by other programmers.

5.2   Objects, messages and methods

A car can be thought of as an object. The car contains complex details and processes that are hidden from the driver. For example, to make the car go faster the driver presses the accelerator pedal. The car receives the message 'go faster' and evokes an internal method to speed up the engine.

In the above description of driving a car many object-oriented ideas have been used. These ideas are as follows:

object	An item that has a hidden internal structure. The hidden structure is manipulated or accessed by messages sent by a user.
message	A request sent to the object to obey one of its methods.
method	A set of actions that manipulates or accesses the internal state of the object. The detail of these actions is hidden from a user of the object.

5.3   Objects, messages and methods in Ada

In Ada an object is an instance of either a user-defined type or an instance of one of the in-built types.

An object for a user-defined type can be imagined diagrammatically as Figure 5.2.

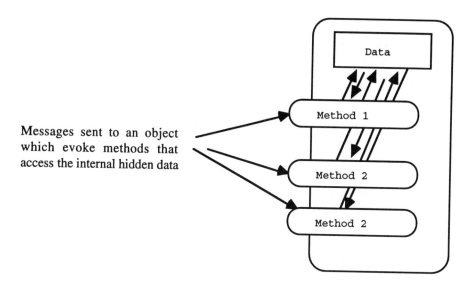

Messages sent to an object which evoke methods that access the internal hidden data

Figure 5.2 Diagrammatic representation of an object.

A message is implemented as either a procedure or function call, the body of which is the method that is evoked when the message is sent to the object. The user of the object has no knowledge of the implementation code contained in the body of the procedure of function.

Note: The idea of binding code and data together in a unit that does not allow direct access to the data is often referred to as encapsulation.

5.3.1 An object for a bank account

Before looking in detail at the implementation of an object that represents a bank account, it is appropriate to consider the messages that might be sent to such an object. For a very simple type of bank account these messages would be:

- Deposit money into the account.
- Withdraw money from the account.
- Deliver the account balance.
- Print a mini statement of the amount in the account.

The following program demonstrates the sending of these messages to an instance of an `Account`.

```
with Ada.Text_io, Class_account;
use  Ada.Text_io, Class_account;
procedure main is
  my_account: Account;
  obtain    : Money;
begin
  statement( my_account );

  put("Deposit £100.00 into account"); new_line;
  deposit( my_account, 100.00 );
  statement( my_account );

  put("Withdraw £80.00 from account"); new_line;
  withdraw( my_account, 80.00, obtain );
  statement( my_account );

  put("Deposit £200.00 into account"); new_line;
  deposit( my_account, 200.00 );
  statement( my_account );

end main;
```

Note: The package Class_account *contains:*

- *The definition of the type* Account *plus the definition of the operations allowed on an instance of an* Account;
- *The subtype* Money *used to define some of the parameters to messages sent to an instance of* Account.

The messages sent to an instance of an Account are: deposit, withdraw, balance, statement. For example, to deposit £100 into my_account the following procedural notation is used:

```
deposit( my_account, 100.00 );
```

This should be read as: send the message deposit to the object my_account with a parameter of 100.00.

To withdraw money from the account a programmer would send the message withdraw to the object my_account with two parameters, the amount to withdraw and a variable that is to be filled with the amount actually withdrawn. The implementation of the method will check that the person has sufficient funds in their account to allow the transaction to take place. This is written as:

```
withdraw( my_account, 80.00, obtain );
```

*Note: In reality the method is a normal Ada procedure that is passed as parameters,
the object on which the action is to take place, plus any additional information as
successive parameters.*

5.3.2 Putting it all together

When compiled with an appropriate package body, the above program unit when run
will produce the following results:

```
Mini statement: The amount on deposit is £ 0.00

Deposit £100.00 into account
Mini statement: The amount on deposit is £100.00

Withdraw £80.00 from account
Mini statement: The amount on deposit is £20.00

Deposit £200.00 into account
Mini statement: The amount on deposit is £220.00
```

5.3.3 Components of a package

The package construct in Ada is split into two distinct parts. These parts contain the
following object-oriented components:

Ada package component	Object-oriented component
Specification	The type used to elaborate the object, plus the specification of the messages that can be sent to an instance of the type.
Implementation	Implementation of the methods that are evoked when a message is sent to the object.

5.3.4 Specification of the package

The specification defines what the packages does, but not how it performs the
implementation. It is used by the Ada compiler to check and enforce the correct usage of
the package by a programmer.

The specification is split into two distinct parts: a public part and a private part. The
public part defines the messages that may be sent to an instance of an `Account`, whilst
the private part defines the representation of the type `Account`.

As the representation of `Account` is defined in the private part of the specification,
a user of an instance of an `Account` will not be allowed to access the internal
representation. The user however, is allowed to declare and, depending on the

description of the type, assign and compare for equality and inequality. In this case the description of the type is private and a user is allowed to declare, assign and compare for equality and inequality instances of Account.

```
package Class_account is

  type Account is private;
  subtype Money  is Float;
  subtype PMoney is Float range 0.0 .. Float'Last;

  procedure statement( the:in Account );
  procedure deposit ( the:in out Account; amount:in PMoney );
  procedure withdraw( the:in out Account; amount:in PMoney;
                      get:out PMoney );
  function  balance ( the:in Account ) return Money;

private
  type Account is record
     balance_of : Money := 0.00;        -- Amount in account
  end record;
end Class_account;
```

The component parts of the specification are illustrated in Figure 5.3.

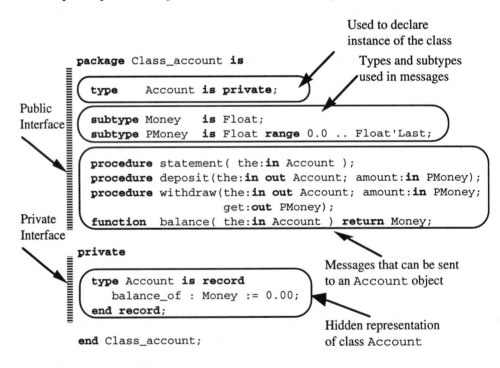

Figure 5.3 Components of the specification part of a package.

The representation of `Account` (which is defined in the private part) is a subtype of a `Float` that will have an initial value of 0.00. An Ada record groups together several type declarations into a single named type. In this case the record type `Account` declares a single object called `balance_of`. Section 6.1 in Chapter 6 describes the **record** type.

Note: The **type** `Account` *is defined in the public part of the specification as* **private***. This means that a user of an instance of the type cannot access the internal contents of the object. Apart from the methods defined in the public part of the specification the only operations that a user can perform on this object is to assign it to another instance of an* `Account` *or compare two instance of an* `Account` *with either = or /=.*

5.3.5 Representation of the balance of the account

The package `Class_account` represents internally the balance of the account as a subtype of a `Float`. A `Float` is an inexact way of representing numbers, as only the most significant digits of the number will be stored. Instances of a type declaration of the form **type** `Money` **is delta** 0.01 **digits** 8; would provide a more reliable way of holding the balance of the account. However, this would require instantiation of a specific package for input and output of objects of this type. To simplify the presentation of this package the representation of the balance of the account is implemented as a subtype of a `Float`. After reading Chapters 13 and 17 the reader may wish to re-implement this package as a generic package which uses an instantiation of `Ada.Text_io.Decimal_io`.

5.3.6 Implementation of the package

The implementation of the package `Class_account` is as follows:

```
with Simple_io; use Simple_io;
package body Class_account is

  procedure statement( the:in Account ) is
  begin
    put("Mini statement: The amount on deposit is £" );
    put( the.balance_of, aft=>2, exp=>0 );
    new_line(2);
  end statement;

  procedure deposit ( the:in out Account; amount:in PMoney ) is
  begin
    the.balance_of := the.balance_of + amount;
  end deposit;
```

```
procedure withdraw( the:in out Account; amount:in PMoney;
                    get:out PMoney ) is
begin
  if the.balance_of >= amount then
    the.balance_of := the.balance_of - amount;
    get := amount;
  else
    get := 0.00;
  end if;
end withdraw;

function  balance( the:in Account ) return Money is
begin
  return the.balance_of;
end balance;

end Class_account;
```

Note: **with** `Simple_io;` **use** `Simple_io;` *has been included in the body of the package.*

The body of the package contains the definition of the procedures and functions defined in the specification part of the package. In accessing the `balance_of` contained in an instance of `Account` the . notation is used. For example, in the function `balance` the result returned is obtained using the statement '`return the.balance_of;`'. The . notation is used to access a component of an instance of a record type. In this case, the instance of the record type is the object `the` and the component of the object is `balance_of`.

5.3.7 Terminology

The following terminology is used to describe the components of a class.

Terminology	Example: in class Account	Explanation
Instance attribute	balance_of	A data component of an object. In Ada this will be a member of the type that is used to declare the object.
Instance method or just method	deposit	A procedure or function used to access the instance attributes in an object.

Note: The terminology comes from the language Smalltalk.

5.4 The package as seen by a user

A user will normally only have access to the specification part of a package. This provides a specification of the messages that can be sent to an object but does not show how the methods invoked by the messages have been implemented. The implementation part will not normally be available, the implementor normally providing only a compiled version of the package.

Unfortunately the details of the private type will normally be visible, though they cannot be accessed.

Note: The details of the private type can be made invisible to a user, but this involves some complexity. One approach to this is shown in Chapter 14, section 14.5.

5.5 The package as seen by an implementor

When building a package the implementor should ensure:

- That a user of the package can make effective use of its facilities.
- That the only visible components are:
  - (a)   The messages that can be sent to an object.
  - (b)   The private type declaration that is used to elaborate an object.

The visibility hierarchy for the package Class_account is shown in Figure 5.4.

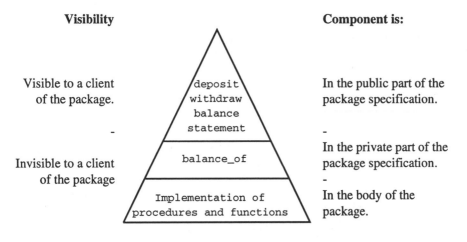

Figure 5.4 Visibility of methods and instance attributes of the package Class_account.

5.6   The class

In object-oriented programming one of the important ideas is that of the class. A class is the collective name for all objects that share the same structure and behaviour. For example, in a program dealing with bank transactions, all the objects that represent a particular type of bank account would belong to the same class.

The class construct in a programming language is used to define objects that share a common structure and behaviour. Ada does not have a class construct.

However, Ada's package construct can be used to simulate the class construct found in other object-oriented programming languages. For example, a class Account is defined by the following package:

```
with Simple_io; use Simple_io;
package Class_account is

  type Account is private;

  procedure statement( the:in Account );
  -- other instance methods

private
  type Account is record
    balance : Money := 0.00;      -- Amount in account
  end record;
end Class_account;
```

```
package body Class_account is
  -- Implementation of the procedures and functions
end Class_account;
```

In defining a class, the following conventions are used:

*   The class is defined in terms of a package which has the class name prefixed with Class_.

*   The package has a single private type which takes the class name and is used to declare instances of the class. Hence all instances of the class will share the same structure and behaviour.

*   Procedures and functions are used to define the behaviour of the class. The first parameter to the procedure or function is an instance of the class.

*   The implementation of the private type is defined as a **record** type, the components of which define the structure of the class.

5.7 **with** and **use**

The clauses '**with** Ada.Text_io; **use** Ada.Text_io;' make available the contents of the package Ada.Text_io to the following program unit. The package Ada.Text_io contains definitions for performing input and output on character and string objects. The exact effect of these clauses are as follows:

- **with** Ada.Text_io;
  Make available to the unit all the public components of the package. However, when components of the package are used in a program they must be prefixed with the package name.

- **use** Ada.Text_io;
  Permit public components of the package to be used without having to prefix their name with that of the package name.

Thus without the **use** clause, the program to process bank transactions would become:

```
with Ada.Text_io, Class_account;
procedure main is
my_account:Class_account.Account;
  obtain    :Money;
begin
  Class_account.statement( my_account );

  Ada.Text_io.put("Deposit £100.00 into account");
  Ada.Text_io.new_line;
  Class_account.deposit( my_account, 100.00 );
  Class_account.statement( my_account );

  Ada.Text_io.put("Withdraw £80.00 from account");
  Ada.Text_io.new_line;
  Class_account.withdraw( my_account, 80.00, obtain );
  Class_account.statement( my_account );

  Ada.Text_io.put("Deposit £200.00 into account");
  Ada.Text_io.new_line;
  Class_account.deposit( my_account, 200.00 );
  Class_account.statement( my_account );
end main;
```

*Note: Some program guidelines will ban the use of a **use** clause.*

5.7.1 To use or not to use the **use** clause

Using a **use** clause	Not using a **use** clause
Program writing is simplified.	A program must explicitly state which package the component is taken from.
Confusion may arise as to which package the item used is a component of.	This can reduce the possibility of program error due to accidental misuse.

5.7.2 The package **Standard**

In Ada the clause '**with** Standard; **use** Standard;' is implicitly added to the start of each program unit. The specification for the package Standard is shown in Section C.4, Appendix C. This package contains definitions for +, -, *, /, etc. The package Standard cannot be directly changed by a programmer.

5.7.3 Positioning of **with** and **use** in a package declaration

The **with** and **use** clauses that appear before a specification of a package are implicitly included for the body of the package. If components of the with'ed and used packages are only used in the body of a package, then the clauses **with** and **use** need only be specified for the body. For example, in the class Account the specification of the package Class_account does not use any components of Simple_io and thus can be written as:

```
package Class_account is
   -- rest of specification
end Class_account;

with Simple_io; use Simple_io;
package body Class_account is
   -- rest of implementation
end Class_account;
```

One consequence of this approach is that the user of the package need not know what packages are used by the implementation code.

5.7.4 Conflict in names in a package

A user may wish to use packages that contain items with the same name. For example, a user of the class Class_account also requires to use the class Class_Account_other. In both classes the name of the type that is used to declare an instance of the class is `Account`. By prefixing the type name with the package name the conflict is resolved.

```
with Ada.Text_io, Class_account, Class_Account_other;
use  Ada.Text_io, Class_account, Class_Account_other;
procedure main is
   my_account      :Class_account.Account;
   other_account  :Class_Account_other.Account;
begin
   statement( my_account );              -- In Class_account
   statement( other_account );           -- In Class_Account_other
end main;
```

Note: Overload resolution is used to resolve which package the procedure `statement` *is implemented in.*

5.8   Mutators and inspectors

The methods in a class can either be inspectors or mutators. The role of each of these methods is illustrated in the table below:

Method is a	Role of method	Example from class `Account`
Inspector	Does not change the state of the object.	`balance`
Mutator	Changes the state of the object.	`withdraw` `deposit`

5.9   Type `private`

In the specification of the class `Account` seen in section 5.3.4, the type of `Account` is **private**. This restricts a user of an instance of the type to the following operations:

- Elaboration of an instance of the type.
- Assigning an instance of the type to another instance of the type.
- Comparing instances of the type for equality or inequality.
- Passing an instance of the type to a procedure of function.

A user of the type is prevented from reading or changing the internal contents other than by the actions of methods in the class.

5.9.1   Type `limited private`

A user can be further restricted in the operations that they can perform on an instance of Account by declaring it as **limited private**. This removes the user's ability to assign or compare an instance of the type by default. Naturally if in the class Account the comparison operations for equality or inequality are provided, then these definitions will be used and will override the restriction. For example, if in the class Account the type Account were defined as **limited private**, a user of an instance of an Account would be prevented from writing the following:

```
with Ada.Text_io, Class_account;
use  Ada.Text_io, Class_account;
procedure devious is
  my_account    : Account;
  other_account : Account;
  get           : Money;
begin
  deposit( my_account, 100.00 );
  other_account := my_account;              -- Copy and
  withdraw( other_account, 100.00, get );  -- Withdraw 100.00

  other_account := my_account;              -- Copy again and
  withdraw( other_account, 100.00, get );  -- Withdraw 100.00

end devious;
```

If Account in the class Account had been made **limited private**, its specifications would be:

```
package Class_account is

  type Account is limited private;

  -- Methods (functions and procedures)
private
  type Account is limited record
    the.balance_of : Money := 0.00;      -- Amount in account
  end record;
end Class_account;
```

*Note: The record declaration in the private part of the class is also of **limited** type.*
*In Ada 83 the use of **limited** in:*
   type Account **is limited record**
is not allowed.

The more traditional reason for making a type limited is that a copy operation will not produce the expected result for an instance of the type. Chapter 16 describes such a type that is built using dynamic storage.

The table below summarizes the allowable uses of **private** and **limited private** types.

Operation involving	`private`	`limited private`
Assignment	✓	×
Comparison using = and / = by default	✓	×
Parameter passing	✓	✓

Note: To pass an object as a parameter, a copy is not necessarily made.

5.10 Initializing an object at declaration time

In Ada it is possible to initialize an object when it is declared, although unfortunately there are restrictions to this initialization. Essentially there are two strategies that can be employed. These strategies are:

- Use a discriminant to specify an initial value. The use of discriminants is fully covered in section 6.4.
- Use an assignment statement to set the object to a specific value.

For example, the following modified class `Account` uses both these approaches to initialize an object on declaration.

```
package Class_account is

  subtype Money  is Float;
  subtype PMoney is Float range 0.0 .. Float'Last;
  type Account( number: Natural:= 0 ) is private;

  procedure statement( the:in Account );
  procedure deposit ( the:in out Account; amount:in PMoney );
  procedure withdraw( the:in out Account; amount:in PMoney;
                          get:out PMoney );
  function  balance ( the:in Account ) return Money;
  procedure new_number( the: in out Account; n:in Natural );
  function  new_account( n:in Natural;
                          amount:in PMoney:=0.0 ) return Account;

private
  type Account( number: Natural:= 0) is record
    balance_of : Float := 0.00;
  end record;
end Class_account;
```

5.10.1   By discriminant

Here a type can be given a discriminant so that a whole family of types may be declared. The discriminant value is held in an instance of the type. Section 6.4 describes in more detail the use of discriminants.

For example, to set `my_account` with a specific account number the following code is written:

```
with Ada.Text_io, Class_account;
use  Ada.Text_io, Class_account;
procedure main is
  my_account: Account(10001);
begin
  deposit( my_account, 200.00 );
  statement( my_account );
  new_number( my_account, 10002 );
  statement( my_account );
end main;
```

Note: The discriminant value 10001 *in the declaration of an instance of* Account.

which when run, will produce:

```
Mini statement: Account #      10001
The amount on deposit is £200.00

Mini statement: Account #      10002
The amount on deposit is £200.00
```

5.10.2   Restrictions

The following restrictions apply, however:

 * Only discrete objects or access values may be used as the discriminant value. If an access value is used then the type must be limited.

 * To change the discriminant value the whole record structure must be changed.

Thus the implementation of the procedure `new_number` that allocates a new account number is:

```
procedure new_number( the: in out Account; n:in Natural ) is
begin
   the := Account'( n, the.balance_of );
end new_number;
```

*Note: The whole record structure needs to be changed to change the discriminant.
Chapter 6 discusses **record** initialization in more detail.*

5.10.3   By assignment

In this case the object is assigned an initial value when it is declared. For example, the
following code sets my_account with an account number and initial balance:

```
with Ada.Text_io, Class_account;
use  Ada.Text_io, Class_account;
procedure main is
   my_account : Account := new_account( 10001, 20.0 );
begin
   statement( my_account );
end main;
```

which when run, will produce:

```
Mini statement: Account #      10001
The amount on deposit is £20.00
```

5.10.4   Restrictions

The following restrictions apply, however.

- As an assignment is used, the type may not be limited.

- The effect of the assignment statement may have undesirable consequences.
  For an explanation of these consequences, see section 16.4.

5.11 A personal account manager

One of the applications on a PDA (Personal Digital Assistant) is a PAM (Personal
Account Manager). The PAM provides facilities for recording the transactions that take
place on the user's bank account. An example of the use of the PAM is shown below:

```
[a]   Deposit

[b]   Withdraw

[c]   Balance

Input selection: a

Amount to deposit : 10.00
```

```
[a]   Deposit

[b]   Withdraw

[c]   Balance

Input selection: b
Amount to withdraw : 4.60
```

```
[a]   Deposit

[b]   Withdraw

[c]   Balance

Input selection: c

Balance is  5. 40
```

The program can be constructed using two classes: Account shown in section 5.3.4 and a new class TUI that will implement the text interface. The responsibilities of the class TUI are:

Method	Responsibility
menu	Set up the menu that will be displayed to the user. Each menu item is described by a string.
event	Return the menu item selected by a user of the TUI.
message	Display a message to the user.
dialog	Solicit a response from the user.

The Ada specification of the class TUI is:

```
package Class_tui is

   type Menu_item is ( M_1, M_2, M_3, M_4, M_QUIT );
   type TUI is private;

   procedure menu( the:in out TUI; m1,m2,m3,m4:in String );
   function  event( the:in TUI ) return Menu_item;
   procedure message( the:in TUI; mes:in String );
   procedure dialog(the:in TUI; mes:in String; res:out Float);
   procedure dialog(the:in TUI; mes:in String; res:out Integer);

private
   -- Not a concern of the client of the class
end Class_tui;
```

For example, if an instance of the TUI had been declared with:

```
screen : TUI;
```

then, to setup the menu system:

```
[a]   Print
[b]   Calculate

Input selection:
```

the following code sequence would be used:

```
menu( screen, "Print", "Calculate", "", "" );
```

Note: Null or empty menu items are not displayed.
A string may be of any length. However, to store a string the receiving object must be of the correct size. Ada strings are fully discussed in section 7.8.

The user's response to this menu is elicited with the function event. The function event returns an enumeration representing the menu item selected. For example, if the user selected option [b] then the code:

```
case event( screen ) is
  when M_1 =>                        -- Print
  when M_2 =>                        -- Calculate
```

associated with label M_2 would be obeyed.

Note: The selected menu item is indicated by an enumeration M_1 for menu item 1, M_2 for menu item 2, etc.

A programmer can display a message onto the TUI by using the procedure message which has the text to be output as its second parameter. Likewise, a programmer can initiate a dialog with the user by using the procedure dialog that returns a floating point number. The TUI currently only supports dialogs that solicit a floating point number or integer number.

The fragment of code below illustrates the use of message and dialog interactions in a program which converts miles to kilometres..

```
message ( screen, "Distance converter" );
dialog  ( screen, "Enter distance in miles", miles );
message ( screen, "Distance in kilometres is " &
                  Float'Image( miles * 1.6093 ) );
```

Note: The operator & concatenates two strings into a single string. For example, "Hello" & " " & "world" delivers the single string "Hello world".

In constructing the main program for the personnel account manager, a nested function float_image is used to simplify the construction of the program.

```
with Simple_io, Class_account, Class_tui;
use  Simple_io, Class_account, Class_tui;
procedure main is
  user     : Account;        -- The user's account
  screen   : TUI;            -- The display screen
  cash     : Money;          --
  received : Money;          --
```

The nested function float_image converts a floating point number into an Ada string. This function is provided so that the format of the number may be controlled.

```
function float_image( f:in Float ) return String is
   res : String( 1 .. 10 );          -- String of 10 characters
begin
   put( res, f, aft=>2, exp=>0 );    -- 2 digits - NO exp
   return res;
end float_image;
```

Note: The declaration of a string of 10 characters is filled with the character
representation for the floating point number res.
The procedure 'put(res, f, aft=>2, exp=>0);' converts a
floating point number into a string.

The main body of the program processes the option selected by the user.

```
begin
  loop
    menu( screen, "Deposit", "Withdraw", "Balance", "" );
    case event( screen ) is
      when M_1 =>                                    -- Deposit
        dialog( screen, "Amount to deposit", cash );
        if cash <= 0.0 then
          message( screen, "Must be >= 0.00" );
        else
          deposit( user, cash );
        end if;
      when M_2 =>                                    -- Withdraw
        dialog( screen, "Amount to withdraw", cash );
        if cash <= 0.0 then
          message( screen, "Must be >= 0.00" );
        else
          withdraw( user, cash, received );
          if received <= 0.0 then
            message( screen, "Not enough money" );
          end if;
        end if;
      when M_3 =>                                    -- Balance
        message( screen, "Balance is " &
                         float_image( balance(user)) );
      when M_QUIT =>                                 -- Exit
        return;
      when others =>                                 -- Not used
        message( screen, "Program error");           -- oops
    end case;
  end loop;
end main;
```

5.12 Class TUI

The full specification for the class TUI is:

```
package Class_tui is

  type Menu_item is ( M_1, M_2, M_3, M_4, M_QUIT );
  type TUI is private;

  procedure menu( the:in out TUI; m1,m2,m3,m4:in String );
  function  event( the:in TUI ) return Menu_item;
  procedure message( the:in TUI; mes:in String );
  procedure dialog(the:in TUI; mes:in String; res:out Float);
  procedure dialog(the:in TUI; mes:in String; res:out Integer);

private
  type TUI is record
     selection : Menu_item := M_QUIT;
  end record;
end Class_tui;
```

In the implementation of the class TUI the most complex method is menu. This method is implemented as a procedure that writes out the menu for the TUI and reads the user's response. It will only complete when a valid response has been received from the user. In the implementation of the procedure the technique of procedural decomposition is used to simplify the code.

In procedural decomposition, a large body of code is split into several procedures or functions. This helps to reduce complexity making construction and maintenance easier.

```
with Ada.Text_io; use Ada.Text_io;
package body Class_tui is
  procedure menu( the:in out TUI; m1,m2,m3,m4:in String ) is

  selection      : Character;
  valid_response : Boolean := FALSE;
```

As a user may inadvertently select a null menu item, the procedure set_response is used to disallow such an action.

```
procedure set_response(choice:in Menu_item; mes:in String) is
begin
  if mes /= "" then                    -- Allowable choice
     the.selection := choice; valid_response := TRUE;
  end if;
end set_response;
```

The procedure `display_menu_item` displays onto the TUI only non null menu items.

```
procedure display_menu_item(prompt, name:in String) is
begin
    if name/="" then put(prompt & name); new_line(2); end if;
end display_menu_item;
```

The main body of the procedure displays the menu on the screen and receives the selected menu choice from the user. If an invalid response is received the menu is re-displayed and the user is asked again to select a menu item.

```
begin
  while not valid_response loop
    display_menu_item( "[a]   ", m1 );
    display_menu_item( "[b]   ", m2 );
    display_menu_item( "[c]   ", m3 );
    display_menu_item( "[d]   ", m4 );
    put( "Input selection: "); get( selection ); skip_line;
    case selection is
      when 'a' | 'A' => set_response( M_1, m1 );
      when 'b' | 'B' => set_response( M_2, m2 );
      when 'c' | 'C' => set_response( M_3, m3 );
      when 'd' | 'D' => set_response( M_4, m4 );
      when 'e' | 'E' => set_response( M_QUIT, "Quit" );
      when others    => valid_response := FALSE;
    end case;
    if not valid_response then
      message( the, "Invalid response" );
    end if;
  end loop;
end menu;
```

The function `event` returns the user's selection.

```
function  event( the:in TUI ) return Menu_item is
begin
  return the.selection;
end;
```

The procedure `message` writes a string onto the screen.

```
procedure message( the:in TUI; mes:in String ) is
begin
  new_line; put( mes ); new_line;
end message;
```

The procedure `dialog` solicits a response from the user.

```
procedure dialog(the:in TUI; mes:in String; res:out Float) is
begin
   new_line(1); put( mes & " : " );
   get( res ); skip_line;
end dialog;

procedure dialog(the:in TUI; mes:in String;
                     res:out Integer) is
begin
   new_line(1); put( mes & " : " );
   get( res ); skip_line;
end dialog;

end Class_tui;
```

*Note: In this case the response must be a floating point number or an integer number.
Other overloaded procedures can be provided for different forms of dialog.*

5.13 Self-assessment

- Why should a program be split into many packages?

- What is a class?

- How do you declare an instance of a class in Ada?

- What is the difference between the declaration of a class and the declaration of an instance of that class?

- When an instance of a class is declared, what happens?

- What is contained in a class?

- How can a user of a class request the execution of a method/function in that class?

- What are the advantages of holding data and the code that operates on the data together?

- Should a function in a class be private? Explain your answer.

- Should a data item in a class be public? Explain your answer.

- How should an implementor of a class allow access to instance attributes contained in an object?

5.14 Exercises

Construct the following classes:

- *Account_with_overdraft*
  Construct a class which represents an account on which a customer is allowed to go overdrawn. You should restrict the amount the customer is allowed to go overdrawn. The methods of this class are:

Method	Responsibility
balance	Deliver the balance of the account.
deposit	Deposit money into the account
set_overdraft_limit	Set the overdraft limit.
statement	Print a statement of the current balance of the account.
withdraw	Withdraw money from the account.

- *Cinema Performance Attendance*
  A class Performance, an instance of which represents the seats at a particular showing of a film, has the following methods:

Method	Responsibility
book_seats	Book n seats at the performance.
cancel	Unbook n seats.
sales	Returns the value of the seats sold at this performance.
seats_free	Return the number of seats that are still unsold.

Thus on an instance of Performance the following actions can be performed :

- Book a number of seats
- Find out the number of unsold seats at the performance
- Cancel the booking for n seats.
- Return the value of the seats sold at this performance.

- *Library Book*

  A class to represent a book in a library, such that the following operations can be processed:

  (a)   Loan the book.

  (b)   Mark the book as being reserved. Only one outstanding reservation is allowed on a book.

  (c)   Ask if a book can be loaned. A book can only be loaned if it is not already on loan or is not reserved.

  (d)   Return the book.

Construct the following program:

- *Cinema*

  A program to deal with the day-to-day administration of bookings for a cinema for a single day. Each day there are three separate performances: an early afternoon performance at 1pm, an early evening performance at 5pm and the main performance at 8.30pm.

  The program should be able to handle the booking of cinema seats for any of these three performances and supply details about the remaining seats for a particular performance.

  Hints:
  - Use the class TUI.
  - Use three instances of the class Performance.
  - Use a case statement.
  - Use a procedure to process transactions on a particular performance.

6   Data structures

This chapter explores the use of data structures. A data structure is used to hold related data items in a program and are built using the Ada construct **record**. However, data structures are a low-level construct and in many cases the use of a class will enable better quality code to be produced. As was seen in the previous chapter a **record** is used to hold the hidden instance attributes in a class.

6.1   The **record** structure

In the construction of a program it is convenient to group like data items together. For example, details about a person may consist of:

* The person's name.
* Their height in centimetres.
* Their sex.

The record structure can be used to group these three distinct data items together into a new type called Person. For example, the above description of a Person can be defined as follows:

```ada
MAX_CHS : constant := 10;
type Gender     is ( FEMALE, MALE );
type Height_cm is range 0 .. 300;

type Person is record
  name   : String( 1 .. MAX_CHS );   -- Name as a String
  height : Height_cm := 0;           -- Height in cm.
  sex    : Gender;                   -- Gender of person
end record;
```

Then an instance of a Person can be declared using the declaration:

```ada
mike    : Person;
```

This is similar to a class declaration as seen in the previous chapter. However, all the members of the data structure are visible to a user of the object `mike`.

6.2 Operations on a data structure

The `.` notation is used to access individual members of a data structure. For example, to set up a description of the person `mike`, the following code can be used.

```
mike.name    := "Mike      ";
mike.height := 183;
mike.sex     := MALE;
```

This initialization can be more elegantly expressed using a record aggregate which is then assigned to the object `mike`.

```
mike    := (name=> "Mike      ", height=> 183, sex=> MALE);
```

Note: The construct:
```
(name => "Mike        ", height => 183, sex => 'M' )
```
is a record aggregate.

The record aggregate can also be defined using the absolute position of the arguments or a mixture of absolute and named arguments. For example, the following assignments are equal in effect.

```
corinna := (         "Corinna   ",             171,         FEMALE);
corinna := (name=> "Corinna   ", sex=> FEMALE, height=> 171);
corinna := (         "Corinna   ", sex=> FEMALE, height=> 171);
```

Note: A record aggregate must have all its components specified even if some components have default values. Once a named parameter in an aggregate has been used, all parameters to the left must also be named.
If there is only one member of the record aggregate then it must still be enclosed in brackets.

A data structure may be compared for equality or assigned. For example, using the declarations:

```
corinna, mike : Person;
taller        : Person;
```

the following code can be written:

```
corinna := (name=> "Corinna   ", height=> 170, sex=> FEMALE );
mike    := (name=> "Mike      ", height=> 183, sex=> MALE );
taller  := mike;

if mike = taller then
  put("Mike taller"); new_line;
end if;
if corinna = taller then
  put("Corinna taller"); new_line;
end if;
```

6.2.1 Other operations allowed on data structures

Chapter 11 describes how new meanings for the inbuilt operators in Ada can be defined. Using these techniques to define an additional meaning for > between instances of a Person would allow the following to be written:

```
if mike > corinna then
  put("Mike taller"); new_line;
else
  put("Corinna taller"); new_line;
end if;
```

6.3 Nested **record** structures

A data structure declaration may be nested as in the following record declaration for a bus:

```
type Bus is record
  driver : Person;      -- Bus driver
  seats  : Positive;    -- Number of seats on bus
end record;

london : Bus;
```

Individual components are accessed using the . notation as follows:

```
london.driver.name   := "Jane      ";
london.driver.sex    := FEMALE;
london.driver.height := 175;
london.seats         := 46;
```

Note: The repeated . is used to access first the `driver` and then the data members name, sex and `height`.

However, a record aggregate may also be used as shown below:

```
london := ( ("Jane       ", 175, FEMALE), 46 );
```

6.4 Discriminants to records

A record type may have a parameter (discriminant) whose value may be an instance of a discrete type or access type. Access types are fully described in Chapter 14. For example, the data structure for a person can be defined with a discriminant which specifies the number of characters for the `String`. This new definition for a `Person` is shown below:

```
type     Gender    is ( FEMALE, MALE );
type     Height_cm is range 0 .. 300;
subtype Str_range is Natural range 0 .. 20;
type     Person( chs: Str_range ) is record  -- Name length
   name   : String( 1 .. chs );              -- Name as String
   height : Height_cm   := 0;                -- Height in cm.
   sex    : Gender;                          -- Gender
end record;
```

Note: The discriminant is a component of the record.

In the declaration of an instance of a `Person` the length of the `String` used for a person's name is specified after the type name as follows:

```
mike     : Person(4);
corinna  : Person(7);
walker   : Person(10);
```

Then an assignment to an instance of `Person` is:

```
mike    := (chs=>4, name=>"Mike"   , height=>183, sex=>MALE);
corinna:= (chs=>7, name=>"Corinna", height=>171, sex=>FEMALE);
```

Note: The value of the discriminant must be specified in the record aggregate.

However, `mike`, `corinna` and `walker` are not of the same type so the assignment:

```
walker := corinna;   -- Fail at run-time
```

will fail at run-time as the discriminants of the record are not identical. The object `walker` contains a `String` of length of 10 whilst the object `corinna` contains a `String` of length 7.

6.5 Default values to a discriminant

A discriminant to a type may have a default value. If a value is not specified with the declaration of a discriminated type then it is an unconstrained discriminated type. An instance of an unconstrained discriminated type may be assigned or compared with other unconstrained discriminants of the same type name.

For example, if the data structure `Person` is now defined as:

```
type     Gender     is ( FEMALE, MALE );
type     Height_cm is range 0 .. 300;
subtype Str_range is Natural range 0 .. 20;
type     Person( chs:Str_range := 0 ) is record -- Length of name
  name   : String( 1 .. chs );                   -- As String
  height : Height_cm    := 0;                     -- Height in cm.
  sex    : Gender;                                -- Gender
end record;
```

then the following code can be written:

```
declare
  mike    : Person;        -- Unconstrained
  corinna: Person;         -- Unconstrained
  walker : Person;         -- Unconstrained
begin
  mike    := (4, name=>"Mike"    , height=>183, sex=>MALE);
  corinna:= (7, name=>"Corinna", height=>171, sex=>FEMALE);
  walker := corinna;

  if mike = walker then
    put("Mike likes walking"); new_line;
  end if;
end;
```

Note: It would still be an error to write:
corinna:=(10,name=>"Corinna",height=>171,sex=>FEMALE);
as the length of "Corinna" is not 10 characters.

6.5.1 Constrained vs. unconstrained discriminants

Using the last definition of type `Person`:

Declaration	The object **Mike** is	Comment
`mike: Person;`	Unconstrained	The variable `mike` may be compared with or assigned any other instance of `Person`.
`mike: Person(4);`	Constrained	May only be assigned or compared with another `Person(4)`.

6.5.2 Restrictions on a discriminant

A discriminant must be a discrete type or access type. If it is an access type then the record must be limited. This unfortunately means that a `Float` cannot be used as a discriminant to a record.

6.6 Variant records

When using a data structure there will be occasions when the use of some of the data items will be mutually exclusive. For example, in a description of a person who may be a LECTURER or a STUDENT the data members are:

Data member	Belongs to	Description
`name`	Both	The name of the person
`class_size`	LECTURER	The size of the group that the lecturer teaches
`full_time`	STUDENT	Whether or not the student is full-time or part-time.
`grade`		The mark out of 100 that the student gains at the end of the course.

Thus the storage for `class_size` can overlay all or part of the storage for `full_time` and `grade` as the two components of the data structure will not both be used simultaneously.

This can be visualized as:

role -> Student	Name	role	full_time	grade
role -> Lecturer	Name	role	class_size

In Ada a variant record allows two or more data items to occupy the same physical storage. This will result in lower memory usage in a program. However, access to the variant components must be carefully controlled to prevent information being stored or extracted as the wrong type. For example, if the record represents a lecturer then it should not be possible to access the component full_time as this is only present when the record represents a student. Ada with its strict typing will prevent such occurrences. The data structure to represent either a lecturer or a student is defined as:

```
type     Occupation is (LECTURER, STUDENT);
type     Mark       is range 0 .. 100;
subtype Str_range  is Natural range 0 .. 20;
type     Person( chs : Str_range :=0;
                 role: Occupation:=STUDENT ) is record
   name    : String( 1 .. chs );      -- Name as string
   case role is                        -- Variant record
     when LECTURER =>                   --  Storage overlaid
       class_size: Positive;            -- Size of taught class
     when STUDENT  =>
       full_time : Boolean := TRUE;     -- Attendance mode
       grade     : Mark;                -- Mark for course
   end case;
end record;
```

Note: If one discriminant item is given a default value than all discriminant items must be given a default value.

Using the above declaration of Person allows the following assignments to be made:

```
declare
  mike : Person;            -- Unconstrained
  clive: Person;            -- Unconstrained
  brian: Person(5,STUDENT); -- Constrained
begin
  mike := (4, LECTURER, name=>"Mike", class_size=>36);
  clive:= (5, STUDENT, name=>"Clive", grade=>70, full_time=>TRUE);
  -- insert --
end;
```

In Ada, this process is safe as the compiler will check and disallow access to a variant part which is not specified by the discriminant. For example, if the following statements were inserted at the point -- insert -- above, they would be flagged as invalid at either compile-time or run-time.

Invalid statement	Reason
adam.role:= STUDENT	Not allowed to change just a discriminant as this would allow data to be modified/extracted as the wrong type. Detectable at compile-time.

Invalid statement	Reason
`mike.grade:= 0`	Access to a component of the data structure which is not active. Mike is a lecturer and hence has no grade score. Detected at run-time.
`brian := (5, LECTURER, name=>"Brian", class_size=>36);`	The object `brian` is constrained to be a student. Detectable at compile-time.

6.7 Data structure vs. class

The table below summarizes the differences between a class and a data structure.

	Data structure	Class
A user of the construct can directly access and change the internal structure.	✓	✕
Can be used where a normal type can be used.	✓	✓
Code to manipulate the data encapsulated with the construct.	✕	✓
Representation of the data items is hidden from the user.	✕	✓

Thus to provide data hiding, a class must be used.

6.8 Self-assessment

- Explain how you can access an individual component of a record.

- What are the major differences between a class and an Ada **record**?

- Is the use of variant records safe in Ada? Explain your answer.

- What is the difference between an unconstrained and a constrained record declaration?

6.9 Exercises

Construct the following:

• An Ada record to describe the computer you are using. This should include for example: the amount of main memory, the amount of cache memory, the amount of disk space.

 You may need a coding scheme for the size of memory components, as in the case of disk space this can be a very large number.

• Generalize this record so that it can hold details about many different types of computer. Include a variant part to allow for the following different types:

 • A computer used for word processing, with no network devices or multimedia components.
 • A multimedia computer with sound and video capability.
 • A workstation with a network and file server connections.

7 Arrays

This chapter introduces arrays that implement a collection facility for objects. With this facility, objects are stored and retrieved using an index of a discrete type.

7.1 Arrays as container objects

An array is a collection of objects that can be accessed using an instance of a discrete type. For example, the number of computer terminals in five rooms could be described with the following declaration:

```
computers_in_room : array ( 1 .. 5 ) of Natural;
```

Note: `computers_in_room` *is a collection of* `Natural` *numbers and the integer numbers 1 through 5 are used to select a particular object in this collection. The compiler will check that the subscript is valid. If it cannot be checked directly, code should be inserted which will perform the check at run-time. The exception* `Constraint_error` *is raised if the index is out of bounds.*

The number of terminals in each room can be recorded in the collection `computers_room` by using an array index to select a particular computer room. For example, to set the number of computers in room 1 to 20, 2 to 30, 3 to 25, 4 to 10 and 5 to 15, the following code can be used:

```
computers_in_room(1)  := 20;
computers_in_room(2)  := 30;
computers_in_room(3)  := 25;
computers_in_room(4)  := 10;
computers_in_room(5)  := 15;
```

This can be visualized diagrammatically as shown in Figure 7.1.

1	2	3	4	5
20	30	25	10	15

Index used to access contents of

array collection `computers_room`

Figure 7.1 Diagrammatic representation of an array.

Once information about the number of computers in each room has been set up, it can be printed with the following code:

```
for i in 1 .. 5 loop
  put("Computers in room "); put( i ); put(" is ");
  put( computers_in_room( i ) ); new_line;
end loop;
```

which when combined with appropriate declarations and run, would produce the following results:

```
Computers in room 1 is 20
Computers in room 2 is 30
Computers in room 3 is 25
Computers in room 4 is 10
Computers in room 5 is 15
```

In the example above, any `Integer` object can be used as an index to the array. This freedom may lead to program errors when a value other than the intended subscript is used. Unfortunately such an error would not be detected until run-time. To allow Ada to perform strict type checking so that such an error may be caught at compile-time, a separate type for the bounds of the array can be defined. This is achieved by defining a range type that is then used to describe the bounds of the array. For example, the previous object `computers_room` could have been defined as:

```
type     Rooms_index is new Integer range 1 .. 5;
subtype Rooms_range is Rooms_index;
type     Rooms_array is array ( Rooms_range ) of Natural;
computers_room : Rooms_array;
```

In the declaration the following types and subtypes have been defined:

Type / Subtype	Description
Rooms_index	A type used to define an object that is used to index the array. This may allow the object to represent out of bound data.
Rooms_range	A subtype of Rooms_index representing the actual range of indices to the array.
Rooms_array	A type representing the array.

Using the above types and subtypes, the **for** loop which prints the number of computers in each room would now become:

```
computers_in_room : Rooms_array;

-- Set up contents of computers_in_room

for i in Rooms_range loop
  put("Computers in room "); put( Integer(i) ); put(" is ");
  put( computers_in_room( i ) ); new_line;
end loop;
```

*Note: As the index i to the **for loop** is now of type Rooms_range it must be
converted to an Integer before it can be output using the procedure put.
Mechanisms to output objects of different discrete types will be explored later in
Chapter 17.*

A compile-time error message will be generated if the programmer incorrectly uses
the above mechanism to index the array, for example, when using an object which is
neither of type Room_index nor a subtype of Room_index.

7.2 Attributes of an array

As arrays in Ada are self-describing, various attributes can be extracted from an instance
of an array. For example, with the following declarations for the array marks:

```
type     Grades_index is new Character range 'a' .. 'f';
subtype Grades_range is Grades_index;
type     Grades_array is array ( Grades_range ) of Natural;
marks : Grades_array;
```

a number of attributes can be extracted:

Attribute	Description	Value
marks'Length	A Universal integer representing the number of elements in the one dimensional array.	6
marks'First	The first subscript of the array which is of type grades_range	'a'
marks'Last	The last subscript of the array which is of type grades_range	'f'
marks'Range	Equivalent to marks'First .. marks'Last	'a'..'f'

A fuller description of the attributes that can be extracted from an object or type are
given in section B.2, Appendix B.

7.3 The game noughts and crosses

The children's game of noughts and crosses or noughts and crosses is played on a three-by-three grid of squares. Players either play X or O. Each player takes it in turn to add their mark to an unoccupied square. The game is won when a player has three of their marks in a row either diagonally, horizontally or vertically. If no unoccupied square remains, the game is a draw (Figure 7.2).

X's first move	O's first move	X's second move	O's second move
X	X	X X / O	X O X / O
X's third move	O's third move	X's fourth move	
X O X / X / O	X O X / X / O O	X O X / X / O O X	As can be seen to go first is a clear advantage

Figure 7.2 A game of noughts and crosses

A program to display the current state of a game of noughts and crosses between two contestants is developed with the aid of a class `Board`. The operations, `add`, `valid`, and `display`, can be performed on an instance of `Board`. The responsibilities of these methods is as follows:

Method	Responsibility
add	Add the player's mark to the board. The player's move is specified by a number in the range 1 to 9 and their mark by a character.
valid	Return true if the presented move is valid. The method checks that the move is in the range 1 to 9 and that the specified cell is not occupied.
display	Display on the screen a representation of the current state of the board.

The specification for the class `Board` is defined by the package `Class_board` as follows:

```
with Simple_io; use Simple_io;
package Class_board is
  type Board is private;
  procedure add(the:in out Board; pos:in Integer;
                piece:in Character);
  function  valid( the:in Board; pos:in Integer ) return Boolean;
  procedure display( the:in Board );
private
  -- Not a concern of the client
end Class_board;
```

Using the above package specification, the following code can be developed which records the moves made on a noughts and crosses board game.

```
with Simple_io, Class_board;
use  Simple_io, Class_board;
procedure main is
  player : Character;          -- Either 'X' or 'O'
  game   : Board;              -- An instance of Class Board
  move   : Integer;            -- Move from user
begin
  player := 'X';                              -- Set player
  put("Player "); put( player );              -- Ask player for
  put(" enter move (1-9) : ");                --   move
  while not end_of_file loop                  -- While pos moves
    get( move ); skip_line;                   --  Get move
    if valid( game, move ) then
      add( game, move, player );              -- Add to board
      display( game );                        -- Display board
      case player is                          -- Next Player
        when 'X'      => player := 'O';       -- 'X' -> 'O'
        when 'O'      => player := 'X';       -- 'O' -> 'X'
        when others   => null;                --
      end case;
    else
      put("Move invalid"); new_line;          -- for board
    end if;
    put("Player "); put( player );            -- Ask player for
    put(" enter move (1-9) : ");              --   move
  end loop;
  new_line(2);
end main;
```

*Note: That the **case** statement which effects the change between the players mark has a **when others** clause. This is required as in theory a player can take any character value. The code for this 'impossible' eventuality is the **null** statement.*

The character object player holds a representation of the current player's mark, in this case either the character 'X' or 'O'. The object player is initially set to 'X', and after each player's move is changed to the other player's mark.

The full specification of the class Board is as follows:

```
with Simple_io; use Simple_io;
package Class_board is
  type Board is private;
  procedure add(the:in out Board; pos:in Integer;
                piece:in Character);
  function  valid( the:in Board; pos:in Integer ) return Boolean;
  procedure display( the:in Board );
private
  SIZE_TTT : constant := 9;                        -- Must be 9
  subtype Board_index is Integer range 1 .. SIZE_TTT;
  subtype Board_range is Board_index;
  type    Board_grid  is array( Board_range ) of Character;
  type Board is record
    sqrs : Board_grid := ( others => ' ');          -- Initialize
  end record;
end Class_board;
```

The noughts and crosses board is represented by a single dimensional array of nine characters. The board is initialized to all spaces with the assignment Board_grid := (**others** => ' '). This style of initialization is explained in section 7.5 *Initializing an array*. In defining the noughts and crosses board the following types and subtypes are used:

Type	Description
Board_index	A subtype used to describe an index object used to access an element of the noughts and crosses board. By making Board_index a subtype of Integer, Integers may be used as an index of the array.
Board_range	A subtype used to describe the range of values that can be used to index the noughts and crosses board.
Board_grid	A type used to describe a noughts and crosses board.

The implementation of the class Board is defined in the body of the package Class_board as follows:

```
with Simple_io; use Simple_io;
package body Class_board is
```

The procedure add adds a counter either the character 'X' or 'O' to the board.

```
procedure add( the:in out Board; pos:in Integer;
               piece:in Character ) is
begin
  the.sqrs( pos ) := piece;
end add;
```

The functions `valid` returns **true** if the square selected is not occupied by a previously played counter.

```
function valid(the:in Board; pos:in Integer) return Boolean is
begin
   return pos in Board_range and then the.sqrs( pos ) = ' ';
end valid;
```

*Note: The use of **and then** so that the check on the board is only made if the position is valid.*

The procedure `display` prints the board on to the player's terminal. The strategy for printing the board is to print each cell followed by a character sequence appropriate for its position on the board. The text to be printed after each square of the array `sqrs` has been printed is as follows:

Printed board showing array index of cell in array `sqrs`	After printing cell:	Text to be printed (Using **Ada.Text_io**)
1 | 2 | 3 --------- 4 | 5 | 6 --------- 5 | 8 | 9	1,2,4,5,7 and 8	`put(" | ");`

	3 and 6	`new_line;`
		`put("---------");`
		`new_line;`

	9	`new_line;`

This results in the printing of a two-dimensional grid for the noughts and crosses board.

```
procedure display( the:in Board ) is
begin
  for i in Board_range loop
    put( the.sqrs( i ) );              -- Display counter;
    case i is                          -- after printing counter
      when 3 | 6  =>                    --   print Row Separator
        new_line; put("---------");
        new_line;
      when 9      =>                   -- print new line
        new_line;
      when 1 | 2 | 4 | 5 | 7 | 8 =>  --  print Col separator
        put(" | ");
    end case;
  end loop;
end display;
end Class_board;
```

7.3.1 Putting it all together

When compiled and run, a possible interaction between two players could be as follows:

X's first move	O's first move	X's second move	O's second move

x | |
--------- 	
  | |
--------- 	
  | |
	x | |
	--------- 	
	  | |
	--------- 	
	  | o |
		x | | x
		--------- 	
		  | |
		--------- 	
		  | o |
			x | o | x
			--------- 	
			  | |
			--------- 	
			  | o |

X's third move	O's third move	X's forth move	

x | o | x
--------- 	
  | x |
--------- 	
  | o |
	x | o | x
	--------- 	
	  | x |
	--------- 	
	o | o |
		x | o | x
		--------- 	
		  | x |
		--------- 	
		o | o | x
			As can be seen to go first is a clear advantage

7.4 Multidimensional arrays

Arrays can have any number of dimensions. For example, the noughts and crosses board could have been represented by a two-dimensional array as follows:

```
SIZE_TTT : constant := 3;
subtype Board_index is Integer range 1 .. SIZE_TTT;
subtype Board_range is Board_index;
type    Board_array is
        array( Board_range, Board_range ) of Character;
type Board is record
  sqrs : Board_array := ( others => (others => ' ') );
end record;
```

Note: The two-dimensional initialization of the board to spaces is as follows:
     `sqrs : Board_grid:=( others => (others => ' ') );`
     This type of initialization is explained in section 7.5 Initializing an array.

Using this new representation of Board the procedure for displaying the board would now become:

```
procedure display( the:in Board ) is
begin
  for i in Board_range loop                  -- For each Row
    for j in Board_range loop                -- For each column
      put( the.sqrs( i,j ) );                --   display counter;
      case j is                              --   column postfix
        when 1 | 2 => put(" | ");
        when 3    => null;
      end case;
    end loop;
    case i is                                -- row postfix
      when 1 | 2  => new_line; put("----------"); new_line;
      when 3      => new_line;
    end case;
  end loop;
end display;
```

Note: The statement **null** has no action, but is necessary as a statement must follow a
when clause. The clause **when** 3 cannot be omitted as this would leave the case
statement not covering all the possible values for j.

7.4.1 Alternative ways of declaring multidimensional arrays

A multidimensional array may be declared in two distinct ways. For example, the board
grid shown above was declared as follows:

```
subtype Board_index is Integer range 1 .. SIZE_TTT;
subtype Board_range is Board_index;
type    Board_array is
        array( Board_range, Board_range ) of Character;
type Board is record
  sqrs : Board_array := ( others => (others => ' ') );
end record;
```

and an instance of the Board the was accessed using a single subscript with two
parameters as follows:

```
put("Using a 2 D array"); new_line;
the.sqrs(1,2) := 'X';
the.sqrs(2,3) := 'X';
the.sqrs(3,2) := 'X';
display( the );
```

Alternatively, Board can be declared as an array of an array as follows:

```
SIZE_TTT : constant := 3;
subtype Board_index is Integer range 1 .. SIZE_TTT;
subtype Board_range is Board_index;
type    Board_row   is array( Board_range ) of Character;
type    Board_array is array( Board_range ) of Board_row ;
type Board is record
  sqrs : Board_array := ( others => (others => ' ') );
end record;
```

To access an instance of Board the, a double subscript is used:

```
put("Using a 1D array of a 1D array"); new_line;
the.sqrs(1)(2) := 'X';
the.sqrs(2)(3) := 'X';
the.sqrs(3)(2) := 'X';
display( the );
```

Note: The initialization of the two-dimensional array is performed in the same way in both cases.

7.4.2 Attributes of multidimensional arrays

Like single dimensional arrays, various attributes can also be extracted from multidimensional arrays. For multidimensional arrays it is, however, necessary to specify which dimension is to be interrogated. This is achieved by appending the appropriate dimension to the attribute. For example, to find the number of elements in the second dimension of the object sqrs use the.sqrs'Length(2). Section B.2, Appendix B lists attributes that can be extracted from an object or type.

7.5 Initializing an array

A pixel on a full colour computer screen is represented by the three primary colours: red, blue, and green. Each colour has an intensity ranging from 0 (dark) to 255 (bright). This is the RGB additive colour model used by computer terminals and TVs, which is different from the CYMB subtractive colour model used in printing. In Ada, a pixel could be represented by an array of three elements representing the intensities of the primary colours. To represent the colour white, the intensity of each of the primary colours would be set to 255. A pixel can be represented by the type Pixel as follows:

```
type Colour      is ( RED, GREEN, BLUE );
type Intensity   is new Integer range 0 .. 255;
type Pixel       is array( Colour ) of Intensity;
```

A single point on the screen could be represented by the object dot as follows:

```
dot            : Pixel;
```

which could be initialized to black or white with the following assignments:

```
dot := ( 0,   0,   0 );                        -- Black
dot := ( 255, 255, 255 );                      -- White
```

The values can be named by using the subscript to the array as follows:

```
dot := ( RED=> 255, GREEN=>255, BLUE=>255);      -- White
```

An **others** clause can be used to let the remaining elements of the array take a particular value as in:

```
dot := Pixel'( RED=>255, others=>0 );            -- Red
```

Note: When the **others** *clause is used, and at least one other element is given a value by a different means, then the type of the constant must be specified. This is achieved by prefixing the constant with its type name followed by a '.*

Using a similar notation to that used in the **case** statement introduced in section 2.8.1, a range of values may also be specified:

```
dot := ( RED | BLUE => 255, GREEN=>0 );        -- Purple
dot := ( RED .. BLUE => 127 );                 -- Grey
dot := Pixel'( RED .. GREEN => 255, others=>0 );  -- Yellow
```

7.5.1 Multidimensional initializations

A cursor on a black and white screen can be defined by the following declaration of an object cursor_style:

```
BITS_CURSOR: constant Positive := 5;
type Bit          is New Integer range 0 .. 1;
type Cursor_range is new Positive range 1 .. BITS_CURSOR;
type Cursor       is array( Cursor_range,
                            Cursor_range ) of Bit;

cursor_style : Cursor;
```

Black is represented by 1

White is represented by 0

Figure 7.3 Black and white cursor.

The cursor as illustrated in Figure 7.3 could be set up in `cursor_style` with any of the following three declarations:

- by initializing every cell in the cursor individually:

```
cursor_style := Cursor'( (1, 0, 0, 0, 1),
                         (0, 1, 1, 1, 0),
                         (0, 0, 1, 0, 0),
                         (0, 1, 1, 1, 0),
                         (1, 0, 0, 0, 1) );
```

Note: The prefix to the array constant is optional in this case.

- by using an **others** clause to set up the white elements:

```
cursor_style := Cursor'( 1=> ( 1=>1, 5=>1, others => 0 ),
                         2=> ( 2..4    =>1, others => 0 ),
                         3=> ( 3=>1,        others => 0 ),
                         4=> ( 2..4    =>1, others => 0 ),
                         5=> ( 1=>1, 5=>1, others => 0 ) );
```

- by using | clauses to combine any identical initializations:

```
cursor_style := Cursor'( 1|5=> ( 1|5 =>1, others => 0 ),
                         2|4=> ( 2..4=>1, others => 0 ),
                         3  => ( 3   =>1, others => 0 ) );
```

In a program using a colour monitor, the cursor could have been described as follows:

```
BITS_CURSOR: constant Positive := 5;
type Colour       is ( RED, GREEN, BLUE );
type Intensity    is new Integer range 0 .. 255;
type Pixel        is array( Colour ) of Intensity;

type Cursor_range is new Positive range 1 .. BITS_CURSOR;
type Cursor       is array( Cursor_range,
                            Cursor_range ) of Pixel;
```

The following code would be used to initialize the cursor to the colour grey:

```
cursor_style :=
Cursor'( 1|5=> ( 1|5 => (others=>127), others => (others=>0) ),
        2|4=> ( 2..4=> (others=>127), others => (others=>0) ),
        3  => ( 3  => (others=>127), others => (others=>0) ) );
```

7.6   A histogram

A program to print a histogram representing the frequency of individual letters occurring in a piece of text can be developed by first implementing a class that performs the following operations on an instance of a `Histogram`.

Method	Responsibility
add_to	Add a character to the histogram, recording the updated total number of characters.
put	Write a histogram to the output source representing the currently gathered data.
reset	Clear any previously gathered data, setting various internal objects to an initial state.

Using the class `Histogram` which has been implemented in the package `Class_histogram`, code can be written which will produce a histogram of the frequency of characters taken from the standard input:

```
with Simple_io, Class_histogram;
use  Simple_io, Class_histogram;
procedure main is
  ch:Character;                          -- Current character
  text_histogram: Histogram;             -- Histogram object
begin
  reset(text_histogram);                 -- Reset to empty

  while not end_of_file loop             -- For each line
    while not end_of_line loop           -- For each character
      get(ch);                           -- Get current character
      add_to( text_histogram, ch );      -- Add to histogram
    end loop;
    skip_line;                           -- Next line
  end loop;

  put( text_histogram );                 -- Print histogram

end main;
```

The class histogram is defined by the following package specification:

```
with Simple_io;
use  Simple_io;
package Class_histogram is
  type Histogram is private;
  DEF_HEIGHT : constant Positive := 14;
  procedure reset( the:in out Histogram );
  procedure add_to( the:in out Histogram; a_ch:in Character );
  procedure put(the:in Histogram; height:in Positive:=DEF_HEIGHT);
private
  type     Alphabet_index is new Character range 'A' .. 'Z';
  subtype Alphabet_range is Alphabet_index;
  type     Alphabet_array is array (Alphabet_range) of Natural;
  type Histogram is record
    number_of    : Alphabet_array := ( others => 0 );
  end record;
end Class_histogram;
```

The histogram is calculated using the individual letter frequencies that are stored in an array of Naturals indexed by the upper case letters 'A' .. 'Z'. The implementation is simplified by allowing each letter to index directly the frequency count for the letter.

In the implementation of the class histogram shown below, the procedure reset is used to set the individual frequency counts for each letter to 0.

```
with Ada.Characters.Handling;
use  Ada.Characters.Handling;
package body Class_histogram is

  procedure reset(the:in out Histogram) is
  begin
    the.number_of := ( others => 0 );   -- Reset counts to 0
  end reset;
```

The procedure add_to uses the functions is_lower, to_upper and is_upper which are contained in the package Ada.Characters.Handling. A full description of these functions can be found in section C.7, Appendix C.

```
  procedure add_to(the:in out Histogram; a_ch:in Character) is
    ch : Character;
  begin
    ch := a_ch;                      -- As write to ch
    if is_lower(ch) then             -- Convert to upper case
      ch := to_upper( ch );
    end if;
    if is_upper( ch ) then           -- so record
      declare
        c : Alphabet_index := Alphabet_index(ch);
      begin
        the.number_of(c) := the.number_of(c) + 1;
      end;
    end if;
  end add_to;
```

The histogram is displayed as a bar graph corresponding to the accuracy of the output device, which in this case is an ANSI terminal. The size of the histogram is set by the defaulted parameter height.

```
procedure put(the:in Histogram;
              height:in Positive:=DEF_HEIGHT) is
   frequency      : Alphabet_array;          -- Copy to process
   max_height     : Natural := 0;            -- Observed max
begin
   frequency := the.number_of;               -- Copy data (Array)
   for ch in Alphabet_range loop             -- Find max frequency
      if frequency(ch) > max_height then
         max_height:= frequency(ch);
      end if;
   end loop;

   if max_height > 0 then
      for ch in Alphabet_range loop          -- Scale to max height
         frequency(ch):=(frequency(ch)*height)/(max_height);
      end loop;
   end if;

   for row in reverse 1 .. height loop       -- Each line
      put( "  |  " );                        -- start of line
      for ch in Alphabet_range loop
         if frequency(ch) >= row then
            put('*');                        -- bar of hist >= col
         else
            put(' ');                        -- bar of hist <  col
         end if;
      end loop;
      put(" | "); new_line;                  -- end of line
   end loop;
   put("   +---------------------------+"); new_line;
   put("    ABCDEFGHIJKLMNOPQRSTUVWXYZ " ); new_line;
   put("  *  = (approx) ");
   put( Float(max_height) / Float(height), aft=>2, exp=>0 );
   put(" characters "); new_line;
end put;
end Class_histogram;
```

7.6.1 Putting it all together

When run with the following data:

```
Ada is a language developed for the American Department
of Defense.
Ada is named after the first programmer Ada (Byron) Lovelace
who helped Charles Babbage with his work on the analytical engine.
She was the daughter of the poet Lord Byron.
```

the program would produce the following output:

```
     |        *                                 |
     |        *                                 |
     |        *                                 |
     |    *   *                                 |
     |    *   *                                 |
     |    *   *                                 |
     |    *   *                                 |
     |    *   *                                 |
     |    *   *           *   * *               |
     |    *  **   *      **   * *               |
     |    *  **   *   *  **   * *               |
     |    *  **  **   *  **   ***               |
     |   ** ******   ***** ***                  |
     |   ********    ***** ***   * *            |
     +---------------------------+
         ABCDEFGHIJKLMNOPQRSTUVWXYZ      *  = 2.071
```

*Note: The exact number of characters shown for each * in the bar graph is guaranteed to be accurate only for the most frequently occurring character.*

7.7 Unconstrained arrays

In earlier sections, the types used to represent an array have been constrained types. These can be used to create only objects that have the specific bounds defined by the type declaration. Ada allows a user to define a type for an array that can be constrained to represent a whole family of instances of arrays, where each member of the family can potentially have different bounds. This mechanism is required when an array of arbitrary size is to be passed as a parameter to a procedure or function. For example, a function sum that sums the contents of an array passed to the function, can be written as follows:

```
function sum( list:in Numbers_array ) return Integer is
total : Integer := 0;
begin
  for i in list'Range loop          -- Depends on # of elements
    total := total + list( i );
  end loop;
  return total;
end sum;
```

The type Numbers_array is an unconstrained array that has the following definition:

```
type Numbers_array is array ( Positive range <> ) of Integer;
```

This defines a type that can be used to elaborate array objects with Positive type bounds. For example, an instance of the type Numbers_array can be declared as follows:

```
computers_in_room :Numbers_array(513..519) := (2,2,2,3,2,1,3);
```

Note: The specific bounds of computers_in_room, *an instance of* Numbers_array *needs to be specified in the declaration.*

7.7.1 Slices of an array

A slice of a one-dimensional array can be obtained by selecting elements from a contiguous range from within the array. For example, to select the computers in rooms 517 to 519 from the object computers_in_room the following slice of the array can be extracted: computers_in_rooms(517 .. 519).

Note: A slice can only be taken from a one-dimensional array.

7.7.2 Putting it all together

A package Pack_types is defined so that any program unit may use the constrained type declaration for Numbers_array.

```
package Pack_types is
   type Numbers_array is array ( Positive range <> ) of Integer;
end Pack_types;
```

Note: No body is required as the specification has no implementation part.

This is then used by a program to illustrate the use of the function sum.

```
with Simple_io, Pack_types;
use  Simple_io, Pack_types;
procedure main is
   computers_in_room: Numbers_array(513 .. 519) := (2,2,2,3,2,1,3);

   -- The function sum

begin
   put("The total number of computers is:        " );
   put( sum( computers_in_room ) ); new_line;
   put("Computers in rooms 517, 518 and 519 is: " );
   put( sum( computers_in_room( 517 .. 519 ) ) ); new_line;
end main;
```

When compiled with the body of the function sum, the above program when run would print the results:

```
The total number of computers is:              15
Computers in rooms 517, 518 and 519 is:         6
```

7.8 Strings

The type String is a predefined, unconstrained array whose definition is:

```
type String is array ( Positive range <> ) of Character;
```

This type is defined in the package Standard listed in section C.4, Appendix C. A limitation of the String type is that in the declaration of each instance of a string the number of characters that are to be assigned to that particular string must be specified. For example, the following program writes out the name and address of the University of Brighton.

```
with Simple_io; use  Simple_io;
procedure main is
   institution : String(1 .. 22);
   address     : String(1 .. 20);
   full_address: String(1 .. 44);
begin
   institution := "University of Brighton";
   address      := "Brighton East Sussex";
   full_address:= institution & ", " & address;
   put( full_address ); new_line;
end main;
```

When run, this would print:

```
University of Brighton, Brighton East Sussex
```

Note: The concatenation operator & is used to deliver the join of two one-dimensional arrays.

7.9 Dynamic arrays

In Ada the bounds of an array need not be fixed at compile-time, as they can be specified by an object whose value is not fixed until run-time. Such an array is known as a dynamic array. However, once elaborated, the bounds of the dynamic array cannot be changed. Unlike many other languages, Ada allows a dynamic array to be returned as the result of a function. For example, a function `reverse_string` can be written which reverses the characters passed to it. An implementation of the function `reverse_string` is as follows:

```
function reverse_string( str:in String ) return String is
   res : String( str'Range );              -- Dynamic bounds
begin
   for i in str'Range loop
      res( str'First+str'Last-i ) := str( i );
   end loop;
   return res;
end reverse_string;
```

7.9.1 Putting it all together

The above function `reverse_string` is used in the following program to illustrate the use of a dynamic array:

```
with Simple_io, reverse_string; use Simple_io;
procedure main is
begin
   put( reverse_string( "madam i'm adam" ) ); new_line;
end main;
```

When run, this would deliver the following results:

```
mada m'i madam
```

Note: Even though dynamic arrays can be created, they can only be used to store an object that is type compatible. In particular, the number and type of the elements in the receiving object must be the same as in the delivered object.

7.10 A name and address class

A class for managing a person's name and address has the following responsibilities.

Method	Responsibility
`set`	Set the name and address of a person. The name and address is specified with a / character separating each line.
`deliver_line`	Deliver the n'th line of the address as a string.
`lines`	Deliver the number of lines in the address.

The specification for the class is as follows:

```
package Class_name_address is
  type Name_address is tagged private;

  procedure set( the:out Name_address; str:in String );
  function deliver_line( the:in Name_address;
                              line:in Positive ) return String;
  function lines( the:in Name_address ) return Positive;
private
  MAX_CHS : constant := 200;
  subtype Line_index is Natural    range 0 .. MAX_CHS;
  subtype Line_range is Line_index range 1 .. MAX_CHS;

  type Name_address is tagged record
    text   : String( Line_range );    -- Details
    length : Line_index := 0;          -- Length of address
  end record;
end Class_name_address;
```

In the implementation of the class the method `set` stores the string given as a parameter into the instance attribute `text`. A check is made to see if the string is too long. If it is, the string is truncated and the procedure recalled recursively with the shortened name.

```
package body Class_name_address is

  function spaces( line:in Positive ) return String;

  procedure set( the:out Name_address; str:in String ) is
  begin
    if str'Length > MAX_CHS then
      set( the, str( str'First .. str'First+MAX_CHS-1 ) );
    else
      the.text( 1 .. str'Length ) := str;
      the.length := str'Length;
    end if;
  end set;
```

The function `deliver_line` returns a string representing the n'th line of the address with a staggered left margin. Spaces for the staggered left margin are delivered by the function `spaces`.

```
function deliver_line( the:in Name_address;
                       line:in Positive ) return String is
  line_on : Positive := 1;
begin
  for i in 1 .. the.length loop
    if line_on = line then
      for j in i .. the.length loop
        if the.text(j) = '/' then
          return spaces(line_on) & the.text(i .. j-1);
        end if;
      end loop;
      return spaces(line_on) & the.text(i..the.length);
    end if;
    if the.text(i) = '/' then line_on := line_on+1; end if;
  end loop;
  return "";
end deliver_line;
```

The number of lines in an address is delivered by the function `lines`. This function counts the number of ' / ' characters in the string `text`.

```
function lines( the:in Name_address ) return Positive is
  no_lines : Positive := 1;
begin
  for i in  1 .. the.length loop
    if the.text(i) = '/' then no_lines := no_lines + 1; end if;
  end loop;
  return no_lines;
end lines;
```

The function `spaces` delivers a string of `line` spaces.

```
function spaces( line:in Positive ) return String is
  spaces_are : String( 1 .. Line ) := (others=>' ');
begin
  return spaces_are;
end spaces;

end Class_name_address;
```

7.10.1　Putting it all together

A program to illustrate the use of the class `Name_address` is shown below:

```
with Simple_io, Class_name_address;
use  Simple_io, Class_name_address;
```

```
procedure main is
  name    : Name_address;
  address : String := "A.N.Other/Brighton/East Sussex/UK";
begin
  set( name, address );
  put( address ); new_line; put("There are ");
  put( lines( name ) ); put(" lines"); new_line;
  for i in 1 .. lines(name)+1 loop
    put("Line #"); put(i); put("   ");
    put( deliver_line(name, i) ); new_line;
  end loop;
end main;
```

which, when compiled and run, will produce the following output:

```
A.N.Other/Brighton/East Sussex/UK
There are          4 lines
Line #        1   A.N.Other
Line #        2    Brighton
Line #        3     East Sussex
Line #        4       UK
Line #        5
```

Note: The standard library packages Ada.Strings.Bounded and Ada.Strings.Unbounded *provide an elegant mechanism for handling strings of variable length. Section C.8, Appendix C lists the members of the package* Ada.Strings.Bounded.

7.11 An electronic piggy bank

Arrays are made up of objects of any type including instances of classes. For example, to implement a program to deal with a small bank's transactions, a class Piggy_bank can be defined which has the following methods:

Method	Responsibility
deposit	Deposit money into a named person's account.
withdraw	Withdraw money from a named person's account.
balance	Obtain the balance in a named person's account.
statement	Print a statement for a named account.
new_account	Allocate a new account number.

The Ada specification of the class `Piggy_bank` is as follows:

```
with Class_account;
package Class_piggy_bank is
  type Piggy_bank is private;              -- Class
  subtype Money  is Class_account.Money;   -- Make visible
  subtype PMoney is Class_account.PMoney;  -- Make visible

  procedure new_account( the:in out Piggy_bank; no:out Positive );
  procedure statement( the:in Piggy_bank; no:in Positive );
  procedure deposit  ( the:in out Piggy_bank; no:in Positive;
                       amount:in PMoney );
  procedure withdraw ( the:in out Piggy_bank; no:in Positive;
                       amount:in PMoney; get:out PMoney );
  function balance( the:in Piggy_bank;
                    no:in Positive) return Money;
  function valid( the:in Piggy_bank;
                  no:in Positive) return Boolean;

private
  NO_ACCOUNTS : constant := 10;
  subtype Accounts_index is Integer range 0 .. NO_ACCOUNTS;
  subtype Accounts_range is Accounts_index range 1 .. NO_ACCOUNTS;
  type    Accounts_array is array ( Accounts_range ) of Account;
  type Piggy_bank is record
    accounts: Accounts_array;        -- Accounts in the bank
    last    : Accounts_index := 0;   -- Last account
  end record;
end Class_piggy_bank;
```

Note: The number of accounts that can be held is fixed and is defined by the constant NO_ACCOUNTS. In Chapter 16, ways of storing a variable number of (in this case instances of Account) objects are explored.

The following code uses the class `Piggy_bank` to perform transactions on a newly allocated account:

```
with Simple_io, Class_piggy_bank;
use  Simple_io, Class_piggy_bank;
procedure main is
  bank_accounts: Piggy_bank;        -- A little bank
  customer     : Positive;          -- Customer's account no
  obtain       : Money;             -- Money processed
begin
  new_account( bank_accounts, customer );
  if valid( bank_accounts, customer ) then
    statement( bank_accounts, customer );

    put("Deposit £100.00 into account"); new_line;
    deposit( bank_accounts, customer, 100.00 );
    statement( bank_accounts, customer );

    put("Withdraw £80.00 from account"); new_line;
    withdraw( bank_accounts, customer, 80.00, obtain );
    statement( bank_accounts, customer );
```

```
        put("Deposit £200.00 into account"); new_line;
        deposit( bank_accounts, customer, 200.00 );
        statement( bank_accounts, customer );
    else
        put("Customer number not valid"); new_line;
    end if;
end main;
```

When compiled and run, the code would produce the following output:

```
Mini statement for account #  1
The amount on deposit is £ 0.00

Deposit £100.00 into account
Mini statement for account #  1
The amount on deposit is £100.00

Withdraw £80.00 from account
Mini statement for account #  1
The amount on deposit is £20.00

Deposit £200.00 into account
Mini statement for account #  1
The amount on deposit is £220.00
```

In the implementation of the package Class_piggy_bank shown below, the function new_account allocates an account number to a new customer.

```
with Simple_io, Class_account;
use  Simple_io, Class_account;
package body Class_piggy_bank is

    procedure new_account(the:in out Piggy_bank; no:out Positive)
    begin
        if the.last = NO_ACCOUNTS then
            raise Constraint_error;
        else
            the.last := the.last + 1;
        end if;
        no := the.last;
    end new_account;
```

Note: The exception Constraint_error is raised if no new accounts can be created. Chapter 12 shows how a user defined exception can be raised.

The procedure `statement` prints details about a customer's account.

```
procedure statement( the:in Piggy_bank; no:in Positive ) is
   in_account : Money;
begin
   put("Mini statement for account #");
   put( no, width=>3 ); new_line;
   put( "The amount on deposit is ú" );
   in_account := balance( the.accounts(no) );
   put( in_account, aft=>2, exp=>0 );
   new_line(2);
end statement;
```

The procedure and functions for `deposit`, `withdraw` and `balance` call the appropriate code from the package `Class_account`.

```
procedure deposit ( the:in out Piggy_bank; no:in Positive;
                    amount:in PMoney ) is
begin
   deposit( the.accounts(no), amount );
end deposit;

procedure withdraw( the:in out Piggy_bank; no:in Positive;
                    amount:in PMoney; get:out PMoney ) is
begin
   withdraw( the.accounts(no), amount, get);
end withdraw;

function balance( the:in Piggy_bank;
                  no:in Positive) return Money is
begin
   return balance( the.accounts(no) );
end balance;

function valid( the:in Piggy_bank;
                no:in Positive) return Boolean is
begin
   return no in 1 .. the.last;
   end valid;
end Class_piggy_bank;
```

7.12 Self-assessment

- Can the index to an array be of type real?

- How can a programmer reduce the possibility of using an incorrect subscript value?

- Are there any restrictions on what type of objects can be used as array elements?

- Are there any limitations on how many dimensions an array might have?

- How is an array of objects declared?

- What is the difference between the two declarations for `Board_array` below, and how may an individual character be accessed in both cases?

```
subtype Board_range is Integer 1 .. 3;
type    Board_array is
        array( Board_range, Board_range ) of Character;
```

```
subtype Board_range is Integer 1 .. 3;
type    Board_row   is array( Board_range ) of Character;
type    Board_array is array( Board_range ) of Board_row;
```

7.13 Exercises

Construct the following programs:

- *A program to play the game noughts and crosses.*

  Using as a base the code for the noughts and crosses program, implement a complete program that checks for a win by a player. A win is when a player has three of their counters in a row, either diagonally, horizontally or vertically.

- *A program which maintains the records of books in a small school library.*

  Each book in the library has a class mark which is a number in the range 1 — 999. A person may:

  (a)   Take a book out of the library.
  (b)   Return a book to the library.
  (c)   Reserve a book that is out on loan.
  (d)   Enquire as to the status of a book.

  The program should be able to handle the recording and extracting of information required by the above transactions. In addition, a facility should be included which will provide a summary about the status of the books in the library.

  Hints:
  - Define the class `Book` to represent individual books in the library.
  - Define a class `Library` to represent the library. The hidden internal structure of `Library` contains an array of `Books`.
  - Re-use the class `TUI` to display a menu.

8 Case study: Design of a game

This chapter looks at the implementation of the game reversi. The problem is analysed using the fusion methodology and from this analysis and design is developed a program to play the game of reversi between two human players.

8.1 Reversi

In the game of reversi two players take it in turn to add counters to a board of 8-by-8 cells. Each player has a stack of counters, black one side and white the other. One player's counters are placed white side up, whilst the other player's are black side up. The object of the game is to capture all your opponent's counters. You do this by adding one of your counters to the board so that your opponent's counter(s) are flanked by two of your counters. When you do this, the counters you have captured are flipped over to become your counters. If you can't capture any of your opponent's counters during your turn, you must pass and let your opponent go.

The game is won when you have captured all your opponent's counters. If neither player can add a counter to the board, then the player with the most counters wins. If the number of counters for each player is equal, then the game is a draw.

The initial starting position is set so that the 4 centre squares in the 8-by-8 board of cells is as follows:

On a reduced board of 4-by-4 cells a game might be as illustrated in Figure 8.1.

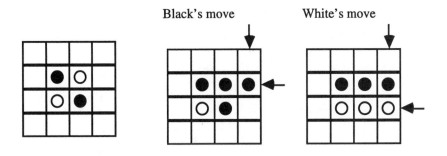

Black's move   White's move

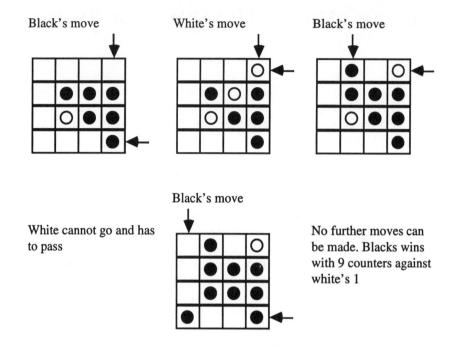

Black's move　　　White's move　　　Black's move

Black's move

White cannot go and has
to pass

No further moves can
be made. Blacks wins
with 9 counters against
white's 1

Figure 8.1 A game of reversi.

8.1.1　A program to play reversi

A controller of the game (games master) asks each player in turn for a move. When a
move is received from a player the board is asked to validate the move. If this is a valid
move the counter of the current player is added to the board. The board is displayed and
the new state of the board is evaluated. This process is repeated until either the board is
filled or neither player can make a move. The player making the last move is asked to
announce the result of the game.

The interactions by the controller with the system are shown in Figure 8.2

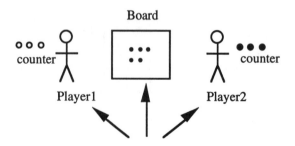

Board

counter　　　Player1　　　Player2　　　counter

Figure 8.2 Interactions by the controller with the objects in the system.

8.2 Analysis and design of the problem

Using a design methodology based on a simplified version of fusion the above specification can be analysed and a design created for an eventual implementation in Ada. In preparation for this it is appropriate to identify the objects and system actions from the written specification. An easy but incomplete way of identifying objects and system actions is to identify the major nouns and verbs. The nouns in the specification become the objects and the major verbs become the system actions.

With the major **nouns** indicated in bold type and the major *verbs* in bold italic type, the specification for the game reversi can now be read as:

In the **game** of reversi two **players** take it in turn to *add* counters to a **board** of 8-by-8 **cells**. Each **player** has a stack of **counters** black one side and white the other. One **player's counters** are placed white side up, whilst the other **player's** are black side up. The object of the game is to *capture* all your opponent's **counters**. You do this by adding one of your **counters** to the **board** so that your opponent's **counter(s)** are flanked by two of your **counters**. When you do this, the **counters** you have captured are *flipped* over to become your **counters**. If you can't capture any of your opponent's **counters** during you turn, you must pass and let your opponent go.

The **game** is won when you have *captured* all your opponent's **counters**. If neither **player** can add a **counter** to the **board**, then the **player** with the most **counters** wins. If the number of **counters** for each **player** is equal, then the game is a draw.

A controller of the **game** (games master) *asks* each player in turn for a move. When a move is received from a **player** the **board** is asked to *validate* the move. If this is a valid move the **counter** of the current **player** is *added* to the **board**. The **board** is *displayed* and the new state of the board is *evaluated*. This process is repeated until either the **board** is filled or neither **player** can make a move. The **player** making the last move is asked to *announce* the result of the **game**.

The major objects and verbs identified are:

Objects (nouns)	System actions (verbs)
board	add
game	announce
cell	ask
counter	evaluated
player	capture
	display
	validate

8.2.1 Analysis

a) Object model

Using the major objects identified, the game of reversi can be represented by the object diagram illustrated in Figure 8.3.

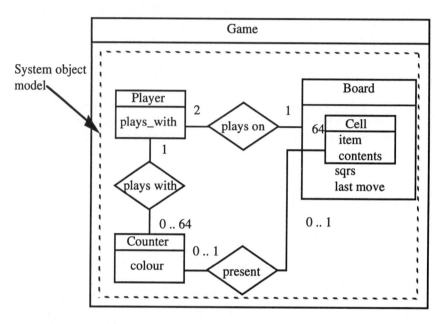

Figure 8.3 Object diagram for the game reversi.

Note: Section 1.3.1 in Chapter 1 explains the notation used.

The 'system object model' is that part of the system to be implemented, which in this case is the components of the object game.

b) Data dictionary

Name	Kind	Description
Board	Class	The playing board used to hold Counters.
Cell	Class	One of 64 cells that make up the playing board.
Counter	Class	A coloured token, white on one side black on the other, is used to represent the current state of the game.
Player	Class	A player of the game.
Game	Class	The board game
plays on	Relationship	The board that the player plays on.
plays with	Relationship	The Counters that a Player plays with.
present	Relationship	The presence or absence of a Counter in a Cell.

Name	Kind	Description
colour	Attribute	The colour of the Counter.
contents	Attribute	The contents of a Cell on the board.
item	Attribute	The actual counter in a cell.
last_move	Attribute	The last move made on the board
plays_with	Attribute	The counter that a player plays with.
sqrs	Attribute	The squares that make up the board.

c)   Interface model

The system is described by the system object model. The behaviour of the system is described in terms of the interface model, in which agents interact with the system model. In the example below there is a single agent 'control' (the games controller) that is responsible for all interactions. These are refined from the verbs identified in the specification of the problem.

System actions (verbs)	Refined action	Explanation
add	add	Add a contestant's counter to the board.
announce	announce	Announce the result of the game.
ask	get_move	Get a move from the player.
display	display	Display a representation of the board.
evaluated	status	Ask the board for the current game state.
validate	check_move	Check if the player's move is valid.
-	now_playing	Tell the board the contestant who is about to play.
-	set_up	Initialize the board for the start of play.

Note: The system actions now_playing *and* set_up *were not identified by looking for verbs in the specification, but were identified by looking at the interactions that occur in the system. The action capture is an effect of add.*

The system interface model is illustrated in Figure 8.4:

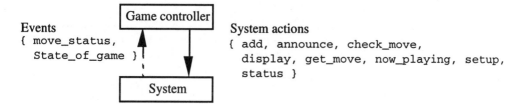

Events
{ move_status,
    State_of_game }

Game controller

System

System actions
{ add, announce, check_move,
    display, get_move, now_playing, setup,
    status }

Figure 8.4 Systems interface model.

Note: An input event is sent by an agent to the system, these events are termed system operations. An output event is sent by the system to an agent.

d) Life-cycle model

The life-cycle model describes communication in the system from its inception to termination. This is in terms of the system actions identified in the interface model.

```
life_cycle:   setup . Turn⁺ . announce
Turn        = Player1 | ( Player1 . Player2 )
Player1     = Make_Move
Player2     = Make_Move
Make_Move = Move . display . status . #state_of_game
Move        = now_playing . Do_Move⁺ . add
Do_Move     = get_move . check_move . #move_status
```

The syntax used is:

Notation	Explanation
*	Zero or more occurrences of the item.
+	One or more occurrences of the item.
.	Followed by
|	Alternative
#name	An output event

The first line is read as:

The `life_cycle` of the game is an initial `setup` followed by 1 or more `turns` followed by an `announcement` of the result of the game.

e) Operational model

The operation model specifies the behaviour of the system operations. This is done in terms of state changes and events that result from these state changes. The operation model shows in high level detail the behaviour of the system. The operation model is composed of the following components:

Item	Description
Operation	The name of the operation modelled. This comes from the life cycle model.
Description	A description in English of the operation.
Reads	Input for the operation. This can come from two distinct sources: • Parameters supplied with the operation. • Objects read.
Changes	The objects that are changed by the operation
Sends	The event returned from the performance of the operation
Assumes	Any assumptions about the state of items before the operation is performed. A precondition to the operation.
Result	An English description of the new state of the item after the operation has been performed. A postcondition for the operation.

The system operations for the system are:

Operation	add
Description	Add a counter into a specific cell on the board.
Reads	Supplied move, Supplied status of move, Board, Cell, Counter
Changes	Board, Cell, Counter
Sends	
Assumes	Move is valid, Board has been reset
Result	The current players counter is dropped into a cell on the board. The state of the game is changed.

Operation	announce
Description	Announce to the world the result of the game.
Reads	Supplied state of game
Changes	
Sends	game_controller { description of result }
Assumes	
Result	Player announces the state of the game.

Operation	check_move
Description	Checks if the counter can be added at a particular position on the board.
Reads	Supplied move, Board, Cell, Counter
Changes	
Sends	game_controller { move_status }
Assumes	Board has been reset
Result	Returns true if a counter can be moved onto the board

Operation	display
Description	Displays a graphical representation of the current state of the game
Reads	Board, Cell, Counter
Changes	
Sends	game_controller { picture of board }
Assumes	Board has been reset
Result	The latest state of the game is displayed

Operation	get_move
Description	Get a move from the player.
Reads	Supplied type of move
Changes	
Sends	game_controller { move }
Assumes	
Result	Returns the players chosen move

Operation	now_playing
Description	Tell the board who is playing next.
Reads	Supplied counter
Changes	Board
Sends	
Assumes	Board has been reset
Result	The board is set for one of the contestants to check their move and make a move.

Operation	setup
Description	Setup the initial board position
Reads	
Changes	Board, Cell
Sends	
Assumes	
Result	The board is set up to an initial configuration

Operation	status
Description	Determines the current sate of the game
Reads	Board
Changes	
Sends	game_controller { state_of_game }
Assumes	Board has been reset
Result	Returns the current state of the game.

8.2.2 Design

a) Object interaction graph

The object interaction graphs show the flow of control between the objects in the system for each of the system operations. The following conventions are used

Diagram	Explanation
object:Class	A single object. This is annotated with the object:Class name.
object:Class	A container object. This is annotated with container object:Class name.

Where there is more than one action these are numbered. The diagrams are annotated with the Ada procedure or function calls that will be used in the final program. The following diagrams show the flow of control for the system operations in the game of reversi.

add

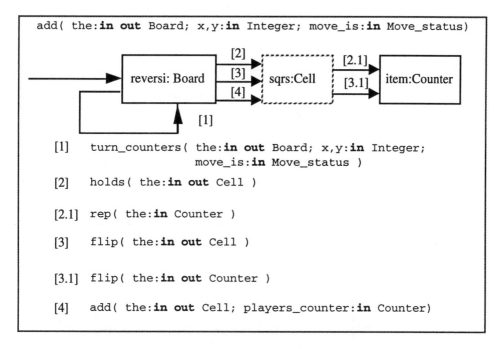

```
add( the:in out Board; x,y:in Integer; move_is:in Move_status)
```

[1]   turn_counters(the:**in out** Board; x,y:**in** Integer;
                      move_is:**in** Move_status)

[2]   holds(the:**in out** Cell)

[2.1] rep(the:**in** Counter)

[3]   flip(the:**in out** Cell)

[3.1] flip(the:**in out** Counter)

[4]   add(the:**in out** Cell; players_counter:**in** Counter)

*Note: In some diagrams the actions are decomposed into more than one operation, in
which case they are numbered in the order in which they occur.
The action 1 is on the object* reversi. *The action 3.1 is called from action 3*

announce

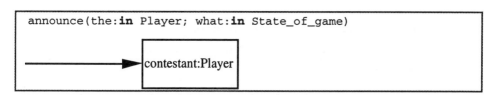

```
announce(the:in Player; what:in State_of_game)
```

contestant:Player

check move

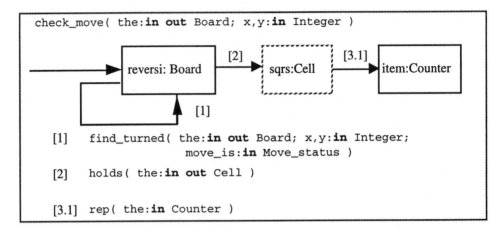

```
check_move( the:in out Board; x,y:in Integer )
```

[1]   find_turned(the:**in out** Board; x,y:**in** Integer;
                    move_is:**in** Move_status)

[2]   holds(the:**in out** Cell)

[3.1] rep(the:**in** Counter)

display

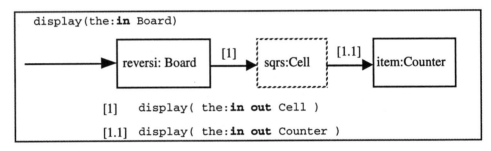

```
display(the:in Board)
```

[1]   display(the:**in out** Cell)

[1.1] display(the:**in out** Counter)

get move

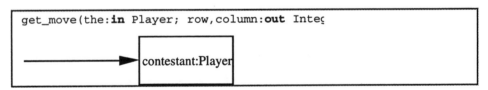

```
get_move(the:in Player; row,column:out Inte
```

now playing

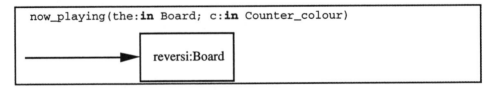

```
now_playing(the:in Board; c:in Counter_colour)
```

setup

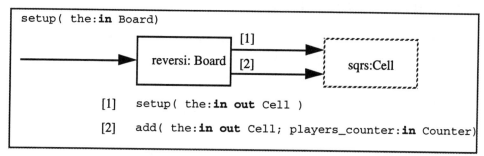

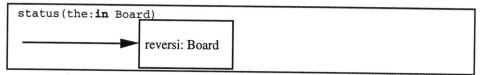

status

b) Event diagram

The sequence of events that happen between the objects in the system can also be shown in an event diagram, Figure 8.5. An event diagram, though not part of the fusion process, is a convenient way of showing the messages in the system. In an event diagram time flows from the top to the bottom of the diagram.

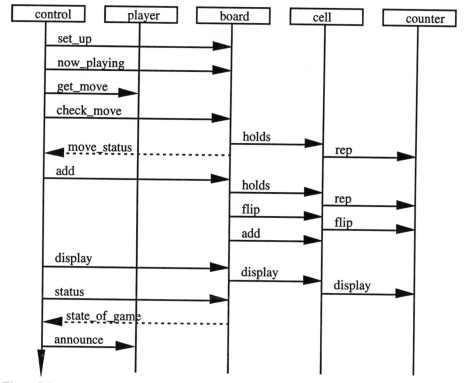

Figure 8.5 Event diagram for the system.

8.3 Implementation (the main program)

Using the design carried out above, the system operations can be used to implement the main processing loop as follows:

```
with Class_board, Class_player, Class_counter;
use  Class_board, Class_player, Class_counter;
procedure play is                          -- Reversi
  reversi       : Board;                   -- The playing board
  contestant    : array(Counter_colour) of Player;
  current_state : State_of_game;           -- State of game
  person        : Counter_colour;          -- Current player
  x, y          : Integer;                 -- Move
  move_is       : Move_status;             -- Last move is
begin
  set_up( reversi );                       -- Set up board
  set( contestant(BLACK), BLACK );         -- Set player black
  set( contestant(WHITE), WHITE );         -- Set player white

  current_state := PLAY;  person := BLACK; -- Black starts

  display( reversi );                      -- Initial board

  while current_state = PLAY loop          -- Playable game
    now_playing( reversi, person );        -- set player

    loop                                   -- Get move
      get_move( contestant(person), x, y );
      move_is := check_move(reversi, x, y);  -- Validate
      exit when move_is=OK or move_is=PASS;  -- OK
    end loop;

    add( reversi, x, y, move_is );         -- Add move to board

    display( reversi );                    -- Display new board
    current_state := status( reversi );    -- State of play is

    if current_state = PLAY then           -- Is still playable
      case person is                       -- next player
        when BLACK  => person := WHITE;
        when WHITE  => person := BLACK;
      end case;
    end if;

  end loop;                                -- Next move

  announce( contestant(person), current_state );  -- Result

end play;
```

8.3.1 Example of a typical game

A typical game might be:

```
--------------------------------------          --------------------------------------
|   |   |   |   |   |   |   |   |   |          |   |   |   |   |   |   |   |   |   |
--------------------------------------          --------------------------------------
|   |   |   |   |   |   |   |   |   |          |   |   |   |   |   |   |   |   |   |
--------------------------------------          --------------------------------------
|   |   |   |   |   |   |   |   |   |          |   |   |   |   |   |   |   |   |   |
--------------------------------------          --------------------------------------
|   |   |   | X | O |   |   |   |   |          |   |   |   | X | X | X |   |   |   |
--------------------------------------          --------------------------------------
|   |   |   | O | X |   |   |   |   |          |   |   |   | O | X |   |   |   |   |
--------------------------------------          --------------------------------------
|   |   |   |   |   |   |   |   |   |          |   |   |   |   |   |   |   |   |   |
--------------------------------------          --------------------------------------
|   |   |   |   |   |   |   |   |   |          |   |   |   |   |   |   |   |   |   |
--------------------------------------          --------------------------------------
|   |   |   |   |   |   |   |   |   |          |   |   |   |   |   |   |   |   |   |
--------------------------------------          --------------------------------------

Player X has 2 counters -               Player X has 4 counters -
Player O has 2 counters                 Player O has 1 counters
Please enter move X row column: 4 6     Please enter move O row column: 5 6
```

```
--------------------------------------          --------------------------------------
|   |   |   |   |   |   |   |   |   |          |   |   |   |   |   |   |   |   |   |
--------------------------------------          --------------------------------------
|   |   |   |   |   |   |   |   |   |          |   |   |   |   |   |   |   |   |   |
--------------------------------------          --------------------------------------
|   |   |   |   |   |   |   |   |   |          |   |   |   |   |   |   |   |   |   |
--------------------------------------          --------------------------------------
|   |   |   | X | X | X |   |   |   |          |   |   |   | X | X | X |   |   |   |
--------------------------------------          --------------------------------------
|   |   |   | O | O | O |   |   |   |          |   |   |   | O | X | X |   |   |   |
--------------------------------------          --------------------------------------
|   |   |   |   |   |   |   |   |   |          |   |   |   |   |   | X |   |   |   |
--------------------------------------          --------------------------------------
|   |   |   |   |   |   |   |   |   |          |   |   |   |   |   |   |   |   |   |
--------------------------------------          --------------------------------------
|   |   |   |   |   |   |   |   |   |          |   |   |   |   |   |   |   |   |   |
--------------------------------------          --------------------------------------

Player X has 3 counters -               Player X has 6 counters -
Player O has 3 counters                 Player O has 1 counters
Please enter move O row column: 6 6     Please enter move O row column: 0 0
```

```
-----------------------------------    -----------------------------------
|   |   |   |   |   |   |   |   |   |    |   |   |   |   |   |   |   |   |   |
-----------------------------------    -----------------------------------
|   |   |   |   |   |   |   |   |   |    |   |   |   |   |   |   |   |   |   |
-----------------------------------    -----------------------------------
|   |   |   |   |   |   |   |   |   |    |   |   |   |   |   |   |   |   |   |
-----------------------------------    -----------------------------------
|   |   |   | X | X | X |   |   |   |    |   |   |   | X | X | X |   |   |   |
-----------------------------------    -----------------------------------
|   |   |   | O | X | X |   |   |   |    |   |   |   | X | X | X |   |   |   |
-----------------------------------    -----------------------------------
|   |   |   |   | X |   |   |   |   |    |   |   |   | X |   | X |   |   |   |
-----------------------------------    -----------------------------------
|   |   |   |   |   |   |   |   |   |    |   |   |   |   |   |   |   |   |   |
-----------------------------------    -----------------------------------
|   |   |   |   |   |   |   |   |   |    |   |   |   |   |   |   |   |   |   |
-----------------------------------    -----------------------------------

Player X has 6 counters -              Player X has 8 counters -
Player O has 1 counters                Player O has 0 counters
Please enter move X row column: 6 4    Player X has won
```

8.4   Implementation of the classes

The main program is implemented using the classes described earlier. The package
Pack_screen is responsible for handling the machine specific action of clearing the
screen. Using an ANSI terminal, its implementation is as follows:

```
package Pack_screen is
  procedure screen_clear;              -- Home clear screen
  procedure screen_home;               -- Home no clear screen
private
  ESC: constant Character := Character'Val(27);
end Pack_screen;
```

The implementation of this package uses ANSI escape sequences to implement these
procedures. If an ANSI compatible terminal is not available, the bodies of these
procedures can be changed to implement an appropriate alternative.

```
with Text_io; use Text_io;
package body Pack_screen is             -- Terminal dependent I/O
  procedure screen_clear is             -- Clear screen
  begin
    put( ESC & "[2J" );                 -- Escape sequence
  end screen_clear;
  procedure screen_home is              -- Home
  begin
    put( ESC & "[0;0H");                -- Escape sequence
  end screen_home;
end Pack_screen;
```

The specification of the class Counter is as follows:

```
package Class_counter is
  type Counter          is private;
  type Counter_colour is ( BLACK, WHITE );
  procedure set( the:in out Counter; rep:in Counter_colour );
  procedure display( the:in Counter );
  procedure display_none( the:in Counter );
  procedure flip( the:in out Counter );
  function  rep( the:in Counter ) return Counter_colour;
private
  type Counter is record
    colour: Counter_colour;        -- Colour of counter
  end record;
end Class_counter;
```

The procedure set sets a counter to a specific colour.

```
with Ada.Text_io; use Ada.Text_io;
package body Class_counter is
  procedure set( the:in out Counter; rep:in Counter_colour ) is
  begin
    the.colour := rep;
  end set;
```

The procedure display and display_none respectively display the contents of a counter or no counter.

```
  procedure display( the:in Counter ) is
  begin
    case the.colour is
      when BLACK  => put('X'); -- Representation of a black piece
      when WHITE  => put('O'); -- Representation of a white piece
    end case;
  end display;


  procedure display_none( the:in Counter ) is
  begin
    put(' ');                    -- Representation of NO piece
  end display_none;
```

The procedure `flip` flips a counter. By flipping a counter the other player's colour is exposed, whilst the procedure `rep` returns the colour of the counter.

```
procedure flip( the:in out Counter ) is
begin
  case the.colour is
    when BLACK => the.colour := WHITE;    -- Flip to White
    when WHITE => the.colour := BLACK;    -- Flip to Black
  end case;
end flip;

function  rep( the:in Counter ) return Counter_colour is
begin
  return the.colour;  -- Representation of the counter colour
end rep;
end Class_counter;
```

The specification for the class `Cell` which holds a counter is as follows:

```
with Class_counter;
use  Class_counter;
package Class_cell is
  type Cell is private;
  type Cell_holds is ( C_WHITE, C_BLACK, EMPTY );

  procedure initialize( the:in out Cell );
  function  holds( the:in Cell ) return Cell_holds;
  procedure add( the:in out Cell; players_counter:in Counter );
  procedure display( the:in Cell );
  procedure flip( the:in out Cell );
  function to_colour( c:in Cell_holds ) return Counter_colour;
private
  type Cell_is is ( EMPTY_CELL, NOT_EMPTY_CELL );
  type Cell is record
    contents: Cell_is := EMPTY_CELL;
    item    : Counter;                  -- The counter
  end record;
end Class_cell;
```

In the implementation of the package the procedure `initialize` sets the contents of the cell to empty.

```
package body Class_cell is
  procedure initialize( the:in out Cell ) is
  begin
    the.contents := EMPTY_CELL;   -- Initialize cell to empty
  end initialize;
```

The procedure `holds` returns the contents of the cell which is defined by the enumeration type `Cell_holds`.

```
function  holds( the:in Cell ) return Cell_holds is
begin
  case the.contents is
    when EMPTY_CELL     =>            -- Empty
      return EMPTY;                   --  No counter
    when NOT_EMPTY_CELL =>            -- Counter
      case rep( the.item ) is
        when WHITE => return C_WHITE; --  white counter
        when BLACK => return C_BLACK; --  black counter
      end case;
  end case;
end holds;
```

The next three procedures implement:

- Adding of a new counter into a cell.
- Displaying the contents of a cell.
- Flipping the counter in the cell to the other colour.

```
procedure add(the:in out Cell; players_counter:in Counter) is
begin
  the := (NOT_EMPTY_CELL,players_counter);
end add;

procedure display( the:in Cell ) is
begin
  if the.contents = NOT_EMPTY_CELL then
    display( the.item );           -- Display the counter
  else
    display_none( the.item );      -- No counter
  end if;
end display;

procedure flip( the:in out Cell ) is
begin
  flip( the.item );                -- Flip counter
end flip;
```

The function `to_colour` converts the enumeration `Cell_holds` to the enumeration `Counter_colour`. This method is required so that the contents of a `Cell` can be processed as a `Counter_colour`. The board holds the colour of the current player. It is an error to ask for the colour of an empty cell.

```
function to_colour(c:in Cell_holds) return Counter_colour is
begin
  case c is                          -- Conversion of enum.
    when C_WHITE => return WHITE;
    when C_BLACK => return BLACK;
    when others  => raise Constraint_error;
  end case;
end to_colour;

end Class_cell;
```

*Note: The code associated with the **when others** clause will never be executed.*

The package `Class_board` is by far the most complex of the packages used in this implementation. As well as several visible functions and procedures, it also has several private functions and procedures. The main complexity occurs in the function `check_move` and the function `add`.

```
with Class_counter, Class_cell;
use  Class_counter, Class_cell;
package Class_board is

  type Board          is private;
  type State_of_game is ( PLAY, WIN, DRAW, LOSE );
  type Move_status   is ( OK, INVALID, PASS );

  procedure set_up( the:in out Board );
  procedure add( the:in out Board; x,y:in Integer;
                 move_is:in Move_status );
  procedure now_playing( the:in out Board; c:in Counter_colour );
  procedure display( the:in Board );
  function  check_move( the:in Board; x,y:in Integer )
                        return Move_status;
  function  status( the:in Board ) return State_of_game;
  function  contents( the:in Board; x,y:in Integer )
                      return Cell_holds;

private
  SIZE: constant := 8;                        -- 8 * 8 Board
  subtype Board_index is Integer range 1 .. SIZE; --
  subtype Board_range is Board_index;         --

  type Board_array is array (Board_range, Board_range) of Cell;
  type Score_array is array (Counter_colour) of Natural;
  type Move_array  is array (Counter_colour) of Move_status;

  type Board is record
    sqrs    : Board_array;            -- Game board
    player  : Counter_colour;         -- Current Player
    opponent : Counter_colour;        -- Opponent
    score   : Score_array;            -- Running score
    last_move: Move_array;            -- Last move is
  end record;
end Class_board;
```

The body of `Class_board` contains specifications of functions and procedures which are used in the decomposition of the methods of the class `Board`.

```
with Simple_io, Pack_screen;
use  Simple_io, Pack_screen;
package body Class_board is

  procedure next( the:in Board; x_co,y_co:in out Board_index;
                   dir:in Natural; res:out Boolean);
  function find_turned( the:in Board; x,y: in Board_index )
                   return Natural;
  procedure turn_counters(the: in out Board; x,y: in Board_index;
                   total: out Natural );
  function no_turned(the:in Board; o_x,o_y:in Board_index;
                   dir:in Natural;
                   n:in Natural := 0 ) return Natural;
  procedure capture(the:in out Board; x_co, y_co:in Board_index;
                   dir:in Natural );
```

The procedure `setup` populates the board with empty cells and the initial central grid of four counters.

```
procedure set_up( the:in out Board ) is
  black_counter: Counter;              -- A white counter
  white_counter: Counter;              -- A black counter
begin
  set( black_counter, BLACK );         -- Set black
  set( white_counter, WHITE );         -- Set white
  for x in the.sqrs'Range(1) loop
    for y in the.sqrs'Range(2) loop
      initialize( the.sqrs(x,y) );     -- To empty
    end loop;
  end loop;
  add( the.sqrs( SIZE/2,   SIZE/2 ),   black_counter );
  add( the.sqrs( SIZE/2,   SIZE/2+1 ), white_counter );
  add( the.sqrs( SIZE/2+1, SIZE/2 ),   white_counter );
  add( the.sqrs( SIZE/2+1, SIZE/2+1 ), black_counter );
  the.score( BLACK ) := 2; the.score( WHITE ) := 2;
end set_up;
```

The procedure `now_playing` records the colour of the current player. This information is used by subsequent methods `add` and `check_move`.

```
procedure now_playing(the:in out Board; c:in Counter_colour) is
begin
  the.player   := c;                   -- Player
  case c is                            -- Opponent
    when WHITE => the.opponent := BLACK;
    when BLACK => the.opponent := WHITE;
  end case;
end now_playing;
```

The procedure `display` displays a representation of the reversi board on the output device. For this implementation of the game, the output device is an ANSI text-based terminal.

```
procedure display( the:in Board ) is
  dashes: String( 1 .. the.sqrs'Length*4+1 ) := (others=>'-');
begin
  screen_clear;                               -- Clear screen
  put( dashes ); new_line;                    -- Top
  for x in the.sqrs'Range(1) loop
    put("|");                                 -- Cells on line
    for y in the.sqrs'Range(2) loop
      put(" "); display( the.sqrs(x,y) ); put(" |");
    end loop;
    new_line; put( dashes ); new_line;        -- Bottom lines
  end loop;
  new_line;
  put( "Player X has " );
  put( Integer(the.score(BLACK)), width=>2 );
  put( " counters" ); new_line;
  put( "Player O has " );
  put( Integer(the.score(WHITE)), width=>2 );
  put( " counters" ); new_line;
end display;
```

The function `check_move` checks the validity of a proposed move on the board. This function is decomposed into the function `find_turned` which calculates the number of pieces that will be turned if a move is made into the specified square.

```
function check_move( the:in Board; x,y:in Integer )
                      return Move_status is
begin
  if x = 0 and then y = 0 then
    return PASS;
  elsif x in Board_index and then y in Board_index then
    if holds( the.sqrs( x, y ) ) = EMPTY then
      if find_turned(the, x, y) > 0 then
        return OK;
      end if;
    end if;
  end if;
  return INVALID;
end check_move;
```

The function `find_turned` finds the number of the opponent's counters that would be turned for a particular move. The strategy for `find_turned` is to sum the number of opponent's counters which will be flipped in each compass direction. For any position on the board there are potentially eight directions to check. The directions are illustrated in Figure 8.6.

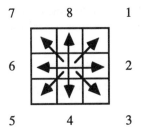

Figure 8.6 Compass direction to check when a new counter is added to the board.

```
function find_turned( the:in Board; x,y: in Board_index )
                      return Natural is
  sum      : Natural := 0;          -- Total stones turned
begin
  if holds( the.sqrs( x, y ) ) = EMPTY then
    for dir in 1 .. 8 loop       -- The 8 possible directions
      sum := sum + no_turned( the, x, y, dir );
    end loop;
  end if;
  return sum;                      -- return total
end find_turned;
```

The recursive function `no_turned` counts the number of the opponent's pieces that would be captured. This may of course be zero.

```
function  no_turned(the:in Board; o_x,o_y:in Board_index;
                    dir:in Natural;
                    n:in Natural := 0 ) return Natural is
  ok : Boolean;                         -- Result from next
  nxt: Cell_holds;                      -- Next in line is
  col: Counter_colour;                  -- Counter colour
  x  : Board_index := o_x;              -- Local copy
  y  : Board_index := o_y;              -- Local copy
begin
  next( the, x,y, dir, ok );            -- Next cell
  if ok then                            -- On the board
    nxt := holds( the.sqrs(x,y) );      -- Contents are
    if nxt = EMPTY then                 -- End of line
      return 0;
    else
      col := to_colour( nxt );          -- Colour
      if col = the.opponent then        -- Opponents counter
        return no_turned(the, x,y, dir, n+1); -- Try next cell
      elsif col = the.player then       -- End of counters
        return n;                       -- Counters turned
      end if;
    end if;
  else
    return 0;                           -- No line
  end if;
end no_turned;
```

The procedure next returns the position of the next cell in the current direction. If there is no such cell because the edge of the board has been reached, then res is set to FALSE.

```
procedure next( the:in Board; x_co,y_co:in out Board_index;
                dir:in Natural; res:out Boolean) is
  x, y   : Natural;
begin
  x := x_co; y := y_co;            -- May go outside Board_range
  case dir is
    when 1 =>            y:=y+1;   --  Direction to move
    when 2 => x:=x+1; y:=y+1;      --      8   1   2
    when 3 => x:=x+1;              --
    when 4 => x:=x+1; y:=y-1;      --      7   *   3
    when 5 =>            y:=y-1;   --
    when 6 => x:=x-1; y:=y-1;      --      6   5   4
    when 7 => x:=x-1;              --
    when 8 => x:=x-1; y:=y+1;      --
    when others => raise Constraint_error;
  end case;
  if x in Board_range and then y in Board_range then
    x_co :=  x; y_co :=  y;        --
    res := TRUE;                   -- Found a next cell
  else
    res := FALSE;                  -- No next cell
  end if;
end next;
```

The procedure add adds a player's move to the board. Naturally this must be a valid move which has previously been validated with the function check_move. The type of move is recorded so that a draw can be detected when both players have passed on their last move.

```
procedure add( the:in out Board; x,y:in Integer;
               move_is:in Move_status ) is
  plays_with: Counter;            -- Current player's counter
  turned    : Natural;            -- Number counters turned
begin
  set( plays_with, the.player );           -- Set current colour
  the.last_move( the.player ) := move_is;  -- Last move is
  if move_is = OK then                     -- Not Pass
    turn_counters(the, x,y, turned);       -- and flip
    add( the.sqrs( x, y ), plays_with );   -- to board
    the.score( the.player ) :=
            the.score( the.player ) + turned + 1;
    the.score( the.opponent ):=
            the.score( the.opponent ) - turned;
  end if;
end add;
```

The procedure `turn_counters` implements the turning of the opponents counters on the board. Naturally, for this to be called, the move made must be valid.

```
procedure turn_counters(the: in out Board; x,y: in Board_index;
                        total: out Natural ) is
  num_cap   : Natural := 0;
  captured  : Natural;
begin
  if holds( the.sqrs( x, y ) ) = EMPTY then
    for dir in 1 .. 8 loop
      captured := no_turned( the, x, y, dir );
      if captured > 0 then
        capture( the, x, y, dir );
        num_cap := num_cap + captured;
      end if;
    end loop;
  end if;
  total := num_cap;
end turn_counters;
```

The recursive procedure `capture` implements the physical capture of the opponent's counters. The strategy is to flip the opponent's counters in the current direction until a square containing the current player's counters is found

```
procedure capture(the:in out Board; x_co, y_co:in Board_index;
                  dir:in Natural ) is
  ok    : Boolean;                -- There is a next cell
  x, y  : Board_index;            -- Coordinates of cell
  nxt   : Cell_holds;             -- Next in line is
begin
  x := x_co; y := y_co;
  next( the, x, y, dir, ok );     -- Calculate pos next cell
  if ok then                      -- Cell exists (Must)
    nxt := holds( the.sqrs(x,y) );
    if to_colour( nxt ) = the.opponent then
      flip( the.sqrs(x, y) );     -- Capture
      capture(the, x, y, dir );   -- Implement capture
    else
      return;                     -- End of line
    end if;
  else
    raise Constraint_error;       -- Will never occur
  end if;
end capture;
```

The procedure `status` returns the current state of the game. This may be a draw if both players have passed on their last go.

```
function  status ( the:in Board ) return State_of_game is
begin
  if the.score( the.opponent ) = 0 then
    return WIN;
  end if;
  if (the.sqrs'Length(1) * the.sqrs'Length(2) =
      the.score(the.opponent)+the.score(the.player)) or
      (the.last_move(BLACK)=PASS and the.last_move(WHITE)=PASS)
  then
    if the.score(the.opponent) = the.score(the.player)
       then return DRAW;
    end if;
    if the.score(the.opponent) < the.score(the.player)
       then return WIN;
    else
       return LOSE;
    end if;
  end if;
  return PLAY;
end;
```

Whilst not used, the function `contents` is provided so that another user of the class `Board` could find the contents of individual cells.

```
function contents( the:in Board; x,y:in Integer )
                   return Cell_holds is
begin
    return holds( the.sqrs( x, y ) );
end contents;

end Class_board;
```

The package `Class_player` is responsible for communicating with the actual human player playing the game.

```
with Class_counter, Class_board;
use  Class_counter, Class_board;
package Class_player is
  type Player is private;

  procedure set( the:in out Player; c:in Counter_colour );
  procedure get_move(the:in Player; row,column:out Integer);
  function  my_counter( the:in Player ) return Counter;
  procedure announce( the:in Player; what:in State_of_game );
private
  type Player is record
    plays_with : Counter;          -- Player's counter
  end record;
end Class_player;
```

In the implementation of the class `Class_player` the procedure `set` sets the colour for the player's counter.

```
with Simple_io;
use  Simple_io;
package body Class_player is
  procedure set(the:in out Player; c:in Counter_colour ) is
    a_counter : Counter;
  begin
    set( a_counter, c );            -- Set colour
    the.plays_with := a_counter;    -- Player is playing with
  end set;
```

The procedure `get_move` communicates with the human player using a simple text based interaction.

```
  procedure get_move(the:in Player; row,column:out Integer) is
    valid_move : Boolean := FALSE;
  begin
    while not valid_move loop
      begin
        put("Please enter move "); display( the.plays_with );
        put(" row column : "); get( row ); get( column );
        valid_move := TRUE;
      exception
        when Data_Error =>
          row := -1; column := -1; skip_line;
        when End_error =>
          row := 0; column := 0;
          return;
      end;
    end loop;
  end get_move;
```

Note: A player can pass a turn by entering a coordinate of 0, 0.

The counter that the player plays with is returned by the function `my_counter`.

```
  function  my_counter( the:in Player ) return Counter is
  begin
    return the.plays_with;
  end my_counter;
```

The procedure `announce` communicates with the human player the result of the game.

```
procedure announce(the:in Player; what:in State_of_game) is
begin
  case what is
    when WIN    =>
      put("Player "); display( the.plays_with );
      put(" has won");
    when LOSE   =>
      put("Player "); display( the.plays_with );
      put(" has lost");
    when DRAW   =>
      put("It's a draw");
    when others =>
      raise Constraint_error;
  end case;
  new_line;
end announce;

end Class_player;
```

8.5 Self-assessment

- What is the function of the class `Player`?

- What is the function of the class `Cell`?

- Could the recursive routine `turned_is` in the class `Board` be written non-recursively?

- The procedure `announce` in the class Board has a `case` statement with a `when others` clause that can never occur. Why is this clause necessary?

8.6 Exercises

- *Better 'reversi'*
  Modify the program to have a separate class for all input and output.

- *Graphic 'reversi'*
  The program could be modified by providing additional classes to present a graphical display of the board. The display could enable the user to drop a counter into a cell selected by a using a mouse. Describe the modifications required to implement this new version.

- *Implementation of a graphic 'Reversi'*
  Implement this new graphical version.

9 Inheritance

This chapter introduces the concept of inheritance in which an existing class can be specialized without modifying the original class. By using this technique software re-use can be become a practical consideration when developing software. Thus a programmer can become a builder of software using previously developed components.

9.1 Introduction

Inheritance is the ability to create a new class by using the methods and instance attributes from an existing class in the creation of a new class. For example, a class Account that provides the methods deposit, withdraw, balance, and statement can be used as the base for a new class that provides the ability to pay interest on the outstanding balance in the account. The new class Interest_account inherits all the methods and instance attributes from the class Account and adds to these the new methods of calc_interest, add_interest, and set_rate plus the instance attribute accumulated_interest. This is illustrated in Figure 9.1.

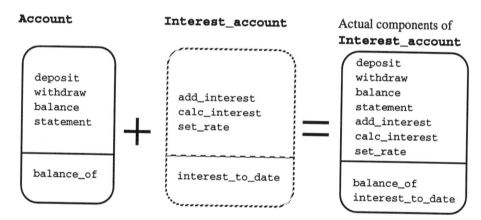

Figure 9.1 components of Account and the derived class Interest_account.

Note: The class Interest_account has the same visibility of components in the base class Account as would a client of the class. In particular, it has no access to the private instance attributes of the base class. Thus methods in the class Interest_account cannot access the base class instance attribute balance_of.

However, for a class type to be fully extended it must be declared as `tagged`. If a class type is not `tagged` then it can only be extended by adding new methods. New instance attributes may not be added.

The consequence of this is that an implementor of a class must explicitly declare the class record type `tagged` if new classes are to be derived from it.

9.2 Tagged types

A `tagged record` type declaration is very similar to an ordinary type declaration. For example, the specification of a class `Account` shown in section 5.3.4 can be amended to allow inheritance to take place. The new specification for the class `Account` is as follows:

```
package Class_account is
  type Account is tagged private;
  subtype Money  is Float;
  subtype PMoney is Float range 0.0 .. Float'Last;

  procedure statement( the:in Account );
  procedure deposit( the:in out Account; amount:in PMoney );
  procedure withdraw( the:in out Account;
                      amount:in PMoney; get:out PMoney );
  function  balance( the:in Account ) return Money;
private
  type Account is tagged record
     balance_of : Money := 0.00;            -- Amount on deposit
  end record;
end Class_account;
```

Note: The only difference from the previous class specification for `Account` *is the inclusion of the keyword* `tagged`.

The implementation of the class `Class_account` remains the same. This implementation is shown in section 5.3.6.

9.2.1 Terminology

Terminology	Explanation
base class	A class from which other classes are derived from.
derived class	A new class that specializes an existing class

9.3 The class `Interest_account`

From the class `Account` can be derived a new type of account that pays interest on the outstanding balance at the end of each day. This new class will have the additional methods of:

Method	Responsibility
`calc_interest`	Calculate at the end of the day the interest due on the balance of the account. This will be accumulated and credited to the account at the end of the accounting period.
`add_interest`	Credit the account with the accumulated interest for the accounting period.
`set_rate`	Set the interest rate for all instances of the class.

The method `set_rate` is special as it has the responsibility of setting the interest rate for all instances of the class. This is implemented by setting the shared class attribute `the_interest_rate`. When a variable is declared outside the class record type there is only a single instance of the attribute and this single class attribute is shared between, and visible to all instances of the class. However, it is not visible outside the class as it is declared within the private part of the package specification. This is illustrated in Figure 9.2

Three instances of the class `Interest_account` sharing the same class attribute `the_interest_rate`.

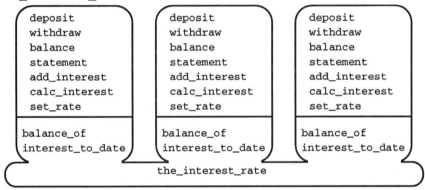

Figure 9.2 Illustration of a class global variable.

The Ada specification for the inherited class `Class_interest_account` is:

```
with Class_account;
use  Class_account;
package Class_interest_account is

  type Interest_account is new Account with private;

  procedure set_rate( rate:in Float );
  procedure calc_interest( the:in out Interest_account );
  procedure add_interest( the:in out Interest_account );
private
  DAILY_INTEREST_RATE: constant Float := 0.00026116; -- 10%
  type Interest_account is new Account with record
    accumulated_interest : Money := 0.00;          -- To date
  end record;
  the_interest_rate      : Float := DAILY_INTEREST_RATE;
end Class_interest_account;
```

164 Adding to an existing package

Note: *The declaration of the class* `Interest_account` *is defined as an extension to the existing class* `Account`. *The specification for the additional procedures are defined in the public part of the specification.*
The class attribute `the_interest_rate` *is shared amongst all the instances of the class* `Interest_account`.
As the procedure `set_rate` *only accesses class attributes, an instance of the class is not required as a parameter. This type of method is referred to as a class method.*

The class `Interest_account` contains:

- The following methods:

Defined in Class_account	Defined in Class_interest_account
deposit	calc_interest
withdraw	add_interest
balance	set_rate
statement	

- The following instance and class attributes:

Defined in Class_account	Defined in Class_interest_account
balance_of	accumulated_interest
	the_interest_rate

Note: *Only* `accumulated_interest` *and* `the_interest_rate` *may be accessed by methods defined in the class* `Interest_account`.

The implementation of the class `Class_interest_account` is:

```
package body Class_interest_account is

  procedure set_rate( rate:in Float ) is
  begin
    the_interest_rate := rate;
  end set_rate;

  procedure calc_interest( the:in out Interest_account ) is
  begin
    the.accumulated_interest := the.accumulated_interest +
      balance(the) * the_interest_rate;
  end calc_interest;

  procedure add_interest( the:in out Interest_account ) is
  begin
    deposit( the, the.accumulated_interest );
    the.accumulated_interest := 0.00;
  end add_interest;

end Class_interest_account;
```

The two classes `Account` and `Interest_account` can be used in a program to perform some simple bank transactions. A program to illustrate the use of the new class `Interest_account` and the original class `Account` is shown below:

```
with Simple_io, Class_account, Class_interest_account;
use  Simple_io, Class_account, Class_interest_account;
procedure main is
  mike     :Account;            -- Normal Account
  corinna :Interest_account;    -- Interest bearing account
  obtained:Money;
begin

  set_rate( 0.00026116 );       -- For all instances of
                                -- interest bearing accounts
  statement( mike );

  put("Deposit £50.00 into Mike's account"); new_line;
  deposit( mike, 50.00 );
  statement( mike );

  put("Withdraw £80.00 from Mike's account"); new_line;
  withdraw( mike, 80.00, obtained );
  statement( mike );

  put("Deposit £500.00 into Corinna's account"); new_line;
  deposit( corinna, 500.00 );
  statement( corinna );

  put("Add interest to Corinna's account"); new_line;
  calc_interest( corinna );
  add_interest( corinna );
  statement( corinna );
end main;
```

which, when compiled and run, would produce the following output:

```
Mini statement: The amount on deposit is £ 0.00

Deposit £50.00 into Mike's account
Mini statement: The amount on deposit is £50.00

Withdraw £80.00 from Mike's account
Mini statement: The amount on deposit is £50.00

Deposit £500.00 into Corinna's account
Mini statement: The amount on deposit is £500.00

Add interest to Corinna's account
Mini statement: The amount on deposit is £500.13
```

9.3.1   Terminology

The following terminology is used to describe the shared components of a class.

Terminology	Example: in class Interest_account	Explanation
Class attribute	`the_interest_rate`	A variable which is shared between all members of the class.
Class method	`set_rate`	A procedure or function used to access only class attributes.

9.4   Visibility rules (Normal inheritance)

The derived class can only access public methods of the base class. As instance attributes are declared in the private part of the base class they are not accessible to the derived class. For example, the class `interest_account` can access the methods `deposit`, `withdraw`, `balance`, and `statement` but cannot access the instance attribute `balance_of`. The visibility of items in the base class and derived class is illustrated in Figure 9.3.

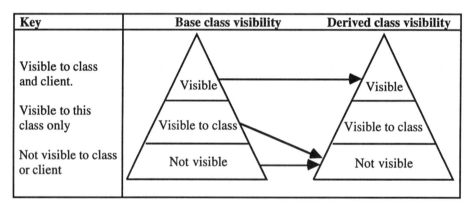

Figure 9.3 Visibility of components in base and derived classes.

9.5   Converting a derived class to a base class

A derived class may be converted to its base class, the effect of which is to remove the instance attributes added by the derived class. For example, in the following program `corinna`'s interest bearing account is converted to a normal account. However, a base class cannot be converted directly to a derived class.

```
with Simple_io, Class_account, Class_Interest_account;
use  Simple_io, Class_account, Class_Interest_account;
procedure main is
  corinna : Interest_account;
  new_acc : Account;
begin
  deposit( corinna, 100.00 );
  statement( corinna );         -- Interest_account
  new_acc := Account(corinna);  -- derived -> base conversion
  statement( new_acc );         -- Account
end main;
```

Note: The effect of a conversion from a derived class to a base class is to remove the additional components that have been defined in the derived class.

which when run, would give the following results:

```
Mini statement: The amount on deposit is £100.00

Mini statement: The amount on deposit is £100.00
```

9.6 Abstract class

If a class is to be used purely as a specification of the facilities that are to be provided by later derived classes, then it can be made abstract. An abstract class therefore has no implementation part. For example, an abstract specification of a bank account is as follows:

```
package Class_abstract_account is

  type Abstract_account is abstract tagged null record;
  subtype Money  is Float;
  subtype PMoney is Float range 0.0 .. Float'Last;

  procedure statement( the:in Abstract_account ) is abstract;
  procedure deposit  ( the:in out Abstract_account;
                       amount:in PMoney ) is abstract;
  procedure withdraw ( the:in out Abstract_account;
                       amount:in PMoney;
                       get:out PMoney ) is abstract;
  function  balance  ( the:in Abstract_account )
                       return Money is abstract;
end Class_abstract_account;
```

Note: An elaboration of an abstract class can never be made.

The keyword `abstract` is used to indicate:

- That the type is abstract, and hence no actual definition will be provided.

- That the methods (functions or procedures) are abstract and consequently there will be no implementation part.

Note: As the type `Abstract_account` *contains no instance attributes it has been left public. It could have been defined as:*

```
type Abstract_account is tagged private;
```

with the private part of the specification containing:

```
type Abstract_account is abstract tagged null record;
```

The component `'null record'` *is shorthand for :*
`'record null end record'`

The abstract class can then be used to derived specific types of bank account. In the following case it has been used to derive a simple bank account.

```
with Class_abstract_account;
use  Class_abstract_account;
package Class_account is

  type Account is new Abstract_account with private;
  subtype Money is Class_abstract_account.Money;
  subtype PMoney is Class_abstract_account.PMoney;

  procedure statement( the:in Account );
  procedure deposit  ( the:in out Account; amount:in PMoney );
  procedure withdraw ( the:in out Account; amount:in PMoney;
                       get:out PMoney );
  function  balance  ( the:in Account ) return Money;
private
  type Account is new Abstract_account with record
    balance_of : Money := 0.00;       -- Amount in account
  end record;
end Class_account;
```

Note: Subtype has been used to make the subtypes `Money` *and* `PMoney` *visible to clients of the class. If this had not been done, users of the class would in most cases have to* **with** *and* **use** *the package* `Class_abstract_account`.

The implementation of which would be the same as the class `Account` shown in section 5.3.6.

Once a class has been derived from an existing class it too may be used as a base class in deriving a new class. For example, an account that allows a customer to only make three withdrawals in a week can be derived from `Class_account` as follows:

```
with Class_account;
use  Class_account;
package Class_account_ltd is

  type Account_ltd is new Account with private;

  procedure withdraw ( the:in out Account_ltd;
                          amount:in PMoney; get:out PMoney );
  procedure reset( the:in out Account_ltd );
private
  WITHDRAWALS_IN_A_WEEK : Natural := 3;
  type Account_ltd is new Account with record
    withdrawals : Natural := WITHDRAWALS_IN_A_WEEK;
  end record;
end Class_account_ltd;
```

Note: The derived class overloads the method `withdraw` *with a new specialized meaning. The method* `reset` *is used to set the number of withdrawals that may be made in the current week to three.*

The implementation for the class is as follows:

```
package body Class_account_ltd is
```

The specialization of the procedure `withdraw` calls the method `withdraw` in class `Account` to process the withdrawal. To avoid infinite recursion, the parameter `the` is converted to type `Account` before it is passed as a parameter to `withdraw`. This is termed a view conversion. Overload resolution is then used to determine which version of `withdraw` to call.

```
  procedure withdraw ( the:in out Account_ltd;
                          amount:in PMoney; get:out PMoney ) is
  begin
    if the.withdrawals > 0 then              -- Not limit
      the.withdrawals := the.withdrawals - 1;
      withdraw( Account(the), amount, get );  -- In Account
    else
      get := 0.00;                           -- Sorry
    end if;
  end withdraw;
```

The function `reset` resets the number of withdrawals that may be made in the current week.

```
procedure reset( the:in out Account_ltd ) is
begin
   the.withdrawals := WITHDRAWALS_IN_A_WEEK;
end reset;

end Class_account_ltd;
```

9.6.1 Putting it all together

A program to illustrate the use of the class `Class_account_ltd` is shown below:

```
with Class_account, Class_account_ltd;
use  Class_account, Class_account_ltd;
procedure main is
  mike  : Account_ltd;
  obtain: Money;
begin
  deposit( mike, 300.00 );              -- In credit
  statement( mike );
  withdraw( mike, 100.00, obtain ); -- Withdraw some money
  withdraw( mike,  10.00, obtain ); -- Withdraw some money
  withdraw( mike,  10.00, obtain ); -- Withdraw some money
  withdraw( mike,  20.00, obtain ); -- Withdraw some money
  statement( mike );
end main;
```

*Note: The **with** and **use** of the package Class_account so that the subtype Money is directly visible.*

which when run, produces the following output:

```
Mini statement: The amount on deposit is £300.00

Mini statement: The amount on deposit is £180.00
```

Note: The final withdrawal of £20 is not processed as three withdrawals have already been made this week.

9.6.2 Visibility of base class methods

It is of course possible to call the base class method `withdraw` directly using:

```
withdraw( Account(mike),  20.00, obtain ); -- In base class
```

as the Class Account is visible. This could have been prevented by not **with**'ing and **use**'ing the package Class_account. This has been done to make the subtype Money directly visible. Remember Money is defined in the class Account (it has not been made visible to class Account_ltd) so that both classes Account and Account_ltd can be **with**'ed and **use**'ed in the same unit.

To avoid the possibility of the accidental use of withdraw in the base class the above program could have been written as:

```
with Class_account, Class_account_ltd;
use  Class_account_ltd;
procedure main is
  mike  : Account_ltd;
  obtain: Class_account.Money;
begin

  -- Body of procedure as before

end main;
```

Note: The package Class_account has been used explicitly to access the subtype Money.

9.7 Multiple inheritance

Multiple inheritance is the ability to create a new class by inheriting from two or more base classes. For example, the class Named_account, a named bank account, can be created from the class Account and the class Name_address. The class Account is described in section 5.3.4 and the class Name_address is described in section 7.10 The inheritance diagram for the class Named_account is illustrated in Figure 9.4.

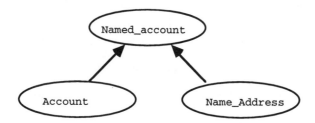

Figure 9.4 Inheritance diagram for a named bank account.

The responsibilities of the class Named_account are all those of the classes Account and Name_address plus the additional responsibility to print the person's name with their printed statement. The new responsibility of printing a statement with the account holder's name overrides the responsibility of printing a statement in Account. The methods in the three classes are:

In Named_account	In Account	In Name_address
statement	deposit	set
	withdraw	print_name
	balance	print_address
	statement	

Note: *The methods of the class* Named_account *will be all the methods of an* Account *plus all the methods of* Name_address *plus any methods of* Named_account *itself.*

Unfortunately multiple inheritance is not directly supported in Ada 95. However, an easy work around is to define the class Named_account whose instance attributes are instances of the classes Account and Name_address. The public methods of the class Named_account have the same specification as the methods of Account and Named_account except that the type of object operated on is an instance of the class Named_account.

The specification for the class Named_account is shown below:

```ada
with Class_account, Class_name_address;
use  Class_account, Class_name_address;
package Class_named_account is

  type Named_account is tagged private;
  subtype PMoney is Class_account.PMoney;
  subtype Money  is Class_account.Money;

  procedure set( the:out Named_account; str:in String );
  function deliver_line( the:in Named_account;
                          line:in Positive ) return String;
  function lines( the:in Named_account ) return Positive;
  procedure statement( the:in Named_account );
  procedure deposit( the:in out Named_account; amount:in PMoney );
  procedure withdraw( the:in out Named_account; amount:in PMoney;
                      get:out PMoney );
  function  balance( the:in Named_account ) return PMoney;
private
  type Named_account is tagged record
    acc : Account;            -- An account object
    naa : Name_address;       -- A Name and address object
  end record;
end Class_named_account;
```

Note: *To allow a client of the class* Named_account *to directly use the subtype* Money *in the class* Account *the declaration :*
        subtype Money **is** Class_account.Money;
has been added to the class.

The implementation of the class Named_Account is split into three distinct parts:

- The implementation of the methods in Name_address.
- The implementation of the methods in Account.
- The implementation of the methods of Named_account itself.

The implementation of the methods in Named_account which are inherited from Name_address are as follows:

```
with Simple_io; use  Simple_io;
package body Class_named_account is

  procedure set( the:out Named_account; str:in String ) is
  begin
    set( the.naa, str );
  end set;

  function deliver_line( the:in Named_account;
                         line:in Positive ) return String is
  begin
    return deliver_line( the.naa, line );
  end deliver_line;

  function lines( the:in Named_account ) return Positive is
  begin
    return lines( the.naa );
  end lines;
```

The implementation of the single method of Named_account is:

```
  procedure statement( the:in Named_account ) is
  begin
    put("Statement for : " );
    put( deliver_line( the.naa, 1 ) ); new_line;
    statement( the.acc );
  end statement;
```

Note: This method overloads the same named method of Account.

The implementation of the methods in Named_account which are inherited from Account are as follows:

```
  procedure deposit(the:in out Named_account; amount:in PMoney)
  begin
    deposit( the.acc, amount );
  end deposit;
```

```
procedure withdraw( the:in out Named_account; amount:in PMoney;
                    get:out PMoney ) is
begin
  withdraw( the.acc, amount, get );
end withdraw;

function balance ( the:in Named_account ) return PMoney is
begin
  return balance( the.acc );
end balance;

end Class_named_account;
```

9.7.1 Putting it all together

A program to illustrate the use of the class Named_account is shown below:

```
with Simple_io, Class_named_account;
use  Simple_io, Class_named_account;
procedure main is
  mike : Named_account;
  get  : Money;
begin
  set( mike, "Mike Smith/University of Brighton/Brighton" );
  deposit( mike, 10.00 );
  statement( mike );
  withdraw( mike, 5.00, get );
  statement( mike );
end main;
```

which when run, produces the following output:

```
Mike Smith
The amount on deposit is 10.00
Mike Smith
The amount on deposit is  5.00
```

9.8 Initialization and finalization

When an instance of a class is created, there can be static initialization of the instance or class attributes in the object. For example, in the class Account in section 5.3.4 the initial amount in the account was set to £0.00 when an instance of the class was elaborated. However, this initialization is limited to a simple assignment. In some cases a more complex initialization is required.

Consider the case of a bank account that records an audit trail of all transactions made on the account. The audit trail consists of a record written to disk for each transaction made on the account. The audit trail file descriptor is shared between all instances of the class and is initialized by the first elaboration of an instance of the class. The file descriptor is closed when the last instance of the class is finalized.

By inheriting from the package Ada.Finalization user defined initialization and finalization can be defined for a class. This takes the form of two user defined procedures initialize and finalize which are called respectively when an instance of the class is elaborated and when an instance of the class is destroyed. For example, the point when initialization and finalization take place is annotated on the following fragment of code.

```ada
procedure main is
   mike : Account_at;              -- Initialization on mike
begin
   deposit( mike, 100.00 );
   declare
      corinna : Account_at;        -- Initialization on corinna
   begin
      deposit( corinna, 100.00 );
                                   -- Finalization on corinna
   end;
                                   -- Finalization on mike
end main;
```

The responsibilities for the class Account_at that provides an audit trail are as follows:

Method	Responsibility
withdraw	Withdraw money from the account and write an audit trail record.
deposit	Deposit money into the account and write an audit trail record.
balance	Return the amount in the account and write an audit trail record.
statement	Write a statement of the current state of the account to the terminal and write an audit trail record.
set_acc_num	Set the number of the account.
initialize	If this is the only active instance of the class Account then open the audit trail file.
finalization	If this is the last active instance of the class Account then close the audit trail file.

The specification for the class Account_at that creates an audit trail of all transactions is:

```
with Ada.Text_io;
with Ada.Finalization; use Ada.Finalization;
package Class_account_at is

  type Account_at is new Limited_controlled with private;
  subtype Money  is Float;
  subtype PMoney is Float range 0.0 .. Float'Last;

  procedure initialize( the:in out Account_at );
  procedure finalize( the:in out Account_at );

  procedure statement( the:in Account_at );
  procedure deposit( the:in out Account_at; amount:in PMoney );
  procedure withdraw( the:in out Account_at;
                      amount:in PMoney; get:out PMoney );
  function  balance( the:in Account_at ) return Money;
private
  type Account_at is new Limited_controlled with record
     balance_of : Money := 0.00;              -- Amount on deposit
  end record;
  the_audit_trail: Ada.Text_io.FILE_TYPE;  -- File handle
  the_active      : Natural := 0;           -- No of accounts
end Class_account_at;
```

Note: `Account_at` *is inherited from* `Limited_Controlled` *that is defined as a limited type. Thus assignments of instances of* `Account_at` *are not allowed.*

The variables `the_audit_trail` and `the_active` are shared amongst all instances of the class and contain respectively the open file descriptor and the number of active instances of the class.

The number of active instances of the class is required so that the file descriptor `the_audit_trail` may be initialized when the first instance of the class is elaborated and closed when the last active instance of the class goes out of scope.

9.8.1 Implementation

The procedure `initialize` is called whenever an instance of `Account_at` is elaborated. This procedure checks if this is the first elaboration, determined by the reference count `the_active`. If it is the first concurrent elaboration then the audit trail file `log.txt` is opened in append mode and associated with the file descriptor `the_audit_trail`.

```
with Simple_io; use Simple_io;
package body Class_Account_at is

  procedure initialize( the:in out Account_at ) is
  begin
    the_active := the_active + 1;     -- Another object
    if the_active = 1 then            --  first time for class
      open( File=>the_audit_trail,
            Mode=>APPEND_FILE, Name=>"log.txt" );
    end if;
  end initialize;
```

The procedure finalize is called when the elaborated storage for an instance of Account_at goes out of scope. The reference count of the number of active instantiations of Account_op is checked and when the last concurrent instance goes out of scope the file descriptor the_audit_trail is closed.

```
procedure finalize( the:in out Account_at ) is
begin
    if the_active = 1 then close( the_audit_trail ); end if;
    the_active:=the_active-1;
end finalize;
```

The rest of the implementation follows very closely the previous implementation of the class Account with the additional functionality of writing the audit trail record for each transaction performed.

```
procedure statement( the:in Account_at ) is
begin
  put( "The amount on deposit is " );
  put( the.balance_of, aft=>2, exp=>0 ); new_line;
  put( the_audit_trail, "Statement : Balance = " );
  put( the_audit_trail, the.balance_of, aft=>2, exp=>0 );
  new_line( the_audit_trail );
end statement;

procedure deposit( the:in out Account_at; amount:in PMoney ) is
begin
  the.balance_of := the.balance_of + amount;
  put( the_audit_trail, "Deposit    : " );
  put( the_audit_trail, amount, aft=>2, exp=>0 );
  new_line( the_audit_trail );
end deposit;
```

```
procedure withdraw( the:in out Account_at;
                    amount:in PMoney; get:out PMoney ) is
begin
  if the.balance_of >= amount then
    the.balance_of := the.balance_of - amount;
    get := amount;
  else
    get := 0.00;
  end if;
  put( the_audit_trail, "Withdraw  : " );
  put( the_audit_trail, get, aft=>2, exp=>0 );
  new_line( the_audit_trail );
end withdraw;

function  balance( the:in Account_at ) return Money is
begin
  return the.balance_of;
  put( the_audit_trail, "Balance    : " );
  put( the_audit_trail, the.balance_of, aft=>2, exp=>0 );
  new_line( the_audit_trail );
end balance;
end Class_Account_at;
```

9.8.2 Putting it all together

The following short test program demonstrates the working of the class `Account_at`.

```
with Class_Account_at;
use  Class_Account_at;
procedure main is
  bank  : array ( 1 .. 10 ) of Account_at;
  get   : Money;
begin
  statement( bank(1) );
  deposit( bank(1), 100.00 );          -- Deposit 100.00
  statement( bank(1) );
  withdraw( bank(1), 80.00, get );     -- Withdraw 80.00
  statement( bank(1) );
  deposit( bank(2), 200.00 );          -- Deposit 200.00
  statement( bank(2) );
end main;
```

Note: The procedure initialize will be called ten times when the object bank is elaborated, once for each element of the array. Likewise when the object bank is finalized, the procedure finalize will be called ten times, once for each element of the array.

This when compiled and run will generate the file `Log.txt` which contains the audit trail of all transactions made. The contents of the audit trail file are illustrated below:

```
Statement : Balance =   0.00
Deposit   : 100.00
Statement : Balance = 100.00
Withdraw  : 80.00
Statement : Balance = 20.00
Deposit   : 200.00
Statement : Balance = 220.00
```

9.8.3 Warning

There are two base types in `Ada.Finalization` from which user defined initialization and finalization is facilitated. These are `Controlled` and `Limited_Controlled` the properties of which are:

Type in Ada.Finalization	Properties
Controlled	Allow user defined initialization and finalization for inheriting types. Instances of these types may be assigned.
Limited_Controlled.	Allow user defined initialization and finalization for inheriting types. Instances of these types may not be assigned.

When the base type for a class is Controlled then as part of an assignment operation Finalization is called on the target of the assignment. This will result in Finalization being called at least twice on an object. The procedure Finalization is called once when an object is assigned too and once when its storage is de-allocated. Thus if you use Controlled as the base type, the code for Finalization must allow for such an eventuality. The code for Finalization in the class Account_at cannot be called twice. The exact details of how to use Controlled are explained in Chapter 16.

9.9 Hiding the base class methods

The base class methods may be hidden in a class by defining the inheritance only in the private part of the specification. For example, a restricted type of account that only allows a statement to be printed and money to be deposited into the account can be created.

For this type of account we wish to prevent the user from calling base class methods. Remember that normally with inheritance the base class members are visible. Even if a base class method is overloaded in the derived class it can still be called.

The specification of the class Restricted_account is:

```
with Class_account;
use  Class_account;
package Class_restricted_account is

  type Restricted_account is private;
  subtype Money  is Class_account.Money;
  subtype PMoney is Class_account.PMoney;

  procedure statement( the:in Restricted_Account );
  procedure deposit( the:in out Restricted_Account;
                     amount:in PMoney );
private
  type Restricted_account is new Account with record
    null;
  end record;
end Class_restricted_account;
```

Note: The use of subtype to make the types from class Account visible.

The implementation of the class is:

```
package body Class_restricted_account is

  procedure statement( the:in Restricted_account ) is
  begin
    statement( Account(the) );
  end statement;
```

```
   procedure deposit( the:in out Restricted_account;
                      amount:in PMoney ) is
   begin
     deposit( Account(the), amount );
   end deposit;

end Class_restricted_account;
```

Note: *The use of* statement(Account(the)) *to call the method* statement
in the class Account.

Here the base class methods are called from within the body of the derived class methods. Remember the body of the package can see the methods of the base class.

9.9.1 Visibility rules (Hidden base class)

The visibility of items in the base class and derived class is illustrated in Figure 9.5.

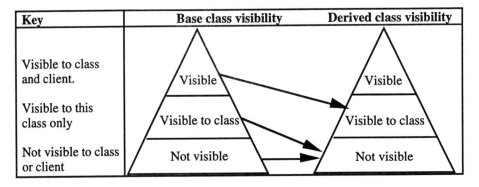

Key	Base class visibility	Derived class visibility
Visible to class and client.	Visible	Visible
Visible to this class only	Visible to class	Visible to class
Not visible to class or client	Not visible	Not visible

Figure 9.5 Visibility of components in base and derived classes.

The consequence of this is that any methods from the base class that a client of the derived class may wish to use have to be explicitly made available by providing an appropriate procedure or function in the derived class.

9.9.2 Putting it all together

The program below illustrates the use of this restricted account.

```
procedure main is
  corinna :Restricted_account;   -- Can only deposit
begin
  statement( corinna );
  deposit( corinna, 50.00 );
  statement( corinna );
end main;
```

which when run would produce the following results:

```
Mini statement: The amount on deposit is £ 0.00

Mini statement: The amount on deposit is £50.00
```

9.10 Self-assessment

- How can the use of inheritance save time in the production of software?

- Can any previously defined class be used as a base class from which other classes are derived?

- Can a derived class see the private data attributes of the base class? Explain why this is so.

- What is the purpose of the pre-defined package `Ada.Finalization`?

- For an object o which is an instance of a derived class, how does a programmer call the method m in the base class which has been overloaded by another method m in the derived class?

- Why can the code of `Finalization` in the class `Account_at` not be called twice?

9.11 Exercises

Construct the following:

- *Employee_pay*
  A class `Employee_pay` which represents a person's salary has the following methods:

Method	Responsibility
set_hourly_rate	Set the hourly rate.
add_hours_worked	Accumulate the number of hours worked so far.
pay	Deliver the pay for this week.
reset	Reset the hours worked back to zero.
hours_worked	Deliver the number of hours worked so far this week.
pay_rate	Deliver the hourly pay rate.

Tax is to be deducted at 20% of total pay.

- `test`
  A program to test the class `Employee_pay`.

- *`Better_employee_pay`*
  A class `Better_employee_pay` which represents a person's salary. This extends the class *`Employee_pay`* to add the additional methods of:

Method	Responsibility
`set_overtime_pay`	Set the overtime pay rate.
`normal_pay_hours`	Set the number of hours in a week that have to be worked before the overtime pay rate is applied.
`pay`	Deliver the pay for this week. This will consist of the hours worked at the normal pay rate plus the hours worked at the overtime rate.

- `test`
  A program to test the class `Better_employee_pay`.

- *`Employee_pay_with_repayment.`*
  A class `Employee_pay_with_repayment` which represents a person's salary after the deduction of the weekly repayment of part of a loan for travel expenses. This extends the class `Better_employee_pay` to add the additional methods of:

Method	Responsibility
`set_deduction`	Set the weekly deduction
`pay`	Deliver the pay for this week. This will include the deduction of the money for the employee loan if possible.

Remember to include the possibility of an employee not being able to repay the weekly repayment of their loan as they have not worked enough hours.

- `test`
  A program to test the class `Employee_pay_with_repayment`.

10 Child libraries

This chapter introduces child libraries. A child library is a way of adding to an existing package without changing the original package. In addition, a child of an existing package is allowed to access the private components of the parent. By using child libraries a large package or class can be split into manageable components.

10.1 Introduction

In developing software, extensions to an existing class are occasionally required which modify or access the private instance attributes. This is not possible with inheritance as an inheriting class is not allowed to access private instance attributes of the base class. Rather than change the code of the class directly, a child library of the class can be created which is a separate entity that is allowed to access private components of a package.

The original class is not re-compiled, and thus does not need re-testing. However, the combined parent and child library needs to be tested as the child library can modify private instance or class attributes of the parent.

This is similar in effect to inheritance, in that new methods are added to an existing class. The class type however, may not be extended. For example, the class `Interest_account` (in section 9.3) can have an additional method `inspect_interest` added which will allow inspection of the accumulating interest that is to be added to the account at the end of the accounting period. This is implemented as a child package whose specification is as follows:

```
package Class_interest_account.inspect_interest is
  function interest_is( the:in Interest_account )
                    return Money;
end Class_interest_account.inspect_interest;
```

The child package name is defined as two components, the original package name followed by the name of the child package. In this case the two components are `Class_interest_account.inspect_interest`.

The implementation of these is as follows:

```
with Class_account; use  Class_account;
package body Class_interest_account.inspect_interest is

   function interest_is( the:in Interest_account )
                           return Money is
   begin
     return the.accumulated_interest;
   end interest_is;

end Class_interest_account.inspect_interest;
```

Note: *You can access private components of the parent package.*

This specialization of an interest bearing account could not be created by inheriting from the class Interest_account as accumulated_interest is a private instance attribute of the class Interest_account. Access to this variable breaks the encapsulation of the class Interest_account.

The intent is for child packages to allow the specialization of an existing package without having to change the parent. In particular, the parent will not need re-testing but the combined parent and child must be tested as the child package may affect the working of the parent.

10.1.1 Putting it all together

The package Interest_account and its child inspect_interest are used as follows:

```
with Simple_io, Class_account, Class_interest_account,
              Class_interest_account.inspect_interest;
use  Simple_io, Class_account, Class_interest_account,
              Class_interest_account.inspect_interest;
procedure main is
  my_account: Interest_account;
  obtained   : Money;
begin
  statement( my_account );
  put("Deposit 100.00 into account"); new_line;
  deposit( my_account, 100.00 );          -- Day 1
  calc_interest( my_account );            -- End of day 1
  calc_interest( my_account );            -- End of day 2
  statement( my_account );                -- Day 3
  obtained := interest_is( my_account );  -- How much interest
  put("Interest accrued so far : £" );
  put( obtained, aft=>2, exp=>0 ); new_line;
end main;
```

Note: *When a child is included, its ancestors are automatically **with**'ed.*

When run it will produce the following output:

```
Mini statement: The amount on deposit is £ 0.00

Deposit 100.00 into account
Mini statement: The amount on deposit is £100.00

Interest accrued so far : £ 0.05
```

10.1.2 Warning

A child package breaks the encapsulation rules of a package. In particular a child package can access the private data components of its parent package. In accessing the private instance attributes of a class, the child package may compromoise the integrity of the parent package.

10.2 Visibility rules of a child package

The private part of a child package can access all components of its ancestors, even the private components. However, the visible part of a child package has no access to the private components of its ancestors. This is to prevent possible renaming allowing a client direct access to the private components of one of the child's ancestors.

A child package allows a programmer the ability to extend an existing package without the need to change or re-compile the package.

For example, Figure 10.1 illustrates a hierarchy of package specifications rooted at package P. The ancestor of packages P.C2 and P.C1 is package P, whilst the ancestors of package P.C2.G1 are the packages P.C2 and P.

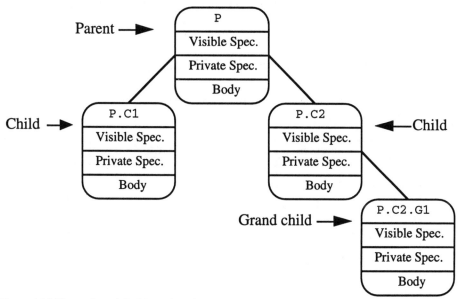

Figure 10.1 Illustration of the hierarchy of child units.

Key	Package specification	Package body

Components of a package in this case package P.	`package P is`
	  `-- Visible specification.`
	`private`
	  `-- Private specification.`
	`end P;`
		`package body P is`
		  `-- Body of package`
		`end P;`

Can access in ->	P	P.C1	P.C2	P.C2.G1
P.C1 Visible specification	Visible spec.	•	Visible spec. when **with**'ed	Visible spec. when **with**'ed
P.C1 Private specification	Visible spec. Private spec.	•	Visible spec. when **with**'ed	Visible spec. when **with**'ed
P.C2.G1 Visible specification	Visible spec.	Visible spec. when **with**'ed	Visible spec.	•
P.C2.G1 Private specification	Visible spec. Private spec.	Visible spec. when **with**'ed	Visible spec. Private spec.	•

*Note: A **with** clause for a child package implies a **with** clause for all its ancestors.*

10.3 Private child

A private child package is like a normal child package except that it is only visible within the sub-tree, which has an ancestor as its root. A private child can be used to hide implementation details from a user of the parent package.

10.3.1 Visibility rules of a private child package

If in Figure 10.1 P.C2 is a private child then the visibility of components is as illustrated in the table below.

Can access in ->	P	P.C2	P.C1
P.C2 Visible specification	Visible spec.	•	Visible spec. when **with**'ed
P.C2 Private specification	Visible spec. Private spec.	•	Visible spec. when **with**'ed

Can access in ->	P	P.C2	P.C1
P.C1 Visible specification	Visible spec.	No access	•
P.C1 Private specification	Visible spec. Private spec.	No access	•

Note: The private part of a child package has access to all components of its parent, even the private components.

10.4 Child packages vs. inheritance

The following table summarizes the differences between the use of a child package and inheritance.

Ability to	Child package	Inheritance
Create a new package	×	✓
Extend a base package by adding new procedures and functions	✓	✓
Extend a type in the base package	×	✓ (1)
Access private components in the base package	✓	×
Override existing procedures and functions in the base package	×	✓

Note: 1. Must be tagged in the base class.

The danger in the use of child libraries is that they can subvert the data hiding of a class. For example, the class Interest_account hides the representation of, and prevents access to the accumulated_interest. A child library of the class Interest_account can allow a client of the class the ability to change or inspect this hidden variable.

10.5 Self-assessment

- How can the use of child libraries save time in the production of software?

- Why is a child library's public specification not allowed to access components in a parent's private specification?

- What is the difference between a normal child package and a private child package?

- What is the difference between the use of a child package and the use of inheritance to build on existing code?

10.6 Exercises

Construct the following:

- *Money*
  A class which manipulates amounts of money held in pounds and pence. This class should allow the following operations to be performed on an instance of the class Money
  - Add monetary amounts using the operator +.
  - Subtract monetary amounts using the operator –.

- *Conversion*
  A child library of the package Class_money which allows the conversion of an amount in pounds to dollars, francs and ECU (European Currency Unit).

11 Defining new operators

This chapter shows how the predefined operators in Ada can be overloaded with a new meaning. This process is best done via the class mechanism using packages.

11.1 Defining operators in Ada

The inbuilt operators in Ada can be overloaded with a new meaning. Ada only allows existing operators to be defined as new operators. These new operators have the same precedence as their existing counterparts. For example, to trace every executed integer + in a program, the operator + can be overloaded by a function that writes trace information to the terminal before delivering the normal integer addition. This is achieved by the following function:

```
function "+" ( f:in Integer; s:in Integer ) return Integer is
begin
  put("[Performing "); put(f); put(" + "); put(s); put("]");
  return Standard."+"( f, s );
end "+";
```

Note: *To perform the inbuilt + the functional notation for the plus operation must be used. This is achieved with* `Standard."+"( f, s )`. *In Ada, the inbuilt operators are considered to belong to the package* `Standard` *which is automatically made visible to all program units.*
Section C.4, Appendicx C gives the specification for the package standard.

The above function can be used to trace the use of + in the following program:

```
with Simple_io; use Simple_io;
procedure main is
  -- The body of the function "+"
begin
  put("The sum of 1 + 2 is: "); put ( 1+2 ); new_line;
  put("The sum of 1 + 2 is: "); put ( Standard."+"(1,2) );
  new_line;
  put("The sum of 1 + 2 is: "); put ( "+"(1,2) ); new_line;
end main;
```

which when compiled and run will deliver the following results:

```
The sum of 1 + 2 is: [Performing 1 + 2]3
The sum of 1 + 2 is: 3
The sum of 1 + 2 is: [Performing 1 + 2]3
```

Note: The way of directly using the operator + defined in the package Standard
  'Standard."+"(1,2)'.
  The function notation for the use of the operator + "+"(1,2).

11.2 A rational arithmetic package

A rational arithmetic package can be developed by defining a class which can create
objects of type Rational. The following operations: +, −, * and /. can be performed
on an instance of a Rational number. The responsibilities of these methods are as
follows:

Method	Responsibility
+	Delivers the sum of two rational numbers as a rational number.
−	Delivers the difference of two rational numbers as a rational number.
*	Delivers the product of two rational numbers as a rational number.
/	Delivers the division of two rational numbers as a rational number.

In addition the following methods are used to create a rational constant and to output
a rational number in a canonical form.

Method	Responsibility
rat_const	Creates a rational number from two Integer numbers
put	Writes a rational constant to the standard output in the canonical form 'a b/c'.

The specification of the package is as follows:

```
package Class_rational is
  type Rational is private;

  function "+" ( f:in Rational; s:in Rational ) return Rational;
  function "-" ( f:in Rational; s:in Rational ) return Rational;
  function "*" ( f:in Rational; s:in Rational ) return Rational;
  function "/" ( f:in Rational; s:in Rational ) return Rational;

  function rat_const( f:in Integer;
                      s:in Integer:=1 ) return Rational;
  procedure put( the:in Rational );
```

```
private
   function sign( the:in Rational ) return Rational;
   function simplify( the:in Rational ) return Rational;
   type Rational is record
      above : Integer := 0;      -- Numerator
      below : Integer := 1;      -- Denominator
   end record;
end Class_rational;
```

The two private functions are used internally to put the stored rational number into a minimal form. The function `sign` makes sure that only the top part of the rational number may be negative and the function `simplify` reduces the rational number to its simplest form.

Using the above package, the following code can be written:

```
with Simple_io, Class_rational;
use  Simple_io, Class_rational;
package body Class_procedures is

procedure main is
   a,b : Rational;
begin
   a := rat_const( 1, 2 );
   b := rat_const( 1, 3 );

   put( "a     = " ); put( a );   new_line;
   put( "b     = " ); put( b );   new_line;
   put( "a + b = " ); put( a+b ); new_line;
   put( "a - b = " ); put( a-b ); new_line;
   put( "b - a = " ); put( b-a ); new_line;
   put( "a * b = " ); put( a*b ); new_line;
   put( "a / b = " ); put( a/b ); new_line;
end main;
```

which when run will deliver the following output:

```
a     = 1/2
b     = 1/3
a + b = 5/6
a - b = 1/6
b - a = -1/6
a * b = 1/6
a / b = 1 1/2
```

The implementation of the package defines the code to implement the overloaded operators between rational numbers as follows:

```ada
with Simple_io; use Simple_io;
package body Class_rational is

  function "+" (f:in Rational; s:in Rational) return Rational is
    res : Rational;
  begin
    res.below := f.below * s.below;
    res.above := f.above * s.below + s.above * f.below;
    return simplify(res);
  end "+";

  function "-" (f:in Rational; s:in Rational) return Rational is
    res : Rational;
  begin
    res.below := f.below * s.below;
    res.above := f.above * s.below - s.above * f.below;
    return simplify(res);
  end "-";

  function "*" (f:in Rational; s:in Rational) return Rational is
    res : Rational;
  begin
    res.above := f.above * s.above;
    res.below := f.below * s.below;
    return simplify(res);
  end "*";

  function "/" (f:in Rational; s:in Rational) return Rational is
    res : Rational;
  begin
    res.above := f.above * s.below;
    res.below := f.below * s.above;
    return simplify(res);
  end "/";
```

The function `rat_const` converts two `Integer` numbers into a rational, the second of which may be omitted to allow a whole integer number to be converted into a rational.

```ada
  function rat_const( f:in Integer;
                      s:in Integer:=1 ) return Rational is
  begin
    if f = 0 then
      return Rational'(0,1);
    else
      return simplify( sign( Rational'( f, s ) ) );
    end if;
  end rat_const;
```

*Note: A rational constant could have been created by overloading the operator /
between two integers to deliver a rational number. The disadvantage of this
approach is that the two distinct meanings for / must be distinguished between
in a program section.*

The output function `put` is defined to output a rational number in a canonical form.

```ada
procedure put( the:in Rational ) is
  above : Integer := the.above;
  below : Integer := the.below;
begin
  if above = 0 then                              -- Rational 0
    put( "0" );
  else
    if above < 0 then
      put("-"); above := -above;                 -- make +ve
    end if;
    if above >= below then                       -- Whole number
      put( above/below, width=>1 ); put(" ");
      above := above rem below;                  -- Fraction
    end if;
    if above /= 0 then
      put( above, width=>1 ); put( "/" );
      put( below, width=>1 );                    -- Fraction
    end if;
  end if;
end put;
```

Finally, the two private functions that convert a rational number into a standard internal form are defined as:

```ada
function sign( the:in Rational ) return Rational is
begin
  if the.below >= 0 then              --    -a/b or a/b
    return the;
  else                                --    a/-b or -a/-b
    return Rational'( -the.above, -the.below );
  end if;
end sign;

function simplify( the:in Rational ) return Rational is
  res: Rational := the;
  d  : Positive;                      -- Divisor to reduce with
begin
  if res.below = 0 then               -- Invalid treat as 0
    res.above := 0; res.below := 1;
  end if;
  d := 2;                             -- Divide by 2, 3, 4 ...
  while d < res.below loop
    while res.below rem d = 0 and then res.above rem d = 0 loop
      res.above := res.above / d;
      res.below := res.below / d;
    end loop;
    d := d + 1;
  end loop;
  return res;
end simplify;

end Class_rational;
```

11.3 A bounded string class

A partial solution to overcome the fixed size limitations of Ada strings is to use a discriminated record that can hold a string of any length up to a pre-defined maximum. The responsibilities of the class `Bounded_string` which holds a variable length string is as follows:

Method	Responsibility
operator: &	Concatenate an Ada string or a `Bounded_string` to a `Bounded_string`.
operators: > >= < <= =	Compare Bounded_strings
`to_string`	Convert an instance of a `Bounded_string` to an Ada string.
`to_bounded_string`	Convert an Ada string to an instance of a `Bounded_string`.
`slice`	Deliver a slice of a `Bounded_string`

11.3.1 Overloading = and /=

The operators = and /= are provided automatically by the Ada system for comparing for equality or not equality. However, if a user redefines the = operator with a function that returns a `Boolean` value, the Ada system automatically provides the definition of /= as simply **not** =.

If the operator = is overloaded by a function that returns a value other than a `Boolean`, then the user must explicitly provide an overload definition for /= if it is to be used.

11.3.2 Specification of the class `Bounded_string`

The Ada specification of the class `Bounded_string` is shown below:

```
with Simple_io; use Simple_io;
package Class_bounded_string is
  type Bounded_string is private;

  function to_bounded_string(str:in String)
    return Bounded_string;

  function to_string(the:in Bounded_string) return String;

  function "&" (f:in Bounded_string; s:in Bounded_string)
    return Bounded_string;
  function "&" (f:in Bounded_string; s:in String)
    return Bounded_string;
  function "&" (f:in String; s:in Bounded_string)
    return Bounded_string;
```

```
    function slice( the:in Bounded_string;
                    low:in Positive; high:in Natural )
        return String;

    function ">"  ( f:in Bounded_string; s:in Bounded_string )
        return Boolean;
    function ">=" ( f:in Bounded_string; s:in Bounded_string )
        return Boolean;
    function "<"  ( f:in Bounded_string; s:in Bounded_string )
        return Boolean;
    function "<=" ( f:in Bounded_string; s:in Bounded_string )
        return Boolean;
    function "="  ( f:in Bounded_string; s:in Bounded_string )
        return Boolean;
private
    MAX_STRING: constant := 80;
    subtype Str_range is Natural range 0 .. MAX_STRING;
    type A_Bounded_string( length: Str_range := 0 ) is record
        chrs: String( 1 .. length );   -- Stored string
    end record;
    type Bounded_string is record
        v_str : A_Bounded_string;
    end record;
end Class_bounded_string;
```

In the specification of the class Bounded_string a discriminated record is used. This discriminated record A_Bounded_string will store strings up to length MAX_STRING characters. The discriminate length is used to specify the upper bound of the string, and has a default value of 0. An instance of Bounded_string may be assigned another instance of Bounded_string that may have a different discriminate value.

Note: The discriminated record will usually be implemented by allocating the maximum amount of storage. Setting MAX_STRING to 10_000 in the package would allow for most eventualities, but would waste large amounts of storage.
As the operator = is overloaded by a function which returns a Boolean value then the operator /= is automatically created.

In the implementation of the package Class_bounded_string shown below, the procedure to_bounded_string is used to convert a 'normal' Ada string into an instance of a Bounded_string.

```
with Simple_io; use Simple_io;
package body Class_bounded_string is

    function to_bounded_string( str:in String )
        return Bounded_string is
    begin
        return (v_str=>(str'Length, str));
    end to_bounded_string;
```

The function `to_string` delivers a normal Ada string from a `Bounded_string`.

```
function to_string(the:in Bounded_string) return String is
begin
  return the.v_str.chrs( 1 .. the.v_str.length );
end to_string;
```

The function `slice` allows slices to be taken off an instance of a `Bounded_string`.

```
function slice( the:in Bounded_string;
                low:in Positive; high:in Natural)
  return String is
begin
  if low <= high and then high <= the.v_str.length then
      return the.v_str.chrs( low .. high );
    end if;
    return "";
end slice;
```

The overloaded definitions of &, >, >=, <, <= allow the normal Ada comparison operators to be used with instances of a `Bounded_string`. The operators for = are used by the Ada system to provide the definition of /=. The implementation for & allows concatenation between instances of a `Bounded_string` and a normal Ada string. This is achieved by overloading & with three different definitions as follows:

```
function "&" ( f:in Bounded_string; s:in Bounded_string )
  return Bounded_string is
begin
  return (v_str=>(f.v_str.chrs'Length + s.v_str.chrs'Length,
                  f.v_str.chrs & s.v_str.chrs));
end "&";

function "&" ( f:in Bounded_string; s:in String )
  return Bounded_string is
begin
  return (v_str=>(f.v_str.chrs'Length + s'Length,
                  f.v_str.chrs & s ) );
end "&";

function "&" ( f:in String; s:in Bounded_string )
  return Bounded_string is
begin
  return ( v_str=>(f'Length + s.v_str.chrs'Length,
                   f & s.v_str.chrs ) );
end "&";
```

The implementation for the relational operators however, only allows comparison between instances of a `Bounded_string`. Their implementation is as follows:

```
function ">"  ( f:in Bounded_string; s:in Bounded_string )
   return Boolean is
begin
   return f.v_str.chrs > s.v_str.chrs;
end ">";

function ">=" ( f:in Bounded_string; s:in Bounded_string )
   return Boolean is
begin
   return f.v_str.chrs >= s.v_str.chrs;
end ">=";

function "<"  ( f:in Bounded_string; s:in Bounded_string )
   return Boolean is
begin
   return f.v_str.chrs < s.v_str.chrs;
end "<";

function "<=" ( f:in Bounded_string; s:in Bounded_string )
   return Boolean is
begin
   return f.v_str.chrs <= s.v_str.chrs;
end "<=";

function "=" ( f:in Bounded_string; s:in Bounded_string )
   return Boolean is
begin
   return f.v_str.chrs = s.v_str.chrs;
end "=";

end Class_bounded_string;
```

Note: *To compare an instance of a* `Bounded_string` *and an instance of an Ada string a user would have to convert the Ada string to a* `Bounded_string`. *For example:*

```
name : Bounded_string;
if name > to_bounded_string( "Brighton" ) then
```

11.3.3 Putting it all together

```
procedure main is
  town, county, address : Bounded_string;
begin
  town    := to_bounded_string( "Brighton" );
  county := to_bounded_string( "East Sussex" );

  address := town & " " & county;

  put( to_string(address) ); new_line;
  put( slice( county & " UK", 6, 14 ) );
  new_line;
end main;
```

When run, this would produce the following results:

```
Brighton East Sussex
Sussex UK
```

11.3.4 `Ada.Strings.Bounded` a standard library

In the standard library there is a package Ada.Strings.Bounded which the above class Bounded_string is based on. The generic library package Ada.Strings.Bounded.Generic_bounded_length allows the maximum length of the stored string to be defined by a user of the package. Chapter 13 describes the concepts of generics. Chapter 28 lists the specification of the library package Ada.Strings.Bounded.

11.3.5 `use type`

A modified form of the **use** clause allows operators from a package to be used without having to prefix the operator with the package name. Other components however, from the package need to be prefixed with the package name when used. This modified form of the use clause is **use type** which is followed by the type name whose operators can be used without prefixing them by the package name. For example, the following program requires all components in the package Bounded_string except for operators to be prefixed with the package name.

```
with Ada.Text_io, Class_bounded_string;
use  type Class_bounded_string.Bounded_string;
procedure main3 is
  town  : Bounded_string :=
    Class_bounded_string.to_bounded_string("Brighton");
  county: Bounded_string :=
    Class_bounded_string.to_bounded_string("E Sussex");
begin
  Ada.Text_io.put(
      Class_bounded_string.to_string( town & " " & county )
  );
end main3;
```

11.4 Self-assessment

- What operators can be overloaded with a new meaning in Ada?

- Can a user invent new operators? For example, could a user define the monadic operator ++ to add one to an integer?

- Why might excessive use of overloading the standard operators lead to a program that is difficult to follow?

- Why is the function rat_const needed in the class Rational?

- How can a user guarantee to use the definition for the operator + in the package standard?

11.5 Exercises

Construct the following class:

- *A very large integer number class .*

which stores an integer number to 200 digits.

Method	Responsibility
+	Delivers the sum of two very long integer numbers as a very long integer number.
−	Delivers the difference between two very long integer numbers as a very long integer number.
VLN_const	Creates a very long integer number from an Integer.
put	Writes a very long integer number.

A user of the class class_very_large_number can write:

```
with class_very_large_number; use class_very_large_number;
procedure fib is
  MAX_TERMS : constant := 50;
  type    Line_index is new Integer range 1 .. MAX_TERMS;
  subtype Line_range is Line_index;
  type    Line_array is array (Line_range) of Very_large_number;

  fibonacci : Line_array;
begin
  fibonacci(1) := VLN_const(1);
  fibonacci(2) := VLN_const(1);
  for i in 3 .. Line_range'Last loop
    fibonacci(i) := fibonacci(i-1) + fibonacci(i-2);
  end loop;

  put("First ");put( Integer(fibonacci'Length), width=>2 );
  put(" numbers in the fibonacci series are:"); new_line;

  for i in Line_range loop
    put( fibonacci(i) ); put(" ");
  end loop;
  new_line;
end fib;
```

which would print out the first 50 terms of the Fibonacci series.

Hint:

- Use an array to store the 200 digits of the number.

12 Exceptions

This chapter looks at the way errors and exceptions are handled by the Ada system. Unlike many languages, Ada allows the user to capture and continue processing after an error or user-defined exception has occurred.

12.1 The exception mechanism

When writing code for an application it is tedious to have to keep testing for exceptional conditions such as "Data store full". The likely outcome is that the user will not test for the exception. Ada provides the elegant solution of allowing code to raise an exception that can be caught by a user of that code. If the user does not provide an exception handler, the exception is propagated upwards to the potential caller of the user's code. If no one has provided an exception handler, then the program will fail with a run-time message of the form 'Exception Data store full not handled'.

The following program reads in an Integer number from the user and prints the corresponding character represented by this number in the Ada character set.

```
with Simple_io; use Simple_io;
procedure main is
  number : Integer;          -- Number read in
  ch      : Character;       -- As a character
begin
  loop
    begin
      put("Enter character code : ");        -- Ask for number
      exit when end_of_file;                 -- EOF ?
      get( number ); skip_line;              -- Read number
      put("Represents the character [");     -- Valid number
      put( Character'Val(number) );
      put("]");                              -- Valid character
      new_line;
    exception
      when Data_Error =>
        put("Not a valid Number"); skip_line;    -- Exception
        new_line;
      when Constraint_Error =>
        put("Not representable as a Character]"); -- Exception
        new_line;
      when End_error =>
        put("Unexpected end of data"); new_line;  -- Exception
      exit;
    end;
  end loop;
end main;
```

In this program the following exceptions may occur:

Exception	Explanation
Constraint_error	An invalid value has been supplied.
Data_error	The data item read is not of the expected type.
End_error	During a read operation the end of file was detected.

Section B.7, Appendix B gives a full list of the exceptions that can occur during the running of an Ada program.

A user may interact with the program as shown below.

```
Enter character code : 96
Represents the character [`]
Enter character code : Invalid
Not a valid Number
Enter character code : 999
Represents the character [Not representable]
Enter character code : ^D
```

Note: The user input is shown in bold type.
*   ^D represents the end of file character, which on an unix system is control - d*

12.2 Raising an exception

An exception is raised by way of the **raise** statement. For example, to raise the exception Constraint_error the following statement is executed:

```
raise Constraint_error;
```

Naturally, a user-defined exception can be raised. Firstly, the exception to be raised is declared:

```
Unexpected_condition : Exception;
```

then the exception can be raised with:

```
raise Unexpected_condition;
```

12.3 Handling any exception

It is possible to capture an exception without knowing its name by the use of a **when others** clause in an exception handler. For example, the additional handler:

```
when others =>
   put("Unexpected exception"); new_line;
```

could have been included with the previous program to capture any unexpected exceptions. If information is required about the exception then the handler can include a name for the exception. For example:

```
when event: others =>
   put("Unexpected exception is ");
   put( exception_name( event ) ); new_line;
```

Note: The object event *is declared as:*

```
event : Exception_ocurrence;
```

and is defined in the package Ada.Exceptions.

In the above exception handler the exception is known by the name event. Information about the exception is obtained by using the following functions:

Function (Defined in **Ada.Exceptions**)	Returns as a string:
exception_name(event)	In upper case the exception name starting with the root library unit.
exception_information(event)	Detailed information about the exception.
exception_message(event)	A short explanation of the exception.

Other functions and procedures in Ada.Exceptions are:

Function / procedure	Action
reraise_occurrence(event)	A procedure which re-raises the exception event.
raise_exception(e,"Mess")	A procedure which raises exception e with the message "Mess".

12.4 The `cat` program revisited

The program to concatenate the contents of files previously seen in section 2.11 can now be re-written to give a sensible error message to the user when an attempt is made to list a file that does not exist. In this program the following exception occure:

Exception	Explanation
Name_error	File does not exist.
Status_error	File is already open.

This new program is:

```ada
with Ada.Text_io, Ada.Command_line;
use  Ada.Text_io, Ada.Command_line;
procedure cat is
  fd  : Ada.Text_io.File_type;    -- File descriptor
  ch  : Character;                -- Current character
begin
  if argument_count >= 1 then
    for i in 1 .. argument_count loop -- Repeat for each file
      begin
        open( File=>fd, Mode=>IN_FILE,  -- Open file
              Name=>argument(i) );
        while not end_of_file(fd) loop  -- For each Line
          while not end_of_line(fd) loop-- For each character
            get(fd,ch); put(ch);        -- Read / Write character
          end loop;
          skip_line(fd); new_line;      -- Next line / new line
        end loop;
        close(fd);                      -- Close file
      exception
        when Name_error =>
          put("cat: " & argument(i) & " no such file" );
          new_line;
        when Status_error =>
          put("cat: " & argument(i) & " all ready open" );
          new_line;
      end;
    end loop;
  else
    put("Usage: cat file1 ... "); new_line;
  end if;
end cat;
```

12.5 A stack

A stack is a structure used to store and retrieve data items. Data items are pushed onto the structure and retrieved in reverse order. This is commonly referred to as 'first in last out'. This process is illustrated in Figure 12.1

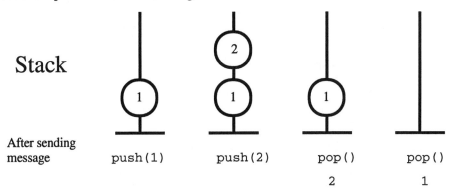

Stack

After sending
message

| push(1) | push(2) | pop() | pop() |
| | | 2 | 1 |

Figure 12.1 Example of operations on a stack.

A program to demonstrate the operation of a stack is developed with the aid of a class Stack. The operations push, pop and reset can be performed on an instance of Stack. The responsibilities of these methods are as follows:

Method	Responsibility
push	Push the current item onto the stack. The exception Stack_error will be raised if this cannot be done.
pop	Return the top item on the stack, whereupon the item is removed from the stack. The exception Stack_error will be raised if this cannot be done.
reset	Resets the stack to an initial state of empty.

The Ada specification of the class Stack is as follows:

```ada
package Class_stack is
  type Stack is private;              -- Copying allowed
  Stack_error: exception;             -- When error

  procedure reset( the:in out Stack);
  procedure push( the:in out Stack; item:in Integer );
  procedure pop(the:in out Stack; item :out Integer );
private
  MAX_STACK: constant := 3;
  type    Stack_index is range 0 .. MAX_STACK;
  subtype Stack_range is Stack_index range 1 .. MAX_STACK;
  type    Stack_array is array ( Stack_range ) of Integer;

  type Stack is record
    elements: Stack_array;            -- Array of elements
    tos     : Stack_index := 0;       -- Index
  end record;

end Class_stack;
```

The following simple program demonstrates the operation of a stack:

```
with Simple_io, Class_stack;
use  Simple_io, Class_stack;
procedure main is
  number_stack : Stack;              -- Stack of numbers
  action       : Character;          -- Action
  number       : Integer;            -- Number processed
begin

  while not end_of_file loop
    while not end_of_line loop
      begin
        get( action );
        case action is               -- Process action
          when '+' =>
            get( number ); push(number_stack,number);
            put("push number = "); put(number); new_line;
          when '-' =>
            pop(number_stack,number);
            put("Pop number  = "); put(number); new_line;
          when others =>
            put("Invalid action"); new_line;
        end case;
      exception
        when Stack_error =>
          put("Stack_error"); new_line;
        when Data_error  =>
          put("Not a number"); new_line;
        when End_error   =>
          put("Unexpected end of file"); new_line; exit;
      end;
    end loop;
    skip_Line;
  end loop;

  reset( number_stack );

end main;
```

12.4.1 Putting it all together

When compiled with a suitable package body the above program when run with the following data:

```
+1+2+3+4----
```

will produce the following output:

```
push number  =       1
push number  =       2
push number  =       3
Stack_error
Pop number   =       3
Pop number   =       2
Pop number   =       1
Stack_error
```

12.4.2 Implementation of the stack

The implementation of the package uses the procedure `reset` to set the stack to a defined state, in this case empty.

```
package body Class_stack is

  procedure reset( the:in out Stack ) is
  begin
    the.tos := 0;   -- Set TOS to 0 (Non existing element)
  end reset;
```

The exception `Stack_error` is raised by the procedure `push` if an attempt is made to add a new item to a full stack.

```
  procedure push( the:in out Stack; item:in Integer ) is
  begin
    if the.tos /= MAX_STACK then
      the.tos := the.tos + 1;            -- Next element
      the.elements( the.tos ) := item;   -- Move in
    else
      raise Stack_error;                 -- Failed
    end if;
  end push;
```

The procedure `pop` similarly raises the exception `Stack_error` if an attempt is made to extract an item from an empty stack.

```
  procedure pop( the:in out Stack; item :out Integer ) is
  begin
    if the.tos > 0 then
      item := the.elements( the.tos );   -- Top element
      the.tos := the.tos - 1;            -- Move down
    else
      raise Stack_error;                 -- Failed
    end if;
  end pop;

end Class_stack;
```

12.5 Self-assessment

- When should an exception be used?

- What happens when an exception is not caught in a user program?

- How can a program catch all exceptions which might be generated when executing a code sequence?

- Can a user program raise one of the system's exceptions such as `Constraint_error`?

12.6 Exercises

Construct the following class which uses exceptions:

- *Average*
  This class has the following methods:

Method	Responsibility
add	Add a new data value.
average	Deliver the average of the data values held.
reset	Reset the object to its initial state.

The exception `No_data` is raised when an attempt is made to calculate the average of zero numbers.

13 Generics

This chapter looks at generics that enable parameterized re-usable code to be written. The degree of re-useability, however, will depend on the skill and foresight of the originator.

13.1 Generic functions and procedures

The main problem in re-using code of previously written functions or procedures is that they are restricted to process specific types of values. For example, the function `order` developed as an exercise in Chapter 4 will only work for `Float` values. To be really useful to a programmer, this procedure should work for all objects for which a 'greater than' value can be defined. Ada allows the definition of generic functions or procedures. In this, the actual type(s) that are to be used are supplied by the user of the function or procedure. This is best illustrated by an example:

```
generic                              -- Specification
  type T is ( <> );                  -- Any discrete type
procedure ord_2( a,b:in out T );     -- Prototype ord_2

procedure ord_2( a,b:in out T ) is   -- Implementation ord_2
  tmp : T;                           -- Temporary
begin
  if a > b then                      -- Compare
    tmp := a; a := b; b := tmp;      --   Swap
  end if;
end ord_2;                           --
```

The declaration of a generic function or procedure is split into two components: a specification part that defines the interface to the outside world, and an implementation part that defines the physical implementation. In the specification part, the type(s) that are to be used in the procedure are specified between the **generic** and the prototype line of the function or procedure. In this example a single type T is to be supplied. The type T must be one of Ada's discrete types. The '(<>)' in the declaration '**type** T **is** (<>)' specifies this restriction. A full list of the restricted types to which a generic parameter can be constrained to are given in section 13.2.

To use this procedure the user must first instantiate a procedure that will operate on a particular type. This is accomplished by the declaration:

```
procedure order is new ord_2( Natural );   -- Instantiate
```

which defines a procedure `order` which will put into ascending order its two `Natural` parameters. It would, of course, be an error detected at compile-time to use the procedure `order` with any parameter of a type other than a `natural` or a subtype of a `natural`.

Another generic procedure can be written which will order its three parameters. This new procedure uses an instantiation of the procedure `ord_2` internally.

```
generic                               -- Specification
  type T is ( <> );                   -- Any discrete type
procedure ord_3( a,b,c:in out T );    -- Prototype ord

with ord_2;
procedure ord_3( a,b,c:in out T ) is  -- Implementation ord
  procedure order is new ord_2( T );  -- Instantiate order
begin
  order( a, b );                      -- S L -
  order( b, c );                      -- ? ? L
  order( a, b );                      -- S M L
end ord_3;                            --
```

*Note: The generic parameter T can only be a member of the discrete types. This is achieved with the declaration of the type T as '**type** T **is** (<>)'*
The procedure `order` *in the procedure* `ord_3` *is an instantiation of the generic procedure* `ord_2` *with an actual parameter of type T.*

Figure 13.1 illustrates the components of a generic procedure.

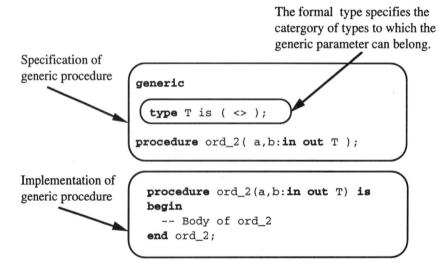

Figure 13.1 Components of a generic procedure declaration.

The above generic procedures `ord_2` and `ord_3` allow the following code to be written:

```
with Simple_io, ord_3;
use  Simple_io;
procedure main is
  procedure order is new ord_3( Natural );        -- Instantiate
  room1 : Natural := 30; -- 30 Square meters
  room2 : Natural := 25; -- 25 Square meters
  room3 : Natural := 20; -- 20 Square meters
begin
  order( room1, room2, room3 );
  put("Rooms in ascending order of size are"); new_line;
  put( room1 ); new_line;
  put( room2 ); new_line;
  put( room3 ); new_line;
end main;
```

which would produce the following results when run:

```
Rooms in ascending order of size are
        20
        25
        30
```

13.1.1   Advantages and disadvantages of generic units

Advantages   •   Facilitate re-use by allowing an implementor to write procedures or functions which process objects of a type determined by the user of the procedure or functiodn.

Disadvantages   •   Extra care must be exercised in writing the procedure or function. This will undoubtedly result in a greater cost to the originator.

•   The implementation of the generic procedure, function or package may not be as efficient as a direct implementation.

13.2 Specification of generic component

The formal type specification constrains the actual type passed as a parameter to belong to a particular category of types. Examples of these categories are listed in the table below:

Formal type specification type T	In Ada 83	Actual parameter can belong to the following types	Note
is private	✓	Any non limited type.	1
is limited private	✓	Any type.	2
is tagged	✗	Any non limited tagged type.	1
is limited tagged	✗	Any tagged type.	2
is (<>)	✓	Any discrete type, constrained type.	1,5
(<>) is private	✗	Any discrete or indefinite non limited type.	2,3
(<>) is limited private	✗	Any discrete or indefinite type.	2,3
is mod <>	✗	Any modular type.	1
is range <>	✓	Any integer type.	1
is digits <>	✓	Any float type.	1
is delta <>	✓	Any fixed ordinary type.	1
is delta <> digits <>	✗	Any fixed decimal type.	1
is access	✓	Any access type.	4
with procedure ...	✓	procedure matching the signiture.	6
with package ...	✗	package matching the signiture.	6

Note 1   *The formal parameter in the generic unit is restricted to a use compatible with the actual parameter.*

Note 2   *The formal parameter is restricted to operations which are compatible with a limited type. Thus, assignment of, and the default comparison for equality and not equality are prohibited.*

Note 3   *Cannot be used to declare an indefinite type without declaring its range. For example, the indefinite type:*
type String **is array** (Positive **range** <>) of Character;
cannot be declared without specifying the range.

Note 4   *Access types are covered in chapter 14.*
May also be **is access all** *or* **is access constant**

Note 5   *Ada 83 has the well-known problem that an indefinite type may be used as a formal parameter. If the formal parameter is used to declare an object in the body of the generic unit, then on the instantiation of the unit an error message will be generated from the body of the generic unit.*

Note 6   *Used to specify a procedure, function or package that is used in the body of the generic unit.*

13.3 Generic stack

The stack illustrated in section 12.4 can be built as a generic package. First, the specification of the package that contains the generic components is defined:

```
generic
  type T is private;              -- Can specify any type
  MAX_STACK:in Positive := 3; -- Has to be typed / not const
package Class_stack is
  type Stack is tagged private;
  Stack_error: exception;

  procedure reset( the:in out Stack);
  procedure push( the:in out Stack; item:in T );
  procedure pop( the:in out Stack; item:out T );
private

  type    Stack_index is new Integer range 0 .. MAX_STACK;
  subtype Stack_range is Stack_index
          range 1 .. Stack_index(MAX_STACK);
  type    Stack_array is array ( Stack_range ) of T;

  type Stack is tagged record
    elements: Stack_array;         -- Array of elements
    tos     : Stack_index := 0;    -- Index
  end record;

end Class_stack;
```

Note: The constant MAX_STACK must be given a type because it is passed as a generic parameter.

The implementation of the package follows the same strategy as seen in section 12.4.2 except that the constant that defines the size of the stack is now typed. The body of the package takes this into account by converting the constant object MAX_STACK into an object of type Stack_index. The body of the package is implemented as follows:

```
package body Class_stack is

  procedure push( the:in out Stack; item:in T ) is
  begin
    if the.tos /= Stack_index(MAX_STACK) then
      the.tos := the.tos + 1;             -- Next element
      the.elements( the.tos ) := item;    -- Move in
    else
      raise Stack_error;                  -- Failed
    end if;
  end push;
```

The procedure pop returns the top item on the stack.

```
procedure pop( the:in out Stack; item: out T ) is
begin
  if the.tos > 0 then
    item := the.elements( the.tos );      -- Top element
    the.tos := the.tos - 1;               -- Move down
  else
    raise Stack_error;                    -- Failed
  end if;
end pop;
```

The procedure reset resets the stack to empty.

```
procedure reset( the:in out Stack ) is
begin
  the.tos := 0;   -- Set TOS to 0 (Non existing element)
end reset;

end Class_stack;
```

A generic package cannot be used directly. An instantiation of the package must first be made for a specific type(s). For example, to instantiate an instance of the above package class_stack to provide an Integer stack, the following declaration is made:

```
with Class_stack;
  package Class_stack_int is new Class_stack(Integer);
```

Note: As the size of the stack is not specified the default value of 3 is used.

The newly created package Class_stack_int can then be used in a program.

13.3.1 Putting it all together

The new package Class_stack_int is tested by the following program unit which is identical to the code seen in section 12.4 except the **with**'ed and **used**'ed package name for the class representing the Stack.

```
with Simple_io, Class_stack_int;
use  Simple_io, Class_stack_int;
procedure main is
  number_stack : Stack;          -- Stack of numbers
  action       : Character;      -- Action
  number       : Integer;        -- Number processed
```

```
begin
  while not end_of_file loop
    while not end_of_line loop
      begin
        get( action );
        case action is                  -- Process action
          when '+' =>
            get( number ); push(number_stack,number);
            put("push number = "); put(number); new_line;
          when '-' =>
            pop(number_stack,number);
            put("Pop number  = "); put(number); new_line;
          when others =>
            put("Invalid action"); new_line;
        end case;
      exception
        when Stack_error =>
          put("Stack_error"); new_line;
        when Data_error  =>
          put("Not a number"); new_line;
        when End_error   =>
          put("Unexpected end of file"); new_line; exit;
      end;
    end loop;
    skip_Line;
  end loop;
end main;
```

When run with the following data:

```
+1+2+3+4----
```

the following results will be produced:

```
push number =          1
push number =          2
push number =          3
Stack_error
Pop number  =          3
Pop number  =          2
Pop number  =          1
Stack_error
```

13.3.2 Implementation techniques for a generic package

The implementation of a generic package is usually performed by one of the following
mechanisms:

- A new package is generated for each unique instantiation of the generic
  package. This is sometimes referred to as the macro implementation.

- A single code body is used which can cater for different formal types.

13.4 Generic formal subprograms

When specifying a generic formal type, the compiler must know how to perform operations on an instance of this type. For example, if the formal type is specified as private, then any Ada private type can be used. The implementor of the body of the generic package may wish to use instances of this type in a comparison. For example, as part of a logical expression:

```
if instance_of_generic > another_instance_of_generic then
   ...
end if;
```

For this to be allowed, the type passed must allow, in this case, for the " > " operation to be performed between instances of the generic type. To enforce this contract the specification part of the generic procedure, function or package must include a generic formal parameter for the " > " logical operation. Remember, the type passed may not have " > " defined between instances of the type. For example, the class Account does not provide any comparison operators between instances of an Account.

The following generic procedure which orders its formal parameters of type **private** is defined with a formal subprogram specification for " > ".

```
generic                                -- Specification
   type T is private;                  -- Any non limited type
   with function ">" ( a, b:in T )
        return Boolean is <>;          -- Need def for >
procedure ord_2( a,b:in out T );       -- Prototype ord_2

procedure ord_2( a,b:in out T ) is     -- Implementation ord_2
   tmp : T;
begin
   if a > b then                       -- Compare
      tmp := a; a := b; b := tmp;      -- Swap
   end if;                             
end ord_2;                             --
```

The generic formal subprogram:

```
   with function ">" ( a, b:in T )
        return Boolean is <>;          -- Specification of ">"
```

specifies that on instantiation of the package, a definition for ">" between instances of the formal parameter T must be provided. The <> part of the generic formal subprogram specifies that this formal parameter has as a default value of the current definition for ">" at the point of instantiation.

Thus, an instantiation of a procedure `order` to order two `Natural` values would be:

```
with ord_2;
  procedure order is new ord_2( Natural );
```

Note: *The default value for the function ">" is the current definition for ">" between* `Naturals` *at the point of instantiation. If the operator ">" has not been overloaded it will be the intrinsic function defined in* `Standard` *for ">".* *Naturally, if the operator ">" is not defined between instances of the formal type* *T, a compile-time error message will be generated.*

If the generic formal subprogram had been of the form:

```
with function ">" ( a, b:in T )
     return Boolean;              -- Specification of ">"
```

then the formal parameter does not have a default value and therefore an actual parameter for a function with signature **function** (a, b:**in** T) must be specified on the instantiation. In this case the instantiation of `order` would be:

```
with ord_2;
  procedure order is new ord_2( Natural, ">" );
```

Note: *If the function ">" has not been overloaded then the function used will be the intrinsic function for ">" in the package* `Standard`. *If the instantiation had been :*

```
with ord_2;
  procedure order is new ord_2( Natural, "<" );
```

Then the items would be ordered in descending order.

13.4.1 Example of the use of the generic procedure `ord_2`

A program to order the height of two people of type `Person` is as follows:

```
with Simple_io, ord_2;
use  Simple_io;
procedure main is
  MAX_CHS : constant := 6;
  type Gender    is ( FEMALE, MALE );
  type Height_cm is range 0 .. 300;
  type Person is record
    name   : String( 1 .. MAX_CHS );   -- Name as a String
    height : Height_cm := 0;           -- Height in cm.
    sex    : Gender;                   -- Gender of person
  end record;

  function ">"( f,s:in Person ) return Boolean is
  begin
    return f.height > s.height;
  end ">";

  procedure order is new ord_2( Person );   -- Instantiate
  person1 : Person := ("Mike    ", 183, MALE );
  person2 : Person := ("Corinna", 171, FEMALE );

begin
  order( person1, person2 );
  put("List of people in ascending height order are"); new_line;
  put( person1.name ); new_line;
  put( person2.name ); new_line;
end main;
```

Note: *The definition for ">" is defaulted to the overloaded definition for ">" at the point of instantiation. The instantiation could, however, have been written as:*

```
    procedure order is new ord_2( Person, ">" );
```

which when run would print:

```
List of people in ascending height order are
Corinna
Mike
```

13.4.2 Summary

The following table summarizes the effect of different subprogram specifications for a formal parameter.

Generic formal subprogram	Explanation
with function ">" (a, b:**in** T) **return** Boolean **is** <>;	Has a default value of the current definition of " > " at the point of instantiation of the generic subprogram.
with function ">" (a, b:**in** T) **return** Boolean;	Takes the value of the formal parameter " > " at the point of instantiation of the generic subprogram.
with procedure exec **is** exec;	Takes the value of the formal parameter at the point of definition of the generic subprogram.

13.5 Sorting

Some of the simplest sorting algorithms are based on the idea of a bubble sort. In an ascending order bubble sort, consecutive pairs of items are compared, and arranged if necessary into their correct ascending order. The effect of this process is to move the larger items to the end of the list. However, in a single pass through the list only the largest item not already in the correct position will be guaranteed to be moved to the correct position. The process of passing through the list exchanging consecutive items is repeated until all the items in the list are in the correct order. For example, the following list of numbers is to be sorted into ascending order:

20	10	17	18	15	11

The first pass of the bubble sort compares consecutive pairs of numbers and orders each pair into ascending order. This is illustrated in Figure 13.2 below.

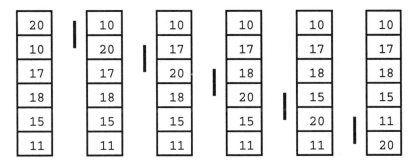

Figure 13.2 The first pass of the bubble sort.

Each pass through the list of numbers moves the larger numbers towards the end of the list and the smaller numbers towards the start of the list. However, only one additional number in the list is guaranteed to be in the correct position. The result of cumulative passes through the list of numbers is illustrated in the table below.

List of numbers	Commentary
20 10 17 18 15 11	The original list.
10 17 18 15 11 20	After the 1st pass through the list.
10 17 15 11 18 20	After the 2nd pass through the list.
10 15 11 17 18 20	After the 3rd pass through the list.
10 11 15 17 18 20	After the 4th pass through the list.

The process is repeated until there have been no swaps during a single pass through the list. Thus, after the 4th pass an additional pass through the list will be made in which no changes will occur. This indicates that the list is sorted.

13.5.1 Efficiency

This variation on the bubble sort is not a very efficient algorithm, as in the worse case it will take n passes through the list to rearrange the data into ascending order, where n is the size of the list. Each pass through the list will result in n-1 comparisons.

The big O notation is used to give an approximation of the order of an algorithm. For this modified bubble sort the order (number of comparisons) will be approximately $O(n^2)$. For a small amount of data this is not important, but if n is large then the number of comparisons will be very large, and hence the time taken to sort the data will be lengthy.

13.6 A generic procedure to sort data

A generic sort procedure using the above variation of the bubble sort algorithm has the following specification:

```
generic
   type T              is private;         -- Any non limited type
   type Vec_range is (<>);                 -- Any discrete type
   type Vec            is array( Vec_range ) of T;
   with function   ">"( first, second:in T ) return Boolean is <>;
procedure sort( items:in out Vec );
```

The generic formal parameters for the procedure `sort` are:

Formal parameter	Description
`type T is private;`	The type of data item to be sorted.
`type Vec_range is (<>);`	The type of the index to the array.
`type Vec is array( Vec_range ) of T;`	The type of the array to be sorted.
`with function ">"(first,second:in T)` `return Boolean is <>;`	A function that the user of the generic procedure provides to compare pairs of data items.

The implementation of the generic procedure is:

```
procedure sort( items:in out Vec ) is
  swaps : Boolean := TRUE;
  tmp   : T;
begin
  while swaps loop
    swaps := false;
    for i in items'First .. Vec_range'Pred(items'Last) loop
      if items( i ) > items( Vec_range'Succ(i) ) then
        swaps := TRUE;
        tmp := items( Vec_range'Succ(i) );
        items( Vec_range'Succ(i) ) := items( i );
        items( i ) := tmp;
      end if;
    end loop;
  end loop;
end sort;
```

Note: *Passes through the data are repeated until there are no more swaps.*
The use of `'Succ` delivers the next index. Remember the array might have an
index of an enumeration type, so + cannot be used.

13.6.1 Putting it all together

The following program illustrates the use of the generic procedure `sort` to sort a list of characters into ascending order.

```
with Ada.Text_io, sort;
use  Ada.Text_io;
procedure main is

  type Chs_range is range 1 .. 6;
  type Chs       is array( Chs_range ) of Character;

  procedure sort_chs is new sort (
    T          => Character,
    Vec_range  => Chs_range,
    Vec        => Chs,
    ">"        => ">" );
  some_characters : Chs := ( 'q', 'w', 'e', 'r', 't', 'y' );
```

```
begin
  sort_chs( some_characters );
  for i in Chs_range loop
    put( some_characters( i ) ); put( " " );
  end loop;
  new_line;
end main;
```

Note: The actual parameters used in the instantiation of the procedure sort_chs.

When run, this will print:

```
e q r t w y
```

13.6.2 Sorting records

A program to sort an array of records is show below. In this program each record represents a person's name and height. First, the declaration of the type Person which is:

```
with Simple_io, sort;
use  Simple_io;
procedure main is
  MAX_CHS : constant := 7;
  type Height_cm is range 0 .. 300;
  type Person is record
    name   : String( 1 .. MAX_CHS );   -- Name as a String
    height : Height_cm := 0;           -- Height in cm.
  end record;
  type People_range is (FIRST, SECOND, THIRD, FORTH );
  type People        is array( People_range ) of Person;
```

Then the declaration of two functions: the function cmp_height that returns true if the first person is taller than the second and the second function cmp_name that returns true if the first person's name collates later in the alphabet than the second.

```
function cmp_height(first, second:in Person) return Boolean is
begin
  return first.height > second.height;
end cmp_height;

function cmp_name( first, second:in Person ) return Boolean is
begin
  return first.name > second.name;
end cmp_name;
```

Two instantiations of the generic procedure `sort` are made, the first to sort people into ascending height order, the second to sort people into ascending name order.

```
procedure sort_people_height is new sort (
   T           => Person,
   Vec_range => People_range,
   Vec         => People,
   ">"         => cmp_height );

procedure sort_people_name is new sort (
   T           => Person,
   Vec_range => People_range,
   Vec         => People,
   ">"         => cmp_name );
```

The body of the program which orders the friends into ascending height and name order is:

```
friends : People := ( ("Paul    ", 146 ), ("Carol  ", 147 ),
                      ("Mike    ", 183 ), ("Corinna", 171 ) );
begin
  sort_people_name( friends );                    -- Name order
  put( "The first in ascending name order is " );
  put( friends( FIRST ).name ); new_line;
  sort_people_height( friends );                  -- Height order
  put( "The first in ascending height order is " );
  put( friends( FIRST ).name ); new_line;
end main;
```

which when run will print:

```
The first in ascending name order is Carol
The first in ascending height order is Paul
```

13.7 Generic child library

The stack seen in section 13.3 can be extended to include the additional methods of:

Method	Responsibility
top	Return the top item of the stack without removing it from the stack.
items	Return the current numbers of items in the stack.

An efficient implementation is to access the private instance attributes of the class `Stack` directly. This can be done by creating a child package of the generic package class_stack. However, as the parent class is generic, its child package must also be generic. The specification of this generic child package is as follows:

```
generic
package Class_stack.Additions is
  function top( the:in Stack ) return T;
  function items( the:in Stack ) return Natural;
private
end Class_stack.Additions;
```

Note: As the child can see the components of the parent, it can also see any generic types.

The implementation of the class is then:

```
with Simple_io; use Simple_io;
package body Class_stack.Additions is

  function top( the:in Stack ) return T is
  begin
    return the.elements( the.tos );
  end top;

  function items( the:in Stack ) return Natural is
  begin
    return Natural(the.tos);
  end items;

end Class_stack.Additions;
```

A generic child of a package is considered to be declared within the generic parent. Thus, to instantiate an instance of the parent and child the following code is used:

```
with Class_stack;
  package Class_stack_pos is new Class_stack(Positive,10);

with Class_stack_pos, Class_stack.Additions;
  package Class_stack_pos_additions is
    new Class_stack_pos.additions;
```

Note: The name of the instantiated child package is an Ada identifier.

13.7.1   Putting it all together

The following program tests the child library:

```
with Simple_io, Class_stack_pos, Class_stack_pos_additions;
use  Simple_io, Class_stack_pos, Class_stack_pos_additions;
procedure main is
  Numbers : Stack;
begin
  push( numbers, 10 );
  push( numbers, 20 );
  put("Top item "); put( top( numbers ) ); new_line;
  put("Items    "); put( items( numbers ) ); new_line;
end main;
```

which when run gives these results:

```
Top item    20
Items        2
```

13.8   Inheriting from a generic class

The class `Stack` seen in section 13.3 and its generic child seen in section 13.7 can be extended to include the additional method of:

Method	Responsibility
depth	Return the maximum depth that the stack reached.

The specification for the new class `Better_stack` is:

```
with Class_stack, Class_stack.Additions;
generic
  type T is private;
  MAX_STACK:in Positive := 3; -- Has to be typed / not const
package Class_better_stack is
  package Class_stack_t is new Class_stack(T,MAX_STACK);
  package Class_stack_t_additions is new Class_stack_t.Additions;

  type Better_stack is new Class_stack_t.Stack with private;

  procedure push( the:in out Better_stack; item:in T );
  function  max_depth( the:in Better_stack ) return Natural;
private
  type Better_stack is new Class_stack_t.Stack with record
    depth : Natural := 0;
  end record;
end Class_better_stack;
```

Note: Be aware of the instantiation of the base class Stack *and its generic child within the body of the inheriting class.*
The procedure push *is overloaded so that it can record the maximum depth reached.*

The implementation of this inherited class is:

```
package body Class_better_stack is
  procedure push( the:in out Better_stack; item:in T ) is
    d : Natural;
  begin
    d := Class_stack_t_additions.items(Class_stack_t.Stack(the));
    if d > the.depth then
      the.depth := d;
    end if;
    Class_stack_t.push( Class_stack_t.Stack(the), item );
  end push;

  function max_depth( the:in Better_stack ) return Natural is
  begin
    return the.depth;
  end max_depth;

end Class_better_stack;
```

13.8.1 Putting it all together

An instantiation of the class Better_stack for Positive numbers is created with the declaration:

```
with Class_better_stack;
  package Class_better_stack_pos is
    new Class_better_stack(Positive,10);
```

This is then used in a small test program of the new class as follows:

```
with Simple_io, Class_better_stack_pos;
use  Simple_io, Class_better_stack_pos;
procedure main is
  Numbers : Better_stack;
  res     : Positive;
begin
  put("Max depth  "); put( max_depth( numbers ) ); new_line;
  push( numbers, 10 );
  push( numbers, 20 );
  put("Max depth  "); put( max_depth( numbers ) ); new_line;
  push( numbers, 20 );
  put("Max depth  "); put( max_depth( numbers ) ); new_line;
  pop( numbers, res );
  put("Max depth  "); put( max_depth( numbers ) ); new_line;
end main;
```

which when run produces the following results:

```
Max depth   0
Max depth   2
Max depth   3
Max depth   3
```

13.9 Self-assessment

- How do generic functions and packages help in producing re-usable code?

- Why can an implementor specify the possible types that can be used as a generic parameter to their package, procedure or function?

- What mechanism(s) prevent a user supplying an inappropriate type as a generic parameter, for example, an instance of the class Account to a generic sort procedure? This would be inappropriate as the comparison operator " > " is not defined between instances of an Account.

13.10 Exercises

Construct the following procedure:

- *Sort (Better)*
  Modify the sort package so that a pass through the data does not consider items that are already in the correct order.

Construct the following classes:

- *Store*
  A store for data items which has as its generic parameters the type of the item stored and the type of the index used. The generic specification of the class is:

```
generic
  type Store_index   is private;      --
  type Store_element is private;      --
package Class_store is
  type Store is limited private;      -- NO copying
  Not_there, Full : exception;

  procedure add    ( the:in out Store;
                     index:in Store_index;
                     item:in Store_element);
  function deliver( the:in Store;
                     index:in Store_index )
                     return Store_element;
private
  --
end Class_store;
```

- *Better Store*

  By adding to the class `store`, provide a class which will give a user of the class information about how many additional items may be added before the store fills up.

14 Dynamic memory allocation

This chapter shows how storage can be allocated and de-allocated arbitrarily by a program. An undisciplined use of this facility can lead to programs that are difficult to debug and fail in unpredictable ways.

14.1 Access values

Ada allows the access value of an object to be taken. An access value is a pointer or reference to an object which can be manipulated and used to access the original object. An access value is usually implemented as the physical address of the object in memory. For example, the declaration shown below elaborates storage for an object which is to hold an integer value.

```
people   :  aliased Integer;
```

Note: In the declaration of people *the prefix* **aliased** *denotes that an access value of the object* people *may be taken. If the prefix is omitted the access value of the object may not be taken.*

The storage for people can be visualized as illustrated in Figure 14.1

people

Figure 14.1 Storage for an instance of an Integer object.

To store a value into the Integer object, a normal assignment statement is used:

```
people   := 24;
```

whilst the declaration:

```
type P_Integer is access all Integer;

p_people : P_Integer;
```

uses the access type `P_Integer` to declare an object `p_people` to hold an access value for an integer object. In the declaration of the access type `P_Integer` the keyword **all** signifies that read and write access may be made to the object described by the access value. The following code assigns to `p_people` the access value of `people`:

```
p_people := people'Access;    -- Access value for people
```

Note: The attribute `'Access` *is used which delivers from an object its access value. Access is used both as a keyword and as an attribute name.*
The attribute 'Access can only be used when the object will exist for all the lifetime of the access value. See section 14.7 for a more detailed explanation of the consequences of this requirement.

The storage for `p_people` can be visualized as illustrated in Figure 14.2

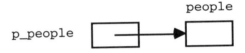

Figure 14.2 Storage for `p_people` after it has been assigned the access value of `people`.

14.1.1 Access to an object via its access value

To access an object via its access value requires the use of `.all` which de-references the access value. This may be thought of as an indirection operator. For example, the following program accesses the object `people` by using the access value for `people` stored in the object `p_people`.

```
with Simple_io;
use  Simple_io;
program main is
   type P_Integer is access all Integer;
   people   : aliased Integer;
   p_people : P_Integer;
begin
   people   := 24;
   p_people := people'Access;    -- Access value for people
   put("The number of people is : "); put( p_people.all );
   new_line;
end main;
```

Note: In the declaration of `P_integer`, ***access all*** *signifies that read and write access may be made to the object via its access value.*

which when run, would produce:

```
The number of people is :    24
```

The ideas described above have their origins in low-level assembly language programming where the address of an item may be freely taken and manipulated. Ada provides a more disciplined way of implementing these concepts.

14.1.2   Lvalues and rvalues

In working with access values it is convenient to think about the lvalue and rvalue of an object. The lvalue is the address of the object, whilst the rvalue is the contents of the object. For example, in the statement:

```
value := amount;
```

the object `amount` will deliver its contents, whilst the object `value` will deliver its address so that the rvalue of `amount` may be assigned to it. The names lvalue and rvalue are an indication of whether the object is on the left or the right hand side of an assignment statement.

In a program it is usual to deal with the contents or rvalue of an object. The access value of an object is its lvalue. For example, after the following fragment of code has been executed:

```
declare
  type P_Integer   is access all Integer;
  type P_P_Integer is access all P_Integer;
  p_p_people : P_P_Integer;
  p_people   : aliased P_Integer;
  people     : aliased Integer;
begin
  people     := 42;
  p_people   := people'Access;
  p_p_people := p_people'Access;

end;
```

the following expressions will deliver the contents of the object `people`:

Expression	Diagram
people	people 24

Expression	Diagram
p_people.**all**	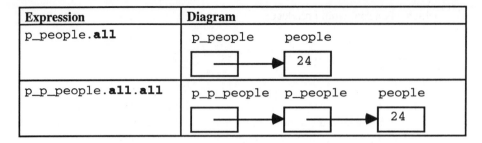
p_p_people.**all**.**all**	

In a similar way the following statements will assign 42 to the object people.

Statement	Explanation
people := 42;	Straight-forward assignment.
p_people.**all** := 42;	Single level of indirection.
p_p_people.**all**.**all** := 42;	Double level of indirection.

14.1.3 Read only access

Access to an object via an access value may be restricted to read only by replacing **all** with **constant** in the declaration of the access type. For example, in the following fragment of code, only read access is allowed to people when using the access value held in p_people.

```
declare
  type P_Integer   is access constant Integer;
  people      : aliased Integer;
  p_people    : P_Integer;
begin
  people      := 42;
  p_people    := people'Access;
  put( "Number of people is   " ); put( p_people.all );
end;
```

14.2 Dynamic allocation of storage

The process described so far has simply used existing storage; the real power of access values accrue when storage is claimed dynamically from a storage pool. In Ada terminology an allocator is used to allocate storage dynamically from a storage pool. For example, storage can be allocated dynamically by using the allocator **new** as follows:

```
declare
  MAX_CHS : constant := 6;
  type Gender    is ( FEMALE, MALE );
  type Height_cm is range 0 .. 300;
  type Person is record
     name   : String( 1 .. MAX_CHS );  -- Name as a String
     height : Height_cm := 0;          -- Height in cm.
     sex    : Gender;                  -- Gender of person
  end record;
  type P_Person is access Person;
  p_mike : P_Person;
begin
  p_mike := new Person'("Mike  ", 183, MALE);
end;
```

Note: *As the storage for a* Person *is always allocated dynamically from a specific storage pool, an access type that declares an object to hold an access value of a* Person *may be declared without the keyword* **all** *or* **constant**.

The expression:

```
new Person'("Mike  ", 183, MALE);
```

returns the lvalue of dynamically allocated storage for a person initialized with the values given in the record aggregate. This could also have been written as:

```
p_mike     := new Person;
p_mike.all := Person'("Mike  ", 183, MALE);
```

One way of managing dynamically allocated storage is to form a daisy chain of the allocated storage. The usual approach when implementing this technique is to include with the record component a value which can hold the access value of the next item in the daisy chain. The end of the chain is indicated by the value **null**. The value **null** is special as it is considered the null value for any access type. The Ada system will guarantee that no allocated access value can ever have the value **null**.

The code below forms a daisy chain of two items of storage which represent individual people.

```
declare
  MAX_CHS : constant := 7;
  type Gender    is ( FEMALE, MALE );
  type Height_cm is range 0 .. 300;
  type Person;                        -- Incomplete declaration
  type P_Person is access Person;
```

```
type Person is record
  name   : String( 1 .. MAX_CHS );   -- Name as a String
  height : Height_cm := 0;            -- Height in cm.
  sex    : Gender;                    -- Gender of person
  next   : P_Person;
  end record;
  people : P_Person;
begin
  people      := new Person'("Mike   ", 183, MALE, null );
  people.next := new Person'("Corinna", 171, FEMALE, null);

end;
```

Note: *P_Person and Person are mutually dependent upon each other as both contain a reference to each other. To fit in with the rule that all items must be declared before they can be used, Ada introduces the concept of a tentative declaration. This is used when Person is defined as 'type Person; '. The full declaration of person is defined a few lines further down.*

The resultant data structure is illustrated in Figure 14.3.

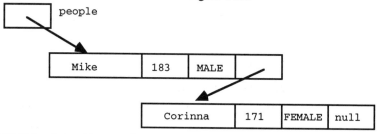

Figure 14.3 Daisy chain of two people.

In the above code the daisy chain of people could have been created with the single assignment statement:

```
people := new Person'("Mike   ", 183, MALE,
            new Person'("Corinna", 171, FEMALE, null) );
```

An iterative procedure to print the names of people represented in this chain is:

```
procedure put( crowd: in P_Person ) is
  cur : P_Person := crowd;
begin
  while cur /= null loop
    put( cur.name ); put(" is ");
    put( Integer(cur.height), width=>3 ); put("cm and is ");
    if cur.sex = FEMALE then put("female");
                        else put("male"); end if;
    new_line;
    cur := cur.next;
  end loop;
end put;
```

whilst a recursive procedure would be:

```
procedure put( cur: in P_Person ) is
begin
  if cur /= null then
    put( cur.name ); put(" is ");
    put( Integer(cur.height), width=>3 ); put("cm and is ");
    if cur.sex = FEMALE then put("female");
                       else put("male"); end if;
    new_line;
    put( cur.next );
  end if;
end put;
```

When executed:

```
declare
  people : P_Person;
begin
  people := new Person'("Mike    ", 183, MALE,
              new Person'("Corinna", 171, FEMALE, null) );
  put( people );
end;
```

either of the above procedures put would produce the following results:

```
Mike    is 183cm and is male
Corinna is 171cm and is female
```

when called to print people.

14.2.1 Problems with dynamically allocated storage

The use of dynamically allocated storage can result in errors which can be difficult to track down in a program. Some of the potential problems associated with dynamic storage allocation are tabled below:

Problem	Result
Memory leak	The storage that is allocated is not always returned to the system. For a program which executes for a long time, this can result in eventual out of memory error messages.

Problem	Result
Accidentally using the same storage twice for different data items.	This will result in corrupt data in the program and probably a crash which is difficult to understand.
Corruption of the chained data structure holding the data.	Most likely a program crash will occur some time after the corruption of the data structure.
Time taken to allocate and de-allocate storage is not always constant.	There may be unpredictable delays in a real-time system. However a worst case Figure can usually be calculated.

14.3 Returning dynamically allocated storage

In Ada there are two processes used for returning dynamically allocated storage to the system. These are:

- The Ada run-time system implicitly returns storage once the type that was used to elaborate the storage goes out of scope.

- The programmer explicitly calls the storage manager to release dynamically allocated storage which is no longer active. This returned storage is then immediately available for further allocation in the program.

The advantages and disadvantages of the two processes described above are as follows:

Process	Advantages	Disadvantages
Storage reclamation implicitly managed by the system.	No problem about de-allocating active storage.	May result in a program consuming large amounts of storage even though its actual use of storage is small. In extreme cases this may prevent a program from continuing to run.
Storage de-allocation explicitly initiated by a programmer.	Prevents inactive storage consuming program address space.	If the programmer makes an error in the de-allocation then this may be very difficult to track down.

Note: The process of explicitly returning storage to the run-time system is described in section 14.4.

As storage de-allocation can be an error-prone process, the best strategies are to either:

- Let the Ada run-time system do the de-allocation automatically for you.

or

- Hide allocation and de-allocation of storage in a class. The methods of the class can then be tested in isolation. The fully tested class can then be incorporated into a program.

14.3.1   Summary: `access all`, `access constant`, `access`

The following table summarizes the choice and restrictions that apply to the use of access values.

Note	Declaration (T is an `Integer` type)	Example of use

1	`type P_T is access all T;`
	`a_t : aliased T;`
	`a_pt: P_T;`
		`a_pt    := a_t'Access;`
		`a_pt.all := 2;`

2	`type P_T is access constant T;`
	`a_t : aliased constant T := 0;`
	`a_pt: P_T;`
		`a_pt    := a_t'Access;`
		`put( a_pt.all );`

3	`type P_T is access T;` `a_pt: P_T;`	`a_pt    := new T;` `a_pt.all := 2;`

Note 1: *Used when it is required to have both read and write access to* a_t *using the access value held in* a_pt. *The storage described by* a_t *may also be dynamically created using an allocator.*

Note 2: *Used when it is required to have only read access to* a_t *using the access value held in* a_pt. *The storage described by* a_t *may also be dynamically created using an allocator.*

Note 3: *Used when the storage for an instance of a* T *is allocated dynamically. Access to an instance of* T *can be read or written to using the access value obtained from* **new.**
*This form may only be used when an access value is created with an allocator (*new *T).*

14.4   Use of dynamic storage

The `Stack` package shown in section 13.3 could be rewritten using dynamic storage allocation. In rewriting this package, the user interface to the package has not been changed. Thus, a user of this package would not need to modify their program.

```
generic
  type Stack_element is private;          --

package Class_stack is
  type Stack is limited private;          -- NO copying
  Stack_error : exception;

  procedure push( the:in out Stack; item:in Stack_element );
  procedure pop(the:in out Stack; item :out Stack_element );
  procedure reset( the:in out Stack );
private

  type Node;                              -- Mutually recursive def
  type P_Node is access Node;             -- Pointer to a Node
  pragma Controlled( P_node );            -- We do deallocation

  type Node is record                     -- Node holds the data
    item   : Stack_element;               -- The stored item
    p_next : P_Node;                      -- Next in list
  end record;

  type Stack is record
    p_head : P_Node := null;              -- First node
  end record;
end Class_stack;
```

Note: The compiler directive **pragma** `Controlled( P_node )` *to inform the compiler that the programmer will explicitly perform the storage de-allocation for data allocated with the type* P_node.

The package body is as follows:

```
with unchecked_deallocation;
package body Class_stack is

  procedure dispose is
    new unchecked_deallocation( Node, P_Node );
```

The package `dispose` is an instantiation of the generic package `unchecked_deallocation` that returns space back to the heap. The parameters to the generic package `unchecked_deallocation` are of two types: firstly, the type of the object to be disposed, and secondly, the access type for this object.

Note: This package does little error checking. It is important not to dispose of storage which is still active.

The empty list is represented by the `p_head` containing the **null** pointer. The **null** pointer is used to indicate that currently the object `p_tos` does not point to any storage. This can be imagined as Figure 14.4:

Figure 14.4 A location containing the **null** access value or pointer.

When an item (in this case an Integer) has been added to the stack it will look like Figure 14.5.

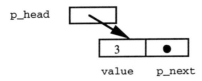

Figure 14.5 A stack containing one element.

To access the component value the . operator is used.

Note: The compiler will generate the appropriate code to reference value. In this case it will involve a de-referencing through the pointer held in p_head.

```
p_head.value = 3;
```

The function push creates a new element and chains this into a linked list of elements which hold the items pushed onto the stack.

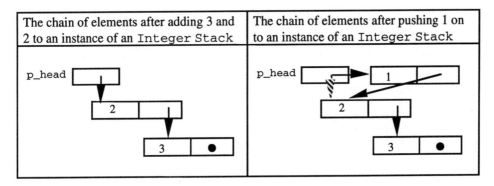

The chain of elements after adding 3 and 2 to an instance of an Integer Stack	The chain of elements after pushing 1 on to an instance of an Integer Stack

```
procedure push( the:in out Stack; item:in Stack_element ) is
   tmp : P_Node;                          -- Allocated node
begin
   tmp := new Node'(item=>item, p_next=>the.p_head);
   the.p_head := tmp;
end push;
```

Pop extracts the top item from the stack, and then releases the storage for this element back to the system.

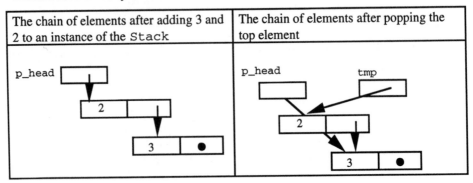

The chain of elements after adding 3 and 2 to an instance of the Stack	The chain of elements after popping the top element

```
procedure pop( the:in out Stack; item :out Stack_element ) is
   tmp : P_Node;                           -- Free node
begin
   if the.p_head /= null then              -- if item available
      tmp := the.p_head;                   -- isolate top node
      item := the.p_head.item;             -- extract item stored
      the.p_head := the.p_head.p_next;     -- Relink
      dispose( tmp );                      -- return storage
   else
      raise Stack_error;                   -- Failure
   end if;
end pop;
```

The procedure reset pops all existing elements from the stack. Remember the procedure pop releases the storage for the held item.

```
procedure reset( the:in out Stack ) is
   tmp : Stack_element;
begin
   while the.p_head /= null loop          -- Re-initialize stack
      pop( the, tmp );
   end loop;
end reset;

end Class_stack;
```

14.4.1 Putting it all together

The following code tests the implementation of the previously compiled Class_stack.

```
with Class_stack;
package Class_stack_int is new Class_stack(Integer);

with Simple_io, Class_stack_int;
use  Simple_io, Class_stack_int;
procedure main is
  number_stack : Stack;            -- Stack of numbers
  action       : Character;        -- Action
  number       : Integer;          -- Number processed
begin
  reset( number_stack );           -- Reset stack to empty
  while not end_of_file loop
    while not end_of_line loop
      begin
        get( action );
        case action is             -- Process action
          when '+' =>
            get( number ); push(number_stack,number);
            put("push number = "); put(number); new_line;
          when '-' =>
            pop(number_stack,number);
            put("Pop number = "); put(number); new_line;
          when others =>
            put("Invalid action"); new_line;
        end case;
      exception
        when Stack_error =>
          put("Pop: Exception Stack_error"); new_line;
        when Data_error  =>
          put("Not a number"); new_line;
        when End_error   =>
          put("End of file"); new_line; exit;
      end;
    end loop;
    skip_Line;
  end loop;
end main;
```

When run with the data:

```
+1+2+3+4-----
```

this will produce the following results:

```
push number = 1
push number = 2
push number = 3
push number = 4
Pop number = 4
Pop number = 3
Pop number = 2
Pop number = 1
Pop: Exception Stack_error
```

This is essentially the same driver code as used on the previous implementation of a stack. This time, however, the stack is using dynamically allocated storage.

14.5 Hiding the structure of an object (opaque type)

So far, even though a client of a class cannot access the instance attributes of an instance of the class the client can still see the type and names of the instance attributes used in the object in the specification of the class. The instance attributes in an object can be hidden by moving the data declarations to the implementation part of the class. The specification part of the class will now contain an access value to a data structure whose contents are defined in the implementation part of the class.

If the specification part of the class no longer defines how much storage is to be used then the storage for an object must be allocated dynamically. The reason for this is that the compiler will not know how much storage to allocate for an object. Remember that the implementation part may have been separately compiled. The specification part of the class defines an access value which points to the storage for the object's instance attributes. For example, the class for a bank account can now be defined as:

```
package Class_account is

  type Account is new Controlled with private;
  subtype Money is Float range 0.0 .. Float'Last;
  procedure initialize( the:in out Account );
  procedure finalize ( the:in out Account );
  procedure statement( the:in Account );
  procedure deposit   ( the:in out Account; amount:in Money );
  procedure withdraw ( the:in out Account; amount:in Money;
                       get:out Money );
  function  balance   ( the:in Account ) return Float;

private
  type Actual_account;                     -- Details In body
  type P_Actual_account is access Actual_account;
  type Account is new Controlled with record
    acc : P_Actual_account;                -- Hidden in body
  end record;
end Class_account;
```

> *Note:* *Apart from the user-defined initialization and finalization, the procedure and function specification is the same as seen in section 5.3.4*
> *The declaration for the type* Actual_account *is tentative.*
> *The base type of the class is* Controlled. *Thus, when an assignment is made to an instance of* Account, *it will be finalized.*

A benifit of the approach taken above is that a client of the class only needs to relink with any new implementation code even though the implementor of the class has changed the data in the object.

The implementation of the revised class Account is as follows:

```
package body Class_account is

  pragma Controlled( P_Actual_Account );   -- We do deallocation
  type Actual_Account is record             -- Hidden declaration
    balance_of : Float := 0.00;             -- Amount in account
  end record;
```

The code for `initialize` allocates the storage for the object automatically when an instance of the class is created. The body of `finalize` releases the storage when the object goes out of scope.

```
  procedure dispose is
    new unchecked_deallocation(Actual_account,P_Actual_account);

  procedure initialize( the:in out Account ) is
  begin
    put("Initialize"); new_line;
    the.acc := new Actual_account;        -- Allocate storage
  end initialize;

  procedure finalize ( the:in out Account ) is
  begin
    if the.acc /= null then               -- Release storage
       dispose(the.acc); the.acc:= null;  -- Note can be called
    end if;                               --   more than once
  end finalize;
```

Note: *The code for* `finalize` *may be called more than once on an object.*
The consequences of an assignment are discussed in Section 16.4.

The code for `statement`, `deposit`, `withdraw` and `deposit` are similar to the previous implementation of `Account`.

```
  procedure statement( the:in Account ) is
  begin
    put("Mini statement: The amount on deposit is £" );
    put( the.acc.balance_of, aft=>2, exp=>0 );
    new_line(2);
  end statement;

  procedure deposit ( the:in out Account; amount:in Money ) is
  begin
    the.acc.balance_of := the.acc.balance_of + amount;
  end deposit;

  procedure withdraw( the:in out Account; amount:in Money;
                      get:out Money ) is
  begin
    if the.acc.balance_of >= amount then
      the.acc.balance_of := the.acc.balance_of - amount;
      get := amount;
    else
      get := 0.00;
    end if;
  end withdraw;
```

```
function  balance( the:in Account ) return Float is
begin
   return the.acc.balance_of;
end balance;

end Class_account;
```

Note: The automatic de-referencing of the.

14.5.1   Putting it all together

The revised version of the class Account can be used in exactly the same way as previously.

```
with Ada.Text_io, Class_account;
use  Ada.Text_io, Class_account;
procedure main is
   my_account:Account;
   obtain    :Money;
begin
   statement( my_account );

   put("Deposit £100.00 into account"); new_line;
   deposit( my_account, 100.00 );
   statement( my_account );

   put("Withdraw £80.00 from account"); new_line;
   withdraw( my_account, 80.00, obtain );
   statement( my_account );

end main;
```

which when run, would produce:

```
Mini statement: The amount on deposit is £  0.00

Deposit £100.00 into account
Mini statement: The amount on deposit is £100.00

Withdraw £80.00 from account
Mini statement: The amount on deposit is £20.00
```

Note: The class Account allows the assignment of an instance of an Account. The consequences of this are that two objects will share the same storage. Section 16.4 in Chapter 16 explores this area.

14.5.2   Hidden vs. visible storage in a class

The main benefit of this approach is that a client of the class does not need to recompile their code when the storage structure of the class is changed. The client code only needs to be relinked with the new implementation code. This would usually occur when a new improved class library is provided by a software supplier. Naturally, this assumes that the interface with the library stays the same.

The pros and cons of the two approaches are:

Criteria	Hidden storage	Visible storage
Compilation efficiency	Fewer resources required, as only a recompile of the class and then a re-link need to be performed.	Greater as all units that use the class need to be recompiled.
Run-time efficiency	Greater as there is the dynamic storage allocation overhead.	No extra run-time overhead.
Client access to data components of an object.	None	None

Note: The extra cost of re-compiling and re-linking all units of a program may be marginal when compared with just re-linking.

14.6   Access value of a function

The access value of a function or procedure may also be taken. This allows a function or procedure to be passed as a parameter to another function or procedure. For example, the procedure `apply` applies the function passed as a parameter to all elements of the array. The implementation of this function is shown below:

```
type P_Fun is access function(item:in Float) return Float;
type Vector is array ( Integer range <> ) of Float;

procedure apply( f:in P_Fun; to:in out Vector ) is
begin
  for i in to'Range loop
    to(i) := f( to(i) );
  end loop;
end apply;
```

*Note: The de-referencing is done automatically when the function f is called. This could have been done explicitly with f.**all**(to(i)). This explicit de-referencing is, however, required if the called function or procedure has no parameters.*

The first parameter to the procedure `apply` can be any function which has the signature:

```
function(item:in Float) return Float;
```

Two such functions are:

```
function square( f:in Float ) return Float is
begin
  return f * f;
end square;

function cube( f:in Float ) return Float is
begin
  return f * f * f;
end cube;
```

14.6.1   Putting it all together

Using the above declarations the following program can be written:

```
procedure main is
  type P_Fun is access function(item:in Float) return Float;
  type Vector is array ( Integer range <> ) of Float;

  -- Body of the procedures apply, square and float

  procedure put( items:in Vector ) is
  begin
    for i in items'Range loop
      put( items(i), fore=>4, exp=>0, aft=>2 ); put(" ");
    end loop;
  end put;
  numbers : Vector(1..5);
begin
  numbers := (1.0, 2.0, 3.0, 4.0, 5.0);
  put("Square list :");
  apply( square'Access, numbers );
  put( numbers ); new_line;
  numbers := (1.0, 2.0, 3.0, 4.0, 5.0);
  put("cube list   :");
  apply( cube'Access, numbers );
  put( numbers ); new_line;
end main;
```

which when run, will produce the following results:

```
Square list :    1.00    4.00    9.00   16.00   25.00
cube list   :    1.00    8.00   27.00   64.00  125.00
```

Note: A program is not allowed to take the address of a predefined operator such as `Standard. "+"`. *This is to ease compiler implementation.*

14.7 Attributes **'Access** and **'Unchecked_Access**

The access value of an object may only be taken if the object is declared at the same lexical level or lower than the type declaration for the access value. If it is not, then a compile time error message will be generated when an attempt is made to take the object's access value. This is to prevent the possibility of holding an access value for an object which does not exist. For example, in the following program:

```
procedure main is
  MAX_CHS : constant := 7;
  type Height_cm is range 0 .. 300;
  type Person is record
    name   : String( 1 .. MAX_CHS );   -- Name as a String
    height : Height_cm := 0;           -- Height in cm.
  end record;
  mike   : aliased Person := Person'("Mike   ",156);
begin
  declare
    type P_Person is access all Person; -- Access type
    p_human: P_Person;
  begin
    p_human:= mike'Access;            -- OK
    declare
      clive : aliased Person := Person'("Clive   ", 171 );
    begin
      p_human := clive'Access;          -- Compile time error
    end;
    put( p_human.name ); new_line;    -- Clive no longer exists
    p_human := mike'Access;           -- Change to Mike
  end;
end main;
```

a compile time error message is generated for the line:

```
      p_human := clive'Access;          -- Compile time error
```

as the object clive does not exist for all the scope of the type P_Person. In fact, there is a serious error in the program, as when the line:

```
  put( p_human.name ); new_line;      -- Clive no longer exists
```

is executed, the storage that p_human points to does not exist. Remember the scope of clive is the **declare** block.

In some circumstances the access value of an object declared in an inner block to the access type declaration is required. If this is so, then the compiler checking can be subverted or overridden by the use of 'Unchecked_Access. Thus, the following code can be written:

```
procedure main is
  -- Declaration of Person, P_Person etc.
begin
  p_human:= mike'Access;                 -- OK
  declare
    clive : aliased Person := Person'("Clive  ", 171 );
  begin
    p_human := clive'Unchecked_Access;
    put( p_human.name ); new_line;     -- Clive
  end;
  p_human := mike'Acess;                 -- Change to Mike
  put( p_human.name ); new_line;       -- Mike
end main;
```

Of course the compiler can no longer help the programmer in detecting possible inconstancies.

14.8 Self-assessment

- What is an access type? What is an access value?

- How is dynamic storage allocated?

- What mechanisms are available to return dynamically allocated storage?

- Why is dynamic storage allocation often considered a potential problem area in a program?

- How do you pass a procedure as a parameter to another procedure?

- Why is it essential to be able to call the procedure Finalize in the class Account more than once on the same object?

- What is the difference between 'Access and 'Unchecked_Access?

14.9 Exercises

Construct the following:

- *Store*

  A store for data items which has as its generic parameters the type of the item stored and the type of the index used. The generic specification of the class is:

```
generic
  type Store_index   is private;        --
  type Store_element is private;        --
package Class_store is
  type Store is limited private;        -- NO copying
  Not_there, Full : exception;

  procedure add    ( the:in out Store;
                     index:in Store_index;
                     item:in Store_element);
  function deliver( the:in Store;
                    index:in Store_index )
                    return Store_element;
private
  --
end Class_store;
```

The implementation of the store uses a linked structure.

- *Queue*

  The class Queue implements a data structure in which items are added to the rear of the queue and extracted from the front. Implement this generic class using dynamic storage allocation.

15 Polymorphism

In the processes described so far, when a message is sent to an object, the method executed has been determinable at compile-time. This is referred to as static binding. If the type of an object that a message is sent to is not known until run-time, the binding between the method and the message is dynamic. Dynamic binding leads to polymorphism, which is when a message sent to an object causes the execution of a method that is dependent on the type of the object.

15.1 Rooms in a building

A partial classification of the different types of accommodation found in an office building is shown in Figure 15.1.

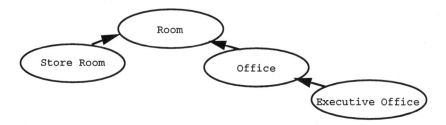

Figure 15.1 Partial classification of types of accommodation in a building.

The type of accommodation in each part of the building can be modelled using the Ada inheritance mechanism. First, a class Room to describe a general room is created. This class is then used as the base class for a series of derived classes that represent more specialized types of room. For example, an executive office is a more luxurious office, perhaps with wall-to-wall carpets and an outside view.

Each class derived from the class Room, including Room, has a function describe which returns a description of the accommodation.

A program is able to send the message describe to an instance of any type of accommodation and have the appropriate code executed. This is accomplished with function name overloading.

Figure 15.2 illustrates the call of a function describe on an instance of a class derived from Room.

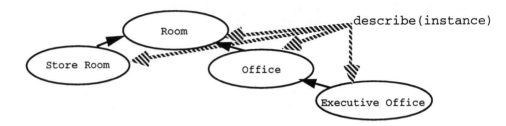

Figure 15.2 Call of describe on any instance of an object derived from Room.

15.1.1 Dynamic binding

Ada introduces the concept of a class-wide type to describe a tagged type and any type derived from the tagged type. The class-wide type is treated as an unconstrained type and is written T'Class, where T is a tagged type. For example, using the above hierarchy of types:

Class wide type	Can describe an instance of the following types
Room'Class	Room, Office, Executive_office or Store_room
Office'Class	Office or Executive_office
Executive_office'Class	Executive_office
Store_room'Class	Store_room

Note: This is a departure from Ada's normal strict type checking, as any derived type of T can be implicitly converted to T'Class.
A class-wide type T'Class is considered to be an unconstrained type which must be initialized and is then only allowed to hold instances of the initialization type.

When a message such as describe is sent to an object of the class-wide type Room'Class the compiler does not know at compile-time which method to execute. The decision as to which method to execute must be determined at run-time by inspecting the object's tag. An object's tag describes its type. The mechanism of dynamic binding between an object and the message sent to it is referred to in Ada terminology as a run-time dispatch.

The object's tag can be explicitly examined using the attribute 'Tag. For example:

```
if w422'Tag = w414'Tag then
  put("Areas are the same type of accommodation");
  new_line;
end if;
```

15.2 A program to maintain details about a building

A program that maintains details about a building stores individual details about rooms and offices. The details stored about a room include a description of its location. For an office, the details stored are all those for a room, plus the number of people who will occupy the room. The program will be required to give details about the individual areas in the building that may be a room or an office.

The responsibilities of a Room are as follows:

Method	Responsibility
initialize	Store a description of the room.
describe	Deliver a string containing a description of the room.
where	Deliver the room's number.

This can be implemented as an Ada class specification as follows:

```
with B_String; use B_String;
package Class_room is
  type Room    is tagged private;

  procedure initialize( the:in out Room; no:in Positive;
                          mes:in String );
  function  where( the:in Room ) return Positive;
  function  describe( the:in Room ) return String;
private
  type Room is tagged record
     desc  : Bounded_string;       -- Description of room
     number: Positive;             -- Room number
  end record;
end Class_room;
```

Note: The package `B_string` *is an instantiation of the package* `Ada.Strings.Bounded.` *For example:*

```
with Ada.Strings.Bounded; use Ada.Strings.Bounded;
  package B_String is
    new Generic_Bounded_Length( 80 );
```

The implementation of the class is:

```
with Simple_io; use  Simple_io;
package body Class_room is

  procedure initialize( the:in out Room;
                          no:in Positive; mes:in String ) is
  begin
    the.desc := to_bounded_string( mes );
    the.number := no;
  end initialize;
```

```
function  where( the:in Room ) return Positive is
begin
  return the.number;
end where;

function  describe( the:in Room ) return String is
  num : String( 1 .. 4 );     -- Room number as string
begin
  put( num, the.number );
  return num & " " & to_string(the.desc);
end describe;

end Class_room;
```

The responsibilities of an Office are those of the Room plus:

Method	Responsibility
initialize	Store a description of the office plus the number of occupants
describe	Returns a String describing an office.
no_of_people	Return the number of people who occupy the room.

The specification for a class Office extends the specification for a class Room as follows:

```
with Class_room; use  Class_room;
package Class_office is
  type Office is new Room with private;

  procedure initialize( the:in out Office; no:in Positive;
                        desc:in String; people:in Natural );
  function no_of_people(the:in Office) return Natural;
  function  describe( the:in Office ) return String;
private
  type Office is new Room with record
    people : Natural := 0;              -- Occupants
  end record;
end Class_office;
```

In the implementation of the class Office the procedure initialize calls the inherited initialize from class Room to store the description of the office. Remember the storage for the description in class Room is inaccessible to the class Office.

```
package body Class_office is

  procedure initialize( the:in out Office; no:in Positive;
                        desc:in String; people:in Natural ) is
  begin
    initialize( the, no, desc );
    the.people := people;
  end initialize;
```

The function `deliver_no_of_people` returns the number of people who occupy the office.

```
function no_of_people( the:in Office ) return Natural is
begin
   return the.people;
end deliver_no_of_people;
```

The function `describe` is overloaded with a new meaning. In the implementation of the method `describe`, a call is made to the method `describe` in the class Room. To call the function `describe` in the class Room, the function is passed an instance of Office viewed as a Room. This is referred to as a view conversion - the view changes, not the object. If this had not been done, a recursive call to `describe` in the class Office would have been made.

```
function  describe( the:in Office ) return String is
   no : String( 1 .. 4 );     -- As string
begin
   put(  no, the.people );
   return describe( Room(the) ) &
          " occupied by" & no & " people";
end describe;

end Class_office;
```

15.2.1 Putting it all together

The above classes can be combined into a program which prints details about various rooms or offices in a building. The program is as follows:

```
with Ada.Text_io, Class_room, Class_Office;
use  Ada.Text_io, Class_room, Class_Office;
procedure main is
   w422 : Room;
   w414 : Office;
```

The procedure `about` can take either an instance of a Room or an Office as a parameter. This is achieved by describing the parameter as Room'Class. The parameter of type Room'Class will match an instance of Room plus an instance of any type which is derived directly or indirectly from a Room. The call to the function `describe( place )` is not resolvable at compile-time, as the object place may be either a Room or an Office. At run-time when the type of place is known to the system, this call can be resolved. Thus, either `describe` in the class Room or `describe` in the class Office will be called.

```
procedure about( place:in Room'Class ) is
begin
  put( "The place is" ); new_line;
  put( "  " & describe( place ) ) ;   -- Run-time dispatch
  new_line;
end about;
```

Note: One way to implement the dynamic binding is for the object to contain information about which function describe *is to be called. This information can then be interrogated at run-time to allow the appropriate version of the function* describe *to be executed. By careful optimization, the overhead of dynamic binding can be limited to a few machine cycles.*

The body of the test program main is:

```
begin
  initialize( w414, 414, "4th Floor west wing", 2 );
  initialize( w422, 422, "4th Floor east wing" );

  about( w422 );                    -- Call with a room
  about( w414 );                    -- Call with an Office
end main;
```

Note: The call to about *with an instance of a* Room *and an* Office *is possible because the type of the formal parameter is* Room'Class.

When run, this program will produce the following output:

```
The place is
   1 4th Floor east wing
The place is
   2 4th Floor west wing occupied by   2 people
```

15.3 Run-time dispatch

For run-time dispatching to take place:

- The function or procedure must have a tagged type as a formal parameter.
- In the call of the function or procedure the actual parameter corresponding to the tagged type must be an instance of a class-wide type.

For example, the call to the function describe(place) in the procedure about will be a dispatching call.

If the actual class-wide type can represent two or more different typed objects which have procedures or functions with the same parameters, except the parameter for the class type, then polymorphism can take place. For example, in class Room and class Office, the function describe has the same signature except for the parameter with the class type.

In class Room	**function** describe(the:**in** Room) **return** String;
In class Office	**function** describe(the:**in** Office) **return** String;

The signatures of the functions and procedures in the class Room and the class Office are:

In class **Room**	In class **Office**
initialize(Room,String)	initialize(Office,String)
describe(Room) -> String	describe(Office) -> String
	no_of_people(Room) -> Integer
	initialize(Office,String,Natural)

Note: The function initialize(Office,String) *in class* Office *is inherited from the class Room.*

15.4 Heterogeneous collections of objects

The real benefits of polymorphism accrue when a heterogeneous collection of related items is created. For example, a program which maintains details about accommodation in a building could use an array to hold objects which represent the different types of accommodation. Unfortunately, this technique cannot be implemented directly in Ada, as the size of individual members of the collection may vary. The solution in Ada is to use an array of pointers to the different kinds of object which represent the accommodation. In Ada, a pointer is referred to as an access value. An access value is usually implemented as the physical address in memory of the referenced object. An array of access values to objects of type Room and Office is illustrated in Figure 15.3.

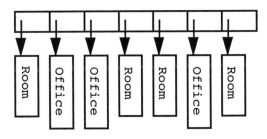

Figure 15.3 Heterogeneous collection of Rooms and Offices.

15.4.1 An array as a heterogeneous collection

A heterogeneous collection of different types of accommodation can be modelled in an array. The array will contain for each type of accommodation a pointer to either an instance of a Room or an instance of an Office. For example:

```
type P_Room      is access all Room'Class;
type Rooms_array is array ( 1 .. 15 ) of P_Room;
```

Note: P_Room is an access type which can declare an object which can hold the access value for a Room or any type derived from a Room.
The keyword null is a predefined value to indicate that the object contains no access value.

The heterogeneous collection is then built using an array of P_Room. The object's access value is used when entering a description of the accommodation into the heterogeneous array. For example, to enter details about room 414 into the heterogeneous array, the following code can be used.

```
declare
   p              : P_Room;
   accommodation: Rooms_array;
begin
   p := new Room;
   initialize( p.all, 422, "4th Floor east wing" );
   accommodation(1) := p;
end;
```

This inelegant code sequence is required as the instance attributes of the class Room are hidden and hence the construct:

```
accommodation(1) := new Office( 414, "4th Floor west wing" ,2 );
```

cannot be used.

15.4.2 Additions to the class Office and Room

To simplify later code, the classes Room and Office are extended to include additional methods to return an access value to an initialized object. These additional methods are:

Method	Responsibility
build_room	Deliver an access value to a dynamically created Room.
build_office	Deliver an access value to a dynamically created Office.

A child package is used to implement this extension to the classes. The specification for the child package of Room is:

```
package Class_room.build is
  type P_Room is access all Room'Class;

  function  build_room( no:in Positive;
                        desc:in String ) return P_Room;
end Class_room.build;
```

whilst its implementation is:

```
package body Class_room.build is
  function  build_room( no:in Positive;
                        desc:in String ) return P_Room is
    p : P_Room;
  begin
    p := new Room; initialize( p.all, no, desc );
    return p;
  end build_room;
end Class_room.build;
```

The specification for the child package of Office is:

```
with Class_room, Class_room.build;
use  Class_room, Class_room.build;
package Class_office.build is

  function  build_office( no:in Positive; desc:in String;
                          people:in Natural ) return P_Room;
end Class_office.build;
```

The implementation of the package is:

```
package body Class_office.build is

  type P_Office is access all Office;

  function  build_office( no:in Positive; desc:in String;
                          people:in Natural ) return P_Room is
    p : P_Office;
  begin
    p := new Office; initialize( p.all, no, desc, people );
    return p.all'Access;
  end build_office;

end Class_office.build;
```

Note: The function build_office *returns an access value to a Room.*

15.5 A building information program

A class `Building`, which is used as a container to store and retrieve details about the accommodation in a building, has the following responsibilities:

Method	Responsibility
add	Add a description of a room
about	Return a description of a specific room

The Ada specification for the class `Building` is:

```
with Class_room, Class_room.build;
use  Class_room, Class_room.build;
use  Ada.Text_io, Class_room, Class_room.build;
package Class_building is

  type Building is tagged private;

  procedure add( the:in out Building; desc:in P_Room );
  function about(the:in Building; no:in Positive) return String;

private
  MAX_ROOMS : constant := 15;
  type    Rooms_index is range 0 .. MAX_ROOMS;
  subtype Rooms_range is Rooms_index range 1 .. MAX_ROOMS;
  type    Rooms_array is array (Rooms_range) of P_Room;

  type Building is tagged record
    last        : Rooms_index := 0;   -- Last slot allocated
    description : Rooms_array;         -- Rooms in building
  end record;
end Class_building;
```

The procedure `add` adds new data to the next available position in the array.

```
package body Class_building is

  procedure add( the:in out Building; desc:in P_Room ) is
  begin
    if the.last < MAX_ROOMS then
      the.last := the.last + 1;
      the.description( the.last ) := desc;
    else
      raise Constraint_error;
    end if;
  end add;
```

Note: The exception constraint error is raised if there is no more free space in the array.

The function about uses a linear search to find the selected room number. If the room number does not exist, the returned string contains the text "Sorry room not known".

```
function about(the:in Building; no:in Positive) return String is
begin
   for i in 1 .. the.last loop
     if where(the.description(i).all) = no then
        return describe(the.description(i).all);
     end if;
   end loop;
   return "Sorry room not known";
end about;
end Class_building;
```

Note: Chapter 16 explores more sophisticated container implementations.
The appending of .all to an access value causes the object described by the access value to be delivered.

15.5.1   Putting it all together

The classes Room, Office and Building can be used to build a program to allow visitors to a building to find out details about individual rooms. The program is split into two procedures. The first procedure declares and sets up details about individual rooms in the building.

```
with Simple_io, Class_room, Class_Office, class_building,
                Class_room.build, Class_Office.build;
with Simple_io, Class_room, Class_Office, class_building,
                Class_room.build, Class_Office.build;
procedure set_up( watts:in out Building ) is
begin
   add( watts, build_office( 414, "4th Floor west wing", 2 ) );
   add( watts, build_room  ( 422, "4th Floor east wing" ) );
end set_up;
```

The second procedure interrogates the object watts to find details about individual rooms.

```
with Simple_io, Class_building, set_up;
use  Simple_io, Class_building;
procedure main is
   watts    : Building;              -- Watts Building
   room_no : Positive;               -- Queried room
begin
```

```
    set_up( watts );                        -- Populate building
  loop
    begin
      put( "Inquiry about room: " );        -- Ask
      exit when end_of_file;
      get( room_no ); skip_line;            -- User response
      put( about( watts, room_no ) );
      new_line;                             -- Display answer
    exception
      when Data_error =>
        put("Please retype the number");    -- Ask again
        new_line; skip_line;
    end;
  end loop;
end main;
```

Note: The program does not release the storage for the descriptions of the individual rooms and offices.

An example interaction using the program would be as follows:

```
Inquiry about room: 414
1 4th Floor west wing occupied by   2 people
Inquiry about room: 422
2 4th Floor east wing
Inquiry about room: 999
Sorry room not known
^D
```

*Note: The user's input is indicated by **bold** type.*

15.6 Program maintenance and polymorphism

To modify the above program so that details about executive offices in the building are also displayed would involve the following changes:

- The creation of a new derived class `Executive_office`.

- The modification of the procedure `set_up` so that details of the executive offices in the building are added to the collection object `watts`.

No other components of the program would need to be changed. In carrying out these modifications, the following points are evident:

- Changes are localized to specific parts of the program.

- The modifier of the program does not have to understand all the details of the program to carry out maintenance.

- Maintenance will be easier.

Thus, if a program using polymorphism is carefully designed, there can be considerable cost saving when the program is maintained/updated.

15.7 Downcasting

Downcasting is the conversion of an instance of a base class to an instance of a derived class. This conversion is normally impossible as extra information needs to be added to the base type object to allow it to be turned into an instance of a derived type. However, in a program it is possible to describe the access value of an instance of a derived type as the access value of the base type. This will usually occur when a heterogeneous collection is created. The data members of a heterogeneous collection, though consisting of many different types, are each defined as an access value of the base type of the collection.

The conversion from a base type to a derived type must, of course be possible. For example, the following code copies the offices in the heterogeneous array `accommodation` into the array `offices`.

```
with Simple_io, Class_room, Class_Office,
             Class_room.build, Class_Office.build;
with Simple_io, Class_room, Class_Office,
             Class_room.build, Class_Office.build;
procedure main is
  MAX_ROOMS : constant := 3;
  type     Rooms_index  is range 0 .. MAX_ROOMS;
  subtype Rooms_range  is Rooms_index range 1 .. MAX_ROOMS;
  type     Rooms_array  is array ( Rooms_range ) of P_Room;
  type     Office_array is array ( Rooms_range ) of Office;
  accommodation : Rooms_array;     -- Rooms and Offices
  offices       : Office_array;    -- Offices only
  no_offices    : Rooms_index;
begin
  accommodation(1):=build_office(414, "4th Floor west wing", 2);
  accommodation(2):=build_room   (518, "5th Floor east wing");
  accommodation(3):=build_office(403, "4th Floor east wing", 1);

  no_offices := 0;
  for i in Rooms_range loop
    if accommodation(i).all'Tag = Office'Tag then
      no_offices := no_offices + 1;
      offices(no_offices) := Office(accommodation(i).all);  --
    end if;
  end loop;

  put("The offices are:" ); new_line;
  for i in 1 .. no_offices loop
    put( describe( offices(i) ) ); new_line;
  end loop;
end main;
```

Note: The use of 'Tag to allow the selection of objects of type `Office`.

This when run, will give the following results:

```
The offices are:
 414 4th Floor west wing occupied by    2 people
 403 4th Floor east wing occupied by    1 people
```

15.7.1 Converting a base class to a derived class

It is possible to convert a base class to a derived class by adding the extra data attributes to an instance of the base class. However, for this to be performed the programmer must have access to the base class components. The implication of this is that the encapsulation of the base class has been broken. In the example below, an instance of `Account` is converted to an instance of an `Account_ltd`.

```
procedure main is
  WITHDRAWALS_IN_A_WEEK : constant Natural := 3;
  subtype Money     is Float;
  type Account      is tagged record
    balance_of : Money := 0.00;        -- Amount in account
  end record;
  type Account_ltd is new Account with record
    withdrawals : Natural := WITHDRAWALS_IN_A_WEEK;
  end record;
  normal     : Account;
  restricted : Account_ltd;
begin
  normal     := ( balance_of => 20.0 );
  restricted := ( normal with 4 );
end main;
```

Note: **with** *ts used to extend* `normal`, *an instance of an* `Account`, *into* `restricted`, *an instance of an* `Account_ltd`.
The components may be named:
`restricted := ( normal with withdrawals => 4 );`
If there are no additional components, **with null record** *is used to form the extension.*

15.8 Self-assessment

- What is the difference between static and dynamic binding?

- What is an object's tag?

- What is a heterogeneous collection of objects? How are heterogeneous collections of objects created and used in Ada?

- What is a view conversion? Why are view conversions required?

- How does the use of polymorphism help in simplifying program maintenance?

- Can you convert a derived class to a base class? Can you convert a base class to a derived class? Are these conversions safe? Explain your answer.

15.9 Exercises

Construct the following:

- The class `Executive_office` which will extend a normal office by including biographical details about the occupants. For example, "Ms C Lord, Programming manager".

- A new information program for a building which will include details about rooms, offices and executive offices. You should try and re-use as much code as possible.

- A program to record transactions made on different types of bank account. For example, the program should be able to deal with at least the following types of account:

  - A deposit account on which interest is paid.

  - An account on which no interest is paid and the user is not allowed to be overdrawn.

16 Containers

This chapter describes the implementation and use of container objects. A container object is a store for objects created in a program. The container will allow a programmer a greater flexibility in storing data items than Ada's array construct.

16.1 List object

A list is a container on which the following operations may be performed:

- Insert a new object into the list at any point.
- Delete an existing object from the list.
- Iterate through the objects held in the list in either a forward or reverse direction.

Note: The number of items held in the list is dependent purely on available storage.

The list object is based on pointer semantics. A 'pointer' is used in this context as an iterator which steps through the elements of the list. For example, a list of three integers and an iterator on the list is illustrated in Figure 16.1.

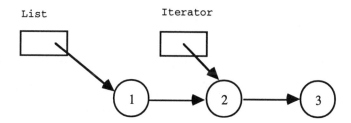

Figure 16.1 A list and its iterator.

Figure 16.2 shows the same list after inserting 99 before the current position of the iterator.

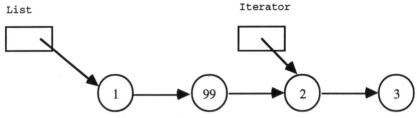

Figure 16.2 After inserting 99 into the container.

Using the iterator, items may be inserted into or deleted from the list. For example, a list object to hold the first 10 Natural numbers can be declared and filled as follows:

```
with Class_list;
  package Class_list_nat is new Class_list(Natural);

with Class_list_nat, Class_list.Iterator;
  package Class_list_nat_iterator is new Class_list_nat.Iterator;

with Simple_io, Class_list_nat, Class_list_nat_iterator;
use  Simple_io, Class_list_nat, Class_list_nat_iterator;
  numbers: List;                      -- List of numbers
  num_it : List_iter;                 --  Iterator
begin
  first( numbers_it, numbers );              -- Initialize
  for number in 1 .. 10 loop
    insert( numbers_it, number );            -- Insert before
    next( numbers_it );                      -- Next item
  end loop;

end main;
```

Note: When an instance of this list is created there is no need to specify the number of items that will be held in the list.

The list numbers has an iterator num_it which is set initially to point to the first element of the list by:

```
first( num_it, numbers );
```

Numbers are then inserted before the current iterator position using the procedure:

```
insert( num_it, number );              -- Insert before
```

The iterator `num_it` is then moved past the inserted number to the end of the list using the procedure:

```
next( num_it );                        -- After last item
```

This mirrors closely the mechanism used to declare and access an array in Ada. The list is implemented as a generic class `list` and its generic child `Iterator`. The two classes allow the elaboration of:

- The object `numbers` which is the list of natural numbers.
- The object `num_it`, an iterator which is used to step through the objects held in the list.

16.1.1   List vs. array

Criteria	List	Array
The number of items held can be increased at run-time.	✓	✗
Deletion of an item leaves no gap when the items are iterated through.	✓	✗
Random access is very efficient.	✗	✓

Note: Ada array's bounds are fixed once the declaration is elaborated.

16.2   Methods implemented in a list

The methods that are implemented in an instance of the class `list` are as follows:

Method	Responsibility
`initialize`	Initialize the container.
`finalize`	Finish using the container object.
`adjust`	Used to facilitate a deep copy.
`=`	Comparison of a list for equality.

Note: A full explanation of `adjust` can be found in section 16.3.

Whilst the methods that are implemented in an instance of the class `list_iter` are:

Method	Responsibility
`initialize`	Initialize the iterator.
`finalize`	Finish using the iterator object.

Method	Responsibility
`deliver`	Deliver the object held at the position indicated by the iterator.
`first`	Set the current position of the iterator to the first object in the list.
`last`	Set the current position of the iterator to the last object in the list.
`insert`	Insert into the list an object before the current position of the iterator.
`delete`	Remove and dispose of the object in the list which is specified by the current position of the iterator.
`is_end`	Deliver true if the iteration on the container has reached the end.
`next`	Move to the next item in the container and make that the current position.
`prev`	Move to the previous item in the container and make that the current position.

16.2.1 Example of use

The following program illustrates the use of a list. In this program natural numbers are read and inserted in ascending order into a list. The contents of the list are then printed.

The strategy used for inserting numbers in ascending order into the list starts by finding the position of the first element in the list that has a value greater than the number to be added. The new number is then inserted into the list before this number. Remember, insertions are always done before the current item.

```
with Class_list;
  package Class_list_nat is new Class_list( Natural );

with Simple_io, Class_list_nat;
use  Simple_io, Class_list_nat;
procedure main is
  numbers: List;                      -- List of numbers
  num_it : List_iter;                 --  Iterator
  num,in_list: Natural;
begin
  first( num_it, numbers );

  while not end_of_file loop          -- Data available
    while not end_of_line loop
      get(num); first(num_it,numbers); -- Read number
      while not is_end( num_it ) loop  -- Scan through list
          in_list := deliver(num_it);
          exit when in_list > num;     -- Exit when larger no.
          next( num_it );              -- Next item
      end loop;
      insert( num_it, num );           -- Before larger no.
    end loop;
    skip_line;                         -- Next line
  end loop;
```

The list is printed out by the following code:

```
put("Numbers sorted are: ");
first(num_it,numbers);              -- Set at start
while not is_end( num_it ) loop
  in_list := deliver( num_it );     -- Current number
  put( in_list,width=>1 ); put(" "); --  Print
  next( num_it );                   -- Next number
end loop;
new_line;
end main;
```

When run with the following data:

```
1 8  6  2  4
```

this would produce:

```
Numbers sorted are:      2      4      6      8      10
```

16.3 Specification and implementation of the list container

The specification of the container list is split between a parent package `Class_list` which contains details of the container and a child package `Class_list.Iterator` which contains details of the iterator. The specification for the container is:

```
with Ada.Finalization, Unchecked_deallocation;
use  Ada.Finalization;
generic
  type T is private;                -- Any type
package Class_list is
  type List is new Controlled with private;

  procedure initialize( the:in out List );
  procedure initialize( the:in out List; data:in T );
  procedure finalize( the:in out List );
  procedure adjust( the:in out List );
  function "="  ( f:in List; s:in List ) return Boolean;
private
  procedure release_storage( the:in out List );

  type Node;                        -- Tentative declaration
  type P_Node is access all Node;   -- Pointer to Node

  type Node is record
    prev    : P_Node;               -- Previous Node
    item    : T;                    -- The physical item
    next    : P_Node;               -- Next Node
  end record;
```

```
   procedure dispose_node is
     new unchecked_deallocation( Node, P_Node );
   type List is new Controlled with record
     first_node : aliased P_Node := null;   -- First item in list
     last_node  : aliased P_Node := null;   -- First item in list
   end record;

end Class_list;
```

The implementation of the List container object uses a linked list to hold the data items. This data structure will allow for a possibly unlimited number of data items to be added as well as the ability to add or remove items from any point in the list. When an instance of the container colour holds three items (Red, Green, Blue) the data structure representing the data would be as shown in Figure 16.3.

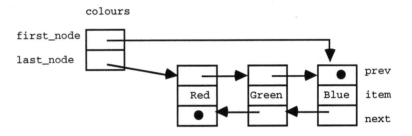

Figure 16.3 Object colour holding the three colours Red,Green and Blue.

Note: The object colours holds a pointer to the root of the linked list.
Adding items to the list is performed by the iterator.

The implementation of the class list is shown below. In the implementation, the procedure initialize sets up either an empty list or a list of one item. The first version of initialize will be automatically called whenever an instance of List is elaborated. Remember List is a controlled type.

```
package body Class_list is

  procedure initialize( the:in out List ) is
  begin
    the.first_node := null;   -- Empty list
    the.last_node  := null;   -- Empty list
  end initialize;

  procedure initialize( the:in out List; data:in T ) is
  begin
    the.first_node := new Node'(null, data, null);
    the.last_node  := the.first_node;
  end initialize;
```

The procedure finalize, which is called when an instance of List goes out of scope, releases any storage used in holding objects in the list. This process is decomposed into the procedure release_storage which performs the actual return of the storage as it iterates along the linked list.

```
procedure finalize( the:in out List ) is
begin
  if the.first_node /= null then
    release_storage( the );
    the.first_node := null;
  end if;
end finalize;

procedure release_storage( the:in out List ) is
  cur : P_Node := the.first_node;  -- Pointer to curr node
  tmp : P_Node;                    -- Node to dispose
begin
  while cur /= null loop           -- For each item in list
    tmp := cur;                    -- Item to dispose
    cur := cur.next;               -- Next node
    dispose_node( tmp );           -- Dispose of item
  end loop;
end release_storage;
```

When an instance of list is assigned, only the direct storage contained in the **record** list will be copied. This will not physically duplicate the list, only the pointers to the list. When a controlled object is assigned, the procedure adjust is called after the assignment has been made. The procedure adjust is used to perform any additional actions required on an assignment. The exact effect of assigning a controlled object is as follows:

Assignment of controlled objects	Actions that take place

a := b;	anon := b;
	  adjust(anon);
	  finalize(a);
	a := anon;
	  adjust(a);
	  finalize(anon);

Action on assignment	Commentary
anon := b	Make a temporary anonymous copy anon.
adjust(anon);	Adjustments required to be made after copying the direct storage of the source object b to anon.
finalize(a);	Finalize the target of the assignment.
a := anon;	Perform the physical assignment of the direct components of the anon object.
adjust(a);	Adjustments required to be made after copying the direct storage of the anon object.
finalize(anon);	Finalize the anonymous object anon.

Note: *If the object's storage does not overlap, which will be the usual case, then the*
compiler may implement the following optimization:

    `finalize(a); a := b; adjust(a);`

Look at the effect of the assignment `a := a;` *to see why this optimization may*
not be performed when the object's storage overlaps.

If the source and target are the same, then the operation may be skipped.

The procedure `adjust` is used to create a new copy of the storage for the list by
duplicating the nodes in the list. When this new copy of the storage for the list has been
created, the target for `adjust` is updated to point to it.

```
procedure adjust( the:in out List ) is
  cur : P_Node := the.first_node;   -- Original list
  lst : P_Node := null;             -- Last created node
  prv : P_Node := null;             -- Previously created node
  fst : P_Node := null;             -- The first node

begin
  while cur /= null loop
    lst := new Node'( prv, cur.item, null );
    if fst = null then fst := lst; end if;
    if prv /= null then prv.next := lst; end if;
    prv := lst;
    cur := cur.next;                -- Next node
  end loop;
  the.first_node := fst;            -- Update
  the.last_node  := lst;
end adjust;
```

When comparing two lists, the physical storage of the list needs to be compared,
rather than the access values which point to the storage for the list. Remember, two lists
may be equal yet contain different physical lists.

```
function "="  ( f:in List; s:in List ) return Boolean is
  f_node : P_Node := f.first_node;  -- First list
  s_node : P_Node := s.first_node;  -- Second list
begin
  while f_node /= null and s_node /= null loop
    if f_node.item /= s_node.item then
      return FALSE;                 -- Different items
    end if;
    f_node := f_node.next; s_node := s_node.next;
  end loop;
  return f_node = s_node;           -- Both null if equal
end "=";
```

Note: *When = is overloaded, /= is also overloaded with the definition of **not** =.*
This is true for = which returns a Boolean value.

16.3.1 The list iterator

The specification for the iterator, which is implemented as a child package of the package Class_list, is:

```
generic
package Class_list.Iterator is

  type List_iter is limited private;

  procedure first( the:in out List_iter; l:in out List );
  procedure last( the:in out List_iter; l:in out List );

  function  deliver( the:in List_iter) return T;
  procedure insert( the:in out List_iter; data:in T );
  procedure delete( the:in out List_iter );
  function  is_end( the:in List_iter ) return Boolean;
  procedure next( the:in out List_iter );
  procedure prev( the:in out List_iter );
private
  type P_P_Node is access all P_Node;
  type List_iter is record
    cur_list_first: P_P_Node := null;     -- First in chain
    cur_list_last : P_P_Node := null;     -- Last in chain
    cur_node      : P_Node   := null;     -- Current item
  end record;
end Class_list.Iterator;
```

Note: The child package Class_list.Iterator *must be generic as its parent is generic.*

When the iterator colours_it has been set at the start of the list colours, the resulting data structure is as illustrated in Figure 16.4.

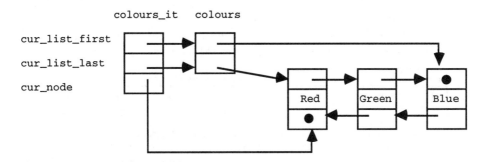

Figure 16.4 The interrelationship between the two objects colours and colours_it.

Note: The iterator holds pointers to the root, current and previous positions in the container.

In the implementation of the iterator for the list, the procedure, `first` and `last` set pointers in the iterator to the first or last object in the list respectively.

```
package body Class_list.Iterator is
  procedure first( the:in out List_iter; l:in out List ) is
  begin
    the.cur_node       := l.first_node;          -- Set to first
    the.cur_list_first:= l.first_node'Unchecked_Access;
    the.cur_list_last := l.last_node'Unchecked_Access;
  end first;

  procedure last( the:in out List_iter; l:in out List ) is
  begin
    the.cur_node       := l.last_node;           -- Set to last
    the.cur_list_first:= l.first_node'Unchecked_Access;
    the.cur_list_last := l.last_node'Unchecked_Access;
  end last;
```

Note: The use of 'Unchecked_Access to deliver the access value of the positions of the first and last access values of items in the list.

The access values of the first and last nodes in the list are recorded in the iterator so that they may be updated should an insertion or deletion take place at the start or the end of the list.

The procedure `deliver` returns a copy of the current item pointed at by the iterator.

```
function deliver( the:in List_iter ) return T is
begin
  return the.cur_node.item;   -- The current item
end deliver;
```

The code for `insert` is complex due to the necessity of handling insertion at different places in the linked list. In particular, the list's access values to the physical storage of the list will need to be updated. Remember, the iterator only knows about the current position in the list.

In the implementation of `insert` there are four distinct cases to handle when a data item is inserted. This is summarized in the table below:

Position	Commentary
On an empty list	Will need to update the list's access values `first` and `last` as well as update the current position in the iterator.
Beyond the last item in the list	Will need to update the list's access value `last` as well as update the current position in the iterator.
Before the first item	Will need to update the list's access value `first`.
In the middle of the list	No updating required to the list's access values nor the current position of the iterator.

The implementation of the insert procedure is as follows:

```
procedure insert( the:in out List_iter; data:in T ) is
   tmp    : P_Node;
   cur    : P_Node    := the.cur_node;    -- Current element
   first  : P_P_Node := the.cur_list_first;
   last   : P_P_Node := the.cur_list_last;
begin
   if cur = null then               -- Empty or last item
      if first.all = null then    --   Empty list
         tmp := new Node'( null, data, null );
         first.all := tmp;
         last.all  := tmp;
         the.cur_node := tmp;
      else                          --   Last
         tmp := new Node'( last.all, data, null );
         last.all.next := tmp;
         last.all      := tmp;
         the.cur_node := tmp;
      end if;
   else
      tmp := new Node'( cur.prev, data, cur );
      if cur.prev = null then       -- First item
         first.all := tmp;
      else
         cur.prev.next := tmp;
      end if;
      cur.prev := tmp;
   end if;
end insert;
```

In the implementation of delete there are two different pointers to fix: the forward pointer and the previous pointer. Each of these cases leads to further specializations depending on whether the object deleted is the first, last or middle object in the list.

```
procedure delete( the:in out List_iter) is
   cur    : P_Node    := the.cur_node;    -- Current element
   first  : P_P_Node := the.cur_list_first;
   last   : P_P_Node := the.cur_list_last;
begin
   if cur /= null then              -- Something to delete
      if cur.prev /= null then      -- Fix forward pointer;
         cur.prev.next := cur.next;  --   Not first in chain
      else
         first.all := cur.next;       --   First in chain
         if first.all = null then
            last.all := null;         --    Empty list
         end if;
      end if;
```

```
        if cur.next /= null then        -- Fix backward pointer;
          cur.next.prev := cur.prev;    --  Not last in chain
        else
          last.all := cur.prev;         --  Last in chain
          if last.all = null then
            first.all := null;          --   Empty list
          end if;
        end if;
        if cur.next /= null then        -- Fix current pointer
          the.cur_node := cur.next;     --  next
        elsif cur.prev /= null then
          the.cur_node := cur.prev;     --  previous
        else
          the.cur_node := null;         --  none empty list
        end if;
        dispose_node( cur );            -- Release storage
      end if;
    end delete;
```

The function `is_end` returns true when the iterator is moved beyond the end of the list, or beyond the start of the list.

```
function  is_end( the:in List_iter ) return Boolean is
begin
  return the.cur_node = null;                -- True if end
end is_end;
```

The procedure `next` and `prev` move the iterator on to the next / previous item in the list. If the iterator is not currently pointing at an item, the iterator is unmodified. The end of the list is indicated by the iterator pointing to a **null** value. By inspecting the list this case can be distinguished from the case of an empty list.

```
procedure next( the:in out List_iter ) is
begin
  if the.cur_node /= null then            --
    the.cur_node  := the.cur_node.next;   -- Next
  end if;
end next;

procedure prev( the:in out List_iter ) is
begin
  if the.cur_node /= null then            --
    the.cur_node  := the.cur_node.prev;   -- Previous
  end if;
end prev;

end Class_list.Iterator;
```

Note: *If you move the iterator to beyond the first element with* `prev` *then it is your responsibility to reset the iterator's position. The* `class` *list will consider the position at the end of the list.*

16.3.2 Relationship between a list and its iterator

The list on which the iterator navigates must be writable. This is because the iterator may be used to insert or delete an item in the list. Another solution would have been to have two distinct iterators for read and write operations on the list.

16.4 Limitations of the list implementation

A limitation of this implementation is that a list object is physically duplicated when it is assigned. This is referred to as a deep copy of an object. A deep copy of an object can involve the use of considerable time and storage space.

There are two options for the implementation of assignment. These options are summarized in the table below:

Type of copy	Commentary
Deep copy	The whole physical data structure is duplicated.
Shallow copy.	Only the pointer held directly in the object is duplicated.

For example, consider the data structure `original` representing a list of colours held as a linked list. This is illustrated in Figure 16.5 which shows the memory layout for the list container `original` which holds the three colours Red, Green and Blue.

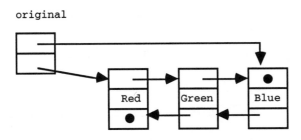

Figure 16.5 Illustration of the memory layout for a linked list of three colours.

A deep copy of this structure:

```
List original, copy;

copy := original;    // Deep copy
```

would give the memory layout as illustrated in Figure 16.6.

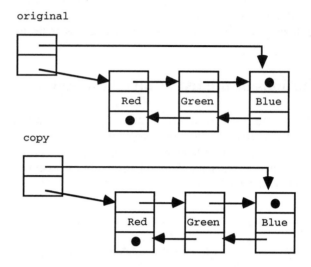

Figure 16.6 Effect of the deep `copy := original;`

A shallow copy :

```
List original, copy;

copy := original;     // Shallow copy
```

would produce the memory layout as illustrated in Figure 16.7.

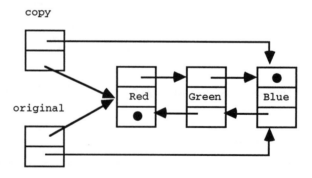

Figure 16.7 Effect of the shallow copy `copy := original;`

The major problem with the shallow copy is that serious errors will occur in a program if a change to the original data structure is made. This is because the copy will change as well. Worse, if the storage for the `original` object is released, then the copy object will be unsafe as it now points to storage that is no longer considered active by the Ada run-time system.

Ada's assignment statement is defined to perform a shallow copy. If a deep copy is required, then the assignment operator must be overloaded with a new meaning. The solution taken in the class list was to make assignment and comparison of a container perform a deep copy, and a shallow equality operation.

16.5 Reference counting

One solution to the problems encountered with a shallow copy is to implement a reference counting scheme. In a reference counting scheme, an additional component is held which is the number of active references to the data structure. A consequence of using this scheme is that additional code needs to be executed on an assignment. For example, the previously described list would be stored as illustrated in Figure 16.8.

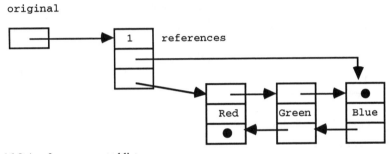

Figure 16.8 A reference counted list.

Note: The root of the list now contains the number of references that are made to this data structure.

When a shallow copy is made, for example, with the assignment:

```
copy := original;
```

the resulting data structure will be as illustrated in Figure 16.9.

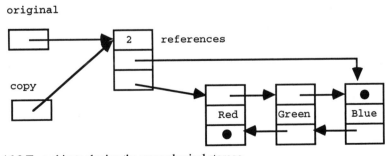

Figure 16.9 Two objects sharing the same physical storage.

The actions that take place for the shallow copy 'copy := original;' are:

- If the objects overlap (share the same storage):

Action on assignment	Commentary
`anon := original;`	Perform the assignment: `'anon := original;'`
`adjust(anon);`	Increment the reference count for the object anon.
`finalize(copy);`	Decrement by one the reference count for the object copy. If this is now zero, release the storage that the object copy points to.
`copy := anon;`	Perform the assignment: `'copy := original;'`
`adjust(copy);`	Increment the reference count for the object copy.
`finalize(anon);`	Decrement by one the reference count for the object anon. If this is now zero release the storage that the object anon points to.

- If the objects do not overlap, the following optimization may be performed:

Action on assignment	Commentary
`finalize(original);`	Decrement by one the reference count for the object original. If this is now zero, release the storage that the object original points to
`copy := original;`	Perform the assignment: `'copy := original;'`
`adjust(copy);`	Increment the reference count for the object copy.

Note: The compiler may generate no code if the target and the source are the same.

When a reference counted item is passed as a parameter to a function or procedure by value, for example:

Procedure	Call of procedure
```procedure put(l:in List) is begin .... end put;```	```declare colours : List; begin put(colours); end;```

then only the following actions are performed:

put(colours)	Commentary
`l := colours;`	Perform the assignment of `colours` to the formal parameter: `'l := colours;'`
`adjust(l);`	Increment the reference count for the actual parameter l.

Note: When the procedure put *is exited,* finalize *will be called on the formal parameter l.*

16.6 Implementation of a reference counting scheme

A generic class which will implement a reference counting scheme for any object has the following specification:

```
with Ada.Finalization; use Ada.Finalization;
generic
   type T is private;                  -- The type
   NULL_VALUE:in T;                    -- Identity element
package Class_object_rc is
   type Object is new Controlled with private;
   type P_T is access T;

   procedure initialize( the:in out Object );
   procedure initialize( the:in out Object; data:in T );
   procedure finalize( the:in out Object );
   procedure adjust( the:in out Object );
   function  deliver( the:in Object) return T;
   function  deliver_ref( the:in Object) return P_T;
   procedure unique( the:in out Object);
private
```

```
type Descriptor;
type P_Descriptor is access all Descriptor;

type Descriptor is record
  refs   : Natural;        -- References to this data
  object : aliased T;      -- The physical data
end record;

type Object is new Controlled with record
  p_desc : P_Descriptor:= null; -- Descriptor for a number
end record;

end Class_object_rc;
```

So that an object can be referenced counted, a new class is instantiated with parameters of the object's type and the null value for the type. For example, to reference count instances of the class `Account`, the following instantiation would be made:

```
null_account: Account;
package Class_rc_account is
  new Class_object_rc(Account, null_account);
```

In this instantiation the null value for the type is simply an instance of `Account` which contains a zero balance.

The implementation of the class is shown below. The procedure `initialize` builds storage for a record which holds the data item and the reference count for the data item. Initially this reference count will be zero.

```
with unchecked_deallocation;
package body Class_object_rc is
  procedure build_storage ( the:in out Object; value:in T );
  procedure release_storage( the:in out Object );

  procedure initialize( the:in out Object ) is
  begin
    build_storage( the, NULL_VALUE );
  end initialize;

  procedure initialize( the:in out Object; data:in T ) is
  begin
    build_storage( the, data );
  end initialize;

  procedure build_storage ( the:in out Object; value:in T ) is
  begin
    the.p_desc            := new Descriptor;
    the.p_desc.object     := value;
    the.p_desc.references := 1;
  end build_storage;
```

The procedure `finalize` is decomposed into the procedure `release_storage` which releases the storage for the managed data item only when the reference count goes to zero.

```
procedure finalize( the:in out Object ) is
begin
  if the.p_desc /= null then
    release_storage( the );
    the.p_desc := null;
  end if;
end finalize;

procedure dispose is
  new unchecked_deallocation( Descriptor, P_Descriptor );

procedure release_storage( the:in out Object ) is
begin
  the.p_desc.references := the.p_desc.references-1;
  if the.p_desc.references = 0 then
    dispose( the.p_desc );
  end if;
end release_storage;
```

The procedure `adjust` is automatically called whenever an assignment or implied assignment of a controlled object takes place. The reason for this is that when an assignment of an object managed by this class is made, there are now two references to the object. The procedure `adjust` has the responsibility of managing this process, which it does by increasing the reference count to the object by 1.

```
procedure adjust( the:in out Object ) is
begin
  the.p_desc.references := the.p_desc.references+1;
end adjust;
```

Remember, when an assignment of a controlled object is made, the following sequence of events occurs:

Assignment of controlled objects	Actions that take place

a := b;	anon := b;
	  adjust(anon);
	  finalize(a);
	a := anon;
	  adjust(a);
	  finalize(anon);

Note: When the storage for the source and target do not overlap, this process can be optimized by the compiler to:
```
finalize(a); a := b; adjust(a);
```

The function `deliver` returns a copy of the managed object

```
function  deliver( the:in Object) return T is
begin
   return the.p_desc.object;
end deliver;
```

whilst the function `deliver_ref` returns an access value to the managed object.

```
function  deliver_ref( the:in Object) return P_T is
begin
   return the.p_desc.object'Access;
end deliver_ref;
```

The procedure `unique` converts the object managed by the class into a unique copy. This may involve a deep copy of the managed object.

```
procedure unique( the:in out Object) is
   tmp : P_Descriptor;
begin
   if the.p_desc.refs > 1 then          -- Make copy
      the.p_desc.refs := the.p_desc.refs-1;
      tmp := new Descriptor'(1,the.p_desc.object);
      the.p_desc := tmp;
   end if;
end unique;
end Class_object_rc;
```

16.6.1   Putting it all together

The program below illustrates the use of the class `Object_rc` to provide a reference counted `Account` class.

```
with Simple_io, Class_account; use Simple_io, Class_account;
procedure main is
   null_account: Account;
   package Class_rc_account is
     new Class_object_rc(Account, null_account);
begin
   declare
     use Class_rc_account;
     original,copy : Class_rc_account.Object;
   begin
     deposit( deliver_ref(original).all, 100.00 );
     put("copy := original; (Shallow copy)"); new_line;
     copy := original;                        -- Shallow copy
     statement( deliver_ref(original).all ); -- The same object
     statement( deliver_ref(copy).all );      --  "    "
     put("Make copy unique (Deep copy if necessary)"); new_line;
     unique( copy );                          -- Deep copy
     deposit( deliver_ref(copy).all, 20.00 );-- copy only
     statement( deliver_ref(original).all ); -- Unique object
     statement( deliver_ref(copy).all );      --  "    "
   end;
end main;
```

Note: **all** *is used to de-reference the access value returned by the function* `deliver_ref`.

When compiled and run will produce the following output:

```
Mini statement: The amount on deposit is £100.00

Mini statement: The amount on deposit is £100.00

Make copy unique (Deep copy if necessary)
Mini statement: The amount on deposit is £100.00

Mini statement: The amount on deposit is £120.00
```

16.7 A set

Using the class `List`, a class to represent a set can be created. The class `set` has the following responsibilities:

Method	Responsibility
put	Display the contents of the set.
+	Form the union of two sets
set_const	Return a set with a single member.
members	Return the numbers of items in the set.

The class `Set` is inherited from the class `List`. The specification for the class `Set` is:

```
with Class_list, Class_list.Iterator;
generic
  type T is private;
  with procedure put( item:in T ) is <>;
  with function  ">" (first,second:in T ) return Boolean is <>;
  with function  "<" (first,second:in T ) return Boolean is <>;
package Class_set is
  type Set is private;
  procedure put( the:in Set );
  function "+"( f:in Set; s:in Set ) return Set;
  function set_const( item: in T )    return Set;
  function members( the:in Set )      return Positive;
private
  package Class_list_t          is new Class_list(T);
  package Class_list_t_iterator is new Class_list_t.Iterator;
  type Set is new Class_list_t.List with record
    elements : Natural := 0;               -- Elements in set
  end record;
end Class_set;
```

Note: On instantiation of the class, a procedure put *and definitions for* > *and* < *must be provided, either explicitly or implicitly.*

In the implementation of the class, the procedure put lists in a conical form the elements of the set.

```
with Simple_io; use Simple_io;
package body Class_set is
  use Class_list_t, Class_list_t_iterator;

  procedure put( the:in Set ) is
    it    : List_iter;
    c_the : List := List(the);
  begin
    put("("); first( it, c_the );
    for i in 1 .. the.elements loop
      put( deliver(it) ); next( it );
      if i /= the.elements then put(","); end if;
    end loop;
    put(")");
  end put;
```

A simple merging process is used to form the union of two sets.

```
function "+"  ( f:in Set; s:in Set ) return Set is
  res_it     : List_iter;
  f_it,s_it  : List_iter;
  res        : Set;
  f_list, s_list: List;
begin
  f_list := List(f); s_list := List(s);
  first( f_it, List(f_list) );
  first( s_it, List(s_list) );
  first( res_it, List(res) );

  while (not is_end(f_it)) or (not is_end(s_it)) loop
    if is_end(f_it) then
      next(res_it); insert(res_it, deliver(s_it));
      next(s_it);
    elsif is_end(s_it) then
      next(res_it); insert(res_it, deliver(f_it));
      next(f_it);
    elsif deliver(f_it) < deliver(s_it) then
      next(res_it); insert(res_it, deliver(f_it));
      next(f_it);
    elsif deliver(f_it) > deliver(s_it) then
      next(res_it); insert(res_it, deliver(s_it));
      next(s_it);
    elsif deliver(f_it) = deliver(s_it) then
      next(res_it); insert(res_it, deliver(f_it) );
      next(f_it); next(s_it);
    end if;
    res.elements := res.elements + 1;
  end loop;
  return res;
end "+";
```

Note: The copying of the list to a new list object which can be written too.

The procedure set_const returns a set with a single element, whilst the function members returns the number of elements in the set.

```
function set_const( item: in T ) return Set is
  res : Set;
begin
  initialize( res, item ); res.elements := 1;
  return res;
end set_const;

function members( the:in Set ) return Positive is
begin
  return the.elements;
end members;

end Class_set;
```

16.7.1   Putting it all together

The program below illustrates the use of a set to record the ingredients in a sandwich.

```
package Pack_types is
  type Filling is ( CHEESE, ONION, HAM, TOMATO );
end Pack_types;

with Simple_io, Pack_types;
use  Simple_io, Pack_types;
procedure put_filling( c:in Filling ) is
begin
  put( Filling'Image( c ) );
end put_filling;

with Pack_types, Class_set, put_filling;
package Class_set_sandwich is
  new Class_set( T => Pack_types.Filling, put => put_filling );

with Pack_types, Simple_io, Class_set_sandwich;
use  Pack_types, Simple_io, Class_set_sandwich;
procedure main1 is
  sandwich : Class_set_sandwich.Set;
begin
  sandwich := sandwich + set_const(CHEESE);
  sandwich := sandwich + set_const(ONION) ;
  put("Contents of sandwich are : ");
  put( sandwich ); new_line;
  put("Number of ingredients is : ");
  put( members(sandwich) ); new_line;
end main1;
```

Note: The instantiation of the class Class_set_sandwich uses the default definitions of > and < taken from the environment.
An instantatiation of a class which is inherited from Controlled must be at the library level.

which when run, will produce the following results:

```
Contents of sandwich are : (CHEESE,ONION)
Number of ingredients is :          2
```

16.8 Self-assessment

- What is the purpose of an iterator?

- When inheriting from `Controlled`, the user can provide the following procedures:
  `finalize, initialize, and adjust.`
  What is the purpose of these procedures?

- If a and b are controlled objects, what happens when the assignment:
  `a := b;`
  is made?

- What is the difference between a deep and a shallow copy?

- What are the semantics of an assignment in Ada for the following assignments:

  (a)   The assignment of an instance of an `Integer`?
  (b)   The assignment of an instance of a linked list?

- With the container `Class_list`, what would be the effect of using an iterator to the container when the storage for the container object has gone out of scope?

- What should happen to the iterator when an item is added to a container on which it is iterating?

16.9 Exercises

Construct the following class:

- `Class_Better_Set`
  A class to implement a better set. A set is an ordered collection of unique items. The operations allowed on a set are:

  - Forming the intersection of two sets.
  - Forming the union of two sets.
  - Forming the set difference of two sets.
  - Testing if an element is a member of the set.

17 Input and output

This chapter describes how input and output of objects other than Float, Integer or Character may be performed.

17.1 The input and output mechanism

In Ada input and output operations are strongly typed. This can cause initial problems as only a mechanism for inputting or outputting characters is provided explicitly in the package Ada.Text_io. The full definition of the package Ada.Text_io is given in section C.5, Appendix C. The package Simple_io described in section C.3, Appendix C provides a package that can input and output instances of Character, Integer, and Float.

The package Ada.Text_io contains generic packages for outputting Float, Integer, String, Fixed or Enumeration types. For example, to output instances of the following types:

```
type Memory is new Integer range 0 .. MAX_MEM;      -- Int
type Cpu    is (M680x0, M80x86, Alpha);             -- Enum
type Mips   is digits 8     range 0.0 .. MAX_MIPS;  -- Float
type Clock  is delta 0.01   range 0.0 .. MAX_CLOCK; -- Fixed
```

the following packages would need to be instantiated:

```
package Class_mem_io   is new Ada.Text_io.Integer_io( Memory );
package Class_cpu_io   is new Ada.Text_io.Enumeration_io( Cpu );
package Class_mips_io  is new Ada.Text_io.Float_io( Mips );
package Class_clock_io is new Ada.Text_io.Fixed_io( Clock );
```

Note: Each of the generic packages has as its generic parameter the type that is to be output.

17.1.1 Putting it all together

The above generic packages are used in the following program that prints out details about the internal specification of a CPU:

```
with Ada.Text_io; use Ada.Text_io;
procedure main is
  MAX_MEM     : constant := 132;
  MAX_MIPS    : constant := 200.0;
  MAX_CLOCK   : constant := 200.0;

  type Memory is range 0 .. MAX_MEM;             -- Int
  type Cpu    is (Alpha, M80x86, Powerpc);       -- Enum
  type Mips   is digits 8    range 0.0 .. MAX_MIPS;   -- Float
  type Clock  is delta 0.01  range 0.0 .. MAX_CLOCK;  -- Fixed

  mc_mem      : Memory;               -- Main memory
  mc_cpu      : Cpu;                  -- Type of CPU
  mc_mips     : Mips;                 -- Raw MIPS
  mc_clock    : Clock;                -- Clock frequency

  package Class_mem_io   is new Ada.Text_io.Integer_io( Memory );
  package Class_cpu_io   is new Ada.Text_io.Enumeration_io( Cpu );
  package Class_mips_io  is new Ada.Text_io.Float_io( Mips );
  package Class_clock_io is new Ada.Text_io.Fixed_io( Clock );
```

the body of the procedure which writes out details about the computer is:

```
begin
  declare
    use Class_mem_io, Class_mips_io,
        Class_clock_io, Class_cpu_io;
  begin
    mc_mem   := 32;        mc_cpu   := M80x86;
    mc_mips  := 27.3;      mc_clock := 65.88;

    put("Memory:"); put( mc_mem );    new_line;
    put("CPU   :"); put( mc_cpu );    new_line;
    put("Mips  :"); put( mc_mips );   new_line;
    put("Clock :"); put( mc_clock );  new_line;

    put("Memory:"); put( mc_mem, width=>3); new_line;
    put("CPU   :"); put( mc_cpu, width=>7, set=>upper_case );
    new_line;
    put("Mips  :"); put( mc_mips, fore=>3, aft=>2, exp=>0 );
    new_line;
    put("Clock :"); put( mc_clock,fore=>3, aft=>2, exp=>0 );
    new_line;
  end;
end main;
```

when run, the program will produce the following output:

```
Memory:  32
CPU    :M80X86
Mips   : 2.7300000E+01
Clock :  65.88
Memory: 32
CPU    :M80X86
Mips   : 27.30
Clock :  65.88
```

17.2   Reading and writing to files

The following program copies input typed in at a terminal to the file named a.txt. The object fd is associated with the newly created file file.txt and is used as a file descriptor in all writing to this file. The exception Name_error is generated if the file cannot be created.

```
with Ada.Text_io; use Ada.Text_io;
procedure main is
   fd        : Ada.Text_io.File_type;        -- File descriptor
   file_name: constant String:= "file.txt";-- Name
   ch        : Character;                     -- Character read
begin
   create( File=>fd, Mode=>OUT_FILE, Name=>file_name );
   while not end_of_file loop                -- For each Line
     while not end_of_line loop              -- For each character
        get(ch); put(fd, ch);                -- Read / Write character
     end loop;
     skip_line;                              -- Next line / new line
   end loop;
   close(fd);
exception
   when Name_Error =>
     put("Cannot create " & file_name ); new_line;
end main;
```

The data in the file file.txt is read by the following program, which copies the contents of the file to the terminal:

```
with Ada.Text_io; use Ada.Text_io;
procedure main is
   fd        : Ada.Text_io.File_type;        -- File descriptor
   file_name: constant String:= "file.txt";-- Name
   ch        : Character;                     -- Character read
begin
   open( File=>fd, Mode=>IN_FILE, Name=>file_name );
   while not end_of_file(fd) loop            -- For each Line
     while not end_of_line(fd) loop          -- For each character
        get(fd, ch); put(ch);                -- Read / Write character
     end loop;
     skip_line(fd); new_line;                -- Next line / new line
   end loop;
   close(fd);
exception
   when Name_Error =>
     put("Cannot open " & file_name ); new_line;
end main;
```

Note: The exception Name_error is generated if the file cannot be opened.

The following program appends instances of Number, one of the integer types to the file file.txt:

```ada
with Ada.Text_io; use Ada.Text_io;
procedure main is
  type Number is Range 1 .. 10;
  fd       : Ada.Text_io.File_type;       -- File descriptor
  file_name: constant String:= "file.txt";-- Name
  package Pack_number_io is new
    Ada.Text_io.Integer_io( Number );
begin
  create( File=>fd, Mode=>APPEND_FILE, Name=>file_name );
  for i in Number loop
    Pack_number_io.put( fd, i ); new_line( fd );
  end loop;
  close(fd);
exception
  when Name_Error =>
    put("Cannot append to " & file_name ); new_line;
end main;
```

17.3 Reading and writing binary data

Any instance of a type may be read and written to a file using the package Ada.Sequential_io. By using this package, binary images of objects may be read and written. For example, the following code writes instances of Person to the file people.txt:

```ada
with Ada.Text_io, Ada.Sequential_io;
use  Ada.Text_io;
procedure main is
  MAX_CHS : constant := 10;
  type Gender    is ( FEMALE, MALE );
  type Height_cm is range 0 .. 300;

  type Person is record
    name   : String( 1 .. MAX_CHS );   -- Name as a String
    height : Height_cm := 0;           -- Height in cm.
    sex    : Gender;                   -- Gender of person
  end record;

  type    Person_index is range 1 .. 2;
  subtype Person_range is Person_index;
  type    Person_array is array ( Person_range ) of Person;

  file_name: constant String:= "people.txt";-- Name
  people   : Person_array;
  package io is new Ada.Sequential_io( Person );
  fd       : io.File_type;             -- File descriptor
```

```
begin
  people(1) := (name=> "Mike      ", height=> 183, sex=> MALE);
  people(2) := (name=> "Corinna   ", sex=> FEMALE, height=> 171);
  io.create( File=>fd, Mode=>io.OUT_FILE, Name=>file_name );
  for i in Person_range loop
    io.write( fd, people(i) );
  end loop;
  io.close(fd);
exception
  when Name_Error =>
    put("Can not create " & file_name ); new_line;
end main;
```

Note: The package Ada.Text_io *is used to provide the definition of the exception* Name_error.

When writing using the generic package Ada.Sequential_io, *the procedures* read *and* write *are used to perform the input and output operations.*

To read back the data written to the file people.txt the following fragment of code is used:

```
-- Declarations as per previous program
begin
  io.open( File=>fd, Mode=>io.IN_FILE, Name=>file_name );
  for i in Person_range loop
    io.read( fd, people(i) );
  end loop;
  io.close(fd);
exception
  when Name_Error =>
    put("Can not open " & file_name ); new_line;
end;
```

17.4 Switching the default input and output streams

It is possible to switch the default input or output stream to another stream using the following procedures in the package Ada.Text_io. The effect is to change the source or sink from which input and output will come from or go to when using the normal input and output procedures put and get without a File parameter.

Procedure	Sets the default
set_input (file:in File_type)	input file descriptor.
set_output(file:in File_type)	output file descriptor.
set_error (file:in File_type)	error file descriptor.

As the file descriptor is of type limited private, it may not be directly assigned. However, an access value of the file descriptor can be saved. The following functions return an access value of the standard input and output file descriptors:

Function	Return the access
standard_input **return** File_access;	value of the input file descriptor.
standard_output **return** File_access;	value of the output file descriptor.
standard_error **return** File_access;	value of the error file descriptor.

17.4.1 Putting it all together

The program below carries out a sequence of switching operations to the default input stream. First, it switches the default input stream to derive input from the file text. After reading a single character, it switches the default input stream back to the original source.

```
with Ada.Text_io;
use  Ada.Text_io;
procedure main is
   fd      : Ada.Text_io.File_type;      -- File descriptor
   p_st_fd : Ada.Text_io.File_Access;    -- Access value of fd
   ch   : Character;                      -- Current character
begin
     p_st_fd := standard_input;          -- Access value of standard

     open( File=>fd, Mode=>IN_FILE, Name=>"text" );
     set_input( fd );
     get(ch);                            -- From file text

     set_input( p_st_fd.all );           -- Back to original fd
     get(ch);                            -- From Keyboard

     close(fd);                          -- Close file
end main;
```

Note: Notice how *.all* has been used to de-reference the access value when using the procedure set_input.

17.5 Self-assessment

- What is the purpose of the package Ada.Sequential_io?

- How can you detect if a file does not exist in Ada?

- How might input and output in Ada be simplified for the novice user?

- How can you write an instance of a record to a file?

17.6 Exercises

Construct the following program:

- *Copy*
  A program to copy a file. A user should be able to run your program by typing:

  ```
  new_copy old_file new_file
  ```

- *Uppercase*
  A program to convert a file in upper and lower case to all upper case. A user should be able to run your program by typing:

  ```
  to_upper_case file
  ```

  Note: The program should create an intermediate file then delete the original file and rename the intermediate file to the original file name. This operation should be safe.

18 Persistence

This chapter shows how to create persistent objects. A persistent object will have a life-time beyond the life-time of the program that created it.

18.1 A persistent indexed collection

The life-time of an object in Ada depends on its declaration, but its life-time will never exist beyond that of the program. For an object to exist beyond the life-time of an individual execution of a program requires the object's state to be saved to disk, allowing the object's state to be restored in another program. The above process makes the object persistent. Normally this process is visible to a programmer.

For example, a program to print the IDC (International Dialling Code) for countries selected by a user could use a persistent object to hold IDC details for individual countries. These details could be amended by the user of the program and the changes would be retained for subsequent re-running of the program.

A program of this kind could uses the persistent object tel_list that is an instance of the class PIC (Persistent Indexed Collection). The class PIC implements a persistent indexed collection of data items. The index can be an arbitrary value as can the data stored with the index. The responsibilities of the class PIC are as follows:

Method	Responsibility
initialize	Initialize the object. When the object is initialized with an identity, the state of the named persistent object is restored into the object.
finalize	If the object has an identity, save the state of the object under this name.
add	Add a new data item to the object.
extract	Extract the data associated with an index.
update	Update the data associated with an index.
set_name	Set the identity of the object.
get_name	Return the identity of the object.

The package Pack_types contains string definitions for the Country and the IDC.

```
package Pack_types is
  subtype  Country is String( 1 .. 12 );
  subtype  IDC     is String( 1 .. 6 );
end Pack_types;
```

The Class Tel_list is an instantiation of the generic class PIC.

```
with Class_pic, Pack_types;
use  Pack_types;
  package Class_tel_list is new
    Class_pic( Country, IDC, ">" );
```

Note: The generic class PIC is described in section 18.2.

A program to implement this telephone aid would be as follows:

```
with Simple_io, Pack_types, Class_tel_list;
use  Simple_io, Pack_types, Class_tel_list;
procedure telephone is
  tel_list : PIC;
  action   : Character;
  name     : Country;
  tel      : IDC;
begin
  initialize( tel_list, "tel_list.per" );
  while not end_of_file loop
    begin
      get( action );                        -- Action to perform
      case action is
        when '+' =>                         -- Add
          get( name ); get( tel );
          add( tel_list, name, tel );
        when '=' =>                         -- Extract
          get( name );
          extract( tel_list, name, tel );
          put( "IDC for " ); put( name );
          put( " is "); put( tel ); new_line;
        when '*' =>                         -- Update
          get( name ); get( tel );
          update( tel_list, name, tel );
        when others =>                      -- Invalid action
          null;
      end case;
    exception
      when Not_there =>                     -- Not there
        put("Name not in directory"); new_line;
      when Exists =>                        -- Exists
        put("Name already in directory"); new_line;
    end;
    skip_line;
  end loop;
end telephone;
```

Note: The usual way of making an object persistent is to save the state of an object to disk using a unique name. This name is the object's identity. In the above program, the object's identity is used as the name of a file in which the state of the object is saved.

18.1.1 Putting it all together

When compiled with the class `Tel_list` and the package `Pack_types` an example interaction using the program would be as follows:

```
=UK                 +    -- Previously stored
IDC for UK               is +44
+New Zealand +64    +    -- Add IDC for New Zealand
+Sweden      +46    +    -- Add IDC for Sweden
+Portugal    +3510  +    -- Invalid IDC
=Portugal           +    -- Lookup IDC for Portugal
IDC for Portugal         is +3510
+Portugal    +351   +    -- Try to add new IDC for Portugal
Name already in directory
*Portugal    +351   +    -- Correct invalid IDC
=Portugal           +    -- Lookup IDC for Portugal
IDC for Portugal         is +351
```

*Note: The user's input is indicated by **bold** type.*
The actions allowed are:

+   *Add country and IDC to collection*
=   *Extract IDC for country*
*   *Change IDC for existing country*

18.2 The class `PIC`

The class `PIC` (Persistent Indexed Collection) implements an indexed collection as a binary tree. An identity is given to an instance of the class `PIC` so that when the object's life-time ends, its state will be saved to disk. The file name used to save the state is the object's identity.

The specification for the class `PIC` is as follows:

```
with Ada.Strings.Bounded; use Ada.Strings.Bounded;
  package B_String is
    new Generic_Bounded_Length( 80 );
```

Note: The package uses an instantiation of the `Generic_Bounded_Length` package to manipulate strings.

```
with B_string, Ada.Finalization;
use  B_string, Ada.Finalization;
generic
  type Index is private;                -- Index for record
  type Data  is private;                -- Data for record
  with function  ">"( f:in Index; s:in Index ) return Boolean;
package Class_pic is
  Not_there, Exists, Per_error : exception; -- Raised Exceptions
  type PIC  is limited private;
  procedure initialize( the:in out PIC );
  procedure initialize( the:in out PIC; id:in String );
  procedure finalize( the:in out PIC );
  procedure discard( the:in out PIC );
  procedure set_name( the:in out PIC; id:in String );
  function  get_name( the:in PIC ) return String;

  procedure add( the:in out PIC; i:in Index; d:in Data );
  procedure extract( the:in out PIC; i:in Index; d:in out Data );
  procedure update( the:in out PIC; i:in Index; d:in out Data );
private
  type Leaf;                            -- Index + Data
  type Subtree is access all Leaf; --
  type PIC is record              -- Persistent Indexed Collection
    tree   : Subtree := null;     --   Storage
    obj_id : Bounded_string;      --   Name of object
  end record;

  function  find( the:in Subtree; i:in Index) return Subtree;
  procedure release_storage( the:in out Subtree );

end Class_pic;
```

Note: The declaration of the type leaf *is a forward declaration so that the type* Subtree, *a pointer to a leaf can be declared. The type* leaf *is fully declared in the package body.*

The two generic parameters, Index and Data represent the type of the index used to access the stored data. As this generic class will need to compare indices for ">" to establish the position of an index in the binary tree, a definition for ">" must be provided by the user of the class. Remember, the index may be of a type for which the operation ">" is not defined between two instances of Index. This forces the user of the package to provide implicitly or explicitly an implementation for the comparison function ">".

The implementation of the class PIC uses the data structure Element to hold the index and the data associated with the index. The data structure Leaf represents a leaf of the binary tree which is composed of a left and right pointer plus the data structure Element.

```
with unchecked_deallocation, sequential_io;
package body Class_pic is

   type Element is record      --
      s_index: Index;          -- The Index
      s_data : Data;           -- The Data
   end record;

   type Leaf is record         --
      left   : Subtree;        -- Possible left node
      rec    : Element;        -- Index + data
      right  : Subtree;        -- Possible right node;
   end record;
```

For example, after the following data is added to the data structure:

Country	IDC
Canada	+1
USA	+1
Belgium	+32
Germany	+49

the resultant tree would be as illustrated in Figure 18.1.

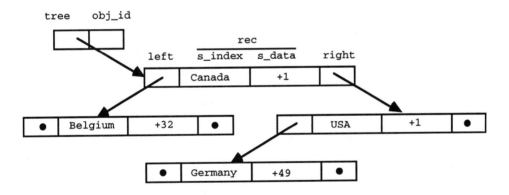

Figure 18.1 Binary tree holding four data items.

The rules for adding items to a binary tree are:

If the current pointer to a leaf is **null**:
- Insert the item at this point.

If the current pointer to a leaf is not **null**
- If the index of the item to be inserted is less than the current index , then recursively call add on the left hand subtree.
- If the index of the item to be inserted is less than the current index , then recursively call add on the right hand subtree.

For example, if the IDC of Norway were added, the resultant tree would be as illustrated in Figure 18.2.

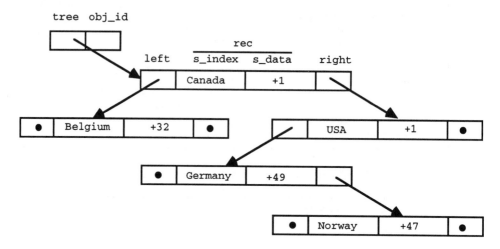

Figure 18.2 Binary tree after adding the country Norway.

The process to add the country Norway to the tree is:

Step	Current leaf contents	Action
1	Canada	Try inserting at RHS leaf
2	USA	Try inserting at LHS leaf
3	Germany	Try inserting at RHS leaf
4	Empty	Insert new leaf (Norway)

The package `sequential_io` is used to hold the saved state of the binary tree. This is simply a file of records of type `Element`. An instantiation of this package `io` is created to allow input and output to take place on instances of `Element`.

```
package io is new Sequential_io( Element );
```

The procedure `initialize` sets the binary tree to a defined empty state.

```
procedure initialize( the:in out PIC ) is
begin
   the.tree := null;     -- No storage
end initialize;
```

Note: This is not necessary as the elaboration of an instance of the class will set the tree *to* null *as its initial value.*

The procedure `initialize` is called to restore the state of the binary tree from a file. The second parameter to the procedure `initialize` is the object's identity. The state of the object is held in a file with the same name as the object's name. This procedure reads in the stored index and data items and uses the procedure `add` to rebuild the tree. The rebuilding of the tree re-creates an exact copy of the structure of the saved tree. This is due to the way the index and data items were stored. The process of saving the state of the binary tree is implemented in the procedure `finalize`.

```
procedure initialize( the:in out PIC; id:in String ) is
  per : io.File_type;      -- File descriptor
  cur : Element;           -- Persistent data record element
begin
  set_name( the, id );                    -- Name object
  io.open( per, io.IN_FILE, id );         -- Open saved state
  while not io.end_of_file( per ) loop    -- Restore saved state
    io.read( per, cur );
    add( the, cur.s_index, cur.s_data );
  end loop;
  io.close( per );
exception                                 -- Return real exception
  when others => raise Per_error;         -- as sub code
end initialize;
```

The procedure `finalize` saves the state of an object which has an identity just before the object is destroyed. The data from the binary tree is saved in the order:

- Item held in the current node.
- The contents of the left hand side.
- The contents of the right hand side.

This unusual ordering saves the index and data item of the leftmost leaves nearest the root first. Thus, when the data is restored the structure of the tree will be the same. For example, if the data structure, illustrated in Figure 18.2 were saved, then the order of saving the data would be:

Canada, Belgium, USA, Germany, Norway.

When added to a binary tree, this would recreate the tree structure present in the original object.

```
procedure finalize( the:in out PIC ) is
  per : io.File_type;      -- File descriptor
  procedure rec_finalize( the:in Subtree ) is -- Save state
  begin
    if the /= null then                  -- Subtree save as
      io.write( per, the.rec );          --   Item
      rec_finalize( the.left );          --   LHS
      rec_finalize( the.right );         --   RHS
    end if;
  end rec_finalize;
```

```
begin
  if to_string(the.obj_id) /= "" then       -- If save state
    io.create( per, io.OUT_FILE, to_string( the.obj_id ) );
    rec_finalize( the.tree );
    io.close( per );
  end if;
  release_storage( the.tree );
exception                              -- Return real exception
  when others => raise Per_error;      --   as sub code
end finalize;
```

The procedure `discard` disassociates the object identity from the object and resets the state of the tree to empty. This procedure should be used when the object's state is not required to be saved to disk.

```
procedure discard( the:in out PIC ) is
begin
  set_name( the, "" );                     -- No name
  release_storage( the.tree );             -- Release storage
end discard;

procedure set_name( the:in out PIC; id:in String ) is
begin
  the.obj_id := to_bounded_string(id); -- Set object name
end set_name;

function  get_name( the:in PIC ) return String is
begin
    return to_string( the.obj_id );      -- Name of object
end get_name;
```

The procedure `add` uses the classic recursive mechanism for adding data items to a binary tree. The process is to add the data item to an empty leaf of the tree. If this is not possible then the current leaf's data item is compared to the data item to be inserted. Depending on how the comparison collates, the process is recursively called on either the left or right hand subtree.

```
procedure add( the:in out PIC; i:in Index; d:in Data ) is
  procedure add_s(the:in out Subtree; i:in Index; d:in Data) is
  begin
    if the = null then
      the := new Leaf'( null, Element'(i,d), null );
    else
      if i = the.rec.s_index then       -- Index all ready exists
        raise Exists;
      elsif i > the.rec.s_index then  -- Try on RHS
        add_s( the.right, i, d );
      else                            -- LHS
        add_s( the.left, i, d );
      end if;
    end if;
  end add_s;
begin
  add_s( the.tree, i, d );
end add;
```

The procedures extract and update respectively read a data value and update a data value using the supplied index. Both these procedures use the function find to find the leaf in which the data item to be accessed is held.

```
procedure extract(the:in out PIC; i:in Index; d:in out Data) is
   node_is : Subtree;
begin
   node_is := find( the.tree, i );      -- Find node with index
   d := node_is.rec.s_data;             -- return data
end extract;

procedure update(the:in out PIC; i:in Index; d:in out Data) is
   node_is : Subtree;
begin
   node_is := find( the.tree, i );      -- Find node with index
   node_is.rec.s_data := d;             -- Update data
end update;
```

The procedure find uses a recursive descent of the tree to find the selected index. If the index is not found, then the exception Not_there is raised.

```
function find( the:in Subtree; i:in Index) return Subtree is
begin
   if the = null then raise Not_there; end if;
   if i = the.rec.s_index then
      return the;                          -- Found
   else
      if i > the.rec.s_index
         then return find( the.right, i ); -- Try RHS
         else return find( the.left,  i ); -- Try LHS
      end if;
   end if;
end find;
```

As the tree is built using dynamic storage, the storage must be released. The procedure release_storage carries out this task:

```
procedure dispose is
   new unchecked_deallocation( Leaf, Subtree );

procedure release_storage( the:in out Subtree ) is
begin
   if the /= null then                       -- Not empty
      release_storage( the.left );           -- Free LHS
      release_storage( the.right );          -- Free RHS
      dispose( the );                        -- Dispose of item
   end if;
   the := null;                              -- Subtree root null
end release_storage;
end Class_pic;
```

Note: The implicit garbage collector could be used, but this would only be called when the instance of the class PIC *went out of scope. If this object is serially re-used then storage used by the program could become excessive.*

19 Tasks

This chapter describes the task mechanism in Ada that allows several threads of execution to take place on a program simultaneously. This facilitates the construction of real-time programs that react to events generated from multiple sources.

19.1 The task mechanism

A program may have sections of code that can be executed concurrently as they have no interaction or dependency. For example, the calculation of the factorial of an integer number and the determination of whether a number is prime, may be done concurrently as separate threads of execution. This can be implemented by means of a **task type** within a package. When elaborated, an instance of the task type will execute as a separate thread. Communication between the executing threads is performed using the **entry** construct which allows a rendezvous to be made between two concurrently executing threads. At the rendezvous, information may be interchanged between the tasks.

The specification for two packages is given below. The first package defines a task to calculate the factorial of a positive number and the second determines whether or not a positive number is a prime.

```ada
package Pack_factorial is
  task type Task_factorial is            -- Specification
    entry start( f:in Positive );        -- Rendezvous
    entry finish( result:out Positive ); -- Rendezvous
  end Task_factorial;
end Pack_factorial;
```

```ada
package Pack_is_a_prime is
  task type Task_is_prime is             -- Specification
    entry start( p:in Positive );        -- Rendezvous
    entry finish( result:out Boolean );  -- Rendezvous
  end Task_is_prime;
end Pack_is_a_prime;
```

Note: *The rendezvous* start *is used to pass data to the task and the rendezvous* finish *is used to pass the result back.*

A task is created using the normal Ada elaboration mechanism. To create an instance of the task `Task_factorial` the following declaration is used:

```
thread_1 : Task_factorial;
```

The task will start executing as an independent thread as soon as the block surrounded by the declaration is entered. A rendezvous with this executing task to pass it the number 5, is written as follows:

```
thread_1.start(5);
```

Note: This can be thought of as sending the message `start` with a parameter of 5 to the task `thread_1`.

The tasks described above may be used as follows:

```
with Simple_io, Pack_factorial, Pack_is_a_prime;
use  Simple_io, Pack_factorial, Pack_is_a_prime;
procedure execute_threads is
thread_1 : Task_factorial;
thread_2 : Task_factorial;
thread_3 : Task_is_prime;
factorial: Positive;
prime    : Boolean;

begin
  thread_1.start(5);              -- Start factorial calculation
  thread_2.start(7);              -- Start factorial calculation
  thread_3.start(97);             -- Start is_prime calculation

  put("Factorial  5 is ");
  thread_1.finish( factorial ); -- Obtain result
  put( factorial ); new_line;

  put("Factorial  8 is ");
  thread_2.finish( factorial ); -- Obtain result
  put( factorial ); new_line;

  put("97 is a prime is ");
  thread_3.finish( prime );       -- Obtain result
  if prime then put("True"); else put("False"); end if; new_line;

end execute_threads;
```

Note: The tasks start executing as soon as the `begin` of the block in which they are elaborated, is entered. The rendezvous point `start` is used to control this wayward behaviour.

This is in essence a client-server relationship between the main program, the client, which requests a service from the server tasks.

19.1.1 Putting it all together

When run, this would deliver the following results:

```
Factorial   5 is 120
Factorial   8 is 5040
1 is a prime is True
```

The execution of the above program can be visualized as Figure 19.1

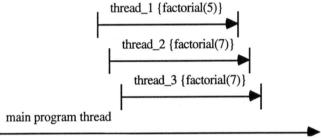

Figure 19.1 Illustration of active threads in the above program.

Once started, each of the threads will execute concurrently until the finish rendezvous is encountered, which is used to deliver the result to the initiator of the tasks.

Note: The actual implementation of the concurrency will depend on the underlying architecture, both software and hardware, of the platform on which the program is executed.

19.1.2 Task rendezvous

The rendezvous mechanism is used for:

- synchronizing two separate threads so that information may be exchanged.
- synchronizing the execution of two threads.

A rendezvous is achieved by one task having an **entry** statement and the other task performing a call on this **entry**. For example, the code for a rendezvous to pass a Positive number to the task object thread_1 the code would be:

Main program (client) which elaborates **thread1**	Body of task **thread_1** (server)
thread_1.start(5);	**accept** start(f:**in** Positive) **do** factorial := f; **end** start;

To achieve this effect, one of the threads of control will be suspended until the other thread catches up. Then at the rendezvous, data, in this case the number 5, is transferred between the tasks. The code between **do** and **end** is executed with the client task suspended. After the code between **do** and **end** has been executed both tasks resume their independent execution.

This rendezvous between the two tasks is illustrated in Figure 19.2.

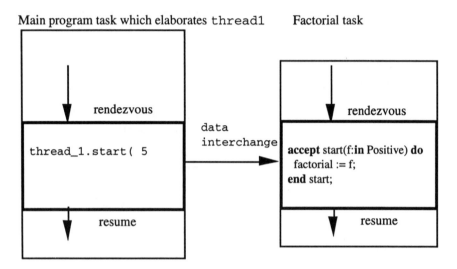

Figure 19.2 Illustration of a rendezvous.

Other variations on the rendezvous are:

Variation	Client	Server task
No information passed	`thread_1.start;`	**accept** `start;`
No information passed but task_1 executes statements during the rendezvous.	`thread_1.start;`	**accept** `start` **do** `    statements;` **end** `start;`

19.1.3 The task's implementation

In the body of the package `Pack_factorial` shown below, the task `Task_factorial` uses two rendezvous points:

-      `start`   to obtain the data to work on
-      `finish`   to deliver the result

When the task's thread of control reaches the end of the task body, the task terminates. Any attempted rendezvous with a terminated task will generate the exception `task_error`.

```
package body Pack_factorial is
   task body Task_factorial is              -- Implementation
      factorial : Positive;
      answer    : Positive := 1;
   begin
      accept start( f:in Positive ) do      -- Factorial
         factorial := f;
      end start;
      for i in 2 .. factorial loop          -- Calculate
         answer := answer * i;
      end loop;
      accept finish( result:out Positive ) do -- Return answer
         result := answer;
      end finish;
   end Task_factorial;
end Pack_factorial;
```

Likewise, the task `Task_is_prime` in the package `Pack_is_a_prime` receives and delivers data to another thread of control.

```
package body Pack_is_a_prime is
   task body Task_is_prime is               -- Implementation
      prime : Positive;
      answer: Boolean := TRUE;
   begin
      accept start( p:in Positive ) do      -- Factorial
         prime := p;
      end start;
      for i in 2 .. prime-1 loop            -- Calculate
         if prime rem i = 0 then
            answer := FALSE; exit;
         end if;
      end loop;
      accept finish( result:out Boolean ) do -- Return answer
         result := answer;
      end finish;
   end Task_is_prime;
end Pack_is_a_prime;
```

19.2 Parameters to a task type

In the previous example, the rendezvous `start` is used to pass initial values to the task. This can be done explicitly, when the task is created by using a discriminated task type. However, the discriminant must be a discrete type or access type. For example, the specification of the task `Task_factorial` can be defined as follows:

```
package Pack_factorial is
  task type Task_factorial(f:Positive) is     -- Specification
    entry finish( result:out Positive );       -- Rendezvous
  end Task_factorial;
end Pack_factorial;
```

Then an instance of the task can be elaborated as follows:

```
    thread_1 : Task_factorial( 7 );                  -- Task is
```

The body of the task type is now:

```
with Simple_io; use Simple_io;
package body Pack_factorial is
  task body Task_factorial is                    -- Implementation
    answer    : Positive := 1;
  begin
    for i in 2 .. f loop                         -- Calculate
      answer := answer * i;
    end loop;
    accept finish( result:out Positive ) do -- Return answer
      result := answer;
    end finish;
  end Task_factorial;
end Pack_factorial;
```

Note: The discriminant to the task type is not specified in the body.

19.2.1 Putting it all together

Using the new definition of the task type in the package `Pack_factorial` the following code can now be written:

```
with Simple_io, Pack_factorial;
use  Simple_io, Pack_factorial;
procedure main is
  num       : Positive;
begin
  num := 7;

  declare
    factorial: Positive;                            -- Answer
    thread_1 : Task_factorial(num);                 -- Task is
  begin
    -- Do some other work as well
    put("Factorial  "); put(num); put(" is ");
    thread_1.finish( factorial );                   -- Obtain result
    put( factorial ); new_line;
  end;

end main;
```

19.3 Mutual exclusion and critical sections

In many cases of real time working, sections of code must not be executed concurrently. The classic example is the adding or removing of data in a shared buffer. For example, to perform a copy operation between two separate devices a shared buffer can be used to even out the differences in response-time. This can be illustrated diagramatically as shown in Figure 19.3.

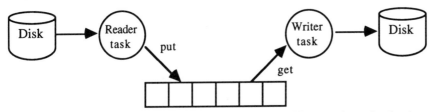

Figure 19.3 Illustration of copy with a buffer to even out the differences in read and write rates.

The problem is how to prevent both the read and write tasks accessing the buffer simultaneously, causing the consequential corruption of indices and data. The solution is to have the buffer as an instance of a protected type.

19.4 Protected type

In essence, an instance of a protected type is an object whose methods (procedures) may not be executed simultaneously. A protected object, an instance of a protected type, is composed of data and the procedures and functions that access the data. The table below summarizes the concurrent access rules for procedures and functions in a protected object.

Unit	Commentary	Access (1)
procedure	A procedure will only execute when no other units are being executed. If necessary the procedure will wait until the currently executing unit(s) have finished.	Read and write
function	A function may execute simultaneously with other executing functions. However, a function cannot execute if a procedure is currently executing.	Read only.
entry	Like a procedure but may also have a barrier condition associated with the entry. If the barrier condition is false the entry is queued until the barrier becomes true.	Read and write

19.5 Implementation

The implementation of a program to perform an efficient copy using an in store buffer to even out differences in response rates can be implemented as two tasks and a protected object, as illustrated in Figure 19.4.

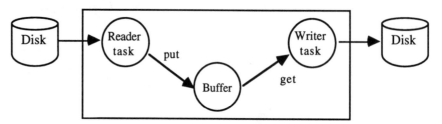

Figure 19.4 Copy implemented using two tasks and a protected object buffer.

The responsibilities of the components are as follows:

Name	Object is	Responsibilities
Task_reader	Task	Read data from the file and then pass the data to the buffer. Note: The task will block if the buffer is full.
Task_writer	Task	Take data from the buffer task and write the data to the file. Note: The task will block if there is no data in the queue.
PT_buffer	Protected type	Serialize the storing and retrieving of data to and from a buffer.

Note: The blocking is achieved with a guard to the accept statement. This is described in the section on guarded accepts.

A package `Pack_types` is defined to allow commonly-used types to be conveniently kept together.

```
with Ada.Text_io;
use  Ada.Text_io;
package Pack_types is
  type P_File_type is access Ada.Text_io.File_type;
  EOT  : constant Character := Character'Val(0);
  CR   : constant Character := Character'Val(15);
  QUEUE_SIZE    : constant := 3;

  type    Queue_no    is new Integer    range 0 .. QUEUE_SIZE;
  type    Queue_index is mod QUEUE_SIZE;
  subtype Queue_range is Queue_index;
  type    Queue_array is array ( Queue_range ) of Character;
end Pack_types;
```

Note: The above package is used to define the type `P_File_type` which is used by several other program units.

The specification for the buffer protected type is as follows:

```
with Pack_types;
use  Pack_types;
package Pack_threads is
  protected type PT_buffer is          -- Task type specification
    entry put( ch:in Character; no_more:in Boolean );
    entry get( ch:in out Character; no_more:out Boolean);
  private
    elements     : Queue_array;          -- Array of elements
    head         : Queue_index := 0;     -- Index
    tail         : Queue_index := 0;     -- Index
    no_in_queue  : Queue_no    := 0;     -- Number in queue
    fin          : Boolean     := FALSE; -- Finish;
  end PT_buffer;

  type P_PT_buffer is access PT_buffer;
```

The specification for the reader and writer tasks are as follows:

```
  task type Task_read(p_buffer:P_PT_buffer;
                      fd_in    :P_File_type) is
    entry finish;
  end Task_read;

  task type Task_write(p_buffer:P_PT_buffer;
                       fd_out   :P_File_type) is
    entry finish;
  end Task_write;
end Pack_threads;
```

Note: To allow the reader and writer tasks to communicate with the buffer, a reference to the buffer protected object is passed to these tasks. A reference to the buffer protected object has to be passed as a protected object is of limited type. The same strategy is used to pass an instance of File_type.

The implementation of the above program is split into two procedures. The procedure do_copy does the actual work of copying between the two files.

```
with Ada.Text_io, Pack_threads, Pack_types;
use  Ada.Text_io, Pack_threads, Pack_types;
procedure do_copy(from:in String; to:in String) is
  type State is ( OPEN_FILE, CREATE_FILE );
  fd_in   : P_File_Type := new Ada.Text_io.File_type;
  fd_out  : P_File_type := new Ada.Text_io.File_type;
  mode    : State := OPEN_FILE;
```

```
begin
  open( File=>fd_in.all, Mode=>IN_FILE, Name=>from);
  mode := CREATE_FILE;
  create(File=>fd_out.all, Mode=>OUT_FILE, Name=>to);
  declare
    buffers : P_PT_buffer := new PT_buffer;
    reader  : Task_read( buffers, fd_in );
    writer  : Task_write( buffers, fd_out );
  begin
    reader.finish; close( fd_in.all );   -- Finish reader task
    writer.finish; close( fd_out.all );  -- Finish writer task
  end;
exception
  when Name_error =>
    case mode is
      when OPEN_FILE =>
        put("Problem opening file " & from ); new_line;
      when CREATE_FILE =>
        put("Problem creating file " & to ); new_line;
    end case;
  when Tasking_error =>
    put("Task error in main program"); new_line;
end do_copy;
```

Note: Explicit de-referencing of instances of a `File_type` *is achieved using* `.all`.

The procedure `copy` extracts the arguments for the copy operation.

```
with do_copy;
with Ada.Text_io, Ada.Command_line;
use  Ada.Text_io, Ada.Command_line;
procedure copy is
begin
  if argument_count = 2 then
    do_copy ( argument(1), argument(2) );
  else
    put("Usage: copy from to"); new_line;
  end if;
end copy;
```

When a pointer to a **protected type** (for example, `PT_buffer`) is elaborated, no object is created. The creation of an instance of the protected type `PT_buffer` is performed using **new** as follows:

```
buffers : P_PT_buffer := new PT_buffer;
```

Note: As a protected object is limited, using an access value is one way of making the protected object visible to several program units.

The implementation of the reader task is then:

```
with Ada.Text_io; use  Ada.Text_io;
   task body Task_read is              -- Task implementation
      ch        : Character;
   begin
      while not end_of_file( fd_in.all ) loop
         while not end_of_line( fd_in.all ) loop
            get( fd_in.all, ch );             -- Get character
            p_buffer.put( ch, FALSE );        -- Add to buffer
         end loop;
         skip_line( fd_in.all );              -- Next line
         p_buffer.put( CR, FALSE );           -- New line
      end loop;
      p_buffer.put( EOT, TRUE );              -- End of characters

      accept finish;
   exception
      when Tasking_error =>
         put("Exception in Task read"); new_line;
   end Task_read;
```

The rendezvous finish is used by the reader to indicate that there is no more data.

Note: As tasking errors are not propagated beyond the task, a specific exception
handler is used to detect this eventuality.
The character constant CR is used to indicate the newline character.

Similarly, the writer task is implemented as follows:

```
   task body Task_write is             -- Task implementation
      last     : Boolean := FALSE;     -- No more data
      ch       : Character;            -- Character read
   begin
      loop
         p_buffer.get( ch, last );           -- From buffer
         exit when last;                     -- No more characters
         if ch = CR then
            new_line( fd_out.all );          -- New line
         else
            put( fd_out.all, ch );           -- Character
         end if;
      end loop;

      accept finish;                   -- Finished
   exception
      when Tasking_error =>
         put("Exception in Task write"); new_line;
   end Task_write;
end Pack_threads;
```

19.5.1 Barrier condition entry

The protected type uses one additional facility, that of a barrier entry. If the buffer becomes full, a mechanism is needed to prevent further data being added. The barrier:

```
entry put( ch:in Character; no_more:in Boolean )
   when no_in_queue < QUEUE_SIZE  is
```

to the **entry** prevents the **entry** being processed until there is room in the buffer. If the buffer is full then the reader task is suspended (blocked) until a successful get **entry** is made. The guards for an **entry** statement are re-evaluated after a successful call on the protected object. The full implementation of the protected type PT_buffer is as follows.:

```
protected body PT_buffer is
```

The queue is implemented in sequential store with the two indices head and tail keeping track of the current extraction and insertion points respectively. A count of the active cells used in the buffer is held in no_of. Figure 19.5 illustrates the queue after adding the characters 't', 'e', 'x', 't'.

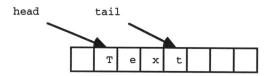

Figure 19.5 Queue holding the characters 't', 'e', 'x', 't'.

The procedure put in the body of the protected object adds new data to the queue. Data can only be added to the queue when there is room. The index tail marks the position of the last data item added. When no more data is available to add to the queue the variable fin is set to true.

```
entry put( ch:in Character; no_more:in Boolean )
  when no_in_queue < QUEUE_SIZE  is
begin
   if no_more then                         -- Last
      fin := TRUE;                         -- Set flag
   else
      elements( tail ) := ch;              -- Add to queue
      tail := tail+1;                      -- Next position
      no_in_queue := no_in_queue + 1;      --
   end if;
end;
```

The procedure get extract data from the queue. The head indexes the data item at the front of the queue. The parameter eof is set to true when no more data is available. This is different from a temporary unavailability of data due to the reader task blocking.

```
   entry get(ch:in out Character; no_more:out Boolean)
     when no_in_queue > 0 or else fin is
   begin
     if no_in_queue > 0 then          -- Item available
        ch := elements( head );       -- Get item
        head := head+1;               -- Next position
        no_in_queue := no_in_queue - 1;  --
        no_more := FALSE;             -- Not end
     else
        no_more := TRUE;              -- End of items
     end if;
   end;

end PT_buffer;
```

Note: *When all the data has been exhausted from the buffer, the procedure* get *will return false in its second parameter.*

19.5.2   Putting it all together

When the above program is compiled and run it will perform a copy operation using the internal buffer to even out differences between the speed of the input and output streams. For example, to copy the contents of from to the file to a user can type:

```
copy from to
```

19.6 Delay

Execution of a program can be delayed for a specific number of seconds or until a specific time is reached. For example, to implement a delay of 2.5 seconds in a program the following **delay** statement is used.

```
delay 2.5;
```

Note: *The delay time is of type* Duration, *which has a range of 0.0 .. 86_400.0 and is defined in the package* Ada.Calendar. *The specification of the package* Ada.Calendar *is contained in section C.15, Appendix C.*

To delay until a specific time the **until** form of the `delay` statement is used. To delay part of a program until the 1st January 2000 the following statement is used:

```
delay until time_of(2000,1,1,0.0); -- Until 1 Jan 2000
```

Note: The package Ada.Calendar *contains the definition for* time_of *which returns the date as an instance of* Time.

19.7 Choice of accepts

The **select** construct is used to select between several different possible rendezvous. The form of the select construct is as follows:

```
select                          -- Choice of accepts
  accept option1 do
    ...
  end;
or
  accept option2 do
    ...
  end;

end select;
```

This can be used when a task can have more than one rendezvous made with it from several different sources. For example, a task controlling output to a terminal may be accessed by either a text interface for information messages, or a block image interface for pictorial data. The `select` construct causes a wait until one of the specified rendezvous is made.

Note: A protected type may be simulated by using a task which consists of a loop in which a select statement is embedded. Each rendezvous within the `select` *statement will then have its execution serialized. For example:*

```
loop
  select                          -- Serialization of code
    accept option1 do ... end;
  or
    accept option2 do ... end;
  end select;
end loop;
```

19.7.1 Accept alternative

An **else** part may be added to a **select** statement. The statements after the **else** will be obeyed if a rendezvous cannot be immediately made with any of the **accept** statements in the **select** construct.

```
select
  accept  ...


else
  statements;            -- Only executed if no call on an
                         --  accept immediately satisfied
end select;
```

19.7.2 Accept time-out

The **select** construct may also include a time-out delay after which, if there is no **accept** called following the statements, the **delay** will be executed. The format of this variation of the select construct is:

```
select
  accept  ...


or
  delay TIME;            -- Time out delay in seconds
  statements;            -- Only executed if no call on an
                         --  accept within TIME seconds
end select;
```

*Note: There may be only one **delay** alternative and no **else** part.*

This construct can be used to implement a watchdog task that will report an error if it has not been polled for a certain time. This watchdog task can act as a safety measure to report that the software is not performing as expected. An implementation of a simple watchdog timer is as follows:

```
package Pack_watchdog is
  task type Task_watchdog is          -- Specification
    entry poll;                       -- Rendezvous
    entry finish;                     -- Rendezvous
  end Task_watchdog;
end Pack_watchdog;
```

The entry `poll` is called at regular intervals to prevent the watchdog task from reporting an error. The task is terminated by a call to `finish`. The implementation of the task is as follows:

```
with Simple_io; use Simple_io;
package body Pack_watchdog is
  task body Task_watchdog is                -- Implementation
  begin
    loop
      select
        accept poll;                        -- Successful poll
      or
        accept finish;                      -- Terminate
        exit;
      or
        delay 0.1;                          -- Time out
        put("WARNING Watchdog failure"); new_line;
      end select;
    end loop;
  end Task_watchdog;
end Pack_watchdog;
```

If a poll is not received every 0.1 seconds then the task will report a warning to the user.

19.8 Alternatives to a task type

Tasks do not have to be defined as a task type. They can be defined as a package or even as part of a program unit.

19.18.1 As part of a package

A task can be specified as a package. For example, the task to calculate a factorial could have been specified as follows:

```
package Pack_factorial is
  task Task_factorial is                    -- Specification
    entry start( f:in Positive);            -- Rendezvous
    entry finish( result:out Positive);     -- Rendezvous
  end Task_factorial;
end Pack_factorial;
```

the implementation of which is:

```
with Simple_io; use Simple_io;
package body Pack_factorial is
  task body Task_factorial is              -- Implementation
  factorial : Positive;
  answer    : Positive := 1;
  begin
    put("Pack_factorial"); new_Line;
    accept start( f:in Positive) do        -- Factorial
      factorial := f;
    end start;
    for i in 2 .. factorial loop           -- Calculate
      answer := answer * i;
    end loop;
    accept finish( result:out Positive ) do -- Return answer
      result := answer;
    end finish;
  end Task_factorial;
end Pack_factorial;
```

The code to interact with this task in a package would be as follows:

```
with Simple_io, Pack_factorial;
use  Simple_io, Pack_factorial;
procedure execute_threads is
factorial: Positive;
begin
  Task_factorial.start(5);        -- Start factorial calculation

  put("Factorial  5 is ");
  Task_factorial.finish( factorial ); -- Obtain result
  put( factorial ); new_line;
end execute_threads;
```

Note: If this form is used, then the task will come into immediate existence as soon as the program is executed.
Only one instance of the factorial task can be created.

19.8.2   As part of a program unit

```
with Simple_io; use  Simple_io;
procedure main is

task Task_factorial is                   -- Specification
  entry start( f:in Positive);           -- Rendezvous
  entry finish( result:out Positive);    -- Rendezvous
end Task_factorial;
```

```
task body Task_factorial is                 -- Implementation
factorial : Positive;
answer    : Positive := 1;
begin
  put("Pack_factorial"); new_Line;
  accept start( f:in Positive) do          -- Factorial
    factorial := f;
  end start;
  for i in 2 .. factorial loop             -- Calculate
    answer := answer * i;
  end loop;
  accept finish( result: out Positive ) do -- Return answer
    result := answer;
  end finish;
end Task_factorial;

begin
  declare
    factorial: Positive;
  begin
    Task_factorial.start(5);     -- Start factorial calculation

    put("Factorial  5 is ");
    Task_factorial.finish( factorial ); -- Obtain result
    put( factorial ); new_line;

  end;
end main;
```

Note: *The task will come into existence as soon as the program unit is executed.*

19.9 Self-assessment

- What is a thread or task in a programming language?

- What Ada construct can be used to implement a thread or task?

- How is information passed between two threads? Explain why a special construct is required for this activity.

- What is the difference between a task type and a normal type?

- What is the difference between execution of a procedure and execution of a function in a protected type?

- What happens when a task type is elaborated ?

- How can a task select the current rendezvous that is made with it, from a number of possible rendezvous?

- Why might a program need to employ a watchdog timer?

- How might a constantly running Ada program execute some code at a particular time of the day?

19.12 Exercises

Construct the following:

- *Fibonacci task*

  A thread or task which will calculate the n'th term of the Fibonacci series. The rendezvous with this task are:

  - ```
    calculate( n );  -- What term to find;
    ```
  - ```
    deliver( res );  -- The result.
    ```

- *Factorial*

  A thread or task which will calculate the factorial of a supplied value. The task should allow multiple serial calculations to be requested. The rendezvous with this task are:

  - ```
    calculate( n );  -- What term to find;
    ```
  - ```
    deliver( res );  -- The result;
    ```
  - ```
    terminate;       -- Terminate the task.
    ```

- *Fast copy*

  A program to perform an optimal block copy using an intermediate buffer of disk blocks to even out any differences in speed between the input and output streams.

- *Communication link*

  A program to allow the sending of data between two computer systems using a serial port. The program should be able to inform the user if the other machine has not responded within the last two minutes.
    ```

20 System programming

This chapter shows how access can be made to low-level facilities of the Ada language. This facilitates the construction of programs which interact with the system at a low level

20.1 Representation clause

An enumeration may be given a specific value by a representation clause. For example, the following enumerations, defined for the type Country:

```
type Country is   (USA, FRANCE, UK, AUSTRALIA);
```

may each be given their international telephone dialling code with the following representation clause:

```
type Country is   (USA, FRANCE, UK, AUSTRALIA);
for  Country use (USA=> 1, FRANCE=> 33, UK=> 44, AUSTRALIA=> 61);
```

Thus, internally the enumeration FRANCE would be represented by the number 33.

Note: The values given to each enumeration must be in ascending order and unique.

However, even though the enumerations may have non-consecutive representations, attributes of the enumeration will be as if there had been no representation clause. For example:

Expression	Delivers
Country'Succ(USA)	FRANCE
Country'Pred(AUSTRALIA)	UK
Country'Pos(FRANCE)	2
Country'Val(2)	UK

To access the value of the enumeration requires the use of the generic package Unchecked_conversion that will deliver an object as a different type without any intermediate conversions. The only restriction with the use of

Unchecked_conversion is that the objects must be of the same size. This can be ensured by informing the compiler of the size in bits required to use for the representation of an object of type Country. To set the size for the enumeration Country to be the same size as the type Integer the following representation clause is used:

```
type Country is   (USA, FRANCE, UK, AUSTRALIA);
for  Country use (USA=> 1, FRANCE=> 33, UK=> 44, AUSTRALIA=> 61);
for  Country'Size use Integer'Size;
```

Note: The attribute 'Size delivers the size in bits of an instance of the type.

For example, to print the international telephone code for France the following code can be used:

```
with Simple_io, unchecked_conversion;
procedure main is
   type Country is   (USA, FRANCE, UK, AUSTRALIA);
   for  Country use (USA=>1, FRANCE=>33, UK=>44, AUSTRALIA=>61);
   for  Country'Size use Integer'Size;

   function idc is new Unchecked_conversion( Country, Integer );
begin
   put( "International dialling code for France is ");
   put( idc(FRANCE) );
   new_line;
end main;
```

when run, it would produce:

```
International dialling code for France is 33
```

It would be convenient to also include Canada in the Country enumeration for telephone codes. However, as Canada has the same code as the USA, this cannot be done directly. The reason for this is that two enumerations may not have the same physical representation. The way round this is to define a renaming for Canada as follows:

```
function CANADA return Country renames USA;
```

which defines CANADA as a function that returns the enumeration USA as its result.

20.2 Binding a variable to a specific address

In some limited situations it is necessary to read or write from absolute locations in memory. In DOS the time of day is stored in locations (in hexadecimal) 46E and 46C. The exact specification is as follows:

Location (hexadecimal)	Contents
046E - 046F	The time of day in hours.
046C - 046D	The ticks past the current hour. Each tick is 5/91 seconds.

A variable may be bound to an absolute location with the for use clause. For example, to bind the integer variable time_high to the absolute location 16#46E# the following declaration can be used:

```
time_high_address : constant Address := to_address( 16#046C# );

type Time        is range 0 .. 65365;        -- Unsigned
for  Time'Size use 16;                        --  in 2 bytes

time_high: Time;
   for time_high'Address use time_high_address;
```

Note: Time is a type describing a 16 bit unsigned integer.
The address 16#046E# must be of type Address that is defined in the package
System. The child package System.Storage_elements contains the
function to_address which converts an integer into an address.

A program to print the current time of day in hours, minutes and seconds is as follows:

```
with Simple_io, System, System.Storage_elements;
use  Simple_io, System, System.Storage_elements;
procedure main is
   time_high_address : constant Address := to_address( 16#046C# );
   time_low_address  : constant Address := to_address( 16#046E# );
   type Seconds_t is range 0 .. 1_000_000_000;  -- up to 65k * 5
   type Time      is range 0 .. 65365;          -- Unsigned
   for  Time'Size use 16;                        --  in 2 bytes
   time_low : Time;
      for time_low'Address  use time_low_address;
   time_high: Time;
      for time_high'Address use time_high_address;
   seconds  : Seconds_t;
begin
   put("Time is ");
   put( Time'Image(time_high) ); put(" :");       -- Hour
   seconds := (Seconds_t(time_low) * 5) / 91;
   put(Seconds_t'Image(seconds/60)); put(" :");  -- Mins
   put(Seconds_t'Image(seconds rem 60));         -- Seconds
   new_line;
end main;
```

which if run on a DOS system would produce:

```
Time is   17 : 54 : 57
```

Note: For this to work, the generated code must be able to access these low locations in DOS.

20.2.1   Access to individual bits

On an MSDOS system memory address 16#0417# contains the status of various keyboard settings. Individual bits in this byte indicate the settings (set or not set) for the scroll lock, number lock, caps and insert keys. The layout of this byte is illustrated in Figure 20.1.

Most significant			Bit position			Least significant	
7	6	5	4	3	2	1	0
Insert	Caps lock	Number lock	Scroll lock				

Figure 20.1 Keyboard status on an MSDOS system.

The following program prints out the status of the insert, caps lock, and number lock keys:

```
with Simple_io, System, System.Storage_elements;
use  Simple_io, System, System.Storage_elements;
procedure main is
  keyboard_address : constant Address := to_address( 16#417# );
  type Status     is  ( NOT_ACTIVE, ACTIVE );
  for  Status     use ( NOT_ACTIVE => 0, ACTIVE => 1 );
  for  Status'Size use 1;
```

The above declarations define the enumeration `Status` to occupy a single bit. The next set of declarations define `Keyboard_status` and access to the individual bits that make up the status byte. This is defined using a record structure with a representation clause for the specific layout of the bits.

```
type Keyboard_status is
  record
    scroll_lock : Status;        -- Scroll lock status
    num_lock    : Status;        -- Num lock status
    caps_lock   : Status;        -- Caps lock status
    insert      : Status;        -- Insert status
  end record;
```

```
for Keyboard_status use
  record
    scroll_lock at 0 range 4..4; -- Storage unit 0 Bit 4
    num_lock    at 0 range 5..5; -- Storage unit 0 Bit 5
    caps_lock   at 0 range 6..6; -- Storage unit 0 Bit 6
    insert      at 0 range 7..7; -- Storage unit 0 Bit 7
  end record;
Keyboardstatus_byte : Keyboard_status;
for Keyboardstatus_byte'Address use Keyboard_address;
```

The representation clause `scroll_lock` **at** 0 **range** 4..4 requests that the
object `scroll_lock` be stored at an offset of 0 storage locations from the start of the
record at bit position 4.

Note: *On a PC the storage unit size is one byte.*
        The bits selected may be outside the storage unit.

The body of the program which interrogates these individual bits using the
individual record components of `keyboard_status_byte` is:

```
begin
  if Keyboardstatus_byte.insert = ACTIVE then
    put("Insert mode set"); new_line;
  else
    put("Insert mode not set"); new_line;
  end if;
  if Keyboardstatus_byte.caps_lock = ACTIVE then
    put("Caps   lock set"); new_line;
  else
    put("Caps   lock not set"); new_line;
  end if;
  if Keyboardstatus_byte.num_lock = ACTIVE then
    put("Number lock set"); new_line;
  else
    put("Number lock not set"); new_line;
  end if;
end main;
```

which when run on an MSDOS system with none of these keys set would print:

```
Insert mode not set
Caps   lock not set
Number lock not set
```

Note: *For this to work, the generated code must be able to access these low locations*
        in DOS.

20.3 Self-assessment

- Using a representation clause, the following enumeration for `Country` defines the IDD (International Dialling Code) for a small selection of countries.

```
type Country is  (USA, FRANCE, UK );
for  Country use (USA=> 1, FRANCE=> 33, UK=> 44 );
```

What do the following deliver?

(a)   `Country'Pos( USA )`
(b)   `Country'Val( 2 ).`

- How can the IDC of France be extracted from the enumeration for `France`?

- As Canada has the same IDC as the USA, how can an enumeration for `Canada` be included in the list of countries above?

- How can the variable `cost` be declared so that its address maps on to the byte at absolute location 040 in programs address space?

20.4 Exercises

Construct the following:

- *Memory dump*
  A program which prints in hexadecimal the contents of the bottom 100 locations of the current program.

21 A text user interface

This chapter defines an API (Application Program Interface) for use by an application program that reads and writes textual information to and from windows on a VDU screen. The TUI (Text User interface) uses the metaphor of non-overlapping windows. The application program is written using an event-driven regime. In this way, call-back functions are written to implement services requested by a user of the application.

The next chapter describes in detail the implementation of the TUI.

21.1 Specification

A TUI (Text User Interface) provides various types of non-overlapping windows on a VDU screen. The windows provided are:

- A text window into which characters from the Ada type Character can be written.
- A dialog window that provides a mechanism for a user to enter character data.
- A menu window from which a user can select an option from a list of available options.

For example, an application that converts miles into kilometres can use the TUI to input and display data as follows:

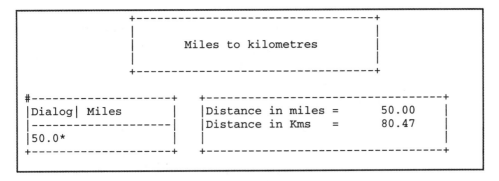

```
                    +-----------------------------------+
                    |                                   |
                    |         Miles to kilometres       |
                    |                                   |
                    +-----------------------------------+

#--------------------+     +-----------------------------------+
|Dialog| Miles       |     |Distance in miles =       50.00    |
|--------------------|     |Distance in Kms    =      80.47    |
|50.0*               |     |                                   |
+--------------------+     +-----------------------------------+
```

Note: A # in the top left hand corner of a window signifies which window has the focus for input.

The interface for this program consists of three windows:

- A text window which displays the title of the program
  "Miles to kilometres"
- A dialog window that solicits input from the user. In this case the dialog window solicits the miles to be converted into kilometres.
- A text window for the display of the results of the conversion.

The TUI supports the display of information into a window using output procedures similar to those implemented in Ada.Text_io. A call-back function is associated with a dialog window and is executed after a user interaction. A call-back function is an Ada function that implements part of the functionality of the program; in effect, the user controls the interactions within the program. This is often referred to as an event-driven metaphor.

The dialog window's call-back function is executed when a user has a message to send to the program. For example, in the miles to kilometres program the dialog window's call-back function is executed when a user has finished typing in a distance in miles. This call-back function calculates the conversion to kilometres and displays the answer in the result's window.

21.2 API for TUI

The API (Application Program Interface) for the TUI consists of a set of function and procedure calls. These are implemented as methods on instances of the different types of windows in the TUI. The windows form an inheritance hierarchy as illustrated in Figure 21.1.

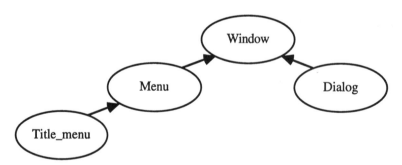

Figure 21.1 Window hierarchy.

The API calls for a Window are inherited to form the base API calls for a Menu and Dialog. Likewise, the base API calls for a Title_menu are inherited from a Menu.

21.2.1   To set up and close down the TUI

The following procedures set up and close down the TUI system. These API calls are independent of any window and thus do not refer to an actual instance of a window. In fact they are class methods of `Input_manager`.

function / procedure	Note
`window_prolog;`	Set up the environment for the TUI. This must be called outside the block in which windows are elaborated.
`window_start;`	After initializing any program-generated windows, start the application by allowing a user to interact with the program.
`window_epilog;`	Close down the window system. This must be called outside the block in which the windows are elaborated.

For example, the structure of a program using the TUI is:

```
procedure main is
begin
  window_prolog;              -- Set-up window system
  declare
                              -- Declaration of windows used in
                              --   the program
  begin
                              -- Initialization of windows
                              --   used in program
    window_start;             -- Start the user interaction
  end;
  window_epilog;              -- Close window system
end main;
```

Note: The reason for this structure is to allow initialization code for any declared windows to be run after the window system has been initiated by the procedure `window_prolog` and to allow any finalization code for the elaborated windows to be executed before the procedure `window_epilog` is called.
To avoid simultaneous access to a window, program initialization of a window must occur before the user is allowed to interact with the system.

21.2.2   Window API calls

A text window is created with a declaration of the form:

```
win : Window;
```

A text window can be created and written to using the following API calls:

Notes	Function / procedure
1	**procedure** framework(the:**in out** Window; abs_x_crd, abs_y_crd: Positive; max_x_crd, max_y_crd: Positive; cb:**in** P_cbf := **null**);
2	**procedure** put(w:**in out** Window; mes:**in** String);
2	**procedure** put(w:**in out** Window; ch:**in** Character);
2	**procedure** put(w:**in out** Window; n:**in** Integer);
3	**procedure** position(w:**in out** Window; x,y:**in** Positive);
4	**procedure** clear(w:**in out** Window);
5	**procedure** new_line(w:**in out** Window);
6	**procedure** make_window(w:**in out** Window; mo:**in** mode);

Notes:

1   Sets the absolute position and size of the window on the screen.
      The top left hand corner position is at:
         (abs_x_crd, abs_y_crd)
      The bottom left corner position is at:
         (abs_x_crd+max_x_crd-1, abs_y_crd+max_y_crd-1)

2   Displays information in a window. These functions are modelled after the procedures in Ada.Text_io.

3   Sets the current output position in the window.

4   Clears the window to all spaces.

5   Writes a newline to the window. This will cause the information in the window to scroll up if the current position is at the last line of the window.

6   Makes the displayed window visible or invisible.

21.2.3 Dialog API calls

A dialog window is created with a declaration of the form:

```
diag : Dialog;
```

A dialog window is inherited from a Window and as well as all the API calls of a Window has the following additional API call:

Note	Function / procedure
1	**procedure** framework (the:**in out** Dialog; abs_x, abs_y:**in** Positive; max_x: **in** Positive; name:**in** String; cb:**in** P_cbf);

Note:

1   *Sets the absolute position of the window on the screen. The size of the window is set with* max_x. *The call-back function* cb *will be called after the user has constructed a message in the dialog box . This is initiated by the user entering the Enter character (return key). When the Enter character is received the menu window calls the call-back function with a string parameter containing the user's entered text. The signature of the call-back function is:*

function cb(mes:**in** String) **return** String

where mes *is the message typed by the user.*

21.2.4   User interaction with the TUI

A user of an application program that is built using the TUI API has the following switch characters defined:

Switch character	Description
TAB	Swaps the focus for user input to another window on the VDU screen. The active window is indicated by a # in the top left hand corner.
ESC	Activates the menu system. The menu system is described in detail in section 21.4.
^E	Terminates the TUI session. All windows will be closed and the user returned to the environment which initiated the program.

A switch character is used to activate a specific window on the system or cause a global effect.

21.2.5   Classes used

The TUI API is contained in the following classes:

API for a	Contained in the package	Notes
Window	Class_window	-
Dialog	Class_dialog	Plus the API inherited from a Window.
Menu	Class_menu	Plus the API inherited from a Window.
Menu_title	Class_menu_title	Plus the API inherited from a Menu
TUI set up	Class_input_manager	Controls the input sent to the TUI.

21.3 An example program using the TUI

A short program to illustrate the use of many of the API calls is shown below. This example program converts a distance entered by the user in miles into kilometres. The package `Pack_globals` contains the global variables which will be used in the program. In this case there is only one, the access value of the results window.

```
with Class_window;
use  Class_window;
package Pack_globals is
  p_result : P_Window;
end Pack_globals;
```

The call-back function `user_input` is executed when a user has pressed the Enter character after entering the distance in miles. This entered distance is converted to a floating point number using the input procedure `get` to convert a string into an instance of a `Float`. If the number is not valid or an error in the calculation occurs, then an appropriate message is displayed to the user.

```
with Simple_io, Class_window, Class_dialog, Pack_globals;
use  Simple_io, Class_window, Class_dialog, Pack_globals;
function user_input( cb_mes:in String ) return String is
  miles : Float;              -- Miles input by user
  last  : Positive;           --
  str_kms: String( 1 .. 10 ); -- As a string in Kms
  str_mls: String( 1 .. 10 ); -- As a string in Miles
begin
  begin
    get( cb_mes & ".", miles, last );
    put( str_kms, miles * 1.609_344, aft=>2, exp=>0 );
    put( str_mls, miles, aft=>2, exp=>0 );
    put( p_result.all, "Distance in miles = " );
    put( p_result.all, str_mls ); new_line( p_result.all );
    put( p_result.all, "Distance in Kms   = " );
    put( p_result.all, str_kms ); new_line( p_result.all );
  exception
    when Data_Error =>
      put( p_result.all, " Not a valid number" );
      new_line( p_result.all );
    when others =>
      put( p_result.all, " [Calculation error]" );
      new_line( p_result.all );
  end;
  return "";
end user_input;
```

Note: The call-back function returns a string as its result. This provides a mechanism for returning information to the environment which called it. In this particular case, no information is returned.

.0 is appended to the user's input to allow a user to enter an integer value and still have the number processed correctly.

The main program declares the three windows that will be displayed:

```
with Class_input_manager, Class_window,
     Class_dialog, Pack_globals, user_input;
use  Class_input_manager, Class_window,
     Class_dialog, Pack_globals;
procedure main is
begin
  window_prolog;                  -- Setup window system
  declare
    result : aliased Window;      -- Result window
    input  : Dialog;              -- Input Window
    title  : Window;              -- title Window
```

Note: The call to window_prolog *initializes the TUI system.*

The main program code calls framework to set the size and position of the various windows on the screen. This initialization is done before a user of the application is allowed to interact with the system.

```
  begin
    framework( title,  20,  1,   36, 5 );    -- Title Window
    framework( result, 30, 10,   36, 5 );    -- Result Window

    position( title, 8, 2 );
    put( title, "Miles to Kilometres" );
    framework( input, 5, 10, 22,             -- Input Window
               "Miles", user_input'Access );
```

Note: The access value of the function user_input *is passed to the function*
*   framework *that sets up the call-back function.*
*   The* title *window top left hand corner is at position (20,1) and the bottom*
*   right hand corner at (20+36-1,1+5-1).*

The access value of the results window is assigned to p_result so that it can be accessed by the call-back function user_input. Remember, the call-back function must be at the library level.

```
    p_result := result'Unchecked_Access;
```

Note: As the type used to declare the access value for a window is at the library level,
*   'Unchecked_Access is used.*

The event-driven component part of the program is activated by a call to the procedure `window_start`. From this point onwards the program flow is driven by the user interacting with windows displayed on the terminal screen. Eventually the user will terminate the program, at which point the procedure `window_start` will return.

```
window_start;                    -- Start the user interaction
```

The procedure `window_epilog` closes down the system. This must be called outside the block in which the instances of the windows were elaborated. This is to allow the finalization code to be called on the elaborated windows before `window_epilog` is called.

```
    end;
    window_epilog;               -- Close window system
end main;
```

21.3.1 Putting it all together

When compiled with the TUI API library code, the screen display with added annotations to show which call of `framework` was used, together with position information is shown below:

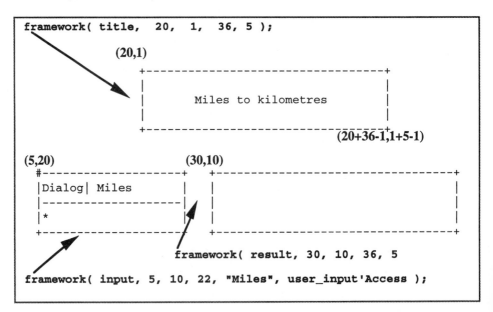

After a user has typed in a distance of 50 miles to be converted to kilometres the screen will display:

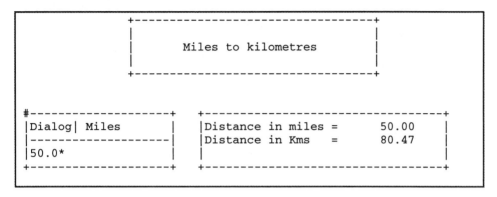

21.4 The menu system

The menu system is based on the metaphor of a menu title bar at the top of the screen which changes as new menu options are selected. When a user selects away from the menu bar, the menu bar is returned to the top level of the menu hierarchy. The menu system is activated by typing the switch character ESC.

For example, a menu title bar of two items:

Menu Component	Effect
About	Prints information about the program
Reset	Resets the program to an initial state

would be displayed as:

The character * indicates the current menu item. To select this menu item the user presses the selection key Enter. To change the current menu item the Arrow keys are used to move between the various options. Left arrow moves left and right arrow moves right the selected component. The effect of going right at the right-most menu item or left at the left-most menu item is to wrap around to the next item.

In addition to the API of a `Window`, the `Menu` and `Menu_title` API have the additional method of:

Note	Function / procedure
1	**procedure** framework(the:**in out** Menu'Class; m1:**in** String:=""; w1:**in** P_Menu:=**null**; cb1:**in** P_cbf:=**null**; m2:**in** String:=""; w2:**in** P_Menu:=**null**; cb2:**in** P_cbf:=**null**; m3:**in** String:=""; w3:**in** P_Menu:=**null**; cb3:**in** P_cbf:=**null**; m4:**in** String:=""; w4:**in** P_Menu:=**null**; cb4:**in** P_cbf:=**null**; m5:**in** String:=""; w5:**in** P_Menu:=**null**; cb5:**in** P_cbf:=**null**; m6:**in** String:=""; w6:**in** P_Menu:=**null**; cb6:**in** P_cbf:=**null**);

Note:

1. This sets up a menu title bar or a menu title. The first parameter can be an instance of either a Menu or a Menu_title. Each menu item in the menu bar has three parameters:

   - The displayed name of the menu item.
   - A possible pointer to another menu bar.
   - A possible pointer to a call-back function which is to be called when the menu is selected.

   The second and third parameter are mutually exclusive. Thus, you can have either another menu bar or a call-back function.
   As the menu bar is always at the top of the screen its position is not selected. It would of course be an error to have a window overlapping the menu bar.
   The type P_cbf is defined as:

   type P_cbf **is access function**(str:**in** String) **return** String;

The following frameworks are used to set up a menu system with a main menu title bar and a selectable secondary menu bar tied to the main menu item Print.

```
with Class_input_manager, Class_window,
     Class_dialog, Class_menu, Class_menu_title,
     laser, ink_jet, about;
use  Class_input_manager, Class_window,
     Class_dialog, Class_menu, Class_menu_title;
procedure main is
begin
  window_prolog;
  declare
    menu_bar     : Menu_title;
    printer_type : aliased Menu;
  begin
    framework( printer_type,
               "Laser",   null, laser'Access,
               "Ink jet", null, ink_jet'Access );
    framework( menu_bar,
               "About",   null, about'Access,
               "Print",   printer_type'Unchecked_Access, null );
    window_start;
  end;
  window_epilog;
end main;
```

Note: The call-back functions `laser, ink_jet,` *and* `about` *process a user request when the appropriate menu option is selected.*
The use of `'Unchecked_Access` *to deliver the access value of* `printer_type.`

When the above code is incorporated into a program the menu system would display as follows:

```
+-----------------------+          +-----------------------+
Main menu bar                      Secondary menu bar

+--------------------+             +----------------------+
| About     |*Print  |             |*Laser   | Ink jet   |
+--------------------+             +----------------------+
```

Note: The secondary menu bar will overwrite the main menu bar regardless of the number of items in the main menu.

21.5 Noughts and crosses program

A program to play the game of noughts and crosses using the TUI API interface is composed of a class `board` which has the following methods:

Method	Responsibility
add	Add a piece to the board.
reset	Reset the board to empty.
state	Return the state of the board.
update	Update onto a window the state of the board.
valid	Check if the move is valid.

The Ada specification for the class `Board` is:

```
with Class_window;
use  Class_window;
package Class_board is
  type Board is private;

  type Game_state is ( WIN, PLAYABLE, DRAW );
  function  valid( the:in Board; pos:in Integer ) return Boolean;
  procedure add(the:in out Board; pos:in Integer;
                piece:in Character);
  function  state( the:in Board ) return Game_state;
  procedure display_board( the:in Board; win:in P_Window );
  procedure update( the:in Board; win:in P_Window );
  procedure reset( the:in out Board );
```

```
private
  SIZE_TTT: constant := 9;                        -- Must be 9
  subtype Board_index is Integer range 1 .. SIZE_TTT;
  subtype Board_range is Board_index;
  type    Board_grid  is array( Board_range ) of Character;
  type Board is record
    sqrs  : Board_grid := ( others => ' ');      -- Initialize
    last  : Board_index := 1;                    -- Last move
    moves : Natural := 0;
  end record;
end Class_board;
```

Note: It would have been elegant to re-use the previous noughts and crosses class for
Board but the functionality is too dissimilar to make this a practical
proposition. Code re-use is not always possible!

In the implementation of the class the function `valid` returns TRUE if the suggested noughts and crosses move is valid.

```
package body Class_board is

  function  valid(the:in Board; pos:in Integer) return Boolean is
  begin
    return pos in Board_range and then the.sqrs( pos ) = ' ';
  end valid;
```

The procedure `add` is responsible for adding a new piece onto the board. The position of the last move made is recorded to simplify the update of the new state of the board.

```
procedure add( the:in out Board; pos:in Integer;
               piece:in Character ) is
begin
  the.last := pos;
  the.sqrs( pos ) := piece;
  the.moves := the.moves + 1;
end add;
```

The function `state` returns the enumeration WIN, DRAW or PLAYABLE depending on the current state of the game. The constant array `cells` holds all possible win lines and the main body of the code uses the values held in this array to determine the current state of the game.

```
function state( the:in Board ) return Game_state is
   type Win_line      is array( 1 .. 3 ) of Positive;
   type All_win_lines is range 1 .. 8;
   cells: constant array ( All_win_lines ) of Win_line :=
      ( (1,2,3), (4,5,6), (7,8,9), (1,4,7),
        (2,5,8), (3,6,9), (1,5,9), (3,5,7) ); -- All win lines
   first : Character;
begin
   for pwl in All_win_lines loop          -- All Pos Win Lines
      first := the.sqrs( cells(pwl)(1) ); -- First cell in line
      if first /= ' ' then                -- Looks promising
         if first = the.sqrs(cells(pwl)(2)) and then
            first = the.sqrs(cells(pwl)(3)) then return WIN;
         end if;
      end if;
   end loop;
   if the.moves >= 9                       -- Check for draw
      then return DRAW;                    --   Board full
      else return PLAYABLE;                --   Still playable
   end if;
end state;
```

The procedure `reset` resets the board to its initial empty state.

```
procedure reset( the:in out Board ) is
begin
   the.sqrs  := ( others => ' ');      -- All spaces
   the.last  := 1;                     -- Last move
   the.moves := 0;                     -- No of moves
end reset;
```

The procedure `display_board` displays in a window the initial state of the board. Each cell is filled with a number corresponding to the keyboard position of a counter to be added.

```
procedure display_board( the:in Board; win:in P_Window ) is
begin
   position( win.all, 1, 2 );
   put(win.all, " 7 | 8 | 9" ); new_line( win.all );
   put(win.all, " ---------" ); new_line( win.all );
   put(win.all, " 4 | 5 | 6" ); new_line( win.all );
   put(win.all, " ---------" ); new_line( win.all );
   put(win.all, " 1 | 2 | 3" ); new_line( win.all );
end display_board;
```

Note: As a window is of type **limited private** *the access value of the window is passed to the procedure.*

The procedure update does a minimal update of the current state of the board into the results window. The constant array pos contains the co-ordinates for each cell on the noughts and crosses board.

```
procedure update( the:in Board; win:in P_Window ) is
   type Co_ordinate is ( X , Y );
   type Cell_pos is array ( Co_ordinate ) of Positive;
   type Board   is array ( 1 .. SIZE_TTT ) of Cell_pos;
   pos: constant Board :=   ( (2,6), (6,6), (10,6),
                              (2,4), (6,4), (10,4),
                              (2,2), (6,2), (10,2) );

begin
   position( win.all, pos(the.last)(X), pos(the.last)(Y) );
   put( win.all, the.sqrs( the.last ) );    -- Display counter;
end update;

end Class_board;
```

In the program, the following global data items are used:

```
with Class_board, Class_window;
use  Class_board, Class_window;
package Pack_globals is
   game      : Board;        -- The board
   p_win_brd : P_Window;     -- Window to display OXO board in
   p_win_bnr : P_Window;     -- Window to display Banner in
   p_win_r   : P_Window;     -- Window to display commentary in
   player    : Character;    -- Either 'X' or 'O'
end Pack_globals;
```

The call-back function user_input for the input dialog validates the move and when a valid move is received, adds the counter to the board calling the procedure update to update the game window.

```
with Simple_io, Class_window, Class_board, Pack_globals;
use  Simple_io, Class_window, Class_board, Pack_globals;
function user_input( cb_mes:in String ) return String is
   move: Integer; last: Positive;
begin
   clear( p_win_r.all );                    -- Clear
   get( cb_mes, move, last );               -- to int
   if valid( game, move ) then              -- Valid
      add( game, move, player );            -- to board
      update( game, p_win_brd );
```

```
     case state( game ) is                    -- Game is
       when WIN       =>
         put(p_win_r.all, " " & player & " wins");
       when PLAYABLE  =>
         case player is                        -- Next player
           when 'X'    => player := 'O';    --   'X' => 'O'
           when 'O'    => player := 'X';    --   'O' => 'X'
           when others => null;             --
         end case;
         put( p_win_r.all, " Player " & player );
       when DRAW      =>
         put( p_win_r.all, " It's a draw " );
     end case;
   else
     put(p_win_r.all, " " & player & " Square invalid");
   end if;
   return "";
exception
   when others =>
     put(p_win_r.all, " " & player & " re-enter move");
     return "";
end user_input;
```

Note: The exception is used to handle invalid input from a user.

The menu system has three call-back functions, the first and second (reset_x and reset_o) reset the board to empty and start the game for either X or O.

```
with Class_window, Class_board, Pack_globals;
use  Class_window, Class_board, Pack_globals;
procedure re_start( first_player:in Character ) is
begin
   player := first_player;                 -- Start with
   reset( game );                          -- Reset Board
   display_board(game, p_win_brd );        -- Display
   clear( p_win_r.all );                   -- Status info
   put( p_win_r.all, " Player " & player ); -- Player name
end re_start;

with re_start;
function reset_x( cb_mes:in String ) return String is
begin
   re_start('X'); return "";
end reset_x;

with re_start;
function reset_o( cb_mes:in String ) return String is
begin
   re_start('O'); return "";
end reset_o;
```

Note: The common code is factored out in the procedure re_start.

The third call-back function displays information about the program in the window win_bnr.

```
with Class_window, Pack_globals;
use  Class_window, Pack_globals;
function about( cb_mes:in String ) return String is
begin
  clear( p_win_bnr.all ); position( p_win_bnr.all, 17, 1 );
  put( p_win_bnr.all, "Written in Ada 95");
  return "";
end about;
```

The procedure play defines the windows that are to be used.

```
with Class_input_manager, Class_board, Class_window,
     Class_dialog, Class_menu, Class_menu_title,
     Pack_globals, reset_x, reset_o, about, user_input;
use  Class_input_manager, Class_board, Class_window,
     Class_dialog, Class_menu, Class_menu_title,
     Pack_globals;
procedure play is
begin
  window_prolog;                  -- Setup window system
  declare
    win_brd  : aliased Window; -- Board Window
    win_r    : aliased Window; -- Result Window
    win_bnr  : aliased Window; -- title Window
    win_usr  : aliased Dialog; -- Input Window
    ttt_reset: aliased Menu;    -- Reset menu
    ttt_menu : Menu_title;      -- Title menu
```

The various windows on the screen are then initialized to their fixed co-ordinate positions.

```
  begin
    framework( win_bnr,  1,  4, 52, 3 );    -- Banner
    framework( win_brd, 32,  8, 13, 9 );    -- OXO board
    framework( win_r,    9, 14, 22, 3 );    -- Results
```

The menu bar sequence is then defined with the following frameworks:

```
    framework( ttt_reset,
               "X start", null,  reset_x'Access,
               "O start", null,  reset_o'Access  );

    framework( ttt_menu,
               "About",  null,   about'Access,
               "Reset",  ttt_reset'Unchecked_Access, null );
```

Following the initialization of global variables the writing of various introductory messages is performed:

```
position( win_bnr, 17, 1 );
put( win_bnr, "Noughts and crosses" );

framework( win_usr,  9, 8, 22,
           "Move (1-9)", user_input'Access );

player := 'X';                                 -- Set player
p_win_brd := win_brd'Unchecked_Access;   -- OXO Board
p_win_bnr := win_bnr'Unchecked_Access;   -- Banner
p_win_r   := win_r'Unchecked_Access;     -- Commentary

display_board( game, p_win_brd );            -- Empty board
new_line( win_r );                           -- Clear
put( win_r, " Player " & player );           -- Players turn is

put( win_usr, "" );          -- Cursor
```

The user is only then allowed to start playing the game.

```
   window_start;                 -- Start the user interaction
 end;
   window_epilog;                -- Close window system
 end play;
```

21.5.1 Putting it all together

When compiled and linked with the TUI API code the opening screen layout is:

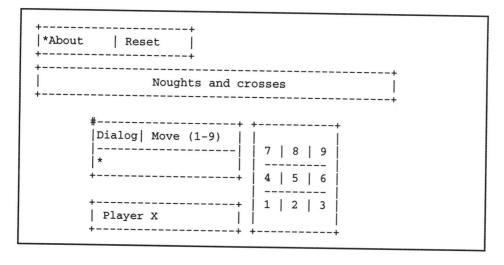

After the following moves have been made:

X's move	Commentary	O's move	Commentary
1	Claim the centre square	2	Not the correct move
3	Setting up a win	4	Block the X's
5	Two win lines	6	Block one of them
7	Win with three X's		

the screen layout will be:

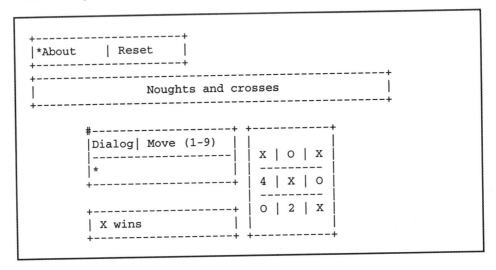

21.6 Self-assessment

- What is a call-back function and how is it used?

- How might the reversi program shown in Chapter 8 be modified so that it can be used with the TUI interface? To what extent is code re-use possible from the original version?

21.7 Exercises

Construct the following programs:

- *Currency converter*
  A program to allow a user to convert between two currencies. The program should allow the input of the current currency rate.

- *Reversi program*

  Re-implement the reversi program to use the TUI interface or any graphical interface that is available.

- *Draughts program*

  Implement the game of draughts to use the TUI interface or any graphical interface that is available.

22 TUI: the implementation

This chapter looks at the implementation of the TUI (Text User Interface) described in Chapter 21. An ANSI terminal or environment that supports ANSI terminal emulation is used as the output screen on which the TUI is implemented.

22.1 Overview of the TUI

The TUI is composed of the following window types: Window, Dialog, Menu and Title_menu. These windows have the following properties:

Type of window	Explanation
Window	A plain scrolling window into which text can be written.
Dialog	A dialog window into which the user can enter text. The text is passed to a call-back function.
Menu	A menu pane, from which a user can select a menu option. The menu option selected either calls a call-back function or selects a new menu pane.
Title_menu	The root of a series of menu panes which overlay each other.

Note: A call-back function is an Ada function called in response to user input.

The relationship between the different types of windows is shown in the inheritance hierarchy illustrated in Figure 22.1.

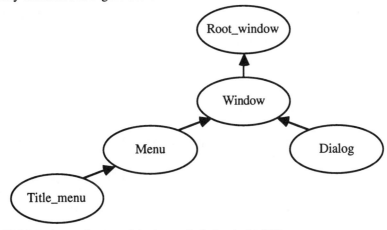

Figure 22.1 Inheritance diagram of the types of window in the TUI.

22.1.1   Structure of the TUI

In essence the TUI is composed of the following components:

Component	Description
Collection of windows	A collection of heterogeneous windows created in the application program.
Event loop	The main processing loop for the program. The event loop obtains the next character from the user and determines which window this should be passed on to.
Display	The displayable representation of the windows in the system. This is an ANSI terminal compatible display area.

The relationship between these components is illustrated in Figure 22.2.

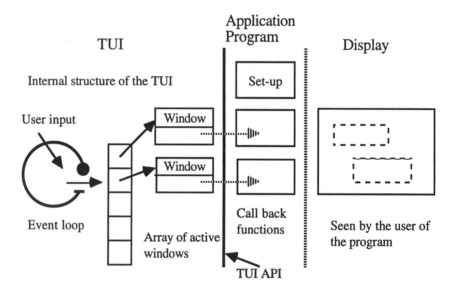

Figure 22.2 Structure of a program using the TUI.

A user of a program which employs the TUI classes interacts with a program by looking at the display, selecting a window capable of receiving input and then sending one or more character(s) to this window. The window selected by the user processes each character independently. For example, a dialog window will accumulate the characters sent to it, displaying the characters as they are received. Then, when the end of message character is received, the whole text string is passed to the call-back function associated with the dialog window. The call-back function implements a service requested by the user.

An application programmer using the TUI's API to implement a program, first constructs the windows used in the program. The application programmer then passes control to the input manager. The input manager accepts input from the user of the application and sends the input onto the window that has the input focus. Text sent to a window may cause the execute of a call-back function provided by the application programmer. The call-back functions implement the functionality of the program.

22.2 Implementation of the TUI

At the heart of the TUI is an event loop that receives characters from the user and dispatches the received characters to the appropriate window. This process is managed by an instance of the class Input_manager.

The input manager accesses the individual windows using an instance of the class Window_control. An instance of class Window_control stores windows in a linear list, the top window in the list representing the window that has the input focus.

Associated with each window is its switch character. A switch character typed by the user selects the window associated with this switch character as the window for input focus. As several windows may have the same switch character, the search mechanism will cycle through windows that have the same switch character.

If the typed character is not a switch character, the character is sent to the window that is the focus for the input.

22.2.1 Constants used in the TUI

The TUI uses several constants to define the state of the TUI and its environment. The size of the screen and the maximum size of windows created on the screen are defined by:

```
package Pack_constants is
   VDT_MAX_X     : constant := 79;    -- Columns on VDT
   VDT_MAX_Y     : constant := 25;    -- Lines on VDT
   WINDOW_MAX_X  : constant := 79;    -- MAX columns window
   WINDOW_MAX_Y  : constant := 25;    -- MAX lines window
```

Various special characters that can be sent to or are used by the TUI, have the following values:

```
   C_CURSOR   : constant Character := Character'Val(04);
   C_BLANK    : constant Character := ' ';
   C_WIN_A    : constant Character := '#';
   C_WIN_PAS  : constant Character := '+';
   C_EXIT     : constant Character := Character'val(05);  --^E
   C_ACTION   : constant Character := Character'Val(13);  --cr
   C_SWITCH   : constant Character := Character'Val(09);  --ht
   C_MENU     : constant Character := Character'Val(27);  --esc
   C_DEL      : constant Character := Character'Val(08);  --^B
```

Various internal states and representations of actions are defined in the list below. In this list, the arrow keys that a user presses to interact with the TUI are internally defined as a single character. This is to simplify the internal code that processes the key's representations.

```
C_NO_CHAR     : constant Character := Character'Val(00);
C_WHERE       : constant Character := ':';    -- Update cursor

C_LEFT        : constant Character := Character'Val(12); --^L
C_RIGHT       : constant Character := Character'Val(18); --^R
C_UP          : constant Character := Character'Val(21); --^U
C_DOWN        : constant Character := Character'Val(04); --^D
end Pack_constants;
```

22.2.2   Raw input and output

The TUI works on the assumption that a character is sent immediately to the screen without any internal processing or buffering. Likewise the TUI receives each character as it is typed without any internal buffering or processing.

An Ada package specification and pseudo implementation for a package to provide these input and output procedures is given below:

```
package raw_io is
  procedure get_immediate( ch:out Character );
  procedure put( ch:in Character );
  procedure put( str:in String );
end raw_io;

with Ada.Text_io;
use  Ada.Text_io;
package body raw_io is

  procedure get_immediate( ch:out Character) is
    c : Character;
  begin
    Ada.Text_io.get_immediate(c);
  end get_immediate;

  procedure put( ch:in Character ) is
  begin
    Ada.Text_io.put( ch ); Ada.Text_io.flush;
  end put;

  procedure put( str:in String ) is
  begin
    Ada.Text_io.put( str ); Ada.Text_io.flush;
  end put;

end raw_io;
```

Note: *The Ada reference manual (V6) does not define whether* get_immediate *echoes the read character.*
Section 24.1.2 describes how this package raw_io *may be written in another language.*

22.2.3   Machine-dependent I/O

In association with the package `raw_io`, the package `Pack_md_io` provides higher
level machine specific input procedures. For output, these allow the use of the
overloaded procedures `put` on a character and a string. For input, the responsibility is
slightly more complex as the arrow keys are mapped onto an internal representation.
The responsibilities for the procedures in the package `Pack_md_io` are:

procedure	Responsibility
put(ch :**in** Character);	Write `ch` immediately to the output screen.
put(str:**in** String);	Write `str` immediately to the output screen.
get_immediate (ch:**out** Character);	Read a character immediately from the keyboard. Do not echo this character onto the screen.

The specification for this package is:

```
package Pack_md_io is
  procedure put( ch :in Character );          -- Put char
  procedure put( str:in String );             -- Put string
  procedure get_immediate( ch:out Character); -- Get character
end Pack_md_io;
```

The implementation code for `get_immediate` is shown mapping two characters
into a single character for arrow keys. The actual character (s) generated will depend on
the operating environment. The arrow key presses are mapped upon input into the
character constants `C_LEFT`, `C_RIGHT`, `C_UP` and `C_DOWN` so that they can be
processed in the program in a machine-independent way.

```
use  raw_io, Pack_constants;
package body Pack_md_io is
  procedure put( ch:in Character ) is
  begin
    raw_io.put( ch );
  end put;

  procedure put( str:in String ) is
  begin
    raw_io.put( str );
  end put;
```

```
procedure get_immediate( ch:out Character) is
begin
  raw_io.get_immediate( ch );
  if ch = character'Val(0) then          -- Function Key
    raw_io.get_immediate( ch );
    case ch is
      when 'H'    => ch := C_UP;         -- Up arrow
      when 'P'    => ch := C_DOWN;       -- Down arrow
      when 'M'    => ch := C_RIGHT;      -- Right arrow
      when 'K'    => ch := C_LEFT;       -- Left arrow
      when others => ch := '?';          -- Unknown
    end case;
  end if;
end get_immediate;

end Pack_md_io;
```

Note: *In the implementation of* get_immediate *the arrow keys are converted into an internal single character. The implementation for* raw_io *that I used returns two characters when an arrow key is pressed.*
One way of simplifying this procedure is to make the user of the TUI use the following control keys for arrow movements.

Single character	Meaning
^L	Same as left arrow key
^R	Same as right arrow key
^U	Same as up arrow key
^D	Same as down arrow key

These definitions can, of course, be changed by modifying the definitions of C_UP *etc. in the package* Pack_constants.

22.2.4 The Class Screen

The package Class_screen implements cursor positioning and output to an ANSI compatible display screen. The responsibilities of the class are:

Method	Responsibility
clear_screen	Clears all the screen.
position_cursor	Position the cursor at x, y on the screen.
put	Write information to the current position on the screen.

Note: The co-ordinate system for the screen is shown in Figure 22.3.

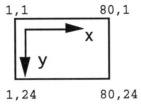

```
1,1              80,1



1,24             80,24
```

Figure 22.3 Co-ordinate system for the screen.

The class specification for `Class_screen` is:

```
package Class_screen is
  procedure put( ch :in Character );      -- Put char
  procedure put( str:in String );         -- Put string
  procedure clear_screen;                 -- Clear screen
  procedure position_cursor(col:in Positive; row:in Positive);
private
end Class_screen;
```

Note: As there is only one instance of a screen the class Screen contains all class methods.

The implementation of the class `Screen` uses the standard ANSI escape sequence to position the cursor onto a text terminal. The overloaded procedures `put` call the relevant `put` procedure in `Pack_md_io`.

```
with Pack_md_io; use  Pack_md_io;
package body Class_screen is
  PREFIX: constant String := Character'Val(27) & "[";
  procedure put( n:in Positive );          -- Write decimal number

  procedure put( ch :in Character ) is
  begin
    Pack_md_io.put( ch );
  end put;

  procedure put( str:in String ) is
  begin
    Pack_md_io.put( str );
  end put;
```

If an ANSI terminal is not available then the bodies of the procedures `clear_screen` and `position_cursor` will need to be amended to reflect the characteristics of the user's terminal or output environment.

```
procedure clear_screen is                    -- Clear screen
begin
   put( PREFIX & "2J");
end clear_screen;

procedure position_cursor(col:in Positive; row:in Positive) is
begin
   put( PREFIX ); put(row); put(";"); put(col); put("H");
end position_cursor;
```

The procedure put, when used to write a positive number without any leading or trailing spaces, is implemented as a recursive procedure. This procedure is used in the package by the public procedure position_cursor.

```
procedure put( n:in Positive ) is    -- Write decimal number
begin
   if n >= 10 then put( n / 10 ); end if;
   put( Character'Val(n rem 10 + Character'Pos('0') ) );
end put;

end Class_screen;
```

22.3 The class Root_window

A root window is the class from which all other windows are eventually derived. Its purpose is to define the minimum responsibilities that any type of window must implement. These minimum responsibilities are:

Method	Responsibility
send_to	Send a character to the window.
switch_to	Inform the window that it is to become the focus for input.
switch_away	Inform the window that it is to lose the focus of input.
refresh	If appropriate, re-display the window.
about	Return information about a window.

Note: There is no requirement that a window has a physical form. Thus, a root window does not need to provide a mechanism for writing into the displayable window.

As no concrete instance of a root window is required, the specification for the class Root_window is abstract. This abstract class will be specialized into the various forms of displayable windows on the screen.

```
with Ada.Text_io, Pack_constants, Ada.Finalization;
use  Ada.Text_io, Pack_constants, Ada.Finalization;
package Class_root_window is
   type Root_window is abstract tagged limited private;
   type P_Root_window is access all Root_window'Class;
   type Attribute is ( TOP, BOTTOM, LEFT, RIGHT, ABS_X, ABS_Y );

   procedure send_to( the:in out Root_window;
                            ch:in Character) is abstract;
   procedure switch_to( the:in out Root_window ) is abstract;
   procedure switch_away( the:in out Root_window ) is abstract;
   procedure refresh( the:in Root_window ) is abstract;
   function  about( the:in Root_window;
                       b:in Attribute) return Natural is abstract;
private
   type Root_window is
     abstract new Limited_controlled with null record;

end Class_root_window;
```

22.4 The classes `Input_manager` and `Window_control`

22.4.1 Specification of the class `Input_manager`

The input manager controls all interactions between a user and the displayed windows. Currently the only input device is the keyboard. The responsibilities of the input manager are:

Method	Responsibility
window_prolog	Set up the initial window environment.
window_start	Start the windowing system by accepting input from a user of the TUI.
window_epilog	Close down the windowing system.

The Ada specification for the class `Input_manager` is:

```
with Ada.Finalization;
use  Ada.Finalization;
package Class_input_manager is
   type Input_manager is abstract tagged limited private;
   procedure window_prolog;        -- Initialize window system
   procedure window_start;         -- Start taking user input
   procedure window_epilog;        -- Clean up
private
   type Input_manager is
     abstract new Limited_controlled with null record;
end Class_input_manager;
```

Note: As there is only one screen the class Screen *has all class methods.*

22.4.2 Specification of the class `Window_control`

The class `Window_control` has overall control of the windows displayed on the TUI screen. The responsibilities of this class are:

Method	Responsibility
`add_to_list`	Add a new window to the list of managed windows.
`remove_from_list`	Remove a window from the list of managed windows.
`top`	Make the supplied window the top window. The top window in the list is the focus for input.
`find`	Search the controlled windows for a window which has the supplied character as its switch character.
`send_to_top`	Send a character to the topmost window
`switch_to_top`	Prepare the top window as the focus of input.
`switch_away_from_top`	Prepare a window to have the focus of input removed from it.
`write_to`	Write to supplied window. Information has already been clipped to fit into the window.
`hide_win`	Remove the window from the screen.
`window_fatal`	Report a serious error in the TUI system.

The Ada specification for this class is:

```ada
with Ada.Finalization, Class_root_window;
use  Ada.Finalization, Class_root_window;
package Class_window_control is

   type Window_control is abstract tagged limited private;
   procedure add_to_list(p_w:in P_Root_window; ch:in Character);
   procedure remove_from_list( p_w:in P_Root_window );
   procedure top( p_w:in P_Root_window );
   procedure find( p_w:out P_Root_window; ch:in Character );

   procedure send_to_top( ch:in Character );
   procedure switch_to_top;
   procedure switch_away_from_top;

   procedure write_to( p_w:in P_Root_window;
                       x,y:in Positive; mes:in String );
   procedure hide_win( p_w:in P_Root_window );
   procedure window_fatal( mes:in String );
private
   type Window_control is
     abstract new Limited_controlled with null record;
   MAX_ITEMS : constant := 10;
   type Active_window is record          -- Active window
     p_w : P_Root_window;                 -- Window
     a_ch: Character;                     -- Activate character
   end record;
```

```
subtype Window_index is Natural      range 0 .. MAX_ITEMS;
subtype Window_range is Window_index range 1 .. MAX_ITEMS;
type    Window_array is array (Window_range) of Active_window;

the_last_win: Window_index := 0;      -- Last active window
the_windows : Window_array;           -- All windows
end Class_window_control;
```

Note: As there is only one screen, the class Window_control *has all class methods.*

Associated with each window is its switch character. When typed by a user this switch character activates the window as the focus for input.

22.4.3   Implementation of the class Input_manager

The Input_manager is started by window_prolog which clears the screen ready for the construction of the individual windows.

```
procedure window_prolog is
begin
  pack_ansi_display.clear_screen;
end window_prolog;
```

The procedure window_start starts the window system by accepting input from the user and sending this input a character at a time to the active window. The input character is first tested (using the procedure find) to see if it is a window switch character. If it is, then the selected window is made the new focus for input.

```
procedure window_start is
  p_w : P_Root_window;                -- A window
  ch  : Character;                    -- Current Char
begin
  loop
    get_immediate( ch );              -- From Keyboard
    exit when ch = C_EXIT;
    find( p_w, ch );                  -- Active window
    if p_w /= null then               -- Window activation
      switch_away_from_top;           --  No longer active
      top( p_w );                     --  Make p_w top
      switch_to_top;                  --  & make active
      send_to_top( C_WHERE );         -- In selected window
    else                              --
      send_to_top( ch );              -- Give to top window
    end if;
  end loop;
end window_start;
```

The window epilog is currently a null procedure as no specific shutdown action is required.

```
procedure window_epilog is
begin
  null;
end window_epilog;

end Class_input_manager;
```

22.4.4 Implementation of the class `Window_control`

In the implementation of the class `Window_control` the managed windows are held in an array. If the user of the TUI creates too many windows then the procedure `window_fatal` will be called. The procedure `add_to_list` adds a new window to the list of controlled windows.

```
procedure add_to_list(p_w:in P_Root_window; ch:in Character) is
begin
  if the_last_win < MAX_ITEMS then
    the_last_win := the_last_win + 1;
    the_windows( the_last_win ) := ( p_w, ch );
  else
    window_fatal("Cannot register window");
  end if;
end add_to_list;
```

A window is removed from the list of controlled windows by the following procedure:

```
procedure remove_from_list( p_w:in P_Root_window ) is
begin
  for i in 1 .. the_last_win loop              -- Look at
    if the_windows( i ).p_w = p_w then         -- Found
      for j in i .. the_last_win-1 loop        -- Delete
        the_windows( j ) := the_windows( j+1 );  --  move up
      end loop;
      the_last_win := the_last_win - 1; exit;  -- Finish
    end if;
end remove_from_list;
```

The procedure `top` makes the supplied window `p_w` the top window and hence the focus for input from a user.

```
procedure top( p_w:in P_Root_window ) is
begin
   for i in 1 .. the_last_win loop                --
      if the_windows( i ).p_w = p_w then          -- Found
         declare
            tmp : Active_window := the_windows( i );
         begin
            for j in i .. the_last_win-1 loop      -- Move down
               the_windows( j ) := the_windows( j+1 );
            end loop;
            the_windows( the_last_win ) := tmp;    -- New top
         end;
         exit;
      end if;
   end loop;
end top;
```

The procedure `find` searches the controlled windows for a window with the supplied `ch` as its switch character. If `ch` is a windows switch character then a pointer to the window is returned.

```
procedure find( p_w:out P_Root_window; ch:in Character ) is
begin
   p_w := null;
   for i in 1 .. the_last_win loop
      if the_windows( i ).a_ch = ch then
         p_w := the_windows( i ).p_w;
         exit;
      end if;
   end loop;
end find;
```

When a character is received from a user of the TUI, and it is not a window switch character, it is sent to the top window.

```
procedure send_to_top( ch:in Character ) is
begin
   if the_last_win >= 1 then
      send_to( the_windows(the_last_win).p_w.all, ch );
   end if;
end send_to_top;
```

When the focus of input is changed, the newly selected window is forewarned that it will become the focus for input by sending it the message `switch_to`. This allows the window to change its appearance to indicate that it is the current focus for input.

```
procedure switch_to_top is
begin
  if the_last_win >= 1 then
    switch_to( the_windows(the_last_win).p_w.all );
  end if;
end switch_to_top;
```

Likewise when the focus of input is taken away from a window it is forewarned by the message switch_away.

```
procedure switch_away_from_top is
begin
  if the_last_win >= 1 then
    switch_away( the_windows(the_last_win).p_w.all );
  end if;
end switch_away_from_top;
```

The procedure write_to writes text to the physical screen. The window is interrogated for its absolute position on the screen so that the physical position to write the text to can be calculated. As no window currently overlaps, no extra clipping needs to be performed.

```
procedure write_to( p_w:in P_Root_window;
                    x,y:in Positive; mes:in String ) is
  abs_x_crd : Positive := about( p_w.all, ABS_X );
  abs_y_crd : Positive := about( p_w.all, ABS_Y );
begin
  position_cursor( abs_x_crd+x-1, abs_y_crd+y-1 );
  Class_screen.put( mes );
end write_to;
```

A window is removed from the screen with the procedure hide_win. As no windows overlap in this implementation, the area that the window occupies is overwritten with spaces.

```
procedure hide_win( p_w:in P_Root_window ) is
  abs_x_crd : Positive := about( p_w.all, ABS_X );
  abs_y_crd : Positive := about( p_w.all, ABS_Y );
  width     : Positive := about( p_w.all, TOP );
  height    : Positive := about( p_w.all, LEFT );
  spaces    : String( 1 .. width ) := ( others => ' ' );
begin
  for h in 1 .. height loop
    position_cursor( abs_x_crd, abs_y_crd+h-1 );
    Class_screen.put( spaces );
  end loop;
end hide_win;
```

The next procedure is concerned with processing a fatal error. The implementation simply writes the error message directly onto the TUI screen.

```
procedure window_fatal( mes:in String ) is
begin
  position_cursor( 1, 1 );
  put( "Window fatal error: "& mes );
end window_fatal;

end Class_window_control;
```

22.5 Overlapping windows

Though not implemented here, only minor code changes are required to allow overlapping windows on the output screen. The order in which windows are held in the class attribute the_windows can be used to indicate the overlapping order as viewed on the screen. For example, the bottom window in the list the_windows is overlapped by all other windows. The top window in the list overlaps all the other windows displayed on the screen. An implementation of overlapping windows requires extra code to be added to write_to, and hide_win in the class Window_control to perform any necessary clipping.

22.6 The class Window

A window object has two main responsibilities:

- To provide an application API for a user program.
- To provide a system API for the manipulation of a window.

22.6.1 Window application API

The application API is available to an application program using the TUI to display and process information to and from a window.

Method	Responsibility
clear	Clear the window to spaces.
framework	Create the framework for a window.
make_window	Make the window visible or invisible.
new_line	Move to the next line in the window. This may involve a rack up of the text in the window.
position	Move to a new position for subsequent output to the window.
put	Write information into a window.

22.6.2 Window system API

The system API should not normally be required by an application program. This API is used internally by the TUI system to manage the windows on the screen.

Method	Responsibility
about	Return information about the window.
call_call_back	Call the call-back function for this window.
create	Create a raw window.
de_register	De-register the window with the Input_manager.
finalize	Destruction of a window.
initialize	Controlled initialization of a window.
mark_border	Set border to indicate state of window active, or inactive.
refresh	Re-display the window.
register	Register window on screen.
send_to	Send a character to the window for processing.
set_call_back	Set a call-back function for this window.
switch_away	Make window non active.
switch_to	Make window active.

22.6.3 The specification for the class `Window`

The specification is as follows:

```
with Pack_constants, Class_root_window,
     Class_input_manager, Class_window_control;
use  Pack_constants, Class_root_window,
     Class_input_manager, Class_window_control;
package Class_window is
  type Window    is new Root_window with private;
  type P_Window is access all Window;

  type Mode    is ( VISIBLE, INVISIBLE );
  type P_cbf   is access function(str:in String) return String;
```

Construction of a window is performed by:

```
  procedure initialize( the:in out Window );
  procedure finalize( the:in out Window );
  procedure framework( the:in out Window;
                       abs_x_crd, abs_y_crd: Positive;
                       max_x_crd, max_y_crd: Positive;
                       cb:in P_cbf := null );
  procedure create     ( the:in out Window;
                       abs_x_crd, abs_y_crd: Positive;
                       max_x_crd, max_y_crd: Positive );
```

A call-back function is set and executed with:

```
procedure set_call_back( the:in out Window; cb:in P_cbf );
function call_call_back( the:in Window;
                         str:in String ) return String;
```

User output to a window is written using:

```
procedure put( the:in out Window; mes:in String );
procedure put( the:in out Window; ch:in Character );
procedure put( the:in out Window; n:in Integer );

procedure position( the:in out Window; x,y:in Positive );
procedure clear( the:in out Window );
procedure new_line( the:in out Window );
procedure refresh( the:in out Window );

procedure make_window( the:in out Window; mo:in Mode );
procedure mark_border( the:in out Window;
                       a_border:in Attribute;
                       pos:in Positive; ch:in Character );
```

Details about a window are obtained using:

```
function about(the:in Window; b:in Attribute) return Natural;
```

The window is controlled by:

```
procedure switch_away( the:in out Window );
procedure switch_to( the:in out Window );
procedure send_to( the:in out Window; ch:in Character );

procedure register( p_w:in P_Root_window; ch:in Character );
procedure de_register( p_w:in P_Root_window );
```

The instance attributes of the class are:

```
private
  subtype Y_Cord is Positive range 1 .. VDT_MAX_Y;
  subtype X_Cord is Positive range 1 .. VDT_MAX_X;

  subtype Line_index  is X_Cord range 1 .. WINDOW_MAX_X;
  subtype Line_range  is Line_index;
  subtype Line        is String( Line_range );
```

```
subtype Pane_index  is Y_Cord range 1 .. WINDOW_MAX_Y;
 subtype Pane_range  is Pane_index;
 type    Pane_array  is array ( Pane_range ) of Line;

 type Window is new Root_window with record
   abs_x    : X_Cord := 1;     -- The position on the vdt
   abs_y    : Y_Cord := 1;     -- The position on the vdt
   c_x      : X_Cord := 1;     -- Current position in window
   c_y      : Y_Cord := 1;     -- Current position in window
   max_x    : X_Cord := 5;     -- X size of window (+Border)
   max_y    : Y_Cord := 5;     -- Y size of window (+Border)
   pane     : Pane_array;       -- Copy of window in memory
   mode_of  : Mode := INVISIBLE;-- Invisible window by default
   call_back: P_cbf := null;   -- Call-back function
 end record;
end Class_window;
```

22.6.4   Implementation of the class `Window`

In the implementation of the class `Window` the procedure `put` is used internally to write to a specific area on the screen.

```
package body Class_window is

  procedure put( the:in out Window;
                 x,y:in Positive; mes:in String );
```

The controlled procedure `finalize` removes a window from the screen and deregisters the window from the input manager.

```
  procedure initialize( the:in out Window ) is
  begin
    null;
  end initialize;

  procedure finalize( the:in out Window ) is
  begin
    make_window( the, INVISIBLE );
    de_register( the'Unchecked_Access );
  end finalize;
```

The procedure `create` sets up the window to be at a defined position on the screen. Some simple validation is performed. If this fails, the procedure `windows_fatal` is called.

```
procedure create( the:in out Window;
                  abs_x_crd, abs_y_crd: Positive;
                  max_x_crd, max_y_crd: Positive ) is
begin
  if max_x_crd < 3 or else max_x_crd > WINDOW_MAX_X or else
     max_y_crd < 3 or else max_y_crd > WINDOW_MAX_Y or else
     abs_x_crd + max_x_crd - 1 > VDT_MAX_X or else
     abs_y_crd + max_y_crd - 1 > VDT_MAX_Y then
     window_fatal("Creation window parameter error");
  end if;
  declare
     top_bottom: String(1..max_x_crd)      := (others => '-');
     spaces    : String(2 .. max_x_crd-1) := (others => ' ');
  begin
     top_bottom(1) := '+'; top_bottom(max_x_crd) := '+';
     the.max_x := max_x_crd - 2;         -- For border
     the.max_y := max_y_crd - 2;         -- For border
     the.abs_y := abs_y_crd;             -- Abs position
     the.abs_x := abs_x_crd;             --
     the.pane(1)(1..max_x_crd) := top_bottom;  -- Clear up
     for y in 2 .. max_y_crd-1 loop
       the.pane(y)(1..max_x_crd):= '|'&spaces&'|';
     end loop;
     the.pane(max_y_crd)(1..max_x_crd) := top_bottom;
     position( the, 1, 1 );              -- Top left hand corner
  end;
end create;
```

The user callable procedure `framework` defines the position of the window on the screen. This procedure uses `create` to do most of the initialization of the window.

```
procedure framework( the:in out Window;
                     abs_x_crd, abs_y_crd: Positive;
                     max_x_crd, max_y_crd: Positive;
                     cb:in P_cbf := null ) is
begin
  create( the, abs_x_crd, abs_y_crd, max_x_crd, max_y_crd );
  make_window( the, VISIBLE );
  if cb /= null then
     set_call_back( the, cb );
     register( the'Unchecked_Access, C_SWITCH );
  else
     register( the'Unchecked_Access, C_NO_CHAR );
  end if;
end framework;
```

The call-back function is set by `set_call_back` and is called via `call_call_back`.

```
procedure set_call_back( the:in out Window; cb:in P_cbf ) is
begin
  the.call_back := cb;
end set_call_back;

function call_call_back( the:in Window;
                          str:in String ) return String is
begin
  if the.call_back /= null then
    return the.call_back(str);
  end if;
  return "No call-back function";
end;
```

Note: The value returned by the call-back function is a string.

The procedure `put` writes text into the selected window from the currently selected position. If the text will not fit in the window it is clipped to fit the window. The text is then added to the stored image of the window. Then, if the window is visible it is written to the screen.

```
procedure put( the:in out Window; mes:in String ) is
  add : Natural;
begin
  add := mes'Length;                    -- Length
  if add + the.c_x > the.max_x then     -- Actual characters
    add := the.max_x - the.c_x + 1;     --  to add
  end if;
  if add >= 1 then                      -- There are some
    the.pane(the.c_y+1)(the.c_x+1 .. the.c_x+add)
        := mes( 1 .. add );
    if the.mode_of = VISIBLE then       -- Add to screen
      put(the, the.c_x+1, the.c_y+1, mes( 1 .. add) );
    end if;
    the.c_x := the.c_x + add;
  else
    put(the, the.c_x+1, the.c_y+1, "" );
  end if;
end put;
```

The two following procedures use the above `put` procedure to write a character and a natural number into the window:

```
procedure put( the:in out Window; ch:in Character ) is
begin
  put( the, "" & ch );                  -- Convert to string
end put;
```

```
procedure put( the:in out Window; n:in Integer ) is
begin
  put( the, Integer'Image(n) );   -- Convert to string
end put;
```

The procedure clear clears a window to spaces. The border of the window is, however, left intact.

```
procedure clear( the:in out Window ) is
  empty : String( 1 .. the.max_x ) := (others => ' ');
begin
  position(the, 1, 1);           -- Top right hand corner
  for y in 1 .. the.max_y loop   -- Clear text
    put( the, empty ); new_line(the);
  end loop;
end clear;
```

The procedure new_line implements the writing of a new line in the selected window. This may result in the information in the window being scrolled. Scrolling is implemented by refreshing the whole window after changing the contents of the remembered window.

```
procedure new_line( the:in out Window ) is
begin
  if the.c_y >= the.max_y then             -- Scroll text
    for y in 2 .. the.max_y loop           --  Copy up
      the.pane(y) := the.pane(y+1);
    end loop;
    the.pane(the.max_y+1)(2..the.max_x+1):= (others=>' ');
    refresh(the);                          --  refresh
  else
    the.c_y := the.c_y + 1;                -- Next line
  end if;
  the.c_x := 1;                            -- At start
end new_line;
```

The procedure position allows a user to set the current writing position in the window.

```
procedure position( the:in out Window; x,y:in Positive ) is
begin
  if x <= the.max_x and y <= the.max_y then
    the.c_x := x; the.c_y := y;
  end if;
end position;
```

The procedure refresh re-draws the whole of the window on the screen.

```
procedure refresh( the:in out Window ) is
begin
  if the.mode_of = VISIBLE then            -- Visible
    for y in 1 .. the.max_y+2 loop         -- Text
      put( the, 1, y,
           the.pane(y)(1 .. the.max_x+2) );
    end loop;
    put( the, "" );                        -- Cursor
  end if;
end refresh;
```

A window can be made visible or invisible by the procedure make_window.

```
procedure make_window( the:in out Window; mo:in Mode ) is
begin
  if the.mode_of /= mo then                -- Change so
    the.mode_of := mo;                     -- Set new mode_of
    case mo is
      when INVISIBLE =>                     -- Clear from screen
        hide_win( the'Unchecked_Access );-- Hide window
      when VISIBLE =>                       -- Redraw on screen
        refresh( the );
    end case;
  end if;
end make_window;
```

The style of the border may be changed by mark_border. A window may be customized to a style to suit the user by using this procedure.

```
procedure mark_border( the:in out Window;
                       a_border:in Attribute;
                       pos:in Positive; ch:in Character ) is
  a_y, a_x : Positive;
begin
  case a_border is
    when TOP    => a_x := pos; a_y := 1;
    when BOTTOM => a_x := pos; a_y := the.max_y+2;
    when LEFT   => a_x := 1; a_y := pos;
    when RIGHT  => a_x := the.max_x+2; a_y := pos;
    when others => null;
  end case;
  if a_x <= the.max_x+2 and then a_y <= the.max_y+2 then
    the.pane(a_y)(a_x) := ch;          -- Store
    if the.mode_of = VISIBLE then      -- Update on screen
      put( the, a_x, a_y, ch & "" );
      put( the, "" );
    end if;
  end if;
end mark_border;
```

The procedure about returns details about the various attributes of a window.

```
function about(the:in Window; b:in Attribute) return Natural is
begin
  case b is
    when TOP   | BOTTOM => return the.max_x+2;
    when LEFT  | RIGHT  => return the.max_y+2;
    when ABS_X          => return the.abs_x;
    when ABS_Y          => return the.abs_y;
    when others         => return 0;
  end case;
end;
```

Whilst publicly visible, the following procedures are not intended to be used by an application programmer. These procedures are used by the event loop to allow a window to:

- Clean up before the focus of user input is removed from the window.
- Prepare for the focus of user input to be directed at the window.

The effect of these procedures is to mark the window with a visual indicator of its state.

```
procedure switch_away( the:in out Window ) is
begin
  mark_border( the, TOP, 1, C_WIN_PAS );
end switch_away;

procedure switch_to( the:in out Window ) is
begin
  mark_border( the, TOP, 1, C_WIN_A );
end switch_to;
```

When a user types a character which is not recognised by the system as a switch character it is sent to the window which has the focus for input. The procedure send_to receives this character. The procedure is simply null, because an instance of a Window does not process user input.

```
procedure send_to( d:in out Window; ch:in Character ) is
begin
  null;
end send_to;
```

The window is registered with the input manager by the procedure register and de-registered with de_register.

```
procedure register( p_w:in P_Root_window;
                    ch:in Character ) is
begin
  switch_away_from_top;              -- Register window focus
  add_to_list( p_w, ch );           -- Register window
  switch_to_top;                    -- Make focus
end register;

procedure de_register( p_w:in P_Root_window ) is
begin
  top( p_w );                       -- Make top
  switch_away_from_top;             --  prepare for demise
  remove_from_list( p_w );          -- De-register window
  switch_to_top;                    -- Make focus
end de_register;
```

The next procedure is used internally by the class to write directly to a position in a window on the screen. This procedure uses `write_to` in the class `Window_control` to perform the actual write.

```
procedure put( the:in out Window;
               x,y:in Positive; mes:in String ) is
begin
  write_to( the'Unchecked_Access, x, y, mes );
end put;
```

22.7 The class `Dialog`

A normal window is specialized to a dialog window by overloading the following windows methods with new responsibilities:

Method	Responsibility
framework	Set up the window as a dialog box.
send_to	Process user input sent to the dialog window.

The Ada specification for the class `Dialog` is as follows:

```
with Pack_constants, Class_root_window, Class_window;
use  Pack_constants, Class_root_window, Class_window;
package Class_dialog is
  type Dialog is new Window with private;

  procedure framework ( the:in out Dialog;
                        abs_x, abs_y:in Positive;
                        max_x: in Positive;
                        name:in String; cb:in P_cbf );

  procedure send_to( the:in out Dialog; ch:in Character );
```

```
private
  subtype Message is String( 1 .. WINDOW_MAX_X );
  type Dialog is new Window with record
    dialog_pos: Positive := 1;   -- Position in input message
    dialog_len: Positive := 1;   -- Length of dialog message
    dialog_mes: Message := ( others => ' ');  -- Input message
  end record;
end Class_dialog;
```

22.7.1 Implementation of the class Dialog

The implementation of the class dialog is:

```
package body Class_dialog is
```

The procedure framework constructs the style of the dialog window and registers the window with the input manager so that user input may be directed to the window:

```
procedure framework( the:in out Dialog;
                     abs_x, abs_y:in Positive;
                     max_x:in Positive;
                     name:in String; cb:in P_cbf ) is
  dashes : String( 1 .. max_x ) := (others=>'-');
begin
  create( the, abs_x, abs_y, max_x, 5 );
  the.dialog_len := max_x-2;                   -- User input
  the.dialog_pos := 1;                         -- In Dialog
  set_call_back( the, cb );                    -- Call-back fun
  put( the, "Dialog| " ); put( the, name );    -- Dialog title
  position( the, 1, 2 ); put( the, dashes );   -- Line
  position( the, 1, 3 ); put( the, C_CURSOR ); -- Cursor
  make_window( the, VISIBLE );
  register( the'Unchecked_Access, C_SWITCH );  -- Activation Ch.
end framework;
```

For example, the fragment of code:

```
declare
  input  : Dialog;                    -- Input Window
  procedure user_input( cb_mes:in String ) is
  begin
    -- Body of procedure
  end user_input;
begin
  framework( input, 5, 10, 22, "Miles", user_input'Access );

end;
```

would produce the following dialog box whose top left hand corner on the screen is at position (5,10):

```
#--------------------+
|Dialog| Miles       |
|--------------------|
|*                   |
+--------------------+
```

User input sent to the dialog window is processed by the procedure send_to. This stores characters in the string dialog_mes. When the user enters C_ACTION this causes a call to an application programmer written call-back function with the string dialog_mes as its parameter. The character C_ACTION is the normal Enter character on the keyboard.

```ada
procedure send_to( the:in out Dialog; ch:in Character ) is
  spaces : String(1 .. about(Window(the),TOP))
                := (others => ' ');
  res    : String(1..0);
begin
  case ch is
    when C_WHERE =>
      put( the, "" );
    when C_ACTION =>
      res := call_call_back( the,
               the.dialog_mes(1..the.dialog_pos-1) )(1..0);
      the.dialog_pos := 1;
      the.dialog_mes := ( others => ' ' );
      position( the, 1, 3 );                    -- Start
      put( the, C_CURSOR & spaces );            -- Clear
      position( the, 2, 3 );                    -- Cursor
      put( the, "" );                           -- Cursor
    when C_DEL =>
      if the.dialog_pos > 1 then                -- Can delete
        the.dialog_pos := the.dialog_pos - 1;   -- Make avail.
        the.dialog_mes(the.dialog_pos):= ' ';   -- Remove
        position( the, the.dialog_pos, 3 );
        put( the, C_CURSOR & " " );             -- Overwrite
        position( the, the.dialog_pos, 3 );
        put( the, "" );                         -- Cursor
      end if;
    when others =>
      if the.dialog_pos <= the.dialog_len then
        if ch in ' ' .. '~' then                -- Add to
          the.dialog_mes( the.dialog_pos ) := ch; -- Save ch
          position( the, the.dialog_pos, 3 );
          put( the, the.dialog_mes(the.dialog_pos) );
          put( the, C_CURSOR );
          the.dialog_pos := the.dialog_pos + 1;
        end if;
      end if;
  end case;
end send_to;
end Class_dialog;
```

22.8 The class **Menu**

A normal window is specialized to a menu window by overloading the following procedures:

Method	Responsibility
framework	Set up the window as a menu window.
send_to	Process user input sent to the menu window.

and adding the procedures:

Method	Responsibility
set_up	Set up the window as a menu window.
menu_spot	Highlight the selected menu item.

The specification of the class Menu is as follows:

```
with Class_root_window, Class_window;
use  Class_root_window, Class_window;
package Class_menu is
  type Menu is new Window with private;
  type P_Menu is access all Menu;

  procedure framework( the:in out Menu'Class;
     m1:in String:=""; w1:in P_Menu:=null; cb1:in P_cbf:=null;
     m2:in String:=""; w2:in P_Menu:=null; cb2:in P_cbf:=null;
     m3:in String:=""; w3:in P_Menu:=null; cb3:in P_cbf:=null;
     m4:in String:=""; w4:in P_Menu:=null; cb4:in P_cbf:=null;
     m5:in String:=""; w5:in P_Menu:=null; cb5:in P_cbf:=null;
     m6:in String:=""; w6:in P_Menu:=null; cb6:in P_cbf:=null );

  procedure set_up( the:in out Menu; active:in Positive);
  procedure menu_spot( the:in out Menu; ch:in Character );
  procedure send_to( the:in out Menu; ch:in Character );

  MAX_MENU  : constant Positive := 10;
  subtype Menu_item is String( 1 .. MAX_MENU );

  procedure get_menu_name( the:in Menu; i:in Positive;
                      n:out Menu_item );
  procedure get_cur_selected_details( the:in P_Menu;
                      w:out P_Menu; cb:out P_cbf );
```

The private part of the specification contains details about how a menu item is stored. A menu consists of the names of menu items and associated with each name is either a call-back function or a link to another menu item.

```
private
  type     Direction is (D_REVERSE, D_FORWARD);
  procedure next( the:in out Menu; dir:in Direction );

  type Menu_desc is record    -- A menu is:
    name: Menu_item;          -- Name of menu item
    p_m : P_Menu;             -- Menu window
    fun : P_cbf;              -- Call-back function
  end record;

  MAX_MENU_ITEMS : constant := 6;     -- Maximum menu items

  type     Menus_index is range 0 .. MAX_MENU_ITEMS;
  subtype Menus_range is Menus_index range 1 .. MAX_MENU_ITEMS;
  type     Menus       is array ( Menus_range ) of Menu_desc;

  type Menu is new Window with record
    number    : Menus_index := 0;   -- Number of menu items
    cur_men   : Menus_index := 1;   -- Currently selected item
    menu_set  : Menus;              -- Components of a menu
  end record;
end Class_menu;
```

22.8.1   Implementation of the class Menu

The implementation of the class is:

```
with Pack_constants;
use  Pack_constants;
package body Class_menu is
```

In the procedure framework the class type is described as Menu'Class. This is so that a run-time dispatch will be performed on inherited procedures or functions in any class derived from this class.

```
procedure framework( the:in out Menu'Class;
  m1:in String:=""; w1:in P_Menu:=null; cb1:in P_cbf:=null;
  m2:in String:=""; w2:in P_Menu:=null; cb2:in P_cbf:=null;
  m3:in String:=""; w3:in P_Menu:=null; cb3:in P_cbf:=null;
  m4:in String:=""; w4:in P_Menu:=null; cb4:in P_cbf:=null;
  m5:in String:=""; w5:in P_Menu:=null; cb5:in P_cbf:=null;
  m6:in String:=""; w6:in P_Menu:=null; cb6:in P_cbf:=null
  ) is
  spaces : Menu_item := ( others => ' ' );
  active : Menus_index := 1;
```

```
   procedure set_up( mi:in String; wi:in P_Menu;
                     cb:in P_cbf; n:in Menus_index ) is
   begin
     if mi /= "" then active := n; end if;    -- A menu item
     the.menu_set( n ) :=
       (" "&mi&spaces(1 .. MAX_MENU-1-mi'Length), wi, cb);
   end set_up;
begin
   set_up( m1, w1, cb1, 1 ); set_up( m2, w2, cb2, 2 );
   set_up( m3, w3, cb3, 3 ); set_up( m4, w4, cb4, 4 );
   set_up( m5, w5, cb5, 5 ); set_up( m6, w6, cb6, 6 );
   the.number := active;
   set_up( the, Positive(active) );
end framework;
```

Note: The procedure set_up *which is called from within* framework *constructs the internal representation for the window.*

The procedure set_up populates the displayed menu window with the names of the menu items.

```
procedure set_up( the:in out Menu;
                  active:in Positive ) is
  me: Menu_item;
begin
  create( the, 1, 1, (1+MAX_MENU)*active+1, 3 );
  for I in 1 .. active loop            -- Display menu names
    get_menu_name( the, i, me );
    put( the, me ); put( the, "|" );
    null;
  end loop;
  menu_spot( the, C_CURSOR );          -- Mark current
end set_up;
```

The procedure menu_spot highlights the menu item selected.

```
procedure menu_spot( the:in out Menu; ch:in Character ) is
begin
  position( the, (MAX_MENU+1)*(Positive(the.cur_men)-1)+1, 1 );
  put( the, ch );
end menu_spot;
```

When user input is focused at the menu window, the arrow keys cause a new menu item to be selected.

```
procedure send_to( the:in out Menu; ch:in Character ) is
begin
  menu_spot( the, C_BLANK );
  case ch is
    when C_RIGHT => next( the, D_FORWARD );
    when C_LEFT  => next( the, D_REVERSE );
    when others  => null;
  end case;
  menu_spot( the, C_CURSOR );
end send_to;
```

The actual calculation of the menu item selected is performed by the procedure next.

```
procedure next( the:in out Menu; dir:in Direction ) is
begin
  case dir is
    when D_FORWARD =>
      the.cur_men := the.cur_men rem the.number + 1;
    when D_REVERSE =>
      if the.cur_men = 1
        then the.cur_men := the.number;
        else the.cur_men := the.cur_men-1;
      end if;
  end case;
end next;
```

The procedure `get_menu_item` returns the name of the menu item selected:

```
procedure get_menu_name( the:in Menu; i:in Positive;
                         n:out Menu_item ) is
begin
  n   := the.menu_set( Menus_index(i) ).name;
end get_menu_name;
```

whilst `get_cur_selected_details` returns a pointer to the selected potential window and call-back function.

```
procedure get_cur_selected_details( the:in P_Menu;
                         w:out P_Menu; cb:out P_cbf ) is
begin
  w   := the.menu_set( the.cur_men ).p_m;
  cb := the.menu_set( the.cur_men ).fun;
end get_cur_selected_details;

end Class_menu;
```

22.9 The class `Menu_title`

A `Menu` window is specialized to a `Menu_title` window by overloading the following procedures:

Method	Responsibility
set_up	Set up the window as a menu title window.
send_to	Process user input sent to the menu title window.
switch_away	Return to the base window.

The Ada specification of the class is:

```ada
with Class_root_window, Class_window, Class_menu;
use  Class_root_window, Class_window, Class_menu;
package Class_menu_title is
   type Menu_title is new Menu with private;
   type P_Menu_title is access all Menu_title;

   procedure set_up( the:in out Menu_title; active:in Positive );
   procedure send_to( the:in out Menu_title; ch:in Character );
   procedure switch_away( the:in out Menu_title );
private

   MAX_ACT_MENU : constant := 6;      -- Maximum depth of menus
   type    Act_index is range 0 .. MAX_ACT_MENU;
   subtype Act_range is Act_index range 1 .. MAX_ACT_MENU;
   type    Act_menus is array ( Act_range ) of P_Menu;

   type Menu_title is new Menu with record
      act_menu   : Act_menus;        -- Stack of displayed menus
      menu_index: Act_index := 0;    -- Top of menu stack
   end record;
end Class_menu_title;
```

22.9.1 Implementation of the class `Menu_title`

In the implementation of the class `Menu_title`:

```ada
with Pack_constants;
use  Pack_constants;
package body Class_menu_title is
```

the procedure `set_up` is called from the inherited procedure `framework` in the class `Menu`. This is because the call of the procedure `set_up` is a dispatching call. Remember, the first parameter to the procedure `framework` is of type `Menu'Class`.

```
procedure set_up( the:in out Menu_title; active:in Positits )
   me: Menu_item;
begin
   create( the, 1, 1, (1+MAX_MENU)*active+1, 3 );  -- Fixed size
   make_window( the, VISIBLE );
   the.act_menu( 1 ) := Menu(the)'Unchecked_Access;-- Title menu
   the.menu_index := 1;
   for i in 1 .. active loop                         -- Get menu
      get_menu_name( the, i, me );                   --   name
      put( the, me ); put( the, "|" );               --   write
   end loop;
   register( the'Unchecked_Access, C_MENU );         -- Register
   menu_spot( the, C_CURSOR );                        -- Cursor on
end set_up;
```

The procedure `send_to` implements the selection of either a new menu bar or the call of a call-back function.

```
procedure send_to( the:in out Menu_title; ch:in Character ) is
   current, next : P_Menu;
   proc          : P_cbf;
   res           : String( 1..0 );
begin
   current := the.act_menu( the.menu_index );   -- Active menu
   get_cur_selected_details( current, next, proc );
   case ch is
     when C_WHERE =>
       put( current.all, "" );
     when C_ACTION =>
       if next /= null and the.menu_index < MAX_ACT_MENU then
          make_window( current.all, INVISIBLE );    -- Hide cur.
          the.menu_index := the.menu_index + 1;      --
          the.act_menu( the.menu_index ) := next;    -- New menu
          make_window( next.all, VISIBLE );          -- Reveal
       else
          if proc /= null then                       -- Call
             res := proc("Action")(1 .. 0 );
          end if;
       end if;
     when others =>
       send_to( current.all , ch );  -- Treat as normal menu
   end case;
end send_to;
```

The procedure `switch_away` replaces the current menu with the top level menu bar. Naturally this replacement is only performed if the displayed menu is not the top level menu.

```
procedure switch_away( the:in out Menu_title ) is
begin
   mark_border( the, TOP, 1, C_WIN_PAS ); -- Now inactive
   if the.menu_index > 1 then           -- Not top level menu
     make_window( the.act_menu(the.menu_index).all, INVISIBLE );
     the.menu_index := 1;
     make_window( the.act_menu( 1 ).all, VISIBLE ); -- Top level
   end if;
end switch_away;

end Class_menu_title;
```

22.10 Self-assessment

- What changes in the implementation of the TUI would be required to allow for overlapping windows?

- The TUI execution is currently serial, in that messages sent to a window are performed before control is returned to the input event loop. What would be the effect of letting code associated with a window execute as a separate task?

22.11 Exercises

Extend the TUI by providing the following new types of window:

- *A window to which Integer and Float numbers may be written*

  This will allow the output of formatted numeric data as well as textual data.

- *A radio button dialog window*

  This will allow a user to create programs in which one of several options may be selected. For example, the conversion program shown in section 21.3 could allow the distance to be input in feet, yards or miles.

- *A check box dialog window*

  This will allow a user to create programs in which several different options may be selected.

- *Noughts and crosses*

  In the previous chapter, in section 21.5, an example program to play the game noughts and crosses was shown. A user entering a square has to press Enter to have the move accepted. Devise and implement a new version where the keystroke for a position is sufficient to activate a call-back function in the application code.

- *Overlapping windows*

  Modify the TUI so that overlapping windows are allowed. A user of the program should also be able to move the windows on the screen.

Build an application framework for the TUI.:

- An application framework allows a user to design the layout of screens used in the program without having to write any code. The application framework will have an interface similar to a drawing editor and allows an application programmer to position the different types of window onto a screen. Then when the user is satisfied with the layout, the application framework program produces an Ada program skeleton of the application.

Graphical Representation

- Modify the TUI so that the screen display is more graphical. You may wish to add procedures and functions that allow for bit mapped data to be written to a window.

23 Scope of declared objects

This chapter describes the access rules for objects and types declared in an Ada program. In Ada the scope or visibility of an item depends on the current lexical position in which the item is introduced.

23.1 Nested procedures

In Ada, nesting of procedures to an arbitrary level is allowed. Each nested procedure introduces a new lexical level. For example, the following program is made up of two procedures outer and inner. The lexical level for each line is shown as a comment.

```
procedure outer is          -- +1
   outer_int : Integer;      --  1
   procedure inner is        --  1
      inner_int: Integer;    -- +2
   begin                     --  2
      inner_int := 1;        --  2
      outer_int := 2;        --  2
   end inner;                -- -2
begin                        --  1
   inner;                    --  1
end outer;                   -- -1
```

Note: + indicates that a new lexical level has been started.
       - indicates that the current lexical level is about to end.

The procedure outer is at lexical level 1 and the procedure inner is at lexical level 2. Code that is at a specific lexical level can access items declared either at that lexical level or declared at a lower surrounding lexical level. For example, in the procedure inner the integer objects inner_int and outer_int can both be accessed. However, in the procedure outer only the integer object outer_int can be accessed. Access to procedures and functions follow the same rules.

It is important to realize that only items that are in a surrounding lower lexical level may be accessed. For example, the following nonsensical program illustrates the variables and procedures that may be accessed at any point in the program.

```
procedure proc_1_1 is                                        -- +1
  int_1_1 : Integer;                                         --  1
  procedure proc_2_1 is                                      --  1
    int_2_1 : Integer;                                       -- +2
    procedure proc_3_1 is                                    --  2
      int_3_1 : Integer;                                     -- +3
    begin                                                    --  3
      int_1_1 := 11; int_2_1 := 21; int_3_1 := 31; --        3
      proc_1_1; proc_2_1; proc_3_1;                          --  3
    end proc_3_1;                                            -- -3
  begin                                                      --  2
    int_1_1 := 11; int_2_1 := 21;                            --  2
    proc_1_1; proc_2_1; proc_3_1;                            --  2
  end proc_2_1;                                              -- -2
  procedure proc_2_2 is                                      --  1
    int_2_2: Integer;                                        -- +2
  begin                                                      --  2
    int_1_1 := 11; int_2_2 := 22;                            --  2
    proc_1_1; proc_2_1; proc_2_2;                            --  2
  end proc_2_2;                                              -- -2
begin                                                        --  1
  int_1_1 := 11;                                             --  1
  proc_1_1; proc_2_1; proc_2_2;                              --  1
end proc_1_1;                                                -- -1
```

Note: *The comment after each line indicates the lexical level of the line.*
A procedure or function, though introducing a new lexical level, is a declaration
of a name at the current lexical level. The parameters of the procedure or
function are of course at the next lexical level.

The layout of the above program can be schematically visualized as:

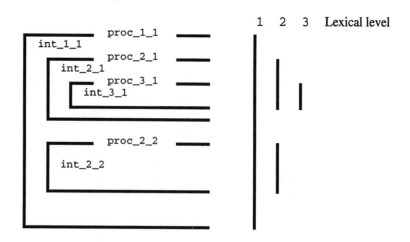

The procedure `proc_3_1` can access the following items:

Procedure	Can access procedures	Can access variables
proc_3_1	proc_1_1 proc_2_1 proc_3_1	int_1_1 int_2_1 int_3_1

However, the procedure `proc_2_2` cannot be accessed as this is declared after the end of `proc_3_1`. The variable `int_2_2` cannot be accessed as even though it is at a lower lexical level as it is not in a surrounding lexical level.

The procedure `proc_2_2` can access the following items:

Procedure	Can access procedures	Can access variables
proc_2_2	proc_1_1 proc_2_1 proc_2_2	int_1_1 int_2_2

However, the variable `int_2_1` cannot be accessed as, even though it is at the same lexical level, it is not in a surrounding lexical level.

23.1.1   Advantages of using nested procedures

Using a nested procedure structure allows a user to hide names used in the solution of different parts of a problem. This helps reduce the pollution of the global name space with items that only have a very limited scope.

23.1.2   Introducing a new lexical level in a procedure or function

The construct **declare** ... **begin** ... **end**; introduces a new lexical level in a procedure or function. For example, in the following program:

```
procedure outer is        -- +1
   outer_int : Integer;    --  1
   procedure inner is      --  1
      inner_int: Integer;  -- +2
   begin                   --  2
      declare              --  2
         i : Integer;      -- +3
      begin                --  3
         i := 2;           --  3
      end;                 -- -3
      inner_int := 1;      --  2
      outer_int := 2;      --  2
   end inner;              -- -2
begin                      --  1
   inner;                  --  1
end outer;                 -- -1
```

the integer object i is at lexical level 3 and can only be accessed within the enclosing **begin ... end**; .

23.1.3 Wholes in visibility

Because names can be overloaded, a whole in the visibility of an item can be created. For example, in the following program the variable i declared immediately in the procedure main is not visible for the extent of the enclosing **begin end** in the declare block.

```
with Simple_io; use  Simple_io;
procedure main is
  i : Integer := 1;     -- First i declaration
begin
  put( i );             -- Accesses first  i => 1
  declare
    i : Integer := 2;   -- Second i declaration
  begin
    put( i );           -- Accesses second i => 2
  end;
  put( i );             -- Accesses first  i => 1
end main;
```

23.1.4 Consequences of lexical levels

There is a performance penalty to pay for this flexibility in accessing items at different lexical levels. This penalty is mostly evident in the lengthy code required to perform procedure entry and exit. Optimizing compiles can drastically simplify the code required for entry and exit to a procedure or function when only a simple nesting structure is used.

The main code complexity arises because procedures and functions may be called recursively. A recursive procedure or function will create each time it is called a new stack frame.

The use of the class construct can drastically reduce the need to use heavily nested procedures.

23.2 Self-assessment

- How might a whole in the visibility of a variable in a program be created.

- Why cannot a procedure or function be called which is in an inner block to the current calling position.

- What procedures and integer variables can code in the body of the procedures main, proc_a, proc_b, and proc_c access in the following program.

```
procedure main is
  a : Integer;
  procedure proc_a is
    b : Integer;
    procedure proc_b is
      c : Integer;
    begin
      -- Code;
    end proc_b;
    procedure proc_c is
      d : Integer;
    begin
      -- Code;
    end proc_c;
  begin
    -- Code;
  end proc_a;
  e : Integer;
begin
  -- Code
end main;
```

24 Mixed language programming

This chapter describes how code written in another language can be called from an Ada program. This allows Ada to take advantage of the wealth of code previously written in other languages.

24.1 Linking to other code

24.1.1 C code

The following program written in Ada calls a function written in the programming language C. The function called is c_double. The Ada program is:

```
function double( n:in Integer ) return Integer is
   function c_double(n:in Integer) return Integer;
   pragma import (C, c_double, "c_double");
begin
   return c_double( n );
end double;

with Simple_io, double;
use  Simple_io;
procedure main is
begin
   put("3 Doubled is "); put( double(3) ); new_Line;
end main;
```

Note: As it is known for the compiler implementations used that the representation of an integer object in the languages C and Ada are the same, no conversion is required.

In the Ada program the **pragma** import is used to request the compiler to link to an externally written procedure or function. In this case the function c_double is written in C.

The implementation of the function `c_double` in C is:

```
int c_double( int n )
{
   return n + n;
}
```

The above program when compiled and linked will produce the following output.

```
3 Doubled is              6
```

24.1.2   An Ada package in C

In section 22.2.2, in the implementation of the class TUI, the package raw_io was used to get a character immediately from the keyboard and write a character and a string immediately to the terminal screen. This package can be implemented by calling C functions to perform the un-buffered I/O. The C functions used are:

C function	Commentary
char c_get_char();	Return immediately the character typed at the keyboard. Do not echo this character.
void c_put_char(char ch);	Write ch immediately, do not buffer output.
void c_put_str(char *str);	Write str immediately, do not buffer output.

The header files and function prototypes used in the implementation of the C functions are:

```
#include <pc.h>
#include <keys.h>
#include <stdio.h>

typedef enum  false, true  bool;

char c_get_char();
void c_put_char( char ch );
void c_put_str( char *str );
```

Note: The use of the machine specific header files pc.h and keys.h.
The compiler used is the djgpp compiler for DOS. This is available free over the internet.

The implementation of the C functions is:

```
/*
 * Make function keys and arrow keys return two characters
 * E.G. Right arrow returns (char) 0, 'M'
 *      Left  arrow        (char) 0, 'K'
 */

char c_get_char()
{
  int c;
  static char the_ch;                /* Remembered character */
  static bool prev_char = false;     /* There is remembered/ch
  if ( prev_char ) {
    prev_char = false; return the_ch;
  }

  c = getkey();                      /* Get char no echo */
  if ( c & 0x100 )  {                /* Function / Arrow key */
    prev_char = true;
    the_ch = (char) ( c & 0xFF );
    return (char) 0;                 /* Marker */
  }
  return (char) (c & 0xFF);          /* Ordinary character */
}
```

Note: On a PC the function keys and arrow keys return a character with a high order bit set. To pass this character onto the Ada code, the character is converted into two Ada characters, an escape character 0 followed by a character representing the bottom 8 bits of the received input.
The function getkey *is machine specific to the djgpp C implementation on a PC.*

```
void c_put_char( char ch )
{
  fputc(ch, stdout); fflush( stdout );   /* Output ch */
}

void c_put_str( char *str )
{
  while (*str) fputc(*str++, stdout);   /* Output String */
  fflush( stdout );                     /* Flush buffer */
}
```

Note: The normal C I/O system is used followed by a call to fflush *that causes the output buffer to be flushed.*

The specification of the package raw_io is:

```
package raw_io is
  procedure get_immediate( ch:out Character );
  procedure put( ch:in Character );
  procedure put( str:in String );
end raw_io;
```

In the implementation of the package raw_io the Ada package Interfaces.C is used to convert between C and Ada representations of a data object.

```
with Interfaces.C;
use  Interfaces.C;
package body raw_io is

procedure get_immediate( ch:out Character ) is
   function c_get_char return Char;
   pragma import (C, c_get_char, "c_get_char");
begin
   ch := to_ada( c_get_char );
end get_immediate;

procedure put( ch:in Character ) is
   procedure c_put_char( ch:in Char );
   pragma import (C, c_put_char, "c_put_char");
begin
   c_put_char( to_c( ch ) );
end put;

procedure put( str:in String ) is
   procedure c_put_str( str:in Char_array );
   pragma import (C, c_put_str, "c_put_str");
begin
   c_put_str( to_c( str, append_nul=>TRUE ) );
end put;
```

Note: The function to_c is used to convert between Ada and C character and string objects.
A null character is appended onto the string passed to the C function.

24.1.3 Linking to FORTRAN and COBOL code

By using the package Interface.Fortran, subprograms written in FORTRAN may be called. By using the package Interface.COBOL subprograms written in COBOL may be called.

Appendix A: The main language features of Ada 95

Simple object declarations

```
ch : Character;      -- An 8 bit character
i  : Integer;        -- A whole number
f  : Float;          -- A floating point number
```

Array declaration

```
numbers : array ( 10 .. 20 ) of Natural;
```

Type and subtype declarations

```
type     Rooms_index is new Integer range 410 .. 419;
subtype Rooms_range is Rooms_index;
type     Rooms_array is array ( Rooms_range ) of Natural;
```

Enumeration declaration

```
type     Colour       is (RED, GREEN, BLUE);
```

Simple statements

```
a := 2 + 3;
deposit( mine, 100.00 );     -- send message deposit to mine
```

Block

```
declare
   ch : Character;
begin
   ch := 'A'; put( ch );
end;
```

Selection statements

```
if temp < 15 then put("Cool"); end if;

if temp < 15 then put("Cool"); else put("Warm"); end if;

case number is
  when 2+3     => put("Is 5");
  when 7       => put("Is 7");
  when others  => put("Not 5 or 7");
end case;
```

Looping statements

```
while raining loop
  work;
end loop;

loop
  play;
  exit when sunny;
end loop;

for i in 1 .. 10 loop
  put(i); new_line;
end loop;
```

Arithmetic operators

```
res := a + b;    -- plus
res := a - b;    -- minus
res := a * b;    -- multiplication
res := a / b;    -- division
res := a mod b;  -- modulus
res := a rem b;  -- remainder
```

Conditional expressions

```
if a = b  then -- Equal to
if a > b  then -- Greater
if a < b  then -- Less than
if a /= b then -- Not equal
if a >= b then -- Greater
               -- or equal
if a <= b then -- Less
               -- or equal
```

```
if wet and jan then  -- and
if dry or  feb then  -- or

if wet and then jan then --
if dry or else  feb then --
```

```
if temp > 15 and dry then play; end if;
```

Note: When using **and then** *or* **or else** *the conditional expression will only be evaluated as far as necessary to produce the result of the condition. Thus in the* if *statement:*

> **if** *fun_one* **or else** *fun_two* **then**

fun_two *will not be called if* fun_one *delivered true.*

Exits from loops

The following code will execute until the condition sunny is met.

```
loop play; exit when sunny; end loop;
```

Class declaration and implementation

```
package Class_account is

  type Account is tagged private;
  subtype Money is Float range 0.0 .. Float'Last;

  procedure statement( the:in Account );
  procedure deposit  ( the:in out Account; amount:in Money );
  procedure withdraw ( the:in out Account; amount:in Money;
                       get:out Money );
  function  balance  ( the:in Account ) return Float;

private
  type Account is tagged record
    balance_of : Float := 0.00;      -- Amount in account
  end record;
end Class_account;
```

```
package body Class_account is
  procedure deposit ( the:in out Account; amount:in Money ) is
  begin
    the.balance_of := the.balance_of + amount;
  end deposit;

  -- Procedures withdraw and balance

end Class_account;
```

Inheritance

```
with Class_account use Class_account;
package Class_interest_account is
  type Interest_account is tagged private;
  procedure calc_interest( the:in out Account );
  procedure add_interest( the:in out Account );
private
  type Interest_account is new Account with record
    accumulated_interest : Float := 0.00;
  end record;
end Class_account;
```

```
package body Class_interest_account is
  procedure add_interest( the:in out Account ) is
  begin
    deposit( Account(the), the.accumulated_interest );
    the.accumulated_interest := 0;
  end add_interest;

  -- Procedure calc_interest

end Class_account;
```

Program delay

delay n.m seconds	delay until a_time;

`delay n.m;`	```
	declare
	  use Ada.Calendar;
	begin
	  delay until time_of(2000,1,1,0.0);
	  -- Until 21st century
	end;
	``

Task

```
task type Task_factorial is              -- Specification
  entry start( f:in Positive );          -- Rendezvous
  entry finish( result:out Positive );   -- Rendezvous
end Task_factorial;
```

```
task body Task_factorial is
begin
  accept start( f:in Positive )          do   end start;
  accept finish( result:out Positive )   do   end finish;
end Task_factorial;
```

Communication with a task

```
procedure main is
  thread    : Task_factorial;
  factorial: Positive;
begin
  thread_1.start(5);              -- Start factorial calculation
  thread_1.finish( factorial );   -- Obtain result
end execute_threads;
```

Rendezvous

select statement	**select** with **else**	**select** with **delay**
```select accept option1 do ... end; or accept option2 do ... end; end select;```	```select accept ... else statements; end select;```	```select accept ... or delay n.m; statements; end select;```

Protected type

```
protected type PT_ex is
   entry put(i:in T);
   entry get(i:out T);
private
   -- variables which cannot be simultaneous accessed
end PT_ex;
```

```
protected body PT_ex is
begin
   entry put(i:in T)   is begin           end put;
   entry get(i:out T)  is begin           end put;
end PT_ex;
```

Appendix B: Components of Ada

B.1 Reserved words and operators in Ada 95

B.1.1 Reserved words

abort	abs	abstract	accept	access	aliased
all	and	array	at	begin	body
case	constant	declare	delay	delta	digits
do	else	elsif	end	entry	exception
exit	for	function	generic	goto	if
in	is	limited	loop	mod	new
not	null	of	or	others	out
package	pragma	private	procedure	protected	raise
range	record	rem	renames	requeue	return
reverse	select	separate	subtype	tagged	task
terminate	then	type	until	use	when
while	with	xor			

B.1.2 Operators

:=	=	/=	>	<
>=	<=	+	-	*
/	rem	mod	**	not
abs	&	and	or	and then
or else	in	not in		

Note: Some of the operators are represented by reserved words.

B.2 Attributes of objects and types

B.2.1 Scalar objects

Attribute	Δ	Description	Type of result
S'Max	1	Delivers the max of the two arguments.	S'Base
S'Min	2	Delivers the min of the two arguments.	S'Base

Δ 1   S'Max denotes a function with specification:
        function S'Max(left, right: S'Base) **return** S'Base;
        This is for all scalar types S.

Δ 2   S'Min may be used in a similar way to S'Max

B.2.2 Array objects and types

Attribute	Δ	Description	Type of result
O'First	1	Delivers the lower bound of the first array index	Type of array index
O'First(n)	1	Delivers the lower bound of the n'th array index	Type of array index
O'Last	1	Delivers the upper bound of the first array index	Type of array index
O'Last(n)	1	Delivers the upper bound of the n'th array index	Type of array index
O'Length	1	Delivers the number of elements in the first array index	Universal Integer
O'Length(n)	1	Delivers the number of elements in the n'th array index	Universal Integer
O'Range	1	Delivers the first array index range	O'First .. O'Last
O'Range	1	Delivers the n'th array index range	O'First .. O'Last

Δ 1   Only an instance of an unconstrained array may be interrogated using the attribute.

B.2.3 Scalar objects and types

Attribute	Δ	Description	Type of result
O'First		Delivers the lower bound of the object or type	Of the type of O
O'Last		Delivers the upper bound of the object or type	Of the type of O

B.2.4 Discrete objects

Attribute	Δ	Description	Type of result
O'Succ(val)	1	Delivers the successor of val which is a value in the base type of T. The exception Constraint_error is raised if the successor of O'Last is taken.	Of the base type of T
O'Pred(val)	1	Delivers the predecessor of val which is a value in the base type of T. The exception Constraint_error is raised if the predecessor of O'First is taken.	Of the base type of T

Δ 1   The attribute will only work on an instance of discrete object and not on a discrete type.

B.2.5 Task objects and types

Attribute	Δ	Description	Type of result
O'Callable	1	Returns TRUE if the task object is callable	Boolean
O'Storage_size		The storage units required for each activation of the task	Universal Integer
O'Terminated	1	Returns TRUE if the task is terminated	Boolean

Δ 1   The attribute will only work on an instance of task object and not on a task type.

B.2.6 Floating point objects and types

Attribute	Description	Type of result
`T'Digits`	The decimal precision.	Universal Integer
`T'Model_epsilon`	The absolute value of the difference between 1.0 and the next representable number above 1.0.	Universal real
`T'Safe_first`	The lower bound of the safe range of T,	Of type T
`T'Safe_last`	The upper bound of the safe range of T,	Of type T

B.3 Literals in Ada

An integer can be expressed in any base from 2 to 16 by prefixing the number by its base. For example, the number 42 to base 10 can be written as:

```
2#101010#    4#222#    8#52#    10#42#    16#2A#
```

Note: The use of #'s to bracket the number.

In a number the underscore character can be used to improve readability. Usually this will be used to separate a number into groups of three digits.

```
1_00         1_234.567_8 3.141_596    1_000_000
```

The number 12.34 can be written as:

```
0.123_4E2    1.234E1
```

a numeric literal is of the type `universal_integer` or `universal_real`, which allows the literal to be used freely with any appropriate type.

B.4 Operators in Ada 95

Operator	Operand(s)	Result
and **or** **xor**	Boolean 1D Boolean array modular	Boolean 1D Boolean array modular
and then **or else**	Boolean	Boolean
< <= > >=	scalar 1D discrete array	Boolean Boolean
= /=	any non limited operands	Boolean
in **not in**	scalar **in** range scalar **not in** range	Boolean
&	1D array & 1D array 1D array & element element & 1D array element & element	1D array 1D array 1D array 1D array
+ - (monadic) + - (dyadic)	numeric numeric	Same as operands Same as operands
*	integer * integer floating * floating fixed * integer integer * fixed universal fixed * universal fixed root real * root integer root integer * root real	integer floating fixed fixed universal fixed root real root real
/	integer / integer floating / floating fixed / integer universal fixed / universal fixed root real / root integer	integer floating fixed universal fixed root real
mod rem	integer	integer
**	integer ** integer (>= 0) floating ** integer (>= 0)	integer floating
not	Boolean 1D Boolean array modular	Boolean 1D Boolean array modular
abs	numeric	numeric

Note: *In the table 1D is a shorthand for a one dimensional array.*

B.4.1 Priority of operators from high to low

`and or xor and then or else`	Logical operators	High
`=  /=  <  <=  >  >=`	Relational operators	
`+  -  *  /  &`	Dyadic arithmetic join operator	
`+  -`	Monadic arithmetic operators	
`*  /  mod rem`	Dyadic arithmetic operators	
`**  abs not`	The others	Low

B.5 Ada type hierarchy

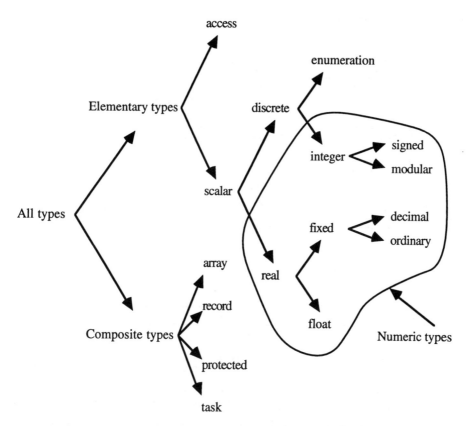

B.6 Implementation requirements of standard types

Type	Min value	Max value	Notes
Integer	-32767	32767	
Long_Integer	-2147483647	2147483647	1
Float	6 dec. places		
Long_float	11 dec. places		2

Min Value   The minimal value that must be representable (smaller values are allowed).

Max Value   The maximum value that must be representable (larger numbers are allowed).

Note: 1 Should be provided by an implementation if the target machine supports 32bit or longer arithmetic.

Note: 2 May be provided.

B.7 Exceptions

B.7.1 Pre-defined exceptions

Exception	Explanation
`Constraint_error`	Raised when an attempt is made to assign a value to a variable which does not satisfy a constraint defined on the variable.
`Storage_error`	Raised when a program tries to allocate more memory than is available to it.
`Program_error`	Raised when an attempt is made to execute an erroneous action. For example, leaving a function without executing a return statement.
`Tasking_error`	Raised when an error occurs in a task.

B.7.2 I/O exceptions

Exception	Explanation
`Data_error`	Raised when a get on a numeric object finds the input is not a valid value of this numeric type.
`End_error`	Raised when an attempt is made to read past the end of the file.
`Mode_error`	Raised when an inappropriate operation is attempted on a file.
`Name_error`	Raised if the name used in an open call does not match a file in the external environment.
`Status_error`	Raised when an operation is attempted on a file that has not been opened or created.
`Use_error`	Raised if the attempted operation is not possible on the external file.

B.8 Sources of information

B.8.1 Copies of the Ada 95 compiler

The main internet site for copies of the GNAT Ada 95 compiler is `cs.nyu.edu`. The latest version of the compiler for a multitude of machines is held in the directory `pub/gnat`.

B.8.2 Ada information on the World Wide Web

Some of the sites offering information about Ada on the World Wide Web are:

URL (Uniform Resource Locator)	Commentary
`http://lglwww.epfl.ch/Ada/`	A wealth of information about Ada. Has links to other sites.
`http://sw-eng.falls-church.va.us/`	The Ada Information Clearinghouse. Many Ada documents, including the reference manual and rational.
`http://wuarchive.wustl.edu/languages/ada/`	The PAL (Public Ada Library): lots of Ada-related software.
`http://www.acm.org/sigada/`	The ACM SIGAda home page

Note: The URL should be typed all on one line:

B.8.3 News groups

The usenet newsgroup `comp.lang.ada` contains a lively discussion about Ada related topics.

B.8.4 CD ROMs

Walnut Creek produce a CD ROM of Ada-related information including the GNAT compiler. For more information e-mail `info@cdrom.com`. Alternatively see the WWW page `http://www.cdrom.com/`.

B.8.5 Additional information on this book

The WWW page `http://www.brighton.ac.uk/ada95/home.html` contains additional information and programs not in this book.

Appendix C: Library functions and packages

The list of library functions and packages except Simple_io is reproduced from the *Ada 95 Reference Manual* ANSI/ISO/IEC-8652:1995. The following copyright notice appears in the manual:

In reproducing the subset of the library functions and packages in the Ada library, the author has made changes to layout, case, and font. This was accomplished by using various software tools and so minor changes may have been introduced without the author's knowledge.

C.1 Generic function Unchecked_Conversion

The generic function Unchecked_Conversion performs a conversion between two dissimilar types. The size of the storage occupied by an instance of the types must be the same.

```
generic
    type source(<>) is limited private;
    type target(<>) is limited private;
function Ada.Unchecked_Conversion(s : source) return target;
pragma convention(intrinsic, Ada.Unchecked_Conversion);
pragma pure(Ada.Unchecked_Conversion);
```

C.2   Generic function `Unchecked_Deallocation`

The generic function `Unchecked_Deallocation` releases storage for storage claimed by an allocator back to the pool of free storage.

```
generic
   type object(<>) is limited private;
   type name        is access   object;
procedure Ada.Unchecked_Deallocation(x : in out name);
pragma convention(intrinsic, Ada.Unchecked_Deallocation);
pragma preelaborate(Ada.Unchecked_Deallocation);
```

C.3   The package `Simple_io`

The following package `Simple_io` can be **with**'ed and **used**'ed in an Ada program to simplify the input and output of objects of type `Character`, `String`, `Integer`, and `Float`. In essence it instantiates instances of the generic packages in `Ada.Text_io` for `Integer` and `Float` input and output. Then by renaming the procedures and functions in these packages it makes the procedures and functions available directly to a user of the package.

In the package `Simple_io` the following parameter arguments are used:

Parameter name	Purpose
aft	The number of digits after the decimal place
base	The base of the number.
exp	The number of characters in the exponent. For the number 123.45678: exp=>0 would give a format of => 123.45678 exp=>2 would give a format of => 1.2345678E+2 exp=>4 would give a format of => 1.2345678E+002
file	file_type: The file descriptor which is read from or written to. file_access: The access value of the file_type.
fore	The number of digits before the decimal place
form	Form of the created output file.
item	The item to be read / written.
last	The last character read from the string.
mode	The mode of the operation read, write or append.
name	The name of the file as a String.
width	The number of characters to be read / written

```
with Ada.Text_io;
package Simple_io is
  package Text_io renames Ada.Text_io;

  package Integer_io is new Text_io.Integer_io (Integer);
  package Float_io   is new Text_io.Float_io (Float);

  subtype File_type       is Text_io.File_type;
  subtype File_mode       is Text_io.File_mode;
  subtype Count           is Text_io.Count;
  subtype Positive_count  is Text_io.Positive_count;
  subtype Field           is Text_io.Field;
  subtype Number_base     is Text_io.Number_base;

  IN_FILE:      constant File_mode := Text_io.IN_FILE;
  OUT_FILE:     constant File_mode := Text_io.OUT_FILE;
  APPEND_FILE: constant File_mode := Text_io.APPEND_FILE;

  -- File management

  procedure create     (file: in out File_type;
                        mode: in File_mode := out_file;
                        name: in String := "";
                        form: in String := "")
                        renames Text_io.create;
  procedure open       (file: in out File_type;
                        mode: in File_mode;
                        name: in String;
                        form: in String := "")
                        renames Text_io.open;
  procedure close      (file: in out File_type)
                        renames Text_io.close;

  -- character i/o:

  procedure get        (item: out character)
                        renames Text_io.get;
  procedure put        (item: in character)
                        renames Text_io.put;
  procedure get        (file: in File_type;
                        item: out character)
                        renames Text_io.get;
  procedure put        (file: in File_type;
                        item: in character)
                        renames Text_io.put;

  -- String i/o:

  procedure get        (item: out String)
                        renames Text_io.get;
  procedure get_line   (item: out String;
                        last: out Natural)
                        renames Text_io.get_line;
  procedure put        (item: in String)
                        renames Text_io.put;
  procedure put_line   (item: in String)
                        renames Text_io.put_line;
  procedure get        (file: in File_type;
                        item: out String)
                        renames Text_io.get;
  procedure get_line   (file: in File_type;
                        item: out String;
                        last: out Natural)
                        renames Text_io.get_line;
  procedure put        (file: in File_type;
                        item: in String)
                        renames Text_io.put;
  procedure put_line   (file: in File_type;
                        item: in String)
                        renames Text_io.put_line;

  -- Integer i/o:

  procedure get        (item: out Integer;
                        width: in Field := 0)
                        renames Integer_io.get;
  procedure put        (item: in Integer;
                        width: in Field := 6; --Integer'width;
                        base: in Number_base := 10)
                        renames Integer_io.put;
```

```
    procedure get          (file: in File_type;
                            item: out Integer;
                            width: in Field := 0)
                            renames Integer_io.get;
    procedure put          (file: in File_type;
                            item: in Integer;
                            width: in Field := 6; --Integer'width;
                            base: in Number_base := 10)
                            renames Integer_io.put;
    procedure get          (from: in String;
                            item: out Integer;
                            last: out Positive)
                            renames Integer_io.get;
    procedure put          (to: out String;
                            item: in Integer;
                            base: in Number_base := 10)
                            renames Integer_io.put;

    -- Floating point i/o:

    procedure get          (item: out Float;
                            width: in Field := 0)
                            renames Float_io.get;
    procedure put          (item: in Float;
                            fore: in Field := 2;
                            aft: in Field := Float'digits-1;
                            exp: in Field := 3)
                            renames Float_io.put;
    procedure get          (from: in String;
                            item: out Float;
                            last: out Positive)
                            renames Float_io.get;
    procedure put          (to: out String;
                            item: in Float;
                            aft: in Field := Float'digits-1;
                            exp: in Field := 3)
                            renames Float_io.put;
    procedure get          (file: in File_type;
                            item: out Float;
                            width: in Field := 0)
                            renames Float_io.get;
    procedure put          (file: in File_type;
                            item: in Float;
                            fore: in Field := 2;
                            aft: in Field := Float'digits-1;
                            exp: in Field := 3)
                            renames Float_io.put;

    -- Cursor control:

    function end_of_file return Boolean
                            renames Text_io.end_of_file;
    function end_of_line return Boolean
                            renames Text_io.end_of_line;
    procedure new_line     (spacing: in Positive_count := 1)
                            renames Text_io.new_line;
    procedure skip_line    (spacing: in Positive_count := 1)
                            renames Text_io.skip_line;
    function end_of_file (file: in File_type) return Boolean
                            renames Text_io.end_of_file;
    function end_of_line (file: in File_type) return Boolean
                            renames Text_io.end_of_line;
    procedure new_line     (file: in File_type;
                            spacing: in Positive_count := 1)
                            renames Text_io.new_line;
    procedure skip_line    (file: in File_type;
                            spacing: in Positive_count := 1)
                            renames Text_io.skip_line;
    -- I/O exceptions

    Status_error:  exception    renames Text_io.Status_error;
    Mode_error:    exception    renames Text_io.Mode_error;
    Name_error:    exception    renames Text_io.Name_error;
    Use_error:     exception    renames Text_io.Use_error;
    Device_error:  exception    renames Text_io.Device_error;
    End_error:     exception    renames Text_io.End_error;
    Data_error:    exception    renames Text_io.Data_error;
    Layout_error:  exception    renames Text_io.Layout_error;

end Simple_io;
```

C.4 The Package Standard

```
package Standard is
   pragma Pure(Standard);
   type Boolean is (False, True);

   -- The predefined relational operators for this type are as follows:

   -- function "="  (Left, Right : Boolean) return Boolean;
   -- function "/=" (Left, Right : Boolean) return Boolean;
   -- function "<"  (Left, Right : Boolean) return Boolean;
   -- function "<=" (Left, Right : Boolean) return Boolean;
   -- function ">"  (Left, Right : Boolean) return Boolean;
   -- function ">=" (Left, Right : Boolean) return Boolean;

   -- The predefined logical operators and the predefined logical
   -- negation operator are as follows:

   -- function "and" (Left, Right : Boolean) return Boolean;
   -- function "or"  (Left, Right : Boolean) return Boolean;
   -- function "xor" (Left, Right : Boolean) return Boolean;

   -- function "not" (Right : Boolean) return Boolean;

   -- The integer type root_integer is predefined.
   -- The corresponding universal type is universal_integer.

   type Integer is range implementation-defined;

   subtype Natural  is Integer range 0 .. Integer'Last;
   subtype Positive is Integer range 1 .. Integer'Last;

   -- The predefined operators for type Integer are as follows:

   -- function "="  (Left, Right : Integer'Base) return Boolean;
   -- function "/=" (Left, Right : Integer'Base) return Boolean;
   -- function "<"  (Left, Right : Integer'Base) return Boolean;
   -- function "<=" (Left, Right : Integer'Base) return Boolean;
   -- function ">"  (Left, Right : Integer'Base) return Boolean;
   -- function ">=" (Left, Right : Integer'Base) return Boolean;

   -- function "+"   (Right : Integer'Base) return Integer'Base;
   -- function "-"   (Right : Integer'Base) return Integer'Base;
   -- function "abs" (Right : Integer'Base) return Integer'Base;

   -- function "+"   (Left, Right : Integer'Base) return Integer'Base;
   -- function "-"   (Left, Right : Integer'Base) return Integer'Base;
   -- function "*"   (Left, Right : Integer'Base) return Integer'Base;
   -- function "/"   (Left, Right : Integer'Base) return Integer'Base;
   -- function "rem" (Left, Right : Integer'Base) return Integer'Base;
   -- function "mod" (Left, Right : Integer'Base) return Integer'Base;

   -- function "**" (Left : Integer'Base; Right : Natural) return Integer'Base;

   -- The specification of each operator for the type
   -- root_integer, or for any additional predefined integer
   -- type, is obtained by replacing Integer by the name of the type
   -- in the specification of the corresponding operator of the type
   -- Integer.  The right operand of the exponentiation operator
   -- remains as subtype Natural.

   -- The floating point type root_real is predefined.
   -- The corresponding universal type is universal_real.

   type Float is digits implementation-defined;

   -- The predefined operators for this type are as follows:

   -- function "="  (Left, Right : Float) return Boolean;
   -- function "/=" (Left, Right : Float) return Boolean;
   -- function "<"  (Left, Right : Float) return Boolean;
   -- function "<=" (Left, Right : Float) return Boolean;
   -- function ">"  (Left, Right : Float) return Boolean;
   -- function ">=" (Left, Right : Float) return Boolean;

   -- function "+"   (Right : Float) return Float;
   -- function "-"   (Right : Float) return Float;
   -- function "abs" (Right : Float) return Float;
```

```ada
-- function "+"    (Left, Right : Float) return Float;
-- function "-"    (Left, Right : Float) return Float;
-- function "*"    (Left, Right : Float) return Float;
-- function "/"    (Left, Right : Float) return Float;

-- function "**"   (Left : Float; Right : Integer'Base) return Float;

-- The specification of each operator for the type  root_real,  or  for
-- any  additional  predefined  floating  point  type,  is obtained by
-- replacing  Float by the name of  the type in the specification of the
-- corresponding  operator  of  the  type  Float.

-- In  addition,  the  following operators are predefined for the root
-- numeric types:

function "*" (Left : root_integer; Right : root_real)
  return root_real;

function "*" (Left : root_real;    Right : root_integer)
  return root_real;

function "/" (Left : root_real;    Right : root_integer)
  return root_real;

-- The type universal_fixed is predefined.
-- The only multiplying operators defined between
-- fixed point types are

function "*" (Left : universal_fixed; Right : universal_fixed)
  return universal_fixed;

function "/" (Left : universal_fixed; Right : universal_fixed)
  return universal_fixed;


   -- The declaration of type Character is based on the
   --   standard ISO 8859-1 character set.
   -- There are no character literals corresponding to the
   --   positions for control characters.
   -- They are indicated in italics in this definition.

type Character is

   (nul,   soh,   stx,   etx,      eot,   enq,   ack,   bel,
    bs,    ht,    lf,    vt,       ff,    cr,    so,    si,

    dle,   dc1,   dc2,   dc3,      dc4,   nak,   syn,   etb,
    can,   em,    sub,   esc,      fs,    gs,    rs,    us,

    ' ',   '!',   '"',   '#',      ' ',   '%',   '&',   ''',
    '(',   ')',   '*',   '+',      ',',   '-',   '.',   '/',

    '0',   '1',   '2',   '3',      '4',   '5',   '6',   '7',
    '8',   '9',   ':',   ';',      '<',   '=',   '>',   '?',

    '@',   'A',   'B',   'C',      'D',   'E',   'F',   'G',
    'H',   'I',   'J',   'K',      'L',   'M',   'N',   'O',

    'P',   'Q',   'R',   'S',      'T',   'U',   'V',   'W',
    'X',   'Y',   'Z',   '[',      '\',   ']',   '^',   '_',

    '`',   'a',   'b',   'c',      'd',   'e',   'f',   'g',
    'h',   'i',   'j',   'k',      'l',   'm',   'n',   'o',

    'p',   'q',   'r',   's',      't',   'u',   'v',   'w',
    'x',   'y',   'z',   '{',      '|',   '}',   '~',   del,


    reserved_128,      reserved_129,  bph,   nbh,
    reserved_132,      nel,    ssa,   esa,

    hts,   htj,   vts,   pld,      plu,   ri,    ss2,   ss3,

    dcs,   pu1,   pu2,   sts,      cch,   mw,    spa,   epa,

    sos, reserved_153, sci, csi,
    st,    osc,   pm,    apc,

... );
```

```
        -- The predefined operators for the type Character are the  same  as  for
        -- any enumeration type.


        -- The declaration of type Wide_Character is based on the
        --  standard ISO 10646 BMP character set.
        -- The first 256 positions have the same contents as type Character.

        type Wide_Character is (nul, soh ... FFFE, FFFF);


        package ASCII is ... end ASCII;  --Obsolescent;

        -- Predefined string types:

        type String is array(Positive range <>) of Character;
        pragma Pack(String);

        -- The predefined operators for this type are as follows:

        -- function "="  (Left, Right: String) return Boolean;
        -- function "/=" (Left, Right: String) return Boolean;
        -- function "<"  (Left, Right: String) return Boolean;
        -- function "<=" (Left, Right: String) return Boolean;
        -- function ">"  (Left, Right: String) return Boolean;
        -- function ">=" (Left, Right: String) return Boolean;

        -- function "&" (Left: String;    Right: String)    return String;
        -- function "&" (Left: Character; Right: String)    return String;
        -- function "&" (Left: String;    Right: Character) return String;
        -- function "&" (Left: Character; Right: Character) return String;

        type Wide_String is array(Positive range <>) of Wide_Character;
        pragma Pack(Wide_String);

        -- The predefined operators for this type correspond to those for String

        type Duration is delta implementation-defined range implementation-defined;

            -- The  predefined  operators for the type Duration are the same as for
            -- any fixed point type.

        -- The predefined exceptions:

        Constraint_Error: exception;
        Program_Error  : exception;
        Storage_Error  : exception;
        Tasking_Error  : exception;

end Standard;
```

C.5 The Package `Ada.Text_io`

In the package `Ada.Standard` the following parameter arguments are used:

Parameter name	Purpose
aft	The number of digits after the decimal place
base	The base of the number.
exp	The number of characters in the exponent. For the number 123.45678: exp=>0 would give a format of => 123.45678 exp=>2 would give a format of => 1.2345678E+2 exp=>4 would give a format of => 1.2345678E+002

Parameter name	Purpose

file	`file_type:`
	The file descriptor which is read from or written to.
	`file_access:`
	The access value of the `file_type`.

fore	The number of digits before the decimal place
form	Form of the created output file.
item	The item to be read / written.
last	The last character read from the string.
mode	The mode of the operation read, write or append.
name	The name of the file as a String.
width	The number of characters to be read / written

```
package Ada.io_exceptions is
   pragma pure(io_exceptions);

   Status_error : exception;
   Mode_error   : exception;
   Name_error   : exception;
   Use_error    : exception;
   Device_error : exception;
   End_error    : exception;
   Data_error   : exception;
   Layout_error : exception;

end Ada.io_exceptions;
```

```
with Ada.io_exceptions;
package Ada.Text_io is

   type File_type is limited private;

   type File_mode is (IN_FILE, OUT_FILE, APPEND_FILE);

   type Count is range 0 .. implementation-defined;
   subtype Positive_count is Count range 1 .. Count'Last;
   unbounded : constant Count := 0; -- line and page length

   subtype Field      is Integer range 0 .. implementation-defined;
   subtype Number_base is Integer range 2 .. 16;

   type type_set is (LOWER_CASE, UPPER_CASE);

   -- file management

   procedure create (file : in out File_type;
                     mode : in File_mode := OUT_FILE;
                     name : in String    := "";
                     form : in String    := "");

   procedure open   (file : in out File_type;
                     mode : in File_mode;
                     name : in String;
                     form : in String := "");

   procedure close  (file : in out File_type);
   procedure delete (file : in out File_type);
   procedure reset  (file : in out File_type; mode : in File_mode);
   procedure reset  (file : in out File_type);

   function  mode   (file : in File_type) return File_mode;
   function  name   (file : in File_type) return String;
   function  form   (file : in File_type) return String;

   function is_open(file : in File_type) return Boolean;
```

```
      -- control of default input and output files
      procedure set_input (file : in File_type);
      procedure set_output(file : in File_type);
      procedure set_error (file : in File_type);

      function standard_input   return File_type;
      function standard_output  return File_type;
      function standard_error   return File_type;

      function current_input    return File_type;
      function current_output   return File_type;
      function current_error    return File_type;

      type File_access is access constant File_type;

      function standard_input   return File_access;
      function standard_output  return File_access;
      function standard_error   return File_access;

      function current_input    return File_access;
      function current_output   return File_access;
      function current_error    return File_access;
--buffer control
      procedure flush (file : in out File_type);
      procedure flush;

      -- specification of line and page lengths

      procedure set_line_length(file : in File_type; to : in Count);
      procedure set_line_length(to    : in Count);

      procedure set_page_length(file : in File_type; to : in Count);
      procedure set_page_length(to    : in Count);

      function line_length(file : in File_type) return Count;
      function line_length return Count;

      function page_length(file : in File_type) return Count;
      function page_length return Count;

      -- column, line, and page control

      procedure new_line    (file    : in File_type;
                             spacing : in Positive_count := 1);
      procedure new_line    (spacing : in Positive_count := 1);

      procedure skip_line   (file    : in File_type;
                             spacing : in Positive_count := 1);
      procedure skip_line   (spacing : in Positive_count := 1);

      function end_of_line(file : in File_type) return Boolean;
      function end_of_line return Boolean;

      procedure new_page    (file : in File_type);
      procedure new_page;

      procedure skip_page   (file : in File_type);
      procedure skip_page;

      function end_of_page(file : in File_type) return Boolean;
      function end_of_page return Boolean;

      function end_of_file(file : in File_type) return Boolean;
      function end_of_file return Boolean;

      procedure set_col (file : in File_type; to : in Positive_count);
      procedure set_col (to    : in Positive_count);

      procedure set_line(file : in File_type; to : in Positive_count);
      procedure set_line(to    : in Positive_count);

      function col (file : in File_type) return Positive_count;
      function col  return Positive_count;

      function line(file : in File_type) return Positive_count;
      function line return Positive_count;

      function page(file : in File_type) return Positive_count;
      function page return Positive_count;
```

```
-- character input-output

procedure get(file : in  File_type; item : out Character);
procedure get(item : out Character);

procedure put(file : in  File_type; item : in Character);
procedure put(item : in  Character);

procedure look_ahead (file       : in  File_type;
                      item       : out Character;
                      end_of_line : out Boolean);
procedure look_ahead (item       : out Character;
                      end_of_line : out Boolean);

procedure get_immediate(file    : in  File_type;
                        item    : out Character);
procedure get_immediate(item    : out Character);

procedure get_immediate(file      : in  File_type;
                        item      : out Character;
                        available : out Boolean);
procedure get_immediate(item      : out Character;
                        available : out Boolean);

-- string input-output

procedure get(file : in  File_type; item : out String);
procedure get(item : out String);

procedure put(file : in  File_type; item : in String);
procedure put(item : in  String);

procedure get_line(file : in  File_type;
                   item : out String;
                   last : out Natural);
procedure get_line(item : out String; last : out Natural);

procedure put_line(file : in  File_type; item : in String);
procedure put_line(item : in  String);

-- generic packages for input-output of integer types

generic
   type num is range <>;
package Integer_io is

   default_width : Field := num'Width;
   default_base  : Number_base := 10;

   procedure get(file  : in  File_type;
                 item  : out num;
                 width : in Field := 0);
   procedure get(item  : out num;
                 width : in  Field := 0);

   procedure put(file  : in File_type;
                 item  : in num;
                 width : in Field := default_width;
                 base  : in Number_base := default_base);
   procedure put(item  : in num;
                 width : in Field := default_width;
                 base  : in Number_base := default_base);
   procedure get(from : in  String;
                 item : out num;
                 last : out Positive);
   procedure put(to   : out String;
                 item : in num;
                 base : in Number_base := default_base);
end Integer_io;

generic
   type num is mod <>;
package modular_io is

   default_width : Field := num'Width;
   default_base  : Number_base := 10;

   procedure get(file  : in  File_type;
                 item  : out num;
                 width : in Field := 0);
```

```
      procedure get(item  : out num;
                    width : in  Field := 0);
      procedure put(file  : in File_type;
                    item  : in num;
                    width : in Field := default_width;
                    base  : in Number_base := default_base);
      procedure put(item  : in num;
                    width : in Field := default_width;
                    base  : in Number_base := default_base);
      procedure get(from : in  String;
                    item : out num;
                    last : out Positive);
      procedure put(to   : out String;
                    item : in num;
                    base : in Number_base := default_base);
   end modular_io;

   -- generic packages for input-output of real types
   generic
      type num is digits <>;
   package Float_io is
      default_fore : Field := 2;
      default_aft  : Field := num'digits-1;
      default_exp  : Field := 3;

      procedure get(file  : in  File_type;
                    item  : out num;
                    width : in  Field := 0);
      procedure get(item  : out num;
                    width : in  Field := 0);
      procedure put(file : in File_type;
                    item : in num;
                    fore : in Field := default_fore;
                    aft  : in Field := default_aft;
                    exp  : in Field := default_exp);
      procedure put(item : in num;
                    fore : in Field := default_fore;
                    aft  : in Field := default_aft;
                    exp  : in Field := default_exp);
      procedure get(from : in String;
                    item : out num;
                    last : out Positive);
      procedure put(to   : out String;
                    item : in num;
                    aft  : in Field := default_aft;
                    exp  : in Field := default_exp);
   end Float_io;

   generic
      type num is delta <>;
   package fixed_io is

      default_fore : Field := num'Fore;
      default_aft  : Field := num'Aft;
      default_exp  : Field := 0;

      procedure get(file  : in  File_type;
                    item  : out num;
                    width : in  Field := 0);
      procedure get(item  : out num;
                    width : in  Field := 0);

      procedure put(file : in File_type;
                    item : in num;
                    fore : in Field := default_fore;
                    aft  : in Field := default_aft;
                    exp  : in Field := default_exp);
      procedure put(item : in num;
                    fore : in Field := default_fore;
                    aft  : in Field := default_aft;
                    exp  : in Field := default_exp);

      procedure get(from : in  String;
                    item : out num;
                    last : out Positive);
      procedure put(to   : out String;
                    item : in num;
                    aft  : in Field := default_aft;
                    exp  : in Field := default_exp);
   end fixed_io;
```

```
generic
   type num is delta <> digits <>;
package decimal_io is

   default_fore : Field := num'Fore;
   default_aft  : Field := num'Aft;
   default_exp  : Field := 0;

   procedure get(file  : in  File_type;
                 item  : out num;
                 width : in  Field := 0);
   procedure get(item  : out num;
                 width : in  Field := 0);

   procedure put(file : in File_type;
                 item : in num;
                 fore : in Field := default_fore;
                 aft  : in Field := default_aft;
                 exp  : in Field := default_exp);
   procedure put(item : in num;
                 fore : in Field := default_fore;
                 aft  : in Field := default_aft;
                 exp  : in Field := default_exp);

   procedure get(from : in  String;
                 item : out num;
                 last : out Positive);
   procedure put(to   : out String;
                 item : in num;
                 aft  : in Field := default_aft;
                 exp  : in Field := default_exp);
end decimal_io;

-- generic package for input-output of enumeration types

generic
   type enum is (<>);
package enumeration_io is

   default_width   : Field := 0;
   default_setting : type_set := UPPER_CASE;

   procedure get(file : in  File_type;
                 item : out enum);
   procedure get(item : out enum);

   procedure put(file  : in File_type;
                 item  : in enum;
                 width : in Field    := default_width;
                 set   : in type_set := default_setting);
   procedure put(item  : in enum;
                 width : in Field    := default_width;
                 set   : in type_set := default_setting);

   procedure get(from : in  String;
                 item : out enum;
                 last : out Positive);
   procedure put(to   : out String;
                 item : in enum;
                 set  : in  type_set := default_setting);
end enumeration_io;

-- exceptions

Status_error : exception renames io_exceptions.Status_error;
Mode_error   : exception renames io_exceptions.Mode_error;
Name_error   : exception renames io_exceptions.Name_error;
Use_error    : exception renames io_exceptions.Use_error;
Device_error : exception renames io_exceptions.Device_error;
End_error    : exception renames io_exceptions.End_error;
Data_error   : exception renames io_exceptions.Data_error;
Layout_error : exception renames io_exceptions.Layout_error;
private
   ... -- not specified by the language
end Ada.Text_io;
```

C.6 The Package `Ada.Sequential_io`

In the package Ada.Sequential_io the following parameter arguments are used:

Parameter name	Purpose
file	file_type: The file descriptor which is read from or written to.
form	Form of the created output file.
mode	The mode of the operation read, write or append.
name	The name of the file as a String.

```
with Ada.io_exceptions;
generic
    type element_type(<>) is private;
package Ada.sequential_io is

    type File_type is limited private;

    type File_mode is (IN_FILE, OUT_FILE, APPEND_FILE);

    -- file management

    procedure create(file : in out File_type;
                     mode : in File_mode := OUT_FILE;
                     name : in String := "";
                     form : in String := "");

    procedure open   (file : in out File_type;
                      mode : in File_mode;
                      name : in String;
                      form : in String := "");

    procedure close (file : in out File_type);
    procedure delete(file : in out File_type);
    procedure reset (file : in out File_type; mode : in File_mode);
    procedure reset (file : in out File_type);

    function mode   (file : in File_type) return File_mode;
    function name   (file : in File_type) return String;
    function form   (file : in File_type) return String;

    function is_open(file : in File_type) return Boolean;

    -- input and output operations

    procedure read  (file : in File_type; item : out element_type);
    procedure write (file : in File_type; item : in element_type);

    function end_of_file(file : in File_type) return Boolean;

    -- exceptions

    Status_error : exception renames io_exceptions.Status_error;
    Mode_error   : exception renames io_exceptions.Mode_error;
    Name_error   : exception renames io_exceptions.Name_error;
    Use_error    : exception renames io_exceptions.Use_error;
    Device_error : exception renames io_exceptions.Device_error;
    End_error    : exception renames io_exceptions.End_error;
    Data_error   : exception renames io_exceptions.Data_error;

private
    ... -- not specified by the language
end Ada.sequential_io;
```

C.7 The Package `Ada.Characters.Handling`

```
package Ada.characters.handling is
  pragma preelaborate(handling);

--character classification functions

  function is_control         (item : in Character) return Boolean;
  function is_graphic         (item : in Character) return Boolean;
  function is_letter          (item : in Character) return Boolean;
  function is_lower           (item : in Character) return Boolean;
  function is_upper           (item : in Character) return Boolean;
  function is_basic           (item : in Character) return Boolean;
  function is_digit           (item : in Character) return Boolean;
  function is_decimal_digit   (item : in Character) return Boolean
                                                    renames_digit;
  function is_hexadecimal_digit (item : in Character) return Boolean;
  function is_alphanumeric    (item : in Character) return Boolean;
  function is_special         (item : in Character) return Boolean;

--conversion functions for character and string

  function to_lower (item : in Character) return Character;
  function to_upper (item : in Character) return Character;
  function to_basic (item : in Character) return Character;

  function to_lower (item : in String) return String;
  function to_upper (item : in String) return String;
  function to_basic (item : in String) return String;

--classifications of and conversions between character and iso 646

  subtype iso_646 is
    Character range Character'val(0) .. Character'val(127);

  function is_iso_646 (item : in Character) return Boolean;
  function is_iso_646 (item : in String)    return Boolean;

  function to_iso_646 (item       : in Character;
                       substitute : in iso_646 := ' ')
    return iso_646;

  function to_iso_646 (item       : in String;
                       substitute : in iso_646 := ' ')
    return String;

--classifications of and conversions between wide_character and character.

  function is_character (item : in Wide_Character) return Boolean;
  function is_string    (item : in wide_string)    return Boolean;

  function to_character (item       : in Wide_Character;
                         substitute : in Character := ' ')
    return Character;

  function to_string    (item       : in wide_string;
                         substitute : in Character := ' ')
    return String;

  function to_wide_character (item : in Character) return Wide_Character;

  function to_wide_string    (item : in String)    return wide_string;

end Ada.characters.handling;
```

C.8 The Package `Ada.Strings.Bounded`

In the package `Ada.Strings.Bounded` the following parameter arguments are used:

Parameter name	Purpose
drop	= Left (Compressing to the right) = Right (Compressing to the left) = Error (Strings Length_error propagated)
going	= Forward (Forward search)

```ada
with Ada.strings.Maps;
package Ada.strings.bounded is
   pragma preelaborate(bounded);

   generic
      max    : Positive;     -- maximum length of a bounded_string
   package generic_bounded_length is

      max_length : constant Positive := max;

      type bounded_string is private;

      null_bounded_string : constant bounded_string;

      subtype length_range is Natural range 0 .. max_length;

      function length (source : in bounded_string) return length_range;

-- conversion, concatenation, and selection functions

      function to_bounded_string (source : in String;
                                  drop   : in truncation := error)
         return bounded_string;

      function to_string (source : in bounded_string) return String;

      function append (left, right : in bounded_string;
                       drop        : in truncation   := error)
         return bounded_string;

      function append (left  : in bounded_string;
                       right : in String;
                       drop  : in truncation := error)
         return bounded_string;

      function append (left  : in String;
                       right : in bounded_string;
                       drop  : in truncation := error)
         return bounded_string;

      function append (left  : in bounded_string;
                       right : in Character;
                       drop  : in truncation := error)
         return bounded_string;

      function append (left  : in Character;
                       right : in bounded_string;
                       drop  : in truncation := error)
         return bounded_string;

      procedure append (source   : in out bounded_string;
                        new_item : in bounded_string;
                        drop     : in truncation  := error);

      procedure append (source   : in out bounded_string;
                        new_item : in String;
                        drop     : in truncation  := error);
```

```
      procedure append (source    : in out bounded_string;
                         new_item  : in Character;
                         drop      : in truncation  := error);

   function "&" (left, right : in bounded_string)
      return bounded_string;

   function "&" (left : in bounded_string; right : in String)
      return bounded_string;

   function "&" (left : in String; right : in bounded_string)
      return bounded_string;

   function "&" (left : in bounded_string; right : in Character)
      return bounded_string;

   function "&" (left : in Character; right : in bounded_string)
      return bounded_string;

   function element (source : in bounded_string;
                     index  : in Positive)
      return Character;

      procedure replace_element (source : in out bounded_string;
                                 index  : in Positive;
                                 by     : in Character);

   function slice (source : in bounded_string;
                   low    : in Positive;
                   high   : in Natural)
      return String;

   function "="  (left, right : in bounded_string) return Boolean;
   function "="  (left : in bounded_string; right : in String)
      return Boolean;

   function "="  (left : in String; right : in bounded_string)
      return Boolean;

   function "<"  (left, right : in bounded_string) return Boolean;

   function "<"  (left : in bounded_string; right : in String)
      return Boolean;

   function "<"  (left : in String; right : in bounded_string)
      return Boolean;

   function "<=" (left, right : in bounded_string) return Boolean;

   function "<=" (left : in bounded_string; right : in String)
      return Boolean;

   function "<=" (left : in String; right : in bounded_string)
      return Boolean;

   function ">"  (left, right : in bounded_string) return Boolean;

   function ">"  (left : in bounded_string; right : in String)
      return Boolean;

   function ">"  (left : in String; right : in bounded_string)
      return Boolean;

   function ">=" (left, right : in bounded_string) return Boolean;

   function ">=" (left : in bounded_string; right : in String)
      return Boolean;

   function ">=" (left : in String; right : in bounded_string)
      return Boolean;

-- search functions

   function index (source  : in bounded_string;
                   pattern : in String;
                   going   : in direction := forward;
                   mapping : in Maps.character_mapping
                             := Maps.identity)
      return Natural;
```

```
    function index (source   : in bounded_string;
                    pattern  : in String;
                    going    : in direction := forward;
                    mapping  : in Maps.character_mapping_function)
       return Natural;

    function index (source : in bounded_string;
                    set    : in Maps.character_set;
                    test   : in membership := inside;
                    going  : in direction  := forward)
       return Natural;

    function index_non_blank (source : in bounded_string;
                              going  : in direction := forward)
       return Natural;

    function Count (source   : in bounded_string;
                    pattern  : in String;
                    mapping  : in Maps.character_mapping
                                  := Maps.identity)
       return Natural;

    function Count (source   : in bounded_string;
                    pattern  : in String;
                    mapping  : in Maps.character_mapping_function)
       return Natural;

    function Count (source   : in bounded_string;
                    set      : in Maps.character_set)
       return Natural;

    procedure find_token (source : in bounded_string;
                          set    : in Maps.character_set;
                          test   : in membership;
                          first  : out Positive;
                          last   : out Natural);

-- string translation subprograms

    function translate (source  : in bounded_string;
                        mapping : in Maps.character_mapping)
       return bounded_string;

    procedure translate (source  : in out bounded_string;
                         mapping : in Maps.character_mapping);

    function translate (source  : in bounded_string;
                        mapping : in Maps.character_mapping_function)
       return bounded_string;

    procedure translate (source  : in out bounded_string;
                         mapping : in Maps.character_mapping_function);

-- string transformation subprograms

    function replace_slice (source : in bounded_string;
                            low    : in Positive;
                            high   : in Natural;
                            by     : in String;
                            drop   : in truncation := error)
       return bounded_string;

    procedure replace_slice (source : in out bounded_string;
                             low    : in Positive;
                             high   : in Natural;
                             by     : in String;
                             drop   : in truncation := error);

    function insert (source   : in bounded_string;
                     before   : in Positive;
                     new_item : in String;
                     drop     : in truncation := error)
       return bounded_string;

    procedure insert (source   : in out bounded_string;
                      before   : in Positive;
                      new_item : in String;
                      drop     : in truncation := error);
```

```
      function overwrite (source    : in bounded_string;
                          position  : in Positive;
                          new_item  : in String;
                          drop      : in truncation := error)
         return bounded_string;

      procedure overwrite (source    : in out bounded_string;
                           position  : in Positive;
                           new_item  : in String;
                           drop      : in truncation := error);

      function delete (source  : in bounded_string;
                       from    : in Positive;
                       through : in Natural)
         return bounded_string;

      procedure delete (source  : in out bounded_string;
                        from    : in Positive;
                        through : in Natural);

--string selector subprograms

      function trim (source : in bounded_string;
                     side   : in trim_end)
         return bounded_string;
      procedure trim (source : in out bounded_string;
                      side   : in trim_end);

      function trim (source : in bounded_string;
                     left   : in Maps.character_set;
                     right  : in Maps.character_set)
         return bounded_string;

      procedure trim (source : in out bounded_string;
                      left   : in Maps.character_set;
                      right  : in Maps.character_set);

      function head (source : in bounded_string;
                     Count  : in Natural;
                     pad    : in Character   := space;
                     drop   : in truncation := error)
         return bounded_string;

      procedure head (source : in out bounded_string;
                      Count  : in Natural;
                      pad    : in Character   := space;
                      drop   : in truncation := error);

      function tail (source : in bounded_string;
                     Count  : in Natural;
                     pad    : in Character   := space;
                     drop   : in truncation := error)
         return bounded_string;

      procedure tail (source : in out bounded_string;
                      Count  : in Natural;
                      pad    : in Character   := space;
                      drop   : in truncation := error);

--string constructor subprograms

      function "*" (left  : in Natural;
                    right : in Character)
         return bounded_string;

      function "*" (left  : in Natural;
                    right : in String)
         return bounded_string;

      function "*" (left  : in Natural;
                    right : in bounded_string)
         return bounded_string;

      function replicate (Count : in Natural;
                          item  : in Character;
                          drop  : in truncation := error)
         return bounded_string;
```

```
        function replicate (Count : in Natural;
                            item  : in String;
                            drop  : in truncation := error)
              return bounded_string;

        function replicate (Count : in Natural;
                            item  : in bounded_string;
                            drop  : in truncation := error)
              return bounded_string;

   private
      ... -- not specified by the language
   end generic_bounded_length;

end Ada.strings.bounded;
```

C.9 The Package Ada.Interfaces.C

```
package interfaces.c is
   pragma pure(c);

   -- declarations based on c's <limits.h>

   char_bit  : constant := implementation-defined;   -- typically 8
   schar_min : constant := implementation-defined;   -- typically -128
   schar_max : constant := implementation-defined;   -- typically 127
   uchar_max : constant := implementation-defined;   -- typically 255

   -- signed and unsigned integers
   type int   is range implementation-defined;
   type short is range implementation-defined;
   type long  is range implementation-defined;

   type signed_char is range schar_min .. schar_max;
   for signed_char'size use char_bit;

   type unsigned       is mod implementation-defined;
   type unsigned_short is mod implementation-defined;
   type unsigned_long  is mod implementation-defined;

   type unsigned_char is mod (uchar_max+1);
   for unsigned_char'size use char_bit;

   subtype plain_char is implementation-defined;

   type ptrdiff_t is range implementation-defined;

   type size_t is mod implementation-defined;

   -- floating point

   type c_float     is digits implementation-defined;

   type double      is digits implementation-defined;

   type long_double is digits implementation-defined;

   -- characters and strings

   type char is <implementation-defined Character type>;

   nul : constant char := char'First;

   function to_c   (item : in Character) return char;

   function to_ada (item : in char) return Character;

   type char_array is array (size_t range <>) of aliased char;
   pragma pack(char_array);
   for char_array'component_size use char_bit;

   function is_nul_terminated (item : in char_array) return Boolean;
```

```
   function to_c  (item       : in String;
                   append_nul : in Boolean := TRUE)
      return char_array;

   function to_ada (item     : in char_array;
                    trim_nul : in Boolean := TRUE)
      return String;

   procedure to_c (item       : in String;
                   target     : out char_array;
                   Count      : out size_t;
                   append_nul : in Boolean := TRUE);

   procedure to_ada (item     : in char_array;
                     target   : out String;
                     Count    : out Natural;
                     trim_nul : in Boolean := TRUE);

   -- wide character and wide string

   type wchar_t is implementation-defined;

   wide_nul : constant wchar_t := wchar_t'First;

   function to_c   (item : in Wide_Character) return wchar_t;
   function to_ada (item : in wchar_t        ) return Wide_Character;

   type wchar_array is array (size_t range <>) of aliased wchar_t;

   pragma pack(wchar_array);

   function is_nul_terminated (item : in wchar_array) return Boolean;

   function to_c  (item       : in wide_string;
                   append_nul : in Boolean := TRUE)
      return wchar_array;

   function to_ada (item     : in wchar_array;
                    trim_nul : in Boolean := TRUE)
      return wide_string;

   procedure to_c (item       : in  wide_string;
                   target     : out wchar_array;
                   Count      : out size_t;
                   append_nul : in  Boolean := TRUE);
   procedure to_ada (item     : in  wchar_array;
                     target   : out wide_string;
                     Count    : out Natural;
                     trim_nul : in  Boolean := TRUE);

   terminator_error : exception;

end interfaces.c;
```

C.10 The Package `Ada.Numerics`

```
package Ada.Numerics is
   pragma pure(Numerics);
   argument_error : exception;
   pi : constant :=
        3.14159_26535_89793_23846_26433_83279_50288_41971_69399_37511;
   e  : constant :=
        2.71828_18284_59045_23536_02874_71352_66249_77572_47093_69996;
end Ada.Numerics;
```

C.11 The Package `Ada.Command_line`

```
generic
   type float_type is digits <>;
package Ada.Numerics.generic_elementary_functions is
   pragma pure(generic_elementary_functions);

   function sqrt     (x            :float_type'Base)    return float_type'Base;
   function log      (x            :float_type'Base)    return float_type'Base;
   function log      (x, base      :float_type'Base)    return float_type'Base;
   function exp      (x            :float_type'Base)    return float_type'Base;
   function "**"     (left, right:float_type'Base)      return float_type'Base;

   function sin      (x            :float_type'Base)    return float_type'Base;
   function sin      (x, cycle     :float_type'Base)    return float_type'Base;
   function cos      (x            :float_type'Base)    return float_type'Base;
   function cos      (x, cycle     :float_type'Base)    return float_type'Base;
   function tan      (x            :float_type'Base)    return float_type'Base;
   function tan      (x, cycle     :float_type'Base)    return float_type'Base;
   function cot      (x            :float_type'Base)    return float_type'Base;
   function cot      (x, cycle     :float_type'Base)    return float_type'Base;

   function arcsin (x            :float_type'Base)    return float_type'Base;
   function arcsin (x, cycle     :float_type'Base)    return float_type'Base;
   function arccos (x            :float_type'Base)    return float_type'Base;
   function arccos (x, cycle     :float_type'Base)    return float_type'Base;
   function arctan (y            :float_type'Base;
                    x            :float_type'Base := 1.0) return float_type'Base;
   function arctan (y            :float_type'Base;
                    x            :float_type'Base := 1.0;
                    cycle        :float_type'Base)    return float_type'Base;
   function arccot (x            :float_type'Base;
                    y            :float_type'Base := 1.0) return float_type'Base;
   function arccot (x            :float_type'Base;
                    y            :float_type'Base := 1.0;
                    cycle        :float_type'Base)    return float_type'Base;

   function sinh     (x            :float_type'Base)    return float_type'Base;
   function cosh     (x            :float_type'Base)    return float_type'Base;
   function tanh     (x            :float_type'Base)    return float_type'Base;
   function coth     (x            :float_type'Base)    return float_type'Base;
   function arcsinh(x            :float_type'Base)    return float_type'Base;
   function arccosh(x            :float_type'Base)    return float_type'Base;
   function arctanh(x            :float_type'Base)    return float_type'Base;
   function arccoth(x            :float_type'Base)    return float_type'Base;

end Ada.Numerics.generic_elementary_functions;
```

C.12 The Package `Ada.Command_line`

```
package Ada.Command_line is
   pragma preelaborate(Command_line);

   function argument_count return Natural;

   function argument (number : in Positive) return String;

   function command_name return String;

   type exit_status is implementation-defined Integer type;

   success : constant exit_status;
   failure : constant exit_status;

   procedure set_exit_status (code : in exit_status);

private
   ... -- not specified by the language
end Ada.Command_line;
```

C.13 The Package `Ada.Finalization`

```
package Ada.Finalization is
    pragma preelaborate(Finalization);

    type controlled is abstract tagged private;

    procedure initialize(object : in out Controlled);
    procedure adjust            (object : in out Controlled);
    procedure finalize          (object : in out Controlled);

    type Limited_Controlled is abstract tagged limited private;


    procedure initialize(object : in out Limited_Controlled);
    procedure finalize  (object : in out Limited_Controlled);
private
    ... -- not specified by the language
end Ada.Finalization;
```

C.14 The Package `Ada.Tags`

```
package Ada.Tags is
    type Tag is private;

    function expanded_name(t : Tag) return String;
    function external_tag(t : Tag) return String;
    function internal_tag(external : String) return Tag;
    tag_error : exception;
private
    ... -- not specified by the language
end Ada.Tags;
```

C.15 The Package `Ada.Calendar`

```
package Ada.Calendar is
    type Time is private;

    subtype year_number  is Integer range 1901 ..  2099;
    subtype month_number is Integer range 1 ..  12;
    subtype day_number   is Integer range 1 ..  31;
    subtype day_duration is duration range 0.0 ..  86_400.0;

    function clock return Time;

    function year   (date : Time) return year_number;
    function month  (date : Time) return month_number;
    function day    (date : Time) return day_number;
    function seconds(date : Time) return day_duration;

    procedure split (date   : in Time;
                     year    : out year_number;
                     month   : out month_number;
                     day     : out day_number;
                     seconds : out day_duration);

    function time_of(year   : year_number;
                     month   : month_number;
                     day     : day_number;
                     seconds : day_duration := 0.0)
      return Time;

    function "+" (left : Time;     right : duration) return Time;
    function "+" (left : duration; right : Time) return Time;
    function "-" (left : Time;     right : duration) return Time;
    function "-" (left : Time;     right : Time) return duration;
```

```
function "<" (left, right : Time) return Boolean;
function "<="(left, right : Time) return Boolean;
function ">" (left, right : Time) return Boolean;
function ">="(left, right : Time) return Boolean;

time_error : exception;

private
   ... -- not specified by the language
end Ada.Calendar;
```

C.16 The Package System

```
package System is
   pragma Preelaborate(System);

   type Name is implementation-defined-enumeration-type;
   System_Name : constant Name := implementation-defined;

   -- System-Dependent Named Numbers:

   Min_Int                : constant := root_integer'First;
   Max_Int                : constant := root_integer'Last;

   Max_Binary_Modulus     : constant := implementation-defined;
   Max_Nonbinary_Modulus  : constant := implementation-defined;

   Max_Base_Digits        : constant := root_real'Digits;
   Max_Digits             : constant := implementation-defined;

   Max_Mantissa           : constant := implementation-defined;
   Fine_Delta             : constant := implementation-defined;

   Tick                   : constant := implementation-defined;

   -- Storage-related Declarations:

   type Address is implementation-defined;
   Null_Address : constant Address;

   Storage_Unit : constant := implementation-defined;
   Word_Size    : constant := implementation-defined * Storage_Unit;
   Memory_Size  : constant := implementation-defined;

   -- Address Comparison:
   function "<" (Left, Right : Address) return Boolean;
   function "<="(Left, Right : Address) return Boolean;
   function ">" (Left, Right : Address) return Boolean;
   function ">="(Left, Right : Address) return Boolean;
   function "=" (Left, Right : Address) return Boolean;
-- function "/=" (Left, Right : Address) return Boolean;
   -- "/=" is implicitly defined
   pragma Convention(Intrinsic, "<");
   ... -- and so on for all language-defined subprograms in this package

   -- Other System-Dependent Declarations:
   type Bit_Order is (High_Order_First, Low_Order_First);
   Default_Bit_Order : constant Bit_Order;

   -- Priority-related declarations (see D.1):
   subtype Any_Priority is Integer range implementation-defined;
   subtype Priority is Any_Priority range
       Any_Priority'First .. implementation-defined;
   subtype Interrupt_Priority is
       Any_Priority range Priority'Last+1 .. Any_Priority'Last;

   Default_Priority : constant Priority :=
       (Priority'First + Priority'Last)/2;

private
   ... -- not specified by the language
end System;
```

Appendix D: Answers to selected exercises

Chapter 2

A program to print the first 20 numbers.

```
with Ada.Text_io; use Ada.Text_io;
procedure main is
begin
  for i in 1 .. 20 loop
    put( Integer'Image( i ) ); new_line;
  end loop;
end main;
```

A program to print the 8 times table.

```
with Ada.Text_io; use Ada.Text_io;
procedure main is
begin
  for i in 1 .. 12 loop
    put( " 8 * " ); put( Integer'Image(i) ); put(" = ");
    put( Integer'Image( i*8 ) ); new_line;
  end loop;
end main;
```

A program to print numbers in the Fibonacci series.

```
with Ada.Text_io; use Ada.Text_io;
procedure main is
  first, second, next : Integer;
begin
  first  := 0;
  second := 1;
  put( Integer'Image(1) ); new_line;
  while second < 10000 loop
    put( Integer'Image( second ) ); new_line;
    next := first + second;
    first  := second;
    second := next;
  end loop;
end main;
```

A program to print a character table.

```
with Ada.Text_io; use Ada.Text_io;
procedure main is
begin
  for i in 32 .. 127 loop
    put( "Character " ); put( Character'Val(i) );
    put( " is represented by code " ); put( Integer'Image(i) );
    new_line;
  end loop;
end main;
```

Chapter 3

A program to print an arbitrary time table in the range 1 .. 20.

```
with Simple_io, Ada.Command_line;
use  Simple_io, Ada.Command_line;
procedure main is
  subtype Valid_times_table is Integer range 1 .. 20;
  table, last : Integer;
begin
  if argument_count >= 1 then
    get( argument(1), table, last );
    if table in Valid_times_table then
      put("The "); put( table, width=>2 );
      put(" times table is"); new_line;
      for i in 1 .. 12 loop
        put( table, width=>2 ); put( " * " );
        put( i, width=>2 ); put("  =  ");
        put( i*table, width=>3 ); new_line;
      end loop;
    else
      put("Number not valid"); new_line;
    end if;
  else
    put("No argument specified"); new_line;
  end if;
end main;
```

A program to determine if a number is prime or not.

```
with Simple_io; use Simple_io;
procedure main is
  num : Integer;
begin
  put("Please enter number : "); get( num );
  put("Number is ");
  if num in Positive then
    for i in 2 .. num-1 loop
      if (num/i)*i = num then
        put("not ");
        exit;
      end if;
    end loop;
    put("prime"); new_line;
  else
    put("Require a positive number"); new_line;
  end if;
end main;
```

A program to covert a temperature in Fahrenheit to centigrade.

```
with Simple_io; use Simple_io;
procedure main is
  subtype Centigrade is Float range -32.0/1.8 .. 212.0/1.8;
  subtype Fahrenheit is Float range 0.0 .. 212.0;
  temp      : Float;
begin
  put("Please enter temperature in Fahrenheit ");
  get( temp );
  if temp in Fahrenheit then
    put("Temperature in Centigrade is ");
    put( ( temp -32.0 ) / 1.8, exp=>0, aft=>2 ); new_line;
  else
    put("Temperature not valid"); new_line;
  end if;
end main;
```

A program to print student marks as grades.

```
with Simple_io; use Simple_io;
procedure main is
  NAME_LENGTH : constant Positive := 20;
  type    Name_range is range 1 .. NAME_LENGTH;
  ch  : Character;
  mark: Integer;
begin
  while not end_of_file loop
    for i in Name_range loop
      get(ch); put(ch);
    end loop;
    get( mark );
    case mark is
      when  0 .. 39 => put("F");
      when 40 .. 49 => put("D");
      when 50 .. 59 => put("C");
      when 60 .. 69 => put("B");
      when 70 ..100 => put("A");
      when others   => put("Invalid data");
    end case;
    skip_line; new_line;
  end loop;
end main;
```

Chapter 4

A program to print statistics on the number of different types of character in a file.

```
with Simple_io; use Simple_io;
procedure main is

  type Char is ( DIGIT, PUNCTUATION, LETTER, OTHER_CH );

  function what_is_char( ch:in Character ) return Char is
  begin
    case ch is
      when 'a' .. 'z' | 'A' .. 'Z' => return LETTER;
      when '0' .. '9'              => return DIGIT;
      when ',' | '.' | ';' | ':'   => return PUNCTUATION;
      when others                  => return OTHER_CH;
    end case;
  end what_is_char;

  no_letters    : Natural := 0;
  no_digits     : Natural := 0;
  no_punct_chs  : Natural := 0;
  no_other_chs  : Natural := 0;
  ch            : Character;
begin
```

```
  while not end_of_file loop
    while not end_of_line loop
      get( ch );
      case what_is_char( ch) is
        when LETTER      => no_letters := no_letters + 1;
        when DIGIT       => no_digits := no_digits + 1;
        when PUNCTUATION => no_punct_chs := no_punct_chs + 1;
        when OTHER_CH    => no_other_chs := no_other_chs + 1;
      end case;
    end loop;
    skip_line;
  end loop;
  put("Letters are        "); put( no_letters ); new_line;
  put("Digits  are        "); put( no_digits ); new_line;
  put("Punctuation chs are "); put( no_punct_chs ); new_line;
  put("Other chs are      "); put( no_punct_chs ); new_line;
end main;
```

Note: This only works for the English character set.

A program to print the average of three rainfall readings.

```
with Simple_io; use Simple_io;
procedure main is
  procedure order3( a,b,c:in out Float ) is
    procedure order2( f,s:in out Float ) is
      tmp : Float;
    begin
      if f > s then
        tmp := f; f := s; s := tmp;
      end if;
    end order2;
  begin
    order2( a, b );    -- S L ?   (a, b,    correct order)
    order2( b, c );    -- ? ? L   (      c is largest)
    order2( a, b );    -- S M L   (a, b, c ordered )
  end order3;
  first,second,third : Float;
begin
  put("Input 3 rainfall reading ");
  get( first ); get( second ); get( third );          -- Data
  put("Rainfall average is     : ");
  put( (first+second+third)/3.0, exp=>0, aft=>2 );   -- Average
  new_line;
  order3( first, second, third );                    -- Order
  put("Data values (sorted) are : ");                -- List
  put( first, exp=>0, aft=>2 ); put(" ");
  put( second, exp=>0, aft=>2 ); put(" ");
  put( third, exp=>0, aft=>2 ); put(" ");
  new_line;
end main;
```

Chapter 5

A class Performance that represents the number of seats at a cinema performance.

```
package Class_performance is

  type Performance is private;
  subtype Money  is Float;

  procedure book_seats( the:in out Performance; n:in Natural );
  procedure cancel( the:in out Performance; n:in Natural );
  function  sales( the:in Performance ) return Money;
  function  seats_free( the:in Performance ) return Natural;

private
  MAX_SEATS : constant Natural := 200;
  SEAT_PRICE: constant Money   := 4.50;
  type Performance is record
      seats_left : Natural := MAX_SEATS;
  end record;
end Class_performance;
```

```
package body Class_performance is

  procedure book_seats( the:in out Performance; n:in Natural ) is
  begin
    if the.seats_left >= n then
      the.seats_left := the.seats_left - n;
    end if;
  end book_seats;

  procedure cancel( the:in out Performance; n:in Natural ) is
  begin
    the.seats_left := the.seats_left + n;
  end cancel;

  function  sales( the:in Performance ) return Money is
  begin
    return Float(MAX_SEATS-the.seats_left) * SEAT_PRICE;
  end sales;

  function  seats_free( the:in Performance ) return Natural is
  begin
    return the.seats_left;
  end seats_free;

end Class_performance;
```

A program to deal with the day-to-day administration for a cinema which has three performances.

```ada
with Simple_io, Class_performance, Class_TUI;
use  Simple_io, Class_performance, Class_TUI;
procedure main is

  procedure process(per:in out Performance; name:in String) is

    function money_image( m:in Money ) return String is
      res : String( 1 .. 10 );
    begin
      put( res, m, aft=>2, exp=>0 );
      return res;
    end money_image;

    screen  : TUI;           -- The TUI screen
    tickets : Integer;       -- Tickets being processed

  begin
    loop
      message( screen, "Performance is " & name );
      menu( screen, "Book", "Cancel", "Seats free", "Sales" );
      case event( screen ) is
        when M_1 =>                              -- Book
          dialog(screen, "Number of seats to book", tickets);
          if tickets>0 and then tickets<=seats_free(per)
          then
            book_seats( per, tickets );
          else
            message(screen, "Not a valid number of tickets");
          end if;
        when M_2 =>                              -- Cancel
          dialog(screen, "Number of seats to return", tickets);
          if tickets > 0 then cancel( per, tickets );
          else
            message( screen, "Not a valid number of tickets" );
          end if;
        when M_3 =>                              -- Free
          message( screen, "Number of seats free is" &
                           Integer'Image( seats_free(per) ) );
        when M_4 =>                              -- Value
          message( screen, "Value of seats sold is ú" &
                           money_image( sales(per) ) );
        when M_QUIT =>
          exit;
      end case;
    end loop;
  end process;
  afternoon, early_evening, evening : Performance;
  main_menu : TUI;
```

```
begin
  loop
    menu(main_menu, "Afternoon", "Early Evening", "Evening", "");
    case event( main_menu ) is
      when M_1    => process( afternoon, "Afternoon" );
      when M_2    => process( early_evening, "Early evening" );
      when M_3    => process( evening, "Evening" );
      when M_QUIT => exit;
      when others => message( main_menu, "Try again");
    end case;
  end loop;
end main;
```

Chapter 6

A fragment of code showing a data structure that represents a computer system.

```
declare
  kb : constant := 1;           -- In Kilobyte units
  Mb : constant := 1024;        -- In Kilobyte units
  Gb : constant := 1024*Mb;     -- In Kilobyte units
  type Main_memory  is range 0 .. 64*Mb;
  type Cache_memory is range 0 .. 2*Mb;
  type Disk_memory  is range 0 .. 16*Gb;
  type Video_memory is range 0 .. 8*Mb;
  type Computer     is (PC, WORKSTATION, MULTIMEDIA );
  type Network      is (EITHER, RING );

  type Computer_system(type_of:Computer:=PC) is record
    main : Main_memory;       -- In Megabytes
    cache: Cache_memory;      -- In Kilobytes
    disk : Disk_memory;       -- In Megabytes
    case type_of is
      when WORKSTATION =>
        connection    : Network;
      when MULTIMEDIA  =>
        display_memory: Video_memory;
      when PC          =>
        null;
    end case;
  end record;
  my_computer: Computer_system(PC);
  at_work    : Computer_system;
begin
  my_computer := ( PC, 16*Mb, 256*Kb, 1*Gb );
  at_work     := ( PC, 16*Mb, 64*Kb, 170*Mb );
end;
```

Note: Kb, Mb, and Gb are scaled so that the number is representable.

Chapter 13

A program to use a generic data store.

The specification for the class Store is

```
generic
  type Store_index   is private;      --
  type Store_element is private;      --
package Class_store is
  type Store is limited private;      -- NO copying
  Not_there, Full : exception;

  procedure add    ( the:in out Store;
                     index:in Store_index;
                     item:in Store_element);
  function deliver( the:in Store;
                    index:in Store_index )
                    return Store_element;
private
  MAX_STORE : constant := 10;
  type     Store_r_index is range 0 .. MAX_STORE;
  subtype Store_r_range is Store_r_index range 1 .. MAX_STORE;
  type Store_record is record
    index: Store_index;       -- Index
    item : Store_element;     -- Data item
  end record;
  type Store_array is array( Store_r_range ) of Store_record;
  type Store is limited record
    data : Store_array;
    items: Store_r_index := 0;
  end record;

end Class_store;
```

A possible implementation of the Class Store is:

```
package body Class_store is

  procedure add    ( the:in out Store;
                     index:in Store_index;
                     item:in Store_element) is
  begin
    if the.items < MAX_STORE then
      the.items := the.items + 1;
      the.data(the.items) := ( index, item );
    else
      raise Full;
    end if;
  end add;
```

```
   function deliver( the:in Store;
                     index:in Store_index)
                     return Store_element is
   begin
     for i in 1 .. Store_r_range(MAX_STORE) loop
       if the.data(i).index = index then
         return the.data(i).item;
       end if;
     end loop;
     raise Not_there;
   end deliver;
end Class_store;
```

```
package Pack_types is
  subtype Name is String( 1..5 );
end Pack_types;
```

The instantiation of a store package to hold student names and exam marks is:

```
with Class_store, Pack_types;
  package Class_store_int_str is
    new Class_store( Pack_types.Name, Integer );
```

A simple test program for this package is:

```
with Simple_io, Class_store_int_str, Pack_types;
use  Simple_io, Class_store_int_str, Pack_types;
procedure main is
  Marks : Store;
begin
  add( marks, "Andy ", 50 );
  add( marks, "Bob  ", 65 );
  add( marks, "Clark", 73 );
  add( marks, "Dave ", 54 );
  put("Mark for Bob  is " );
   put( deliver(marks, "Bob  "), width=> 3 ); new_line;
  put("Mark for Dave is " );
   put( deliver(marks, "Dave "), width=> 3 ); new_line;
end main;
```

Chapter 14

A queue implemented using dynamically allocated storage. The specification of the class Queue:

```ada
with Ada.Finalization;
use  Ada.Finalization;
generic
  type T is private;              -- Can specify any type
package Class_queue is
  type Queue is new Limited_Controlled with private;
  Queue_error: exception;

  procedure add( the:in out Queue; item:in T );
  procedure sub( the:in out Queue; item:out T );
  procedure finalize( the:in out Queue );
private
  type Node;                      -- Mutually recursive def
  type P_Node is access Node;     -- Pointer to a Queue
  pragma Controlled( P_Node );    -- We do deallocation

  type Node is record             -- Node holds the data
    item    : T;                  -- The stored item
    p_next  : P_Node;             -- Next in list
  end record;

  type Queue is new Limited_Controlled with record
    head    : P_Node := null;     -- Head of Queue
    tail    : P_Node := null;     -- Tail of Queue
    no_of   : Natural:= 0;        -- Number in queue
  end record;
end Class_queue;
```

The implementation of the class Queue.

```ada
with unchecked_deallocation;
package body Class_queue is

  procedure dispose is
    new unchecked_deallocation( Node, P_Node );

  procedure add( the:in out Queue; item:in T ) is
    tmp : P_Node := new Node'( item, null );
  begin
    if the.no_of > 0 then
      the.tail.p_next := tmp;           -- Chain in
    else
      the.head         := tmp;          -- Also head
    end if;
    the.tail         := tmp;            -- New Tail
    the.no_of        := the.no_of + 1;  -- Inc no.
  end add;
```

```
   procedure sub( the:in out Queue; item :out T ) is
     tmp : P_Node;
   begin
     if the.no_of > 0 then
        item      := the.head.item;    -- Recovered item
        tmp       := the.head;         -- Node finished with
        the.head := the.head.p_next;   -- new head
        dispose( tmp );                -- Free storage
        the.no_of := the.no_of - 1;    -- 1 less in queue
     else
        raise Queue_error;             -- Error
     end if;
   end sub;

   procedure finalize( the:in out Queue ) is
     discard : T;
   begin
     for i in 1 .. the.no_of loop     -- Free storage
        sub( the, discard );
     end loop;
   end finalize;

end Class_queue;
```

The instantiation of an integer instance of the class Queue.

```
with Class_queue;
  package Class_queue_int is new Class_queue(Integer);
```

A small test program to test the class Queue.

```
with Simple_io, Class_queue_int;
use  Simple_io, Class_queue_int;
procedure main is
  number_queue : Queue;              -- Queue of numbers
  action       : Character;          -- Action
  number       : Integer;            -- Number processed
begin
  while not end_of_file loop
    while not end_of_line loop
      begin
        get( action );
        case action is               -- Process action
          when '+' =>
            get( number ); add(number_queue,number);
            put("add number    = "); put(number); new_line;
          when '-' =>
            sub(number_queue,number);
            put("remove number = "); put(number); new_line;
          when others =>
            put("Invalid action"); new_line;
        end case;
```

```
      exception
        when Queue_error =>
          put("Exception Queue_error"); new_line;
        when Data_error   =>
          put("Not a number"); new_line;
        when End_error    =>
          put("Unexpected end of file"); new_line; exit;
      end;
    end loop;
    skip_Line;
  end loop;
end main;
```

Chapter 19

A task type which allows repeated calculations of a factorial value to be made is:

```
package Pack_factorial is
  task type Task_factorial is            -- Specification
    entry start( f:in Positive );        -- Rendezvous
    entry deliver( res:out Positive );   -- Rendezvous
    entry finish;                        -- Rendezvous
  end Task_factorial;
end Pack_factorial;
```

```
with Simple_io; use Simple_io;
package body Pack_factorial is
  task body Task_factorial is            -- Implementation
    factorial : Positive;
    answer    : Positive := 1;
  begin
    loop
      select                             -- Store in buffer
        accept start( f:in Positive ) do -- Factorial
          factorial := f;
        end start;
        for i in 2 .. factorial loop     -- Calculate
          answer := answer * i;
        end loop;
        accept deliver( res:out Positive ) do -- Return answer
          res := answer;
        end deliver;
      or                                 -- Get from buffer
        accept finish;                   -- Finished
      end select;
    end loop;

  end Task_factorial;
end Pack_factorial;
```

A short test program for this task is:

```
with Simple_io, Pack_factorial;
use  Simple_io, Pack_factorial;
procedure main is
  fac    : Task_factorial;
  num    : Integer;
  answer : Integer;
begin
  while not end_of_file loop
    get( num ); new_line;
    fac.start( num );
    put("Factorial "); put( num, width=>2 ); put("is ");
    fac.deliver( answer );
    put( answer, width=> 2 ); new_line;
  end loop;
end main;
```

References

Intermetrics (1995) *Ada 95 Rational,* Intermetrics, Inc, Cambridge, Massachusetts.

Intermetrics (1995) *Ada 95 Reference Manual* , Intermetrics, Inc, Cambridge, Massachusetts.

Coleman, D. *et al* (1994) *Object-Oriented Development (The fusion method)* Prentice Hall, London.

Taylor, B. (1995) Ada 95 Compatibility Guide in *Ada Yearbook 1995* (Ed Mark Ratcliffe), IOS press, pp. 260-313.

Whitaker, W.A. (1993) Ada - The Project. *ACM SIGPLAN Notices*, **28**(3), 299-331.

Index